Sanctify
the
Congregation

VAN + JUDY GALE
345 DUANE ST #101
GLEN ELLYN, IL 60137

Sanctify
the
Congregation

A Call to the
Solemn Assembly
and to
Corporate Repentance

Edited By

Richard Owen Roberts

INTERNATIONAL
AWAKENING
PRESS

Wheaton, Illinois
1994

Published By
INTERNATIONAL AWAKENING PRESS
P. O. Box 232
Wheaton, Illinois 60189 U.S.A.
A Division Of
International Awakening Ministries, Inc.

Printed in the United States of America

ISBN 0-926474-10-3

Library of Congress
Catalogue Card Number 93-080173

Table of Contents

Introduction

While sin is a very real personal problem, it is not exclusively individuals who fall short of the mark God sets for them. Whole churches sin grievously as do all other religious entities, including mission boards, evangelistic agencies and entire denominations. Even nations can be guilty of sin as nations. A generation that does not know how to put away corporate sin is a generation in trouble with itself and with God.

In his first letter to the Corinthians, the Apostle Paul charges the church with numerous corporate sins of immense consequence. He declared them guilty of a divisive spirit, some saying, "I am of Paul," others, "I am of Apollos," still others, "I am of Cephas," and some even piously declaring, "and I am of Christ" (1 Corinthians 1). He pinpoints their problem of tolerance towards immorality in allowing a man to have his father's wife, linking this filthy sin with corporate arrogance in not even mourning the existence of such wickedness among themselves (1 Corinthians 5). He accuses them of corporate misuse of the Lord's Supper and warns that some have already suffered the righteous judgment of sickness and death because of this sin of the church body (1 Corinthians 11). Tragically, the Corinthian Church even sinned against the Holy Spirit in the misuse and abuse of His spiritual gifts (1 Corinthians 12, 14).

The second letter Paul wrote to this church demonstrated the great concern with which he wrote that first epistle and the normal human apprehension he felt in sending it. Churches do not tend to be any more open to rebuke and correction than individuals and Paul knew this well. In the seventh chapter he described the uneasiness he experienced, "For though I caused you sorrow by my letter, I do not regret it; though I did regret it——for I see that that letter caused you sorrow, though only for a while" (2 Corinthians 7:8). At the same time he had reason to rejoice, "not that you were made sorrowful, but that you were made sorrowful to the point of repentance; for you were made sorrowful according to the will of God, in order that you might not suffer loss in anything through us" (2 Corinthians 7:9). He then made a distinction of vast importance, "For the sorrow that is according to the will of God produces a repentance without regret, leading to salvation; but the sorrow of the world produces death" (2 Corinthians 7:10).

Do you realize there is a repentance to be repented of—a repentance to be regretted? Both individuals and corporate bodies can experience a sorrow over sin that does not lead to salvation but leads instead to death. Paul rejoiced that when the Corinthians received his first epistle they felt a true and godly sorrow over the awful sins both he and the Holy Spirit specified, and they dealt with those sins in appropriate ways, putting them away, making wrongs right, demonstrating they were truly a Church of Jesus Christ. In fact, they provided us a most excellent example of corporate repentance. Notice the commendation given them, "For behold what earnestness this very thing, this godly sorrow, has produced in you: what vindication of yourselves, what indignation, what fear, what longing, what zeal, what avenging of wrong! In everything you demonstrated yourselves to be innocent in the matter" (2 Corinthians 7:11). From the words of verse eleven we need to draw a list of the salient features of that genuine corporate repentance that springs from a sorrow over sin that is according to the will of God.

First, true repentance is always marked by a genuine earnestness: "for behold what earnestness this very thing, this godly sorrow, has produced in you!" The unrepentant church is marked by a spirit of carelessness, indifference, and neglect concerning sin, but godly sorrow provokes an earnest solicitude and overwhelming eagerness to deal with it at its very roots. True repentance includes careful study and serious looking into the matter of sin, searching it out fully and seeing that nothing remains that is odious in God's sight and that nothing is left undone that God wants done. By earnest searching, sins which previously appeared too slight to contemplate are brought into true proportion and put away. The human tendency is to sorrow over the sins that hurt us, but the truly repentant learn to sorrow over all sins because they hurt God, including those corporate sins which bring His Church under remedial judgment. Where true earnestness prevails in repentance, there will be no lingering affection toward the sins that have been put away and no pious fondling of the things that God abhors. This earnestness in repentance will lead the church to diligence, dexterity, vigilance, watching, wakefulness and strife against all that robs her of favor with God and power among men.

Second, true repentance is always marked by vindication: "for behold...what vindication of yourselves!" This speaks, not of self-justification, but of great eagerness to be totally clear, to be truly and finally free of both the guilt and the error of sin. The truly repentant church is possessed of an urgent determination to make a clean breast of things and is absolutely unwilling to leave anything unsettled. Ambrose declared, "Repentance hath no excuse, but confession." Godly sorrow leads to that repentance which provokes open acknowledgement—not denial, not excuses, not covering-up, but clear and full confession of every evil the Holy Spirit pin-points. As the circle of confession must be as broad as the effect of the sin, a church seeking to vindicate itself will not balk at open confession before God and the world, both of whom it has harmed and both of whom deserve to see evidence of genuine change. When a corporate body resists open confession, it obviously seeks to hinder this vindication that is such a crucial part of the repentance produced by godly sorrow.

Third, true repentance is always marked by indignation: "For behold...what indignation!" The word translated "indignation" appears only here in the Scriptures and speaks specifically of wrath unto grief. The repentant are filled with rage against their sin and, in the height of their anger against it, can be described as fretting unto fuming. As an individual, you may have been so angry against yourself for your sin that you were speechless or that you fumed against yourself, asking over and over, "How could I do such a wicked thing against the God I love?" David felt deeply this indignation and said, "I have sinned greatly in what I have done. But now, O Lord, please take away the iniquity of Thy servant, for I have acted very foolishly" (2 Samuel 24:10). The Psalmist understood it and said in agony, "When my heart was embittered, and I was pierced within, then I was senseless and ignorant; I was like a beast before Thee" (Psalm 73:21,22). Ancient Job wrestled his way from a sorrowful repentance that led to death to, by the grace of his God, that true repentance resulting from godly sorrow and summarized his experience declaring, "I have heard of Thee by the hearing of the ear; but now my eye sees Thee; Therefore I retract [I abhor myself], And I repent in dust and ashes" (Job 42:5,6). In the truly repentant, sin is the object of hatred, scorn, rage, reproach, shame, grief, anger and fixed determination to see it destroyed forever.

Fourth, true repentance is always marked by fear: "For behold...what fear!" All repentant entities are of a trembling and timid spirit. Just as the burned child fears the fire, so the repentant know that sin costs dearly: they know what sin cost the Saviour, they know what sin costs them in separation from Him, and they want no part of another round of the same. This fear of the Lord is described as the beginning of wisdom (Psalm 111:10). Jesus warned, "Do not fear those who kill the body, but are unable to kill the soul; but rather fear Him who is able to destroy both soul and body in hell" (Matthew 10:28). The fear of God is at the very heart of the Christian message, "What does the Lord your God require of you, but to fear the Lord your God, to walk in all His ways and love Him, and to serve the Lord your God with all your heart and with all your soul" (Deuteronomy 10:12). It is only by fearing God that one can be kept from sin, "The fear of the Lord is to hate evil; Pride and arrogance and the evil way..." (Proverbs 8:13). "By the fear of the Lord one keeps away from evil" (Proverbs 16:6). True repentance provokes fear lest our great God be offended again; fear lest our Saviour's blood be spilt in vain in our case; fear lest the Holy Spirit be offended and driven away; fear lest the measure of our sins be filled up; fear lest poor souls be damaged by our ill-conduct; fear lest we be hardened through the deceitfulness of sin; fear lest the church and Christian organizations of which we are a part bring shame upon the Gospel and encourage the world in its downward plunge to perdition.

Fifth, true repentance is always marked by longing: "For behold... what longing!" Godly sorrow shapes the appetite of holy desire to such an extent that the repentant are gripped by a fervency of spirit that admits no delay or hindrance in being altogether right before God. Just as the hunted deer seeks the relief of the wooded pool, so the sin-wearied thirst for the true satisfaction of total repentance. Think of the longing to be wholly rid of sin forever manifested in Paul's words, "Wretched man that I am! Who will set me free from the body of this death? (Romans 7:24). Consider the excellent illustration of longing for all the sin-subduing and grace-strengthening mercies of God brought to focus in Peter's words, "Like newborn babes, long for the pure milk of the word, that by it you may grow in respect to salvation" (1 Peter 2:2). True repentance causes churches to yearn to be holy as God is holy, to never again lapse back into the God-dishonoring patterns of the past; to live above the world and its degradation and to hear the Saviour's approbation, "Well done, good and faithful servants." A church that is not distinguished by such longings after the heart of God knows altogether too little of the repentance that came to Corinth.

Sixth, true repentance is always marked by zeal: "For behold...what zeal!" The unrepentant are obviously disinterested in repentance. The barely repentant do whatever they think they have to do to get what they want. The truly repentant believe heartily with Paul that it is good to be zealously affected always in a good thing (Galatians 4:18) and with great zeal they grasp every opportunity to fling off sin and all that contributes to it in this life. They weigh seriously the words of the Saviour, "And if your hand or your foot causes you to stumble, cut it off and throw it from you; it is better for you to enter life crippled or lame, than having two hands or two feet, to be cast into the eternal fire. And if your eye causes you to stumble, pluck it out, and throw it from you. It is better for you to enter life with one eye, than having two eyes, to be cast into the hell of fire" (Matthew 18:8,9). They understand and appreciate the zeal of New Testament believers who Luke describes saying: "many...who practiced magic brought their books together and began burning them in the sight of all; and they counted up the price of them and found it fifty thousand pieces of silver" (Acts 19:19). With vehement zeal they refuse to let any opposition or difficulty stand in the way of their full biblical repentance. They are even willing to stand absolutely alone, if need be, and do not shrink from being considered "fools" for Christ's sake. They, like the Apostle of old, buffet their bodies and make them slaves, lest possibly after preaching to others they themselves should be disqualified (1 Corinthians 9:27). When the church is repentant, its zeal in keeping the channels of grace clear of even minor obstructions will usher it into a whole new day of joyous victory for Christ.

Seventh, true repentance is always marked by avenging of wrong: "For behold...what avenging of wrong!" This does not speak of getting even with those who have wronged us but of that moral persuasion that sin must be punished and all wrongs righted. For the corporate body, it involves the deliberate, specific act of bringing each sin under the blood of Christ and facing squarely the fact that either Christ pays the price of every sin or we do, for no sin can go unpunished. When a church or a denomination sins, that sin will either be repented of and paid for by Christ or the body will be judged for that sin and punished by God Himself. Consider the sin of falsely reported statistics which is so prevalent among churches and denominations who commonly claim more members than really exist. To keep their statistics up, some count the dead, those who have moved away or have not attended church at all for years, and some churches, including Baptist, even count the cradle-roll. There are denominations that would immediately shrink to half their reputed size if they just turned honest. Obviously to repent of this sin requires both a lot of grace and a totally new way of counting. True repentance will make it impossible to go on with this sin of exaggeration for the determination to be right with God will be stronger than the desire to look good before men. To avenge the wrong will require open confession of this long-standing sin and published reports replacing those previously circulated to the media. The church that is avenging wrong will be just as thorough in dealing with sins of racial prejudice, esteeming the wealthy above others, compromising truth, and countless other corporate sins of the day. This avenging of wrong will require restitution, for some sins will never be righted until old debts are settled and broken relationships restored.

Fortunately, Paul knew what to do about corporate sin in the

Corinthian church. Thankfully also, when he confronted the church they heard his word as the Word of God and responded affirmatively in the verifiable repentance noted above.

But what about corporate Christianity today? Altogether too little is said about the repentance of individuals while virtually nothing is being said about corporate repentance. In fact the evidence seems almost overwhelming that most corporate religious entities know nothing at all about this urgent and necessary task.

However, we can be grateful that what we do not know, the Scriptures and our own history can teach us. If you will browse through the early volumes of "American Bibliography by Charles Evans: a Chronological Dictionary of all Books, Pamphlets and Periodical Publications Printed in the United States from the Genesis of Printing in 1639 down to and including the year 1820," you will be amazed and benefited to learn how much attention the founding fathers of America gave to this issue of corporate repentance, for there you will find listed multitudes of messages preached on days of fasting and solemn assemblies.

In this book you will find more than a dozen of these fast day messages described by Evans along with calls to corporate repentance issued by government bodies and church leaders. Early Americans, despite their faults, knew that God hated sin and punished it in the unrepentant, including unrepentant believers and churches. Because they feared God and His ability to punish, they sought to lead their people in quick and thorough repentance.

They were alert to signs of God's manifest displeasure among them. Natural calamities, which some of us treat with the shrug of a shoulder, were dutifully examined, prayed over and improved by godly men of old. Even the unexpected death of a pastor, a youth, a government official, a farmer or a housewife had power to provoke them to inquire if God had a grievance against His people.

Their attitude of brokenness and contrition before God made them sensitive to what He was saying to them, just as the arrogancy and self-sufficiency of today's church make it virtually immune to the voice of God and the promptings of His Spirit. If they passed into dry seasons spiritually, they took this as a message from God and sought His face in renewed repentance and dedication. If others were experiencing manifestations of the enlargement of God's heart toward them, those without such blessings rejoiced with the blest but humbled themselves before the Lord to enquire if their lack of prosperity was because they had grieved the Almighty.

Although no thinking man would dare to describe the Puritan fathers, whose messages are found in this book, as sinless, they were at least possessed of some significant spiritual qualities of which we are sadly deficient. While we cannot and must not copy them in every regard, let us at least have the grace to learn from them the urgent necessity of corporate repentance and the divinely appointed means of bringing it about.

When you consider that the Solemn Assembly Sermons of this book were preached during a span of more than one-hundred years, 1645 to 1753, you can readily understand that of necessity they have been altered for inclusion here. I have edited each message, updating the sermon framework, sentence structure, paragraph arrangement, spelling and punctuation. Where necessary, I have altered wording to make the messages more understandable to today's Christians and have sought to eliminate at least some of the redundancy that is typical of printed sermons. I have carefully sought to avoid putting words in another man's pen or removing essential things he wrote. Hopefully, I have not altered any author's meaning or intent or done anything to cause him other than joy if it is possible for him to know that "he being dead yet speaketh."

In keeping with the times in which they were written, the Biblical quotations in the sermons are from the King James text, whereas my own quotes in this introduction and in The Solemn Assembly are from the New American Standard version.

Richard Owen Roberts
January 1994

CHAPTER ONE

The Solemn Assembly

By
Richard Owen Roberts

This article first appeared in pamphlet form under the title *The Solemn Assembly by Richard Owen Roberts.* It was published in Wheaton, Illinois by The International Awakening Press in 1989 and reprinted in various forms thereafter.

The Solemn Assembly

The Sad Fact

Most professing Christians have never heard of a Solemn Assembly. Of the relatively small number who have, a substantial portion consider it as merely an Old Testament practice of no particular relevance today.

The Biblical Background

There are not less than twelve revival movements in the Old Testament. While each of these revivals is very different from the others, there are at least four factors preceding each revival which they all hold in common:

1. A Tragic Declension. Every revival of the Old Testament is preceded by a period of moral and spiritual decline among the people of God. As illustrations of this problem, consider that preceding the revival of Exodus 32-33, the decline included the building of the golden calf and its worship, while the revival under David was preceded by a period of more than six decades in which the Ark of the Covenant of God was out of its rightful place in Jerusalem.

2. A Righteous Judgment from God. Without any exception, Old Testament revivals have always been preceded by some kind of a righteous judgment from God. While some of these judgments are immediate and final, resulting in deaths among the wicked; others are gracious and remedial, resulting in brokenness, prayer, repentance and extraordinary seeking of God's face.

3. The Raising Up of an Immensely Burdened Leader or Leaders. This fact can be illustrated by a simple listing of the Old Testament revivals themselves:

a) The Revival under Moses — Exodus 32ff.
b) The Revival under Samuel — Samuel 7 [with chapters 1-6 providing the background].
c) The Revival under David — Samuel 6, 7.
d) The Revival under Asa — Chronicles 14-16.
e) The Revival under Jehoshaphat — Chronicles 17-20.
f) The Revival under Jehoiada — Chronicles 23-24.

g) The Revival under Hezekiah — Chronicles 29-32.
h) The Revival under Josiah — Chronicles 34-35.
i) The Revival under Zerubbabel — Ezra 1-6.
j) The Revival under Ezra — Ezra 7-10.
k) The Revival under Nehemiah — Nehemiah 1-13.
l) The Revival under Joel — Joel 1:1-2:27.

Obviously, in each case God Himself raised up a leader who was under the heavy burden of the moral and spiritual needs of his people. The words of Moses in Exodus 32:32 forcefully emphasize this, "But now, if Thou wilt, forgive their sin——and if not, please blot me out from Thy book which Thou hast written."

4. Some Extraordinary Action. While this action varies from revival to revival, the most common action taken was that of a solemn assembly. Again, note the record in the revivals themselves:

a) Exodus 33:7-11 — Moses took the tent and pitched it outside the camp, a good distance from the camp. He called it the place of meeting and required everyone who sought the Lord to go outside the camp, away from the place of sin, to the tabernacle to meet the Lord.

b) I Samuel 7:5,6 — Samuel required all of Israel to gather at Mizpah in a Solemn Assembly where he prayed for them and they fasted and confessed their sins.

c) 2 Samuel 6:14 an I Chronicles 13-18 — After a bad start in sinning against the Lord by moving the Ark of the Covenant on a new cart [the Philistine method], David and the people moved it according to the Word of the Lord and in joyful humiliation, he danced before the Lord with all his might in a linen ephod——having laid aside his crown and royal robes, he acted as a common man among common men. While no mention is made of a Solemn Assembly in the Second Samuel account, it is detailed in the parallel passage in First Chronicles.

d) 2 Chronicles 15:9-15 —Asa called a Solemn Assembly in Jerusalem where the people entered into a covenant to seek the Lord God of their fathers with all their hearts and with all their souls.

e) 2 Chronicles 20:3-13ff — Jehoshaphat called a Solemn Assembly throughout all Judah and Jerusalem and the people fasted and sought the Lord.

f) 2 Chronicles 23:16 — Jehoiada, in a Solemn Assembly, made a covenant between himself and all the people and the king that they should be the Lord's people. They then proceeded to cleanse the land of the evil.

g) 2 Chronicles 29:5ff — Hezekiah and the leaders established a decree which was very extensivly circulated requiring all the people to gather for a Solemn Assembly and the celebration of the Passover. An entire fourteen days were devoted to seeking the Lord and worshiping Him.

h) 2 Chronicles 34:31-33 — Josiah gathered the people together in a Solemn Assembly, and they entered into a covenant with the Lord to walk in all his ways and to perform all the words of the covenant written in the Book.

i) Ezra 6:16-22 — Zerubbabel led the people in a Solemn Assembly and a seven day celebration of the Passover in which they separated themselves from the impurity of the nations and pledged themselves to seek the Lord God of Israel.

j) Ezra 8:21-23; 9:5-15 — a proclaimed a fast at the River Ahava that they might all humble themselves and seek the Lord. They later engaged in public humiliation and putting away of sin in the form of a Solemn Assembly.

k) Nehemiah 8:1ff — A Solemn Assembly was held in front of the Water Gate where the Book of the Law of Moses was read by the hour and an agreement was made in writing to put away sin and to seek the Lord with all their hearts.

l) Joel 1:13; 2:12-17, etc. — Joel called a Solemn Assembly in which all the people were required to be in attendance and where all were required to return to the Lord with all their hearts, with fasting, weeping and mourning, and where they were required to rend their hearts and not their garments.

Consider the situation at the time of the Solemn Assembly called by the Prophet Joel. The people, as was common, were guilty of flagrant sin which had not been confessed and put away. God visited them with a remedial judgment—a plague of locusts of such proportion that nothing like it had happened before: "What the gnawing locust has left, the swarming locust has eaten; and what the swarming locust has left, the creeping locust has eaten; and what the creeping locust has left, the stripping locust has eaten." In addition to the terrible plague of insects, a fierce drought had afflicted the land. The drunkards wailed because they had no new wine to drink, the priests mourned because the grain offering and the libation were cut off from the house of the Lord, the fields were ruined and the land itself mourned, the vinedressers wailed, and the beasts groaned while the herds of cattle wandered aimlessly because there was no pasture for them. The people themselves wailed like a virgin girded with sackcloth for the bridegroom of her youth.

The Prophet issued orders: "Gird yourselves with sackcloth, and lament, O priests; Wail, O ministers of the altar! Come, spend the night in sackcloth, O ministers of my God." "Consecrate a fast, proclaim a solemn assembly; gather the elders and all the inhabitants of the land to the house of the Lord your God, and cry out to the Lord." "Blow a trumpet in Zion, and sound an alarm on My holy mountain! Let all the inhabitants of the land tremble." "Yet even now, declares the Lord, return to Me with all your heart, and with fasting, weeping and mourning; and rend your heart and not your garments. Now return to the Lord your God." "Blow a trumpet in Zion, consecrate a fast, proclaim a solemn assembly, gather the people, sanctify the congregation, assemble the elders, gather the children and the nursing infants. Let the bridegroom come out of his room and the bride out of her bridal chamber. Let the priests, the Lord's ministers, weep between the porch and the altar, and let them say, 'Spare Thy people, O Lord, and do not make Thine inheritance a reproach, a byword among the nations.'"

Promises were offered as encouragement: "Then the Lord will be zealous for His land, and will have pity on His people. And the Lord will answer and say to His people, 'Behold I am going to send you grain, new wine and oil, and you will be satisfied in full with them; and I will never again make you a reproach among the nations. But I will remove the northern army far from you [the horrendous swarm of locusts], and I will drive it into a parched and desolate land, and its vanguard into the eastern sea, and its rear guard into the western sea. And its stench [of rotting carcasses] will arise and its foul smell will come up...'"

And in response to the corporate repentance of the people through the use of the divinely ordained means of the Solemn Assembly, the land rejoiced and was made glad. The pastures of the wilderness turned green. The trees and the vines bore fruit. And the fruit borne was not ordinary but extraordinary for God moved the rainy seasons closer together, and caused the sun to shine upon the earth, so that the threshing floors were full and the vats overflowing. So great was the blessing bestowed by the God who delights in a broken and contrite people that He made up to them the years that were lost to the mighty army of locusts. The people had plenty and were satisfied and praised the name of the Lord who had dealt wondrously with them.They knew that God was in their midst, that He only was God, and that there was none other!

Unfortunately, some professed Christians will be disinclined to seriously think of a Solemn Assembly because the illustrations above are all Old Testament. They would do well to weigh the entire season of preparation prior to Pentecost in the light of the Solemn Assembly and see that those days in the Upper Room were indeed a Solemn Assembly if ever in the history of the world one was held.

Historical Foundations

Not only were Solemn Assemblies a very common aspect in the revivals of the Bible, but they were a very important part of the life of believers in America during all its early years. For verification of this one has only to consult the Sprague Collection of Early American Pamphlets at the Weidener Library at Harvard University. There will be found a large number of sermons that were preached at the Fast Days and Solemn Assemblies which were frequently called and earnestly attended by American believers prior to the general decline of true Christianity which characterizes twentieth-century America.

Our Fathers believed God was offended by sin. They themselves were deeply troubled both by the existence of personal sin in their own lives and by the presence of unconfessed corporate sins in the churches and in the nation. They regarded natural calamities as manifestations of the displeasure of God Almighty against sin and allowed such events as earthquakes, fires, volcanoes, epidemics, floods, and droughts to prompt them to special seeking of God's face in fasting, prayer, and corporate repentance. They also sought the Lord in Solemn Assemblies in connection with wars, murders, rapes, etc., believing such outbursts of wickedness to be directly related to the general decline of moral and spiritual life in the churches.

Misuse of the Solemn Assembly

Like any other God-ordained means of grace, the Solemn Assembly has the potential of being corrupted. The very severe denunciations of Isaiah 1:10-15 clearly indicate God's contempt for Solemn Assemblies that have lost their heart and have become mere form and ritual: "Bring your worthless offerings no longer, their incense is an abomination to Me. New moons and sabbath, the calling of assemblies—I cannot endure iniquity and the Solemn Assembly. I hate your new moon festivals and your appointed feasts, they have become a burden to Me. I am weary of bearing them..."

But we must not think professed American Christians have abandoned the Solemn Assembly because of its perpetual misuse and abuse. More accurately, as God has been degraded to a being scarcely a half inch bigger than man, humans have assumed gigantic proportions in their own eyes. In consequence of this, professed Christians have felt at liberty to neglect major portions of Scripture and to be virtually untaught in and unaffected by the long history of the Christian Church. The Solemn Assembly has simply fallen into oblivion at the hands of a people too arrogant to know that their own corporate sins—especially those heart sins of pride, unbelief, and rebellion—have created a nation ripe for destruction.

Getting the Foundation In Place

One's view of the Solemn Assembly will be affected to a very large degree by their understanding of the righteous judgments of God. As noted above, all Old Testament revivals have been preceded by some form of a righteous judgment. It must be understood that these righteous judgments are the result of unconfessed corporate sins. When the people of God sin against Him and do not repent, He judges them. While some of these judgments may be called final and consist of death and destruction, the more standard form of judgment is both remedial and gracious and consists of the withdrawal of certain evidences of His manifest presence and merciful favors. In the absence of God's manifest presence there is always an immediate and extensive increase in iniquity. This may be compared to the effect upon a city of the police force going on strike. It is the visible manifestation of law and order in the form of policemen, police cars, etc. that keeps crime somewhat restrained. When the police are on strike, when they are known to be corrupt themselves, or when it is known that arrests are meaningless because of the laxity of judges, a community must anticipate a tragic increase in crime. Just so, when God withdraws evidences of His manifest presence from a people, there is always a horrendous increase in iniquity and decline in spirituality.

That there has been a very great increase of immorality and decrease of true biblical spirituality in America in recent years is a fact beyond controversy. Why has this very great change occurred? Is it because the devil is more powerful than he used to be or because God is older and not nearly as able to defend Himself, His people and His church against wickedness? Obviously not. It is because God has judged America with the remedial judgment of the withdrawal of certain manifestations of his gracious presence and mercy.

As soon as it becomes evident that immorality is on the increase and spirituality is on the decline, the biblically sound and spiritually lively Church will not foolishly blame the world but will immediately recognize its own complicity. The Church must first repent, for the righteous judgment was not against the world but against the church. Therefore, in times of spiritual declension and moral decadence, the great duty of every Christian is both to discover those sins which have caused the judgment and to put them away by that method which God Himself has chosen. The method God has chosen is the Solemn Assembly. Corporate sin must be dealt with by corporate repentance according to divinely ordained methods.

Practical Suggestions

1. A Solemn Assembly is to be a time when all normal daily work is set aside. This is clearly the instruction of Leviticus 23:34-36; Numbers 29:35 and Deuteronomy 16:8. While the overwhelming teaching of Scripture is in favor of hard work, it is absolutely clear that all work must be subjugated to spiritual concerns. Just as man is to labor six days, and six days only, and then rest on the seventh, so also man is to labor in times of spiritual and moral advance; but he is to set aside this normal daily work in order to seek the face of God during times of righteous judgment.

2. A Solemn Assembly is a time when the entire body of people affected by the righteous judgment are required to be in attendance. This is clear in the several passages on Old Testament revivals noted above, but nowhere more clear than in Joel where even the honeymooners had their honeymoon revoked, and the mother with an infant at her breast was required to be present (Joel 2:16). Part of the corporate sin that must be put away is that spirit of rebellion that exists in many professed Christians that causes them to believe that no spiritual leader can order them about. Such wicked sinners would do well to observe the severity of the denunciations against rebellion and stubbornness recorded in I Samuel 15:23.

3. A Solemn Assembly is a time of fasting. Rather than wondering concerning the physical significance of fasting, professed Christians would do well to face squarely the immediate spiritual importance. On a normal basis we realize that the care of our bodies is a proper responsibility we assume before God. The care of ourselves is part of our normal service to God. But there are issues vastly more important than the care of our bodies. In fasting, a believing people acknowledge to God that the urgent concerns of the spiritual take precedence over the normal concerns of the physical. In short, fasting is an outward means of demonstrating that humility before God which acknowledges that the discovery of all those sins that have provoked His judgment and the putting away of them in an orderly corporate manner is of vastly greater consequence than the feeding of the body. There are times when the bodies of believers must be brought into subjection so that the overwhelming necessities of the spiritual may receive their due attention.

4. A Solemn Assembly is a time for sacrifice. Numerous Old Testament passages dealing with the Solemn Assembly make this clear (including Numbers 10:10 and 15:3). One of the greatest blessings God has given to mankind is the gift of time. What sacrifice could be more significant than the sacrifice of time in order to participate fully in God's commanded method of reversing a righteous judgment against a church or nation?

5. A Solemn Assembly is of protracted duration. While most professed Christians may content themselves with hour long "worship" services, the call to a Solemn Assembly is a call to a greatly elongated meeting. In many of the passages where Solemn Assemblies are described, the assembly met for days on end——even as long as seven or fourteen days. On other occasions, however, it would appear that a full day was sufficient. In 2 Chronicles 7:8,9 it is noted that the feast was observed for seven days and then on the eighth day a Solemn Assembly was observed. It was at this solemn assembly that God said, "If My people, which are called by my name, shall humble themselves, and pray, and seek My face, and turn from their wicked ways; then will I hear from heaven, and will forgive their sin, and will heal their land" (verse 14). No Solemn Assembly would be worth the name that did not allow at least an entire day for the great tasks of humiliation, prayer, repentance and seeking God's face.

6. A Solemn Assembly is a season of earnest prayer. Churches in general allot altogether too little time for prayer. Enough time may be taken to present requests to God but precious little time is given corporately for God to present requests to men. But not only should much time be given to prayer at a Solemn Assembly, much time in prayer should be given in preparation for a Solemn Assembly. If the Solemn Assembly is to be held throughout the day on Saturday, the people of a church would do well to give considerable time to prayer throughout each day of the preceding week in preparation for the day itself.

7. A Solemn Assembly is a mandatory occasion for corporate repentance. In preparation for this, a catalogue of the sins to be corporately confessed and put away should be prepared in advance. Some churches have solicited the involvement of the entire congregation in this catalogue. Various entities within the fellowship have been asked to prepare lists of the offenses against both God and man that they know the church has never corporately put away. The leaders have then gone over these lists and compiled them into a catalogue. The intent is not to manufacture wrongs but to seriously investigate any and all matters that might have contributed to the righteous judgment.

8. A Solemn Assembly is an opportunity for Spirit-anointed preaching of the searching truths of Scripture to deeply touch afresh the lives of God's people. In Solemn Assemblies where only a single day is devoted, it is not uncommon to have at least one or possibly two such sermons specifically aimed at the issues of the day and assisting the people in fulfillment of the responsibilities and grasping the opportunities the day presents.

9. A Solemn Assembly is a most wonderful opportunity for children to see their parents and elders demonstrating Christianity at its deepest corporate levels. In that the entire family is summoned, the youth and older children have a very special privilege of being deeply touched by the solemnities of the day. In some churches, outside baby-sitters have been hired to look after infants and the smallest children so that parents can devote their full attention to the work of the day.

10. A Solemn Assembly gives God an opportunity to respond to His people at a level He cannot possibly do when they are living in neglect of His Word or in direct violation of His commandments. Historically, God has responded to Solemn Assemblies by sending fresh waves of blessings into both the personal and corporate lives of believers and, on some occasions even, glorious revivals have resulted. One of the most amazing instances of this is the Revival of the General Assembly in the Church of Scotland in 1596.

Illustrations

John Davidson of Prestonpans, Scotland became burdened for the welfare of his beloved Church and gave expressions of concern at the Synod of Fife in 1593 and the Assembly in 1594. His Presbytery of Haddington joined with him in petitioning the General Assembly of the Church to set aside time for a Solemn Assembly at the annual meeting of 1596. The Assembly met at St. Giles Cathedral, Edinburgh in March. A very thorough catalogue of sins was prepared which covered the misdeeds of every class of persons from the King on down to the meanest subjects. More space was given to the sins of ministers than to the wickedness of all other classes put together. The Solemn Assembly occurred on the Tuesday of the second week of the General Assembly and some 400 men, mostly ministers, participated. Davidson preached on Ezekiel 13 and 34 and dealt with the lying prophets and the shepherds who feed themselves and not their flocks. He then exhorted his brethren to enter into private meditation and confession and it was then that the Holy Spirit of God came down and the ancient Cathedral Church resounded with the sobs and cries of hundreds of ministers humbling themselves before God on the dirt floor. A public pledge of fresh surrender to God Almighty was called for and all but one of the men present joined in waving their hands as evidence of binding commitment. This spirit of corporate repentance was carried into all the Presbyteries and the revival of 1596 followed.

But Solemn Assemblies must not be thought of merely as vestiges of the past. Recently the First Baptist Church of Pagosa Springs, Colorado was grievously affected by a divisive spirit. Two of the censorious persons, a husband and wife, were removed from membership because of their continued trouble-making activities. Rather than church discipline bringing them to repentance of their wickedness, these persons led the way in filing three lawsuits against the church, claiming that the two of them plus eleven of their friends and relatives were the true First Baptist Church of that community. The first suit was for all the church property and bank accounts. The second suit was for seventeen million dollars in damages: four million each for the husband and wife, four million each for their two daughters, plus an additional million in family damages against the pastor, Grant Adkisson. The third suit was a temporary injunction against the church, seeking to prevent the members from the use of their own building and finances. After much prayer and consultation the congregation determined to obey the Word of God in the resolution of the matter and called a Solemn Assembly. For three weeks prior to the day of Assembly extensive prayer was uttered. The fourth to second days prior to the Solemn Assembly were devoted to general prayer and fasting. The day immediately preceding the Assembly was given to round-the-clock prayer with fasting. Virtually the entire congregation met for the Solemn Assembly itself and spent nine hours together in prayer, fasting, and corporate repentance. Three days after the Solemn Assembly the four members of the family that had brought the suits against the church were all killed in the crash of a private airplane. As a direct result of divine intervention, the damages suit was dismissed, the temporary injunction was settled in favor of the church, the suit for the church property and bank accounts was dropped, and God Himself crowned the faithfulness of the dear people of that congregation with a season of most blessed nearness.

God's work, done in God's way, still triumphs!

Encouragement

Historically, unheeded remedial judgments have turned into final judgments. America, as a nation, is ripe for destruction. The evangelical movement in this country is characterized by an arrogance that is almost beyond belief. The neglect of prayer, the involvement in Philistine methodology, the moral evils, and the doctrinal corruptions that characterize the movement are sufficient to cause Sodomites to wonder at God's justice in destroying their city while sparing the United States.

If the youth of the nation are to live out their lives in a land of freedom and opportunity, they will do so because their parents had grace sufficient to humble themselves, pray, repent of their sins, and seek God's face in Solemn Assemblies.

Obedience is still better than sacrifice. Joel's call requires prompt response, "Consecrate a fast, proclaim a Solemn Assembly; gather the elders and all the inhabitants of the land to the house of the Lord your God, and cry out to the Lord."

CHAPTER TWO

The Necessity of Reformation

The Synod Of Boston in New-England, September 10, 1679

First published as: *The Necessity of Reformation with the Expedients Subservient Thereunto, Asserted; in Answer to Two Questions I. What are the Evils that have Provoked the Lord to Bring His Judgments on New-England? II. What is to be Done so that Those Evils May be Reformed? Agreed Upon by the Elders and Messengers of the Churches Assembled in the Synod at Boston in New-England, September 10, 1679.* Boston: Printed by John Foster, 1679

To the Much Honored
General Court
of the Massachusetts Colony
now sitting at Boston
in New-England

Right worshipful, worshipful and much honored in our Lord Jesus!

The ways of God toward His people in New-England have, in many respects, been like His dealings with Israel of old. It was a great and noble undertaking when our Fathers ventured themselves and their little ones upon the rude waves of the vast ocean so that they might follow the Lord into this land of America. It would be difficult to find parallel instances other than those of our Father Abraham when he left Ur of the Chaldees or of his seed when they left the land of Egypt. In all three instances, the Lord alone lead them and there was no strange God with them.

In this wilderness where we dwell, we are made the subjects of most peculiar mercies and privileges. The good will of Him that dwelt in the burning-bush has been upon the heads of those that were separated from their brethren. The Lord has, by turning a wilderness into a fruitful land, brought us into a wealthy place. As He did with Israel of old, He has planted a vine, having cast out the heathen and prepared room for it. He has caused it to take deep root and to fill the land so that it has sent out its boughs unto the sea and its branches to the river. If we search the days that are past and look from the one side of heaven to the other, where can we find another instance of this great thing which the Lord has done?

His planting us under these heavens and laying our foundations on this part of earth must be reckoned among the most wonderful works of God which this age has seen. If we look abroad over the face of the whole earth, where shall we see a place or people brought to such perfection and considerableness in so short a time? Let our adversaries themselves be the judges, has this been true of any of the existing nations? We must, then, ascribe all these things to the grace and abundant goodness of the

Lord our God, who has owned the religious designs and interests of New-England in its primitive constitution. Our fathers never sought for nor thought of great things for themselves, but they did seek first the Kingdom of God and His righteousness and, in consequence, all these things were added to them.

They did not come into this wilderness to see a man clothed in soft raiment, but we have, in too many respects, been forgetting the errand upon which the Lord sent us hither. All the world is witness of our failure and therefore we must not wonder that God has changed the tenor of His dispensations toward us, turning to do us hurt and consuming us after He has done us good. If we had continued as we once were, the Lord would have continued to do for us as once He did.

Notwithstanding this, we must not deny or disown what of God remains among us. There is cause to fear that the same evils for which the Lord is contending with us are found too in other Reformed Churches and perhaps even to a higher degree than are yet visible with us. Thankfully, our churches still, through the grace of Christ, own both the faith and order of the Gospel that was professed in the days of our fathers. There are yet a number of precious souls, we hope in every congregation, that have not defiled their garments with the sins of the times. Nonetheless, in respect to the practice and power of godliness, the present generation in New-England as a body is far short of those whom God saw fit to use in the laying of the foundation of His temple here. Our iniquities admit of sadder aggravations than those of others because we sin against greater light and means and mercies than any other people, all circumstances considered, have ever done. Therefore the Lord is righteous in all the evils that have befallen us.

It is high time for us to be earnest in an impartial scrutiny concerning the causes of God's holy displeasure against us and to fervently seek the proper remedies or Scripture expedients for reformation, so that the Lord, who has said, "Return unto Me, and I will return unto you," may be at peace with us. Attempts respecting this matter have not been altogether wanting, but hitherto they have not met with any great degree of success.

Therefore, it has pleased God to so dispose you, the honored General Court of this Colony, to call upon all the churches herein to send their Elders and Messengers that they might meet in the form of a Synod to make most serious enquiry into the questions here propounded and answered.

We cannot but hope that this motion was of God since, after the prayers of His people have been solemnly and abundantly poured out before Him that it might be so, evident tokens of the Lord's gracious presence in and with that Reverend Assembly have been observed, especially in that He was pleased to so enlighten the minds and incline the hearts of His servants, the Messengers and Representatives of the churches, that there was an unanimity in their votes and determinations, not only with reference to the answers to those questions but also concerning other things then discussed and decided upon.

Several days were spent in discoursing upon the questions herewith presented. Every member of the Synod was given full liberty to express himself. After this, some were chosen to draw up what appeared to be the mind of the Assembly and the mind of Christ, in whose name we came together and considered these matters. The document made by those who had been appointed unto that service was read once and again, each paragraph being duly and distinctly weighed in the balance and then, upon mature deliberation, the whole Synod voted unanimously as to the substance, end and scope thereof. Many of the things here insisted on have been often mentioned and inculcated by those whom the Lord has set as Watchmen to the House of Israel, although alas, not with that success which their souls have desired. It is not a small matter, nor should it seem little in our eyes, that the churches have in this way confessed and declared the Truth. Coming from a Synod, as their concurring testimony, will carry more authority with it than if one man only, or many in their single capacities, should speak the same things.

Undoubtedly, the outcome of this undertaking will be most signal, either as to mercy or misery. If New-England remembers from whence she is fallen and does the first works, there is reason to hope that it will be better with us than at our beginnings. But if this, after all other means in and by which the Lord has been striving to redeem us, shall be despised or become ineffectual, we may dread what is likely to follow. It is a solemn thought that the Jewish Church had, as the Churches in New-England have this day, an opportunity to reform in Josiah's time, but because they had no heart for it, the Lord quickly removed them out of His sight. What God, in His sovereignty, may do for us, no man can say, but if He acts according to His accustomed dispensations, we are a perishing people if we do not now reform.

May the Lord help you His Servants, under whose influence and by whose encouragements this Synod has convened, to promote this matter, both by your recommendations of these conclusions unto the churches for their consideration and acceptance in the Lord and otherwise, according to your respective relations and capacities. The Lord strengthen your hearts and hands therein, for much depends upon your courage, prudence, zeal and activity.

We do not read in Scripture or in history of any notable general reformation among a people, except the leaders helped forward the work. Haggai's and Zechariah's sermons would never have built the temple, if Zerubbabel and Shealtiel, both godly magistrates, had not improved their authority to that end. Luther, Calvin, Zwingli and other reformers would have labored in vain, had not the princes and senators among whom they lived, promoted the interest of the Reformation. Nor have we any record of the civil authorities in any place doing their utmost toward the suppression of growing evils but what there was, at least for the moment, some good effect therefrom.

Therefore these things are commended to your most serious consideration. It is, under God, by you that we enjoy great quietness. May the Lord continue the present government and governors, under whose shadow, as was the case with the remnant of Judah under Gedaliah, we have sat with great delight and grant that every one, both leaders and people, in their proper place and order, may up and be doing. May the Lord our God be with us as He was with our Fathers.

"Yet now be strong, O Zerubbabel, saith the Lord; and be strong, O Joshua... and be strong, all ye people of the land, saith the Lord, and work: for I am with you, saith the Lord of hosts: according to the word that I covenanted with you when ye came out of Egypt, so My Spirit remaineth among you: fear ye not" (Haggai 2:4,5).

Increase Mather

The Synod of 1679

QUESTION ONE. What are the evils that have provoked the Lord to bring His judgments on New-England?

Scriptures make it clear that God sometimes has and pleads a controversy with His people (Hosea 4:1; 12:2; Micah 6:1,2). In such passages, God plainly and fully proposes, states and pleads His controversy in all the parts and causes of it. Therein He justifies Himself by the declaration of His own infinite mercy, grace, goodness, justice, righteousness, truth and faithfulness in all His proceedings with them. He judges His people, charging them with all those provoking evils which had been the causes of that controversy. He accuses them of high and heavy aggravation of their sins and blames them for the increase of their guilt and punishment, making it clear that He would have been just if He had carried out His controversy with them unto the utmost extremity of justice and judgment.

That God has a controversy with His New-England people is undeniable. The Lord has written His displeasure in dismal characters against us. Though personal afflictions often come only or chiefly for testing, with public judgments this is not normally so, especially when by a continued series of Providences, the Lord appears and pleads against His people (2 Samuel 21:1). as has been the case with us from year to year. Would the Lord have whetted His glittering sword and His hand have taken hold on judgment? Would He have sent such a moral contagion like a tidal wave of destruction in the midst of us? Would He have said, "Sword! go through the land and cut off man and beast?" Or would He have kindled such devouring fires and made such fearful desolations in the earth, if He had not been angry? It is not for nothing that the merciful God, who does not willingly afflict nor grieve the children of men, has done all these things unto us. Yes, sometimes he has even covered Himself with a cloud so that our prayer should not pass through.

Although it is possible that the Lord may contend with us partly on account of secret unobserved sins (Joshua 7:11,12; 2 Kings 17:9; Psalm 90:8), (in which respect, a deep and most serious enquiry into the causes of His controversy ought to be attended) nevertheless, it is sadly evident that there are visible, manifest evils which, without doubt, the Lord is provoked by.

ANSWER ONE. There is a great and visible decay of the power of godliness amongst many professors in these churches. It may be feared that there is in too many a spiritual and heart apostasy from God. For this reason communion with Him in the ways of His worship, especially in secret, is much neglected and thus men cease to know and fear and love and trust in Him but take up their contentment and satisfaction in something else. This was the ground and bottom of the Lord's controversy with His people of old (Psalm 78:8,37; 81:11; Jeremiah 2:5,11,12) and with His people under the New Testament also (Revelation 2:4-5).

ANSWER TWO. The pride that abounds in New-England testifies against us (Hosea 5:5; Ezekiel 7:10). There is spiritual pride (Zephaniah 3:11), from whence two great evils and provocations have proceeded and prevailed among us.

1. A refusing to submit to order according to divine appointment (Numbers 16:3; 1 Peter 5:5).

2. A spirit of contention (Proverbs 13:10). This is an evil that is most eminently against the solemn charge of the Lord Jesus (John 13:34,35) and that for which God has, by severe judgments, punished His people, both in former and latter ages. This malady has been very general in the country. We have, therefore, cause to fear that the wolves which God in His holy Providence has let loose upon us, have been sent to chasten His sheep for their dividing and straying from one another, and that the wars and fightings which have proceeded from the lust of pride in particular, have been punished with the sword (James 4:1; Job 19:29).

Pride in respect to apparel has also greatly abounded. Servants and the poorer sort of people are notoriously guilty in this matter. Far too many of them have gone above their estates and degrees, thereby transgressing the laws both of God and man (Matthew 11:8). This is a sin that even the light of nature and the laws of civil nations have condemned. Also, many who are not of the poor, have offended God by strange apparel not becoming serious Christians, especially in these days of affliction and misery, wherein the Lord calls upon men to put off their ornaments (Exodus 33:5; Jeremiah 4:30). This is a sin which brings wrath upon the greatest that shall be found guilty of it (Zephaniah 1:8 with Jeremiah 53:13). We note particularly that the Lord has threatened to visit with the sword, with sickness and with loathsome diseases for this very sin (Isaiah 3:16).

ANSWER THREE. Inasmuch as our Fathers followed the Lord into this wilderness while it was a land not sown, out of particular regard for the second commandment, we may fear that the breaches of this commandment form some part of the Lord's controversy with New-England. Church fellowship and other divine institutions are greatly neglected. Many of the rising generation are not mindful of the obligations their baptism engages them unto, that is to use their utmost endeavors that they may be fit for and so partake in all the holy ordinances of the Lord Jesus (Matthew 28:20). There are too many that, with profane Esau, slight spiritual privileges. Nor is there as much discipline extending toward the children of the Covenant as we are generally agreed ought to be done. On the other hand, human inventions and will-worship have been set up even in Jerusalem. Men have set up their thresholds by God's threshold and their posts by His post. Some have arisen among us who, in opposition to the Churches of the Lord Jesus, receive into their societies those that have been delivered unto Satan because of scandalous conduct, and even allow to serve as ministers of holy things those who are justly under church censures, thereby setting up their altar against the Lord's altar. It must surely be provoking to God if these evils are not duly and fully testified against by everyone in position to do so (Joshua 22:19; 2 Kings 23:13; Psalm 99:9; Ezekiel 43:8; Hosea 11:6).

ANSWER FOUR. The holy and glorious name of God has been polluted and profaned among us. This is happening by the use of oaths and imprecations in ordinary discourse. It is too common a thing for men in a most solemn way to swear unnecessary oaths whereas it is a breach of the third commandment to use the blessed name of God this way. Many, if not most, of those that swear do not consider the rule of oaths (Jeremiah 4:2) and so we may justly fear that because of swearing, the land mourns (Jeremiah 23:10).

There is also a great profaneness in respect to irreverent behavior in the solemn worship of God. It is a frequent thing for men, although not required by any infirmity, to sit during prayer time and some even with their heads almost covered. Others give way to their own sloth and sleepiness when they should be serving God with attention and intention, under the solemn dispensations of His ordinances. We read of only one man in Scripture that slept at a sermon and that sin nearly cost him his life (Acts 20:9).

ANSWER FIVE. There is much Sabbath breaking. There are multitudes who profanely absent themselves from the public worship of God on His holy day, especially in the most populous places of the land. Many, under pretence of differing apprehensions about the beginning of the

Sabbath, do not keep a seventh part of their time holy unto the Lord, as the fourth commandment requires. Walking abroad and travelling, not merely to reach the place of worship or to attend works of necessity or mercy, are a common practice on the Sabbath day. This is contrary to that rest enjoined by the commandment. Some attend their particular servile callings and employments after the Sabbath is begun or before it is ended. Worldly, unsuitable discourses are very common upon the Lord's day which are contrary to the Scripture which requires that men should not find their own pleasures on holy times nor speak their own words (Isaiah 58:13). There are many that do not take care to dispatch their worldly business so that they are free and fit for the duties of the Sabbath. There are others who, if not wholly neglectful do, after a careless, heartless manner perform the duties that concern the sanctification of the Sabbath. This brings wrath and the fires of judgment upon a professing people (Nehemiah 13:17,18; Jeremiah 17:27).

ANSWER SIX. There is much amiss concerning families and the government thereof. There are many families that do not pray to God constantly, morning and evening, and many more where the Scriptures are not daily read so that the Word of Christ might dwell richly in them. There are too many houses that are full of ignorance and profaneness and that are not duly examined and for this cause wrath may come upon others round about them as well as upon themselves (Joshua 22:20; Jeremiah 5:7; 10:25). Many householders who profess religion, do not cause all that are within their gates to become subject unto good order as they ought (Exodus 20:10). There are children and servants that are not kept in due subjection, their masters and parents especially, being sinfully indulgent toward them. This is a sin which brings great judgments, as we see in Eli's and David's families. In this respect, Christians in this land have become too much like the Indians natives. Do we then need to wonder why the Lord has afflicted us by them? Sometimes a sin is discerned by the instrument that Providence punishes with. Most of the evils that abound among us proceed from defects in family government.

ANSWER SEVEN. Inordinate passions. There are sinful heats and hatreds and reproachful and reviling expressions among church members themselves, who abound with evil surmising, uncharitable and unrighteous censures, back-biting and hearing and telling tales. There are few that remember and duly observe the rule to drive away the tale bearer with an angry countenance. Hence law suits are frequent, brother going to law with brother and provoking and abasing one another in public courts of justice to the scandal of their holy profession (Isaiah 58:4; 1 Corinthians

6:6,7). In managing the discipline of Christ's Church there are far too many who act by their passions and prejudices more than by a spirit of love and faithfulness towards their brother's soul. All these things are against the law of Christ and therefore dreadful violations of the Church Covenant made in the presence of God.

ANSWER EIGHT. There is much intemperance. That heathenish and idolatrous practice of drinking to one's health is altogether too common and the shameful iniquity of sinful drinking is become a general provocation. Days of training and other public solemnities have been abused in this respect. Not only have the English been guilty of these sins themselves but the Indians have been debauched by those that call themselves Christians, pushing their bottles on them and making them drunk also. This is a crying sin and all the more aggravated by the fact that the first Planters of this Colony came into this land, as the Patent expressed, with a design to convert the heathen unto Christ. But if instead of winning them for Christ, we teach them wickedness which they were never before guilty of, the Lord may well punish us by them.

Moreover, the sword, sickness, poverty and almost all the other judgments which have been upon New-England, are mentioned in the Scripture as the woeful fruit of this sin of intemperance (Isaiah 5:11,12; 28:1,2; 56:12; Proverbs 21:17; 23:21,29-32; Hosea 2:8,9; 7:5). There are more temptations and occasions unto this sin which are publicly allowed than any necessity requires. The proper end of taverns, etc., is for the entertainment of strangers. If they were utilized to that end only, a far smaller number of them would be sufficient. But it is a common practice for town-dwellers and even church members to frequent public houses and there to misspend precious time to the dishonor of the Gospel and the scandalizing of others who are, by such examples, induced to sin against God. Thus for church members to be unnecessarily in such houses is sinful, scandalous and provoking to God (Matthew 17:27; 18:7; Romans 14:21; 1 Corinthians 8:9,10).

There are also other heinous breaches of the seventh commandment. Temptations thereunto have become too common especially those of immodest apparel (Proverbs 7:10), the decking out of the hair, the ornamentation of garments, the exposure of naked necks, arms and even more abominable, of naked breasts, mixed dancing, light behavior and expressions, sinful company-keeping with light and vain persons, unlawful gaming, an abundance of idleness which brought ruinous judgments upon Sodom and much more upon Jerusalem (Ezekiel 16:49) and doth sorely threaten New-England, unless effectual remedies are thoroughly and timely applied.

ANSWER NINE. There is a great lack of truthfulness among men. Promise breaking is a common sin and for it New-England is spoken ill of in the world. For this transgression the Lord has threatened to give His people into the hands of their enemies and that their dead bodies should be meat for the fowls of heaven and to the beasts of the earth. These judgments have been verified as being upon us (Jeremiah 34:18-20). False reports have been too common among us as have slanders and reproaches, and that sometimes against the most faithful and eminent servants of God. The Lord is not inclined to allow such iniquity to pass unpunished (Numbers 16:41-50; Jeremiah 9:4,5).

ANSWER TEN. Inordinate affections to the world. Idolatry is a God-provoking, judgment procuring sin. And covetousness is idolatry (Ephesians 5:5). There has been, in many professed Christians, an insatiable desire after land and worldly accommodations. This has even led to forsaking the church and its ordinances and to living like the heathen so that they might have enough elbowroom in the world. Farms and merchandising have been preferred before the things of God.

In this respect, the interest of New-England seems to be drastically changed. We in New-England are different from other parts of our nation. It was not for any worldly consideration that our Fathers came into this wilderness but for religious purposes, so that they could build a sanctuary unto the Lord's name. But now religion is made subservient to worldly interests. Such iniquity causes war to be in the gates and cities to be burned up (Judges 5:8; Matthew 22:5-7).

Therefore we cannot help but solemnly bear witness against that practice of settling plantations without any ministry among them, for this is the same as preferring the world before the Gospel. When Lot forsook the Land of Canaan and the Church which was in Abraham's family, so that he might have better worldly accommodations in Sodom, God found it necessary to bring judgment upon that wicked place and Lot was constrained to leave his goodly pastures which his heart, though he was otherwise a good man, was too much set upon.

That many among us are under the prevailing power of the sin of worldliness is evident,

1. From that oppression which the land groans under. There are some traders who sell their goods at excessive rates; there are day laborers and mechanics who are unreasonable in their demands; there have even been those that have dealt deceitfully and oppressively with the heathen among whom we live, whereby they have been scandalized and prejudiced against

the name of Christ. The Scriptures frequently threaten judgments for the sin of oppression and especially the judgment of an oppressing sword that comes as a just punishment for that evil (Proverbs 28:8; Isaiah 5:7; Ezekiel 7:11; 22:15).

2. It is also evident that men are under the prevailing power of a worldly spirit by their stinginess as to public concerns. God, by a continued series of Providences, has for many years been blasting the fruits of the earth in great measure. It has happened this year even more so than before. Now if we search the Scriptures, we shall find that when the Lord has been provoked to destroy the fruits of the earth, either by noxious creatures or by His own immediate hand in blastings or droughts or in excessive rains, all of which judgments we have experienced, it has been mostly for this sin of stinginess with reference to public and pious concerns (Haggai 1:9; Malachi 3:8-11). When peoples' hearts and hands are enlarged upon these accounts, God has promised (and is sure by his faithful Providence to do accordingly) to bless with outward plenty and prosperity (2 Chronicles 31:10; Proverbs 3:9,10; Malachi 3:10; 1 Corinthians 9:5-10). So on the other hand, when men withhold more than is meet, the Lord sends impoverishing judgments upon them (Proverbs 11:24).

ANSWER ELEVEN. There has been opposition to the work of reformation. Although the Lord has been calling upon us, not only by the voice of His servants but by awful judgments, that we should return unto Him who has been smiting us, yet men will not return every one from his evil way. Notwithstanding all the good laws that are established for the suppression of growing evils, there has been great incorrigibleness under lesser judgments. Sin and sinners have many advocates. They that have been zealous in bearing witness against the sins of the times have been reproached and in other ways discouraged. This proves that there are hearts that are unwilling to reform. Hence the Lord's controversy is not yet done but His hand is stretched out still (Leviticus 26:23,24; Isaiah 5:12,13).

ANSWER TWELVE. A public spirit is greatly wanting in most men. There are few that are of Nehemiah's spirit (Nehemiah 5:15). All seek their own, not the things which are Jesus Christ's (Philippians 2:21). They serve themselves even while pretending to serve Christ and His holy ordinances. Matters pertaining to the kingdom of God are either not regarded at all or not in the first place. Consequently schools of learning and other public concerns are in a languishing state. There is a wicked spirit of complaining and murmuring because of public expenses, which is a great sin. A private, self-seeking spirit is one of those evils that renders the last times perilous (2 Timothy 3:1-5).

ANSWER THIRTEEN. There are sins against the Gospel, whereby the Lord has been provoked. Christ is not prized and embraced in all His offices and ordinances as He ought to be. His manna has been loathed and the pleasant land despised (Psalm 106:24). Although the Gospel and the Covenant of Grace call upon men to repent, yet there are multitudes that refuse to repent, even when the Lord grants them time and means. No sins provoke the Lord more than impenitence and unbelief (Jeremiah 8:6; Zechariah 7:11-14; Hebrews 3:17; Revelation 2:21,22). There is great unfruitfulness under the means of grace and that brings the most desolating judgments (Isaiah 5:4,5; Matthew 3:10; 21:43).

ANSWER FOURTEEN. Finally, there are several considerations which seem to prove that the evils mentioned are the matters of the Lord's controversy with us.

1. They are sins of which, for the most part, a great many are guilty.

2. They are sins which have already been acknowledged before the Lord on days of humiliation appointed by authority and yet not reformed.

3. They are sins which have not been punished (and some of them not punishable) by men, therefore the Lord Himself punishes for them.

QUESTION TWO. What is to be done so that these evils may be reformed?

ANSWER ONE. It would tend much to promote the interest of reformation, if all that are in places above others become, as to themselves and their families, exemplary in every way possible. Moses, purposing to reform others, began with what concerned himself and his own household. People are apt to follow the example of those that are above them (2 Chronicles 12:1; Galatians 2:14). If any leaders, either civil or ecclesiastical, have divided hearts or have tolerated any other sins of the times, their reformation would have a great and happy influence upon many.

ANSWER TWO. The present standing generation, both leaders and people, is for the greater part a different generation than was in New-England forty years ago. Thus for us to declare our adherence unto the faith and order of the Gospel, according to what is from the Scripture expressed in the Platform of Discipline, may be likewise a good means both to recover those that have erred from the truth and to prevent apostasy in the future.

ANSWER THREE. It is requisite that persons not be admitted unto communion in the Lord's Supper without making a personal and public profession of their faith and repentance, either orally or in some other way to the just satisfaction of the church. Therefore both elders and churches must be duly watchful and circumspect in this matter (Ezekiel 44:7-9; Acts 2:41,42; 1 Corinthians 11:28,29).

ANSWER FOUR. It is essential to reformation that the discipline of Christ, in the power of it, should be upheld in the churches. It is evident from Christ's Epistles to the Churches in Asia Minor, that the evils and degeneracy then prevailing among Christians, proceeded chiefly from the neglect of discipline. It is a known and true observation that when we are remiss in the exercise of discipline, the attendant corruption of manners will provoke the Lord to give men up to strong delusions in matters of faith. Discipline is Christ's ordinance, both for the prevention of apostasy in churches and to recover them when collapsed. Our New-England Churches are under peculiar engagements to be faithful unto Christ and unto His truth in this matter. Faithfulness to the Church Covenant and the correct management of discipline according to the Scriptures were the special design of our Fathers in coming into this wilderness. The degeneracy of the rising generation, so much complained of, is in a great measure to be attributed to neglect of these matters. If all church duty in these respects is faithfully and diligently attended, not only toward parents but also toward the children of the church, according to the rules of Christ, we may wisely hope that the sunk and dying interests of religion will be revived and a world of sin prevented in the future.

ANSWER FIVE. It is requisite that utmost endeavors should be made to assure a full supply of officers in the churches, according to Christ's institution. The defect of many churches on this account is very lamentable. In many of our churches there is only one teaching officer to bear the burden of the whole congregation. The Lord Christ would not have instituted pastors, teachers and ruling elders, nor would the apostles have ordained elders in every church (Acts 14:23; Titus 1:5), if He had not seen the need of them for the good of His people. Therefore, for men to think they can do well enough without them is both to break the second commandment and to reflect upon the wisdom of Christ, as if He appointed unnecessary officers in His church. Experience has proven that personal instruction and discipline have been the happy means of reforming degenerated congregations and have been owned by the Lord for the conversion of many souls. But where there are large congregations, it is impossible for one man, besides his labors in public, to fully

attend all the necessary things of great importance that must be done in
order to an effectual reformation of families and congregations.

ANSWER SIX. It is incumbent upon responsible persons to take care
that officers of the church have adequate encouragement and maintenance. It is high injustice and oppression, yes, even a sin that cries in the
Lord's ears for judgment, when wages are withheld from faithful and
diligent laborers (James 5:4). If this is true of those that labor about
carnal things, how much more true is it of those that labor night and day
over the spiritual and eternal welfare of souls (1 Corinthians 9:11-14). The
Scriptures make it clear that not only members of churches, but all that
are taught in the Word, are bound to share with him that teaches and
that in all good things (Luke 10:7; Galatians 6:6; 1 Timothy 5:17, 18). If,
therefore, people are unwilling to do what justice and reason calls for, the
authorities are to see that they do their duty in this matter. Wherefore,
those in civil authority are said to be the churches' nursing fathers (Isaiah
49:23), for it is their concern to see that the churches are nourished with
the Bread and Water of Life. The magistrate is to be a keeper of both
tables, which as a magistrate he cannot be if he does not promote the
interest of religion by all those means which are of the Lord's appointment. We find in Scripture that when the Lord's ministers have been
forced to neglect the House of God and to go into the field to work
because the people did not provide them the maintenance which was
necessary (and there has been too much of this among us), the magistrate
saw himself as concerned to bring about a reformation (Nehemiah 13:10-
13).

ANSWER SEVEN. Due care and faithfulness with respect unto the
establishment and execution of wholesome laws would very much promote
the interest of reformation. If there are no laws established in the
Commonwealth but what have Scripture warrant, and those laws are so
worded that they may not become a snare unto any that are bound to
censure the violators of them so that they may be impartially executed,
profaneness, heresy, schism, disorders in families, towns and churches will
be happily prevented and reformed. It is especially necessary that those
laws for reformation of provoking evils, which have been determined by
the General Court in the day of our calamity, should be duly considered,
lest we become guilty of dissembling and dallying with the Almighty and
thereby wrath is augmented upon us. In particular, we speak of those laws
respecting the regulation of houses of public entertainment that assure
that the number of such houses does not exceed what is necessary, that
guarantee that the keeping of such houses is entrusted only to persons of

known piety and fidelity, that prohibits inhabitants from drinking in such houses, and that assure that any who shall without license sell any sort of strong drink shall be exemplarily punished.

If civil authorities of every rank are chosen constantly from the ablest and most prudent in the place, authorized and sworn to a faithful discharge of their respective trusts, and duly encouraged to take just action against any that transgress the laws so established, we may hope that much of that profaneness which threatens the ruin of the rising generation will be prevented.

ANSWER EIGHT. Solemn and explicit renewal of Covenant is a Scripture expedient for reformation. We seldom read of any solemn reformation but what was accomplished in this way, as the Scriptures abundantly declare and testify. As the judgments which befell the Lord's people of old are recorded for our admonition (1 Corinthians 10:11), so the course which God led them to observe in order to gain reformation and to avert those judgments is recorded for our imitation. And this was an explicit renovation of covenant. That the Lord calls us to this work, the following considerations seem to prove.

1. If implicit renewal of Covenant is an expedient for reformation and to divert impending wrath and judgment, then much more an explicit renewal is so. The first of these is too obvious to doubt. In prayer and more especially on days of solemn humiliation before the Lord, there is an implicit renewal of Covenant. The very dictates of natural conscience put men upon such duties when they are apprehensive of a day of wrath approaching. If we are afraid to renew our Covenants with God for fear some men will not be true and faithful in doing what they promise, then we must not observe days of fasting and prayers. None will say this.

2. When the church was overrun with idolatry and superstition, those whom the Lord raised up as reformers called for the solemn renewal of the Covenant. You can find this in the records of Asa, Jehoiada, Hezekiah and Josiah. By a parity of reason, when churches are overgrown with worldliness (which is spiritual idolatry) and other corruptions, the same course may and should be observed in order to provoke Reformation.

3. We find in Scripture that when corruption in manners (though not in worship) has prevailed in the church, renovation of Covenant has been the expedient whereby reformation has been attempted and in some measure attained. The Jews have dreaded the sin of idolatry ever since the Babylonian captivity (John 8:41). In Ezra's and Nehemiah's time, sensuality, Sabbath breaking, oppression, strait-handedness respecting the

public worship of God (the very same sins that are found among us) were common, prevailing iniquities. In consequence, those reformers called the people to renew their covenant and to solemnly promise God that they would endeavor not to offend by those evils as formerly (Ezra 10:3; Nehemiah 5:12,13; chapter 10 in total; 13:15).

4. The things which are mentioned in the Scriptures as grounds for renewing Covenant are applicable unto us. The averting of divine wrath is expressed as a sufficient reason for attendance upon this duty (2 Chronicles 29:10; Ezra 10:14). Again, being circumstanced with difficulties and distresses is mentioned as the ground of explicit renovation of Covenant (Nehemiah 9:36-38). Hence, the Lord's servants, when so circumstanced, have been accustomed to make solemn vows, an express form of covenanting (Genesis 28:20,21; Numbers 28:1,2; Judges 11:30). Clouds of wrath are now hanging over our churches. Every one sees that we are circumstanced with some distressing difficulties. This consideration alone ought to be enough to bring us to the renewal of our solemn engagements unto the Lord our God.

5. Men are hereby brought under a stronger obligation to better obedience. There is an awe of God upon the consciences of men when so obliged. Just as is true in respect to oaths, those that have any conscience in them, when under such bonds, are afraid to violate them. Some that are merely legalists and hypocrites may, under solemn Covenants with God, feel such an awe that they are brought at least to an outward reformation, but this may be sufficient to divert temporal judgments. Those that are sincere will, thereby, be engaged unto a closer and more holy walk before the Lord and so become eminent blessings unto the societies and places whereto they belong.

6. This is the way both to prevent and to recover from apostasy. In this respect, even if there were no visible degeneracy among us, this renovation of Covenant would be of singular advantage. There was no public idolatry nor other outward transgressions allowed in the days of Joshua (Joshua 23:8; Judges 2:7). Yet Joshua persuaded the children of Israel to renew their covenant. This was doubtless so that he might thereby restrain them from future idolatry and apostasy (Joshua 24:25).

7. The churches which have lately and solemnly attended this Scripture expedient for reformation have experienced the presence of God with them, signally owning them therein. Think how much more of a blessing might be expected if there should be a general concurrence in this matter!

ANSWER NINE. In renewing Covenant, it is needful that the sins of the times should be engaged against and reformation thereof, in the name and by the help of Christ, promised before the Lord (Ezra 10:3; Nehemiah 5:12,13; and chapter 10).

ANSWER TEN. It seems to be most conducive to edification and reformation, that in renewing Covenant, such things as are clear and indisputable be expressed, so that all the churches may agree in Covenanting to promote the interest of holiness and close walking with God.

ANSWER ELEVEN. As an expedient for reformation, it is good that effectual care should be taken respecting schools of learning. The interest of religion and good literature have been accustomed to rise and fall together. We read in the Scriptures of masters and scholars, of schools and colleges (1 Chronicles 25:8; Malachi 2:12; Acts 19:9; 22:3). The most eminent reformers among the Lord's people of old thought it their concern to erect and uphold them. Was not Samuel, that great reformer, President of the College at Naioth (1 Samuel 19:18-20) and is he not thought to be one of the first founders of colleges? Did not Elijah and Elisha restore the schools erected in the land of Israel and Josiah? Another great reformer showed respect to the College at Jerusalem (2 Kings 22:14). Ecclesiastical tradition informs us that great care was taken by the apostles and by their immediate successors to settle schools in all places where the Gospel had been preached so that the interest of religion might be preserved and the truth propagated to succeeding generations. It is mentioned as one of the greatest mercies that God ever bestowed upon His people Israel, that He raised up of their sons for prophets (Amos 2:11). This statement refers to their education in schools of learning.

We all have cause to bless God that He put it into the hearts of our fathers to take care concerning this matter. These churches would have been in a most deplorable state if the Lord had not blessed the College.[1] It has supplied most of the churches with pastors to this day. When New-England was poor and we were but few in number comparatively, there was a spirit to encourage learning. The college was then full of the students whom God has made a blessing not only in this land but in other places as well. It is to be deeply lamented that now when we have become many and are more able than previously, that the College and other inferior schools are in such a low and languishing state. Therefore, as we desire that reformation and religion should flourish, it concerns us to endeavor that both the College and all other schools of learning in every

---

[1]Harvard College in Cambridge, Massachusetts.

place be duly inspected and encouraged.

ANSWER TWELVE. Inasmuch as a thorough and a heart-felt reformation is necessary in order to obtain peace with God (Jeremiah 3:10) and that all outward means will be ineffectual unto that end unless the Lord pour down His Spirit from on high, it therefore concerns us to cry mightily unto God, both in ordinary and extraordinary ways, that He will be pleased to rain down righteousness upon us (Isaiah 32:5; Ezekiel 39:29; Hosea 10:12; Luke 11:13). Amen!

CHAPTER THREE

Wine for Gospel Wantons: or, Cautions against Spiritual Drunkenness

By
Thomas Shepard

Thomas Shepard, 1605-1649

Thomas Shepard was born in Towcester, near Northampton, England on November 5, in either 1604 or 1605. His father, a prudent and peaceable Puritan, was a grocer. He had eight brothers and sisters of whom he was the youngest. Shepard's childhood was disturbed by much moving about as the result of his mother's death when he was about four and his father's when he was ten. Eventually he was sent to live with his older brother John toward whom Thomas thereafter felt a great obligation. He studied at Emmanuel College, Cambridge receiving from there the B.A. degree in 1624 and the M.A. in 1627. It was while a second year student at the College that an attack of the smallpox combined with the hearing of some powerful preaching aroused him to some serious, albeit temporary, concerns of soul. This was followed by a grievous season of debauchery and doubt but before the end of his College course he entered into a vital spiritual walk with Christ.

About this time he became acquainted with Thomas Hooker whose ministry profoundly affected him. His first regular place of service was at Earles-Colne where for three years he maintained an affecting ministry. Although ordained both Deacon and Priest in the Anglican Church, Shepard was a non-conformist and suffered as such under the hands of Archbishop Laud, being persecuted by him and removed from his charge. After brief service as chaplain to Sir Richard Darley in Yorkshire, where he met and married Margaret Toutville, he labored a short time at two places in Northumberland before the persecutions again reached him.

In June of 1634 Thomas determined to flee England for the new world. Every indication is that he fled in disguise and sailed under an assumed name, but as the result of storms, sickness and a variety of afflictions it was October of 1635 before the Shepards landed in Boston. On February 1st, 1636 he organized the first permanent Church in Cambridge [the eleventh in Massachusetts] where he became the pastor. He was eminent not only in reaching many for Christ but also as an instrument in bringing Harvard College to Cambridge in 1636.

Thomas Shepard was a deeply committed believer who withstood false teachers of his own times, including the Antinomians, whose pernicious doctrines had affected him for ill during his college days. He was a Member of the Synod of Cambridge which solidly condemned them in 1637. He also keenly recognized the extreme dangers facing the church when moral and spiritual declines were tolerated as his sermon on "Spiritual Drunkenness" clearly reveals.

High on his lists of priorities were the evangelization of the American Indians (he was a close friend of John Eliot) and the thorough education of the young (he was the founder of the first academic scholarship program in America).

Among his most popular writings were his diary which first appeared in 1747 but was edited and popularized as "The Autobiography of Thomas Shepard" by Nehemiah Adams in 1832; "The Sincere Convert;" "The Parable of the Ten Virgins Opened and Applied," 1660 and "The Clear Sun Shine of the Gospel Breaking Forth Upon the Indians of New-England," 1648.

For a very fruitful and inspiring study of this great New England preacher, readers are referred to "Thomas Shepard Pilgrim Father and Founder of Harvard. His Spiritual Experience and Experimental Preaching" by Alexander Whyte. Edinburgh. 1909. Also worth reading is the biography by John Adams Albro, "The Life of Thomas Shepard," Boston, 1847. Shepard's Autobiography was reprinted in "First Planters of the Colony of Massachusetts Bay," 1846.

First Published as: *Wine for Gospel Wantons: or, Cautions Against Spiritual Drunkenness. Being the brief notes of a sermon preached at Cambridge in New-England, upon a day of public fasting and prayer throughout the Colony, June 25, 1645. In reference to the sad estate of the Lord's people in England. By that Reverend Servant of the Lord Mr. Thomas Shepard deceased, Sometime the Pastor of the Church of Christ there.* Cambridge: Printed in the year 1668.

Wine for Gospel Wantons

"Therefore thou shalt speak unto them this word; Thus saith the Lord God of Israel, Every bottle shall be filled with wine: and they shall say unto thee, Do we not certainly know that every bottle shall be filled with wine? Then shalt thou say unto them, Thus saith the Lord, Behold, I will fill all the inhabitants of this land, even the kings that sit upon David's throne, and the priests, and the prophets, and all the inhabitants of Jerusalem, with drunkenness. And I will dash them one against another, even the fathers and the sons together, saith the Lord: I will not pity, nor spare, nor have mercy, but destroy them. Here ye and give ear; be not proud: for the Lord hath spoken."
Jeremiah 13:12-15.

This chapter contains a prophecy of the captivity of God's Church in Babylon which is set down to make a deeper impression on their hearts. It is first portrayed under the type of an unwashed girdle which the Prophet took from his loins and hid in a hole in the rocks near the Euphrates River. After a time Jeremiah was instructed to dig it up and when he did found it was so marred that it was good for nothing. The Word of the Lord then came to the Prophet saying, "Thus saith the Lord, After this manner will I mar the pride of Judah, and the great pride of Jerusalem" (Jeremiah 13:9). When a people will not be vile in their own eyes, God has a time to make them vile; when they will not be the glory and praise of God, He will make them the filth and shame of the world.

Then there follows a series of sundry similitudes, the first of which constitutes our text. We must consider it with particular care. Here I ask you to observe two things: First, the similitude itself wherein God compares them to bottles into which wine was put. Here a plain command is recorded, "Thus saith the Lord God of Israel, Every bottle shall be filled with wine." The Prophet was to preach and testify of this fact. Second, the ignorant and disdainful way this message was received from God, "Do we not certainly know that every bottle shall be filled with wine?" It is as if they responded, "Everybody knows that! What great matter is this? Why do you publish and press upon us such an obvious fact? We know that every bottle shall be filled with wine."

Now the Lord had caught them and made them yield thus far. So He comes upon them with the second thing, viz. the explication of the similitude. Similitudes prove nothing, but when God applies them, then there is proof enough. Briefly, to open up the meaning of the text a little consider that,

By "every bottle" is meant all the inhabitants of the land and more particularly even the Kings and the Priests and the Prophets.

By "wine" is meant that spirit of drunkenness wherewith the Lord will fill them.

By "the filling of the vessels" is meant they shall be full of drunkenness.

By the "bottles" is meant their weak condition, for they thought themselves vessels to honor that could withstand the dint of any stroke but the Lord says, "I will dash them one against another."

"I will do it," says the Lord, by filling them with a spirit of drunkenness, and by dashing them one against another. I will break all relations asunder and will not pity nor spare but destroy.

It would take much time to open all these particulars so I shall only speak concerning one of them, viz. what is meant by a spirit of drunkenness. Sometimes it is taken for the drunkenness of men's bodies. Other times it speaks of the soul-calamities that men are under which are so drastic that they know not what to do. The Prophet laments, "He hath made me drunken with wormwood" (lamentations 3:15), that is, with sore and bitter afflictions. Sometimes it is taken for the spiritual judgments that come on the souls of men because of sin and therefore refers not so much to misery in general as to spiritual misery, when the Lord gives men up to a reprobate spirit. It is often used this way in Scripture, "They are drunken, but not with wine; they stagger but not with strong drink. For the Lord hath poured out upon you the spirit of deep sleep, and hath closed your eyes" (Isaiah 29:9,10). Jeremiah expresses the calamity of the people in speaking of their being dashed one against another. But drunkenness goes before as that which prepares the people for this misery: "Thus saith the Lord God of Israel... I will fill all the inhabitants of this land... with drunkenness... I will not pity, nor spare, nor have mercy, but destroy them." From this passage I observe this,

DOCTRINE: Spiritual drunkenness is a certain forerunner of merciless destruction unto a people.

"I will show them no pity, nor spare them, but destroy them," saith the Lord. That is the way it was with Belshazzar. He had been drinking through the evening and that same night the hand-writing of the Lord appeared against him on the wall: "MENE, MENE, TEKEL, UPHAR-SIN... God hath numbered thy kingdom, and finished it... Thou art weighed in the balances, and art found wanting... Thy kingdom is divided" (Daniel 5:25-28). "While they are drunken as drunkards, they shall be devoured as stubble fully dry" (Nahum 1:10).

For the explication of the point I shall show you,

I. What Are the Causes of This Spiritual Drunkenness?

II. By What Effects Does This Spirit of Drunkenness Manifest Itself?

III. When Is This Spirit of Drunkenness a Forerunner of Destruction?

IV. What Are the Reasons Why the Spirit of Drunkenness Is the Forerunner of Merciless Destruction?

I. WHAT ARE THE CAUSES OF THIS SPIRITUAL DRUNKENNESS?

Just as bodily drunkenness arises from inordinate drinking of wine or strong drink, so this spiritual drunkenness arises from excessive indulgence in those things which God opposes.

1. Spiritual Drunkenness Occurs as the Result of the Excessive Drinking of the Pleasures of Sin. When the wills and affections of men inordinately drink at the fountains of pleasure forbidden by God, He will cause them to experience spiritual drunkenness. When they insist on drinking the things their hearts should be weaned from, things which should in comparison with better things be bitter to them, then God will give them up to this. Thus you find that it is in this sense the Prophet calls the Kings and the Priests and the People, "The drunkards of Ephraim" (Isaiah 28:1). for they filled and satiated themselves with sins and the lusts of their own hearts. It is a fearful judgment of God when the Lord shall give men their contentment in this way. "For thus saith the Lord God of Israel unto me: Take the wine cup of this fury at my hand, and cause all the nations, to whom I send thee, to drink it. And they shall drink, and be moved [stagger], and be mad, because of the sword that I will send among them. Then took I the cup at the LORD'S hand, and made all the nations to drink, unto whom the Lord had sent me... to make them a desolation, an astonishment, an hissing, and a curse: as it is this day" (Jeremiah 25:15-18). This is often the case with sinners whom the Lord intends to destroy. They have many sad fears which are vastly multiplied when the Lord puts His cup of just judgments into their hands and bids them take their pleasure in their sins. By this very means they come to be hardened against the fear of death and judgment even when both death and judgment are at their very doors.

2. Spiritual Drunkenness Occurs When the Mind and Judgment of

Man Drinks in the Wine of Any Delusion or Corrupt Counsel. The Apostle Paul speaks of those who were attracted to lying wonders and would not receive the love of the truth. Concerning them he said, "And for this cause God shall send them strong delusion, that they should believe a lie: That they all might be damned who believed not the truth, but had pleasure in unrighteousness" (2 Thessalonians 2:12). Corrupt doctrines make men drunk in their very understanding. When antichrist corrupts the judgments of men with false doctrine they may be said to have a cup in their hand full of abominations and of their fornications (Revelation 17:4).

II. BY WHAT EFFECTS DOES THIS SPIRIT OF DRUNKENNESS MANIFEST ITSELF?

Drunkenness shows itself in staggering and reeling, in unsteadiness and unsettledness, in sottishness and blindness, in rage and fierceness, in deep slumber and in shamelessness. This is how spiritual drunkenness appears also.

1. Spiritual Drunkenness Manifests Itself in Staggering and Reeling. Those who are spiritually drunken demonstrate unsteadfastness and unsettledness in holy resolutions, in matters of faith, in spiritual opinions and in matters of judgment. Faith can have no real hold on the drunken and thus they stagger from doctrine to doctrine, from viewpoint to viewpoint, from good practice to evil practice. "They are drunken, but not with wine; they stagger, but not with strong drink" (Isaiah 29:9). The Lord can never forgive this sin until they come to Him in shame and confess the particular sin of imbibing in all manner of doctrines and religions. Until the sin is confessed and forsaken they will stagger about and as the raging waves of the sea continually foam out their own shame.

It is true that there is a staggering that arises from weakness which you may observe in a child or an elderly person. I am not speaking of that unsteadiness but of men who stagger because they are drunk with their own lusts. This is that spirit of drunkenness which goes before ruin. This is the drunkenness that takes away the use of reason and makes men act foolishly.

2. Spiritual Drunkenness Manifests Itself in a Spirit of Sottishness and Blindness. The Lord inflicts this just judgment upon men who do not receive the truth in the love of it. "The vision... is become unto you as the words of a book that is sealed, which men deliver to one that is learned, saying, Read this, I pray thee: and he saith, I cannot; for it is sealed: And the book is delivered to him that is not learned, saying, Read this, I pray thee: and he saith, I am not learned... the wisdom of their wise men shall perish, and the understanding of their prudent men shall be hid" (Isaiah 29:11-14). "But they also have erred through wine, and through strong drink are out of the way; the priest and the prophet have erred through strong drink, they are swallowed up of wine, they are out of the way through strong drink; they err in vision, they stumble in judgment" (Isaiah 28:7). It is with the spiritually drunken just as it is with those who are drunk with wine; although their reason is not taken away,the ability to use it is gone from them. Their own minds befoul them and make them sottish, giddy and stupefied in their understanding and senses. "The Lord hath mingled a perverse spirit in the midst thereof: and they... err in every work thereof, as a drunken man staggereth in his vomit" (Isaiah 19:14). Men in this condition cannot be moved by reason; they act against common sense and good judgment,and thus I say that when the Lord gives men up to a spirit of delusion,it is like a spirit of drunkenness.

3. Spiritual Drunkenness Manifests Itself in a Spirit of Rage and Fierceness. The spiritually drunken fight against one another. This is especially tragic when there can be found no true reason for it. When the Lord gives men up to a spirit of rage, division and contention they are apt to remain in this condition for a very long time. The Lord Himself will leave them there until they come to true repentance. I am speaking of God's own dear people who hope one day to meet in heaven and yet by no means will be friends on earth. No man can persuade them to agree for God Himself has given them up to a spirit of wrangling and contention. This is that which goes before the calamity of a people as Micah lamented, "The best of them is as a brier: the most upright is sharper than a thorn hedge: the day of thy watchmen and thy visitation cometh; now shall be their perplexity" (Micah 7:4). You will find it is often this way with drunken men. No counsels can persuade them to be quiet. Sometimes only violence used against them can keep them down and by then they usually are very much gone. When men are in a wrangling condition, as was Nabal in his drunkenness, no counsel can be heard. In their rage and drunken fits they think themselves wiser than others. Just so the spiritually drunken fight and rage until the Lord Himself brings them down with His strong hand.

4. Spiritual Drunkenness Manifests Itself in Deep Sleep and Prolonged Stupors. In describing those who were drunk, but not with wine, Isaiah declared, "The Lord hath poured out upon you the spirit of deep sleep, and hath closed your eyes" (Isaiah 29:10). A man drunk with wine may stagger about, fume and rage, but eventually he will fall down in a stupor and sleep off his drunkenness. But when the Lord gives men over to such false security as is portrayed in the deep sleep of the drunkard- ,they cannot sleep off their spiritual lethargy. Only the awakening providences of the Lord can stir them and unless He awakens them they will sleep on until awakened by the horrors of a Christless eternity. "In their heat I will make their feasts, and I will make them drunken, that they may rejoice, and sleep a perpetual sleep, and not wake, saith the Lord" (Jeremiah 51:39), and thus you will find it in sundry other places in Scripture as well.

5. Spiritual Drunkenness Manifests Itself in the Exposing of One's Nakedness. Drunken men tell their choicest secrets and expose their nakedness without shame. You find this in the tragic story of Noah's later life. You see it again in the account of Lot after the destruction of Sodom. The spiritually drunken expose the shame of their spiritual nakedness without awareness and like the Laodicean church say, "I am rich, and increased with goods, and have need of nothing; and knowest not that thou art wretched, and miserable, and poor, and blind, and naked" (Revelation 3:17). As they deepen in their drunkenness they manifest their filthy hidden sins and suppose all the world rejoices with them in their iniquity.

6. Spiritual Drunkenness Manifests Itself by Vomiting Up Corruption and Thoroughly Soiling Oneself and Surroundings. "All [their] tables are full of vomit and filthiness, so that there is no place clean" (Isaiah 28:8). The spiritually drunken seem to have almost unlimited capacity to sully and defile. The stench of their wickedness makes the church an unpleasant place and rises up as an offence to the nostrils of God.

III. WHEN IS THIS SPIRIT OF DRUNKENNESS A FORERUNNER OF DESTRUCTION?

Every spirit of drunkenness is not a forerunner of destruction, but mark this carefully, when the Lord leaves men in such a spirit of unsteadfastness in the truth, a spirit of sottishness and blindness, a spirit of rage and fierceness, a spirit of deep sleep and security so that they manifest their secret wickedness like Sodom and lie all day long in their filth—I say, when God leaves men to such a spirit as this, it is then most certainly a forerunner of destruction. But when precisely is this spirit of drunkenness a forerunner of destruction? I answer this with three particulars from the text.

Answer One. When the Lord fills all the inhabitants of Jerusalem, from the King that sits upon David's throne and the priests and the prophets to all the inhabitants of the land with this drunkenness.

Answer Two. When God not only fills men with that which makes them drunk, leaving them some room for wholesome counsel, but when they are filled so full with their own delusions that there is no room for wholesome counsel and they are incapable of receiving the truth.

Answer Three. When the Lord gives men over to drunkenness as a judgment, and when the Lord gives men over to such a spirit of delusion that truth, which was meant to do them good, only makes them worse. Under this circumstance, men in the mildest of contention allow the means of peace to make them more troublesome. In this condition the Word of God that should awaken men only makes them more secure. In this state the judgments of God abroad in the world, which are calculated to bring them to repentance, only harden them the more.

IV. WHAT ARE THE REASONS WHY THE SPIRIT OF DRUNKEN-NESS IS THE FORERUNNER OF MERCILESS DESTRUCTION?

Reason One. Because in this condition of spiritual drunkenness a man is immediately disposed unto all wickedness; he is filling up the measure of his sin very fast.

Reason Two. Because when the Lord gives men over to a spirit of drunkenness, they cannot understand the cause of their ruin; they are besotted and blinded; they do not seek that the plague of the Lord upon them be removed, nor do they know the cause of it.

Reason Three. This spirit of drunkenness brings division among a people which is a forerunner of all other misery. Under such circumstances you need not wonder if a judgment from God may fall, for it has already begun.

IMPROVEMENT ONE. From this learn, when you see any nation, church or people given over to a spirit of spiritual drunkenness, to bemoan and bewail their condition bitterly, for they have the tokens of certain ruin upon them.

To this end let us take pains to consider the state of God's people at this day in England. Let us investigate whether the cup of this wine is not given to the godly party there. There can be no doubt that this cup has been given to the wicked but in considering if it has been given to the godly part of the nation let us examine it in three particulars.

First. Has not the Lord given them up to a spirit of blindness in matters of doctrine? I will not mention the thousands of persons doubting and staggering with unsettled souls, not knowing what to do or what side to take, for many of whom any religion will serve their turn so long as it requires little of them and allows them peace and quiet.

1. Some in England are Antinomians. They deny the use of the law as a rule of life to any that are in Christ. Those in Christ, they say, are not under the law but under grace. Hence it follows that they will not take any comfort of their good estate from any conformity of their hearts to the law of God nor from any law of God written in their hearts. What, they ask, have we to do with the law? We are under grace. We look to grace only! But in truth they have become patrons of free vice under the mask of free grace. Hence, not being under the law and having nothing to do with it, their consciences have such liberty that they refuse to be discomforted by any sin against the law of God or rule broken, reasoning, if we are not under the law, then there is no sin, and if there is no sin, why should there be sorrow for sin? This sort of deluded persons now abound there. You know that their false doctrine is the very thing that leavened that poor country and for which the wrath of God has broken out against the patrons of it. These very delusions are now given sufficient elbow-room to spread here and they are being spread far and wide.

2. Others are rigid separatists. They refuse to hear a holy minister preach or communicate in their assemblies because he is not altogether purified according to their understanding of the purification of the sanctuary. Hence they forsake the servants of Christ before Christ Himself forsakes them. Their whole course is full of confusion and scandal. They either edify themselves by their own gifts, thus clearly indicating their arrogance, or by choosing only unlearned ministers. They abhor bishops and other human leaders and refuse in any way to submit themselves or to be ruled or spiritually governed by others.

3. Some call themselves seekers. They deny the validity of all churches. Some that have risen up of late think there are no churches or ministers or ordinances of God any place in the world but say they are in a seeking, waiting condition, looking for Apostles to be sent to make a reformation and bring a whole new order. This error is spreading far and wide.

4. There are false teachers. Some think that the soul of man is mortal and dies with the body. They print this heresy and speak it widely so that many are deceived by them. Because they suppose that both soul and body are mortal they deny the resurrection and in so doing prove their unfitness for the work in which they engage.

5. There are others who desire that liberty and toleration be given to all religions for all, they say, lead to the same place. The principal flag they wave is that no man should be punished for his conscience. It is amazing to think how this dazzles the eyes of so many men. For my own part, I believe and judge this false teaching to be the foundation of all other errors and abominations in the churches of God. Once it gains a stronghold among a people it is certain to bring them under divine judgment. Twice in the Book of Judges we read, "In those days there was no king in Israel, but every man did that which was right in his own eyes" (Judges 17:6; 21:25). It is very sad that the same evil which brought a heavy judgment of God against the people of Israel—every man doing what was right in his own eyes—should now be thought to be and taught as a right way. Indeed, what could portray a condition of spiritual drunkenness more thoroughly than to have a people teaching a way to God which has already been brought under divine condemnation as a completely erroneous course? When God turns a people over to such error, it is a heavy judgment indeed against a people and nation.

Have we not sufficient grounds in these brief considerations for mourning to God for poor England that she should be abandoned under such delusions? When the Lord loves a wayward people, He brings them very low, even putting them in the stocks and whipping them. God's judgments will either make their hearts sober and humble or else, mark what I say, they will harden them the more.

Second. What other explanation of this situation can we offer than that the Lord has allowed this spirit of division to increase year by year and grow worse and worse. In former times the people of God, when the Word of God has been abroad, were glad to be of one mind; but now, when God Himself has come with a drawn sword and stands at the door, that there should be such divisions, methinks should provoke deep sobriety in the people of God. The hand of God on the one side is very dreadful; the mercy of God on the other side is working for them. This, I say, should make them very sober and cause them to lie down and mourn at the feet of the Lord. Humiliation and praise should now be the work of God's people in England; but in reality, how is it? The Lord has filled all the inhabitants of the land with a spirit of drunkenness. Sermon is preached against sermon. Men revile one another. The head fights against the body. They go out into the camp, but who can they trust? Religion is the occasion of the breech of the peace. And look into the Parliament: The Upper House is against the Lower House, and many pretended friends are but secret enemies. By these means the great enemy is encouraged and religion is scoffed at. Which of the many religions would you have men hold onto? Many godly people are discouraged and some of God's servants, desiring to say nothing, lie hidden and mourn for their own sins and the sins of the people of the land. Let me now say, you will find it certainly true, at this very moment the principal strength of the land lies with persons that seem to be friends to the Parliament but are truly secret enemies to the truth of God, His ordinances, His people and His ways. They are deadly enemies too.

Third. We mourn the deep security of England under the sins that are now laid open. I will tell you what is their complaint still here in the words of one who in former times published as glorious works as any in that kingdom, "I would I could speak it with tears, never more talking of reformation, but never less practice of reformation; our churches are reformed, but our hearts and houses never less reformed; our high altars are pulled down, but our high minds are not brought down; the worship of God is more pure, but the worshippers as impure as ever; we have less idolatries, but more adulteries and fornications; I do not say more punishment, but never less punished, and more committed. Is there a law against scandalous ministers, and none against scandalous Lords and great ones? Men are not ashamed to profess their adulteries before the face of the sun. We never lived in such days, wherein there is more judging of others, and less of ourselves. Never more sad days in England, and yet never such pride in apparel; never such formality in God's worship, never such murmuring, never such censuring; never more talk of reformation, never less reformed; never more security, than when the ship is sinking, never times wherein fewer converted, and the power of godliness more decayed, and sin abounding; never more controversies how churches should be gathered, never fewer added to the church than in these times; never such controversies over how the churches should be governed, and yet never less care of the government of Christ in our houses and hearts. Godly men have not leisure to study faith and repentance and brokenness for sin." I speak to this end, that the Lord may affect our hearts with the estate of England, for there is some hope that although they are as described, yet they are not all filled with drunkenness yet, and there is some room left for counsel.

Bend your prayers against some persons, even though you know them not, that make others drunk. Give the Lord no rest until He shames them and makes them examples to the world. It is far better to pray rather than that the whole Church of God should be made drunk and, being made drunk, should be dashed one against another and destroyed.

IMPROVEMENT TWO. Let it be used as a warning to all of us that we take heed against all sin, lest because of some sins for which we have not repented, the Lord may give us over to a spirit of drunkenness. Judgment is a great work of God in this day. The time has come for Him to give all the world this same cup to drink, this cup of just and heavy judgment upon men for their contempt of the Gospel of peace. Christ came to make believers one and not to divide them by doctrinal distractions and confusions in all that they do. As the result of quarrels among Christians, most men of the world have seen an end of the perfections of God's ordinances and Gospel and as things becoming stale and ready to be discarded. Therefore the Lord will put His cup into our hands and every bottle shall be filled with wine unless the Lord in great mercy preserves some of us. When once the Lord leaves any man to a spirit of drunkenness, misery shall be coming upon him and even at his door, and he shall not know it.

Are there not many iniquities among us? What is the cause of the Lord's hand being against us in dashing our ships to pieces? Why is the Lord breaking us in our infancy as a nation? Why has he taken so many of our precious ones from us? Would you know the cause of this? You will never know it until the Lord takes away this drunken distemper from us! So long as we are not sober, kept in the love of the truth, we shall never know the true reasons why the Lord is thus angry with us.

Thankfully we cannot say the Lord has filled all the inhabitants of the land with drunkenness. But yet the cup is given to us in part. The head begins to stagger in a great measure. Do we not see this great staggering? We are suffering from unsettledness in the Covenant of God. We are walking with God in an uncertain fashion. There are great hankerings after the whoredoms of the world at this time. There are likewise divisions and distractions among us. Little is done though much time is spent and the country is burdened with charges, and nothing that is done is done without much division and contention. Certainly something is amiss. Everything threatens some sudden blow to New-England.

Yet blessed be the Lord, He has not filled every one with a spirit of drunkenness. Let us not cease to be thankful that the Lord has brought us here and has given us peace in the church, in the commonwealth and in all our colonies. Let us look upon this as a rare and singular mercy of the Lord that He has kept us here in peace, and saved us from being poisoned with the delusions of the world.

You will say, "How shall we continually be preserved from this spirit of drunkenness?"

There are many things that I might say but focus on this: has not the

Lord given us other things and better things to take delight in? The Lord has given us His blessed Scriptures to solace ourselves in, otherwise we would have been like herds of beasts going to the slaughter. We have Jehovah Himself, the infinite God, to whom we can go at any time.

But that we may be preserved from this spirit of delusion, let me suggest the following particulars for our help.

First. Beware of drunken company. I would not have a godly man to go into the company of an erroneous person; his words are infectious.

Second. Let God's people take heed of being deceived by mere color and pretense of things. The color of free grace is attractive but beware of those that bring in free-vice. The color of liberty of conscience is alluring but look out for liberty to sin. Many good men have been deceived in the past and why not you and I? What if what you receive as truth is but an error?

Third. Love dearly the truth that you know already, such truths as reveal your sins unto you and make much of them, putting them in their correct light, then certainly the Lord will make much more known to you and preserve you from error. "I will pray the Father," saith Christ, "and He shall give you another Comforter, that He may abide with you for ever; even the Spirit of truth; whom the world cannot receive, because it seeth Him not, neither knoweth Him: but ye know Him; for He dwelleth with you, and shall be in you" (John 14:16,17). You can see that when a man has had a good drink he will not be apt to drink poison. Love the truth that you know and the Lord will teach you more and more of His ways.

Fourth. Drink no more than will do you good. My meaning is this: Drink in those truths that you know will do you good; take fast hold of them and do not let them go. "I will never forget Thy precepts," saith David, "for with them Thou hast quickened me" (Psalm 119:93). Likewise take no more than you have need of and can make use of. If you are faithful you will find that you need every truth of God. At one moment you may be tempted to deny the Lord but you have evidence of His grace in the conditional promises He has given. At another time you may doubt God's loving care over you but by such promises as the Lord has given you will find Him doing you good. Whatever you need to know you will find in the Truth of God's Word. You will also find warnings there with doctrine that teach you how to behave before Him. Do you not need to know that only the pure in heart shall see God? Do you not need this in time of temptation even although for the present you can walk with a bold conscience.

Fifth. When the Lord leaves you under the sense of your own weakness so that you know not the truth or the Lord is withdrawn from you because of some known sin in your heart which has brought the judgment of His withdrawal upon you, take the counsel of skilful and merciful physicians, go to the servants of the Lord who are sober and understanding men, old acquaintances with the truth of God. Ask their counsel. Go to them with a humble and meek spirit and the Lord will teach you His mind and will. In England, the great reason why so many are deluded is because they lack instructors.

There are but these three things that can hinder you from knowing the truth of the Lord:

1. Unthankfulness.
2. Want of prayer.
3. Contempt of the message of those whom the Lord sends to be His ministers.

CHAPTER FOUR

A Fast
of God's Choosing,
Plainly Opened

By
Thomas Thacher

Thomas Thacher, 1620-1678

The son of Rev. Peter Thacher, pastor at Salisbury, England, Thomas Thacher was born on May 1, 1620. He received a good grammar school education but religious scruples prevented his matriculating at an English University. With his parents permission he sailed for New England, arriving in Boston on June 4, 1635. Soon after arrival there Thacher had a very affecting experience of divine providence. Needing to go from Newbury to Marblehead, he refused to go by water because of a strong presentiment that the voyage would be problematical. The twenty-three persons who made the voyage were ship-wrecked and only two survived.

Charles Chauncy, then minister at Scituate but later President of Harvard, took the young Englishman under his wing, preparing him for the ministry. Thomas was a serious student, excelling in his theological studies and in Arabic, Syriac and Hebrew, even compiling a Hebrew lexicon. In addition to his religious studies, Thacher was interested in medicine and wrote the first medical tract ever published in New England, "A Brief Rule to Guide the Common People of New-England How to Order Themselves and Theirs in the Small Pox or Measles," 1677. Preserved copies of his beautiful hand-writing show an extraordinary gift in this realm as well.

Thacher married the daughter of Rev. Ralph Partridge of Duxbury in 1643. She bore him three sons and a daughter. He was ordained to the ministry at the Church in Weymouth where he served effectively for more than twenty years. It appears that Thacher left the Weymouth pastorate after the death of his first wife and then moved to Boston where he married again. Some time elapsed between leaving Weymouth and accepting the pastorate of the Third [Old South] Church in February of 1669. During this interval he practiced medicine. Not long before his death on October 15, 1678, Samuel Willard became his colleague.

Thacher was one of the most popular and useful ministers in the Colony. His preaching was both careful and affecting. He was a deeply pious man who took great pains to live what he preached and to preach only what he knew experientially. He took particular care with his own family and with children and youth of his parishes. But it was in prayer, according to Cotton Mather, that "he had an eminency above most men living, for his copious, his fluent, his fervent manner of performing that sacred exercise." Records indicate that the blessing of God was considerable upon both his pastoral ministries. In each place there were numerous conversions and major spiritual strengthening of those under his pastoral care.

According to Sprague, just prior to his death, Thacher was preaching a sermon on I Peter 4:18 the last words of which were, "When a saint comes to die, then often it is the hour and power of darkness with him; then is the last opportunity that the devil has to vex the people of God; and hence they then sometimes have the greatest of their distresses. Don't think him no godly man, that then meets with doubts and fears. Our Lord Jesus Christ then cried out, 'My God, My God, why hast Thou forsaken Me?' God help us, that as we live by faith, so we may walk in it." This was the last sermon which he ever preached on earth, for immediately upon leaving the assembly he went to visit a sick person, caught a cold which settled into a fever and claimed his life. By grace Thacher "died in great peace, a stranger to those gloomy doubts and apprehensions to which he had so significantly alluded in the close of his discourse."

Two of Thacher's sons survived him and became men of great value in the Colonies: Peter was Pastor of the Church at Milton and Ralph ministered on Martha's Vineyard.

First published as *A Fast of God's Choosing, Plainly Opened For the Help of Those Poor in Spirit whose Hearts are Set to Seek the Lord their God in New-England, in the Solemn Ordinance of a Fast. Preached on a Fast Called by Public Authority on January 26, 1674. By Thomas Thacher, Pastor of a Church in Boston.* Boston: Printed by John Foster, 1678. The above sketch was extracted from the brief article on Thacher in volume one of William B. Sprague's "Annals of the American Pulpit."

A Fast of God's Choosing, Plainly Opened.

"Is it such a fast that I have chosen?
a day for a man to afflict his soul...
Is not this the fast that I have chosen..."
Isaiah 58:5,6.

It is hard work, in fact one of the hardest parts of the work of the ministry, to awaken people that are rocked to sleep in sin. This is especially true of professed Christians who are lifted to eminent degrees in their profession, exalted with great privileges, and have their hearts raised by these things to great pride. It is just such a people that the prophet deals with in our text. Therefore, in verse one you see what he was required to do. "Cry aloud, spare not, lift up thy voice like a trumpet, and shew My people their transgression, and the house of Jacob their sins." They had watchmen among them but they did not watch. "His watchmen are blind: they are all ignorant, they are all dumb dogs, they cannot bark..." (Isaiah 56:10). Thus the prophet must cry aloud and show them their sins.

Why were they so vile a people? They were eminent in profession, exalted in privileges and arrogant in both. This appears in several things that are said in verse two:

1. "They seek me daily."
2. "They delight to know my ways."
3. "They did righteousness, and forsook not the ordinance of their God."
4. "They ask of Me the ordinances of justice; they take delight in approaching to God," indicating that they were a practicing people as well as a knowing people.

They excelled not only in common and ordinary duties but, as verse three makes plain, in extraordinary duties as well, for they could rightly claim to have fasted and to have afflicted their souls in their fasting. Yet God says to the prophet: "Cry aloud, spare not, lift up thy voice like a trumpet, and shew My people their transgression and the house of Jacob their sins." Despite all their religious acts they were still a people that needed to be awakened.

When were this people in this frame and when did God have such items of complaint against them? In general, I answer, when they kept the hypocritical fasts which are described in verses three and four. They fasted but yet they did not fast. Their fast was to be seen externally but it was not a fast of spiritual efficacy involving the right performance of holy service. They were lifted up with pride in the service performed and quarrelled with God, complaining as if some notable injury were done them in that they had used God's remedy for their malady and yet their malady was not removed.

More particularly, I answer, this rejected fast seems to me to have reference to the days of Hezekiah. You know what glorious days they were and how zealous he was in reformation, even breaking in pieces the brazen serpent which Moses had made and which they had so long admired and to which they had burned incense (2 Kings 18:4). They had very solemn fasts which they kept at that time and took delight in approaching unto God. "And the children of Israel that were present at Jerusalem kept the feast of unleavened bread seven days with great gladness: and the Levites and the priests praised the Lord day by day, singing with loud instruments unto the Lord" (2 Chronicles 30:21). There was great joy for the moment, but alas, as is so often the case, as soon as these things were over and they had purged out idolatry we read, "After these things, and the establishment thereof, Sennacherib King of Assyria came and entered into Judah, and encamped against the fenced cities, and thought to win them for himself" (2 Chronicles 32:1), making it apparent that their political problems were not healed. In the sixth year of Hezekiah the ten tribes were led away by Shalmaneser King of Assyria (2 Kings 18:10). Samaria was taken "because they obeyed not the voice of the Lord their God, but transgressed His covenant, and all that Moses the servant of the Lord commanded, and would not hear them, nor do them. Now in the fourteenth year of King Hezekiah, did Sennacherib King of Assyria, come up against all the fenced cities of Judah, and took them" (2 Kings 18:12,13).

Here Israel is carried away captive despite Judah's fast in King Hezekiah's days. Here Judah is set upon and its fenced cities taken. Were Hezekiah and the people asleep during all this? No! they fasted and prayed, yet the outcome was Jerusalem's being besieged and Ranshekah's blaspheming. Here people fast and pray but not withstanding all this, Jerusalem is in danger of destruction. Why? "Wherefore have we fasted, say they, and thou seest not? Wherefore have we afflicted our soul, and thou takest no knowledge?" (Isaiah 58:3). In these words their quarrel with God is stated. Consider God's answer in the verses that follow:

Verse 3. "Behold, in the day of your fast ye find pleasure, and exact all your labors."

Verse 4. "Behold, ye fast for strife and debate, and to smite with the fist of wickedness: ye shall not fast as ye do this day, to make your voice to be heard on high."

Verse 5. "Is it such a fast that I have chosen? a day for a man to afflict his soul? is it to bow down his head as a bulrush, and to spread sackcloth and ashes under him? wilt thou call this a fast and an acceptable day to the Lord?"

Verse 6. "Is not this the fast that I have chosen? to loose the bands of wickedness, to undo the heavy burdens, and to let the oppressed go free, and that ye break every yoke?"

Verse 7. "Is it not to deal thy bread to the hungry, and that thou bring the poor that are cast out to thy house? when thou seest the naked, that thou cover him; and that thou hide not thyself from thine own flesh?"

By revealing their sins that still remained, notwithstanding their fasts, God demonstrates that their fasts were no fasts at all. The benefits they would have obtained if their fast had been a fast indeed are lost to them by their hypocrisy. From this we may observe an important doctrine:

DOCTRINE: A fast of God's choosing will certainly bring seasonable evidences of God's gracious acceptance.

When the heart is right with God and the fast is ordered by God, it will certainly obtain mercy and bring home help and succor from God. Prayer, especially extraordinary prayer, is not only the key to all earthly treasures of goodness which God has laid up for the sons of men on earth, but the key to heavenly treasures in Christ Jesus also.

The points that I shall observe in opening this subject unto you are:

1. The Nature of the Fast which God Chooses.

2. The Testimony God Gives of His Acceptance of the Fast which He Chooses.

3. The Seasons for the Fast which God Chooses.

4. The Evidence that the Fast which God Chooses Benefits as He Intends.

5. The Reasons God Has for Benefiting His People when They Fast the Fast which He Chooses.

Improvements.

I. THE NATURE OF THE FAST WHICH GOD CHOOSES.

Consider this imperfect definition or description: a fast is an extraordinary part or act of Gospel worship wherein, for a convenient season, we abstain from the comforts of this life and upon due examination of our ways toward God and consideration of God's ways toward us, we make a solemn and real profession that we justify God in bringing the evil affliction upon us that we either feel or fear, and we judge ourselves for the evil of the transgressions which we find within us or know have passed from us. We solemnly proclaim that we seek mercy and grace from God in Jesus Christ to save us from our sins and sorrows. We solemnly promise that we will with all readiness forgive others that have offended us just as we hope to be forgiven by God. We solemnly engage and bind ourselves to reform the evil of our ways and to walk before God in new obedience according to His Word for all time to come.

The very idea of a fast speaks of abstinence. A fast is a time of extraordinary worship and seeking of God's face which includes denial of self and of the use of ordinary and even necessary things for a special season and for a particular reason. If there is no worship and seeking of God's face, there is no fast. If there is no self-denial, there is no fast. This self denial includes at least three things.

1. It requires abstainence from meat and drink. This should be wholly, if strength of nature will bear it, or if not, as much abstinence from meat and drink as mercy and necessity will permit. Queen Esther commanded such a fast of all the people, "Neither eat nor drink three days, night or day" (Esther 4:16). The King of Ninevah published a decree saying "Let neither man nor beast, herd nor flock, taste any thing: let them not feed, nor drink water" (Jonah 3:7).

2. It is part of the abstinence requisite to this duty to abstain from our accustomed ornaments. To adorn the body in the day of fast is a transgression of the rule of fasting. God spoke a very sobering word to the people through Moses, "Say unto the children of Israel, Ye are a stiffnecked people: I will come up into the midst of thee in a moment, and consume thee: therefore now put off thy ornaments from thee, that I may know what to do unto thee. And the children of Israel stripped themselves of their ornaments by the mount Horeb" (Exodus 33:5,6). Clothing themselves in sackcloth and putting dust or ashes on their heads further showed the seriousness of such occcasions. While the rigor of the shadowy time under the Old Covenant is not exacted from us, yet there must be a proportion to be observed. The King of Ninevah, although but the King of Ninevah and not the King of Israel, laid aside his robes and put on sackcloth, and the fast he called was a prevailing fast for it was a self-

A FAST OF GOD'S CHOOSING

57

humbling fast that God honored. If you are reluctant to put off your ornaments then it is evident you need a humbling, and if you cannot be humbled you cannot expect the fast you observe will be the fast of God's choosing.

3. It anticipates abstaining from all your normal relaxations, sports and recreations, and even the pleasures of the marriage bed. "Defraud ye not one the other, except it be with consent for a time, that ye may give yourselves to fasting and prayer" (1 Corinthians 7:5). "Let the bridegroom go forth out of his chamber, and the bride out of her closet" (Joel 2:16). During a fast there should be no sports, pastimes or normal recreations.

In a word, such abstinence is required whereby the body may be afflicted. "For whatsoever soul it be that shall not be afflicted in that same day, he shall be cut off from among his people" (Leviticus 23:29). "In those days I Daniel was mourning three full weeks. I ate no pleasant bread, neither came flesh nor wine in my mouth, neither did I anoint myself at all..." (Daniel 10:2,3). Then the Lord said to him, "Fear not Daniel: for from the first day that thou didst set thine heart to understand, and chasten thyself before thy God, thy words were heard" (verse 12).

This abstinence must continue at least from evening to evening, for so must you keep the sabbaths, not only your weekly sabbaths, but fasting and feasting sabbaths, "It shall be unto you a sabbath of rest, and ye shall afflict your souls... from even unto even" (Leviticus 23:32).

This outward abstinence, contrary to the view of some, is a Gospel duty, that is, it is a duty directed under the Covenant of Grace and not pertaining only to the Covenant of Works. It is required in the Gospel, for our Saviour asked, "Can the children of the bridechamber mourn as long as the Bridegroom is with them?" The answer to this is obviously, No! But then He said, "The days will come when the Bridegroom shall be taken from them, and then shall they fast" (Matthew 9:15). The Bridegroom is Christ and the children of the Bridegroom are believers under the Gospel Covenant. When He is absent, that is, in heaven, before He returns again, there shall be times of fasting. The Apostle Paul directed the Corinthians in managing themselves in fasting and prayer (1 Corinthians 7:5). Clearly, fasting is a Gospel duty.

Although it is a Gospel duty, it is an extraordinary duty. Fasting is not an every week duty or something for constant usage, as the Pharisees thought, saying "I fast twice in the week" (Luke 18:12). God has appointed six days for labor and one for a Sabbath. For men to appoint to themselves constant Sabbaths besides the Sabbath of the Lord is will worship and not acceptable to God. Fasting is not for ordinary but special occasions like times of notable or eminent public danger as in the days of Jehoshaphat (2 Chronicles 20:3-5) or when some notable duty is to be performed which is very difficult and hazardous as was the case in Queen Esther's day (Esther 4:14-16).

We should fast when there is some great sickness lying upon those that are near and dear to us. "But as for me, when they were sick, my clothing was sackcloth: I humbled my soul with fasting... I behaved myself as though he had been my friend or brother: I bowed down heavily, as one that mourneth for his mother" (Psalm 35:13,14). When a friend, brother, mother or near relative is sick, weak and in dangerous condition, it calls for fasting. Here is then an opportunity and occasion for this duty.

We should fast when there is some notable blessing wanting or that we are in danger of loosing. It is time to fast and mourn when a person or people are fallen into some great transgression whereby God's indignation may be provoked against them. Ezra sensed this in the case of his men marrying strange wives and polluting the holy seed (Ezra 9:4-6). It is also time to fast when God goes forth against a people in some notable calamity or threatening judgment, as when Israel fled before the enemy as a result of Achan's sin. Knowing the reason for the defeat, Joshua rent his clothes and fell to the earth upon his face before the ark of the Lord where he remained fasting until evening, he and the Elders of Israel, putting dust upon their heads (Joshua 7:6). Ezra fasted and mourned when he was going up from Babylon (Ezra 8:21-23). So we see that a fast is not a standing duty but an occasionally extraordinary measure to be observed in the days of the Gospel just as in former days.

Concerning the spiritual performance of a fast, we need to consider the preparation thereto. There must be examination of our own ways and a consideration of the works of God. Both of these are preparatory and it is for want of these that men's hearts are utterly indisposed to such spiritual service as is described in Joshua 7:6 to 12 and Lamentations 3:38 to 44 in which you find the people considering and bewailing both their own sins and God's judgments upon them for those sins.

It is necessary to distinguish between an acceptable and an unacceptable fast. In our text, the people professed great delight in God's ordinances and sought the Lord daily saying that they did and would cleave to God in His appointments. They enquired after His mind and made great professions of how they would serve Him. So exact were they in their fasts that they afflicted their souls, bowed down their heads like a bulrush and cried mournfully, spreading sackcloth and ashes on themselves. What more could they do as an outward profession? But their hearts were not engaged in it. Their activity was a lie. They attempted to flatter God and therefore He upbraids them asking, "Is this the fast that I have chosen?"

1. In a true fast there is an acknowledgement of the justice of God for the evil affliction that He brings upon His people and a condemnation of self for the evil of all transgressions against the Lord our God. "O Lord, righteousness belongeth unto Thee, but unto us confusion of faces, as at this day... O Lord, to us belongeth confusion of face, to our kings, to our princes, and to our fathers, because we have sinned against Thee. To the Lord our God belong mercies and forgivenesses, though we have rebelled against Him" (Daniel 9:7-9). Daniel ascribed righteousness to God although He had laid waste Jerusalem, burnt the city, destroyed the temple, scattered the people and led them into captivity. In a true fast, all join with Daniel in saying, "Thou art righteous and we have sinned." Just so, Ezra made a solemn and heart breaking prayer, "O my God, I am ashamed and blush to lift up my face to Thee, my God: for our iniquities are increased over our head, and our trespass is grown up unto the heavens" (Ezra 9:6).

2. In a true fast there is a solemn expression of godly sorrow and repentance of the evil of transgressions which we have committed against the Lord. "Therefore also now, saith the Lord, turn ye even to me with all your heart, and with fasting, and with weeping, and with mourning: And rend your heart and not your garments, and turn unto the Lord your God..." (Joel 2:12,13). Under Nehemiah's leadership the people confessed their sins from the beginning of their being a people and allowed such a load of guilt upon themselves that their hearts were made heavy with godly sorrow (Nehemiah 9).

3. In a true fast there is a genuine commitment to fly for refuge to the hope of grace and mercy that is set before us in the atonement made by Jesus Christ. Thus David lamented the plague of sin in His heart that brought on the sickness of his child and fasted and lay all night on the earth (2 Samuel 12:15,16) crying out, "Create in me a clean heart, O God; and renew a right spirit within me" (Psalm 51:10). This is the commitment of every one that fasts aright, that he will fly for refuge to the precious blood of Christ for mercy to save him from his sin and from God's righteous judgments and that he may have peace and grace and return no more to folly.

4. In true fasting and prayer there is an honest intention to forgive

others as we desire to be forgiven by God. "When ye stand praying, forgive, if ye have ought against any: that your Father also which is in heaven may forgive you your trespasses" (Mark 11:25). Thus in our text the people are warned that they do not fast aright for they are wanting this intention, being willing to "fast for strife and debate" (Isaiah 58:4). They did not heal but rather strengthened their divisions by fasting, therefore their fast was hypocritical and not according to their profession.

5. In a true fast there is a solemn promise to bind ourselves to reform what is amiss and to walk with God in new obedience. It is a true observation concerning prayer that you can put no petition to God for mercy but what it implies a promise unto God of new obedience. This is especially true when you come to God in such a solemn way and manner as in a fast, for you come that you may obtain help against your sin, help to obey or to continue in obedience. In every fast there is an implicit making and renewing of a Covenant with God. This is very apparent in Nehemiah (Nehemiah 9:38; 10:1-39).

In sum, at a fast you solemnly profess that you are grieved for your transgressions and seek God's grace in Christ to pardon and heal you; that all your hope is in the atonement of Jesus; that you freely forgive all that have trespassed against you; laying aside all anger, wrath, malice, envy, evil-speaking and whatever may be the fruits of such duplicity of spirit against others, you profess that you put the thoughts of these from you as you desire your sins should be put away from God's sight; you engage not to walk in the former course of iniquity but vow that you are determined to do the will of God in all duties according to the rules of obedience. It is but a mocking of God, a flattering of Him with your lips, a lying unto Him with your tongues, if your spirits are not thus disposed and inclined in such a solemn duty.

Is it all that God requires of you that you hang down your heads like a bulrush for a day, putting on a sad face and sad clothes, thinking sad thoughts or breathing a sigh or two in your closets, a prayer in your families, a little public worship and when the day is over to be as you were before, making no conscience of answering the expectation justly raised by your profession but the proud left proud still and the filthy left filthy still? Surely this is not the fast which God has chosen. If you will show me your fast I will ask, "Where are the fruits thereof?" Sin is gaining ground among us notwithstanding our fasts. All our days of atonement prevail not to consume, waste and destroy abominations out of the land. These cannot be the fasts which God has chosen. God's fasts will break the heart for sin and from sin. But your fasts keep the heart whole and the life of sin whole within you. You never look for a tender heart but only to see if you can fast away the sense of your sin and sorrow for sin and your care and diligent endeavors to walk with God. My heart aches to think of the unfruitful fasts that are among us as a body of people, though I thank God that there are some precious souls among us that mourn over these things.

Ah, New-England, New-England! How will you be able to bear the burden of your fasts? There is not a soul that hears me but fasts either the fast that God has chosen or the fast that God has not chosen. All of you do fast. Your presence here proves that. In fasting you profess that you are sensible of the displeasure of God hanging over your heads and that you are sorry with all your hearts that you have provoked God. This is the profession of your actions, otherwise what are you doing here? You profess that with all your hearts you entertain motions of love and kindness where there has been strife. By participating in this fast you profess that you forgive others as God has forgiven you and that your hearts are full of compassion to afflicted ones and your hands open to relieve them according to your ability. Can any of you come to seek mercy from God and have your hearts shut up against the poor and needy without great hypocrisy? How do your hearts respond toward these things? Consider, in the fear of God, this question, "What is the fast which God has chosen?"

The fast which God has chosen is when the heart is sincerely and entirely carried forth in a holy conformity to that which the duty makes profession of? "Son, give me thy heart," says God. God cares not for external performances without the heart. It is an high abomination when you come to a day of humiliation without a suitable heart. There are four indicators of a heart that is suitable for a day of humiliation.

First, a suitable heart is a broken and contrite heart. When the heart is right, a holy trembling seizes a man lest he provoke God and procure His indignation in drawing near to Him. When the spirit is indeed suited to the duty, a broken heart and a contrite spirit begins the day, ends the day and continues throughout the day.

Second, a suitable heart manifests a penitent self-abasement before God in fulfilling duty. The false-hearted Jews quarrelled with God, "Wherefore have we fasted, say they, and Thou seest not? wherefore have we afflicted our soul, and Thou takest no knowledge?" (Isaiah 58:3). But sincere souls are humbled in the recognition of God's refusal to listen to their prayers, knowing that God is righteous and owes them nothing and therefore they strongly resolve, the grace of God assisting them, that they will no more return unto vanity.

Third, a suitable heart does not defer or delay doing that work which is necessary to promote the purpose of the fast. You draw near to God that your hearts and ways may be reformed. Do you respond to whatever God shows you immediately? The delaying soul that puts off his reformation and renovation does not keep such a fast as God has chosen. If it is not time for you to do your duty, it is time for you to suffer affliction. If it is not time for you to carry on a thorough reformation, it is time for God to carry on your sorrows and afflictions toward your desolation. Delaying souls do not keep a fast unto God. When you determine a fast you must resolve to begin and prosecute the work of turning unto God that very day and carry it on to the end.

Lastly, a suitable heart leaves a warm impression of love one toward another and to all mankind as God gives opportunity. When you have tasted mercy from God it makes you merciful to others. When men are hard-hearted, cruel and harsh and their spirits not inclined to mercy, they have certainly not been with God in the fast which He has chosen.

Why is this called the fast which God has chosen? I answer briefly.

Reason One. Because such a fast exactly answers the counsel of God's will about it, which He had eternally in Himself and which He gives forth to us in His Holy Word.

Reason Two. It is a fast that God has chosen because God prefers this above any other kind of fast. There are many fasts but God prefers this fast above all. There are fasts which obtain some answers from God and yet are not like these. King Ahab sold himself to work wickedness in the sight of the Lord and thus doom was pronounced upon him. Despite his evil heart he rent his clothes, put sackcloth upon his flesh and fasted and prayed. God responded to his fasting and humility, and Ahab obtained a reprieve whereby the judgment threatened was not executed in his days (1 Kings 21:27-29), and yet Ahab did not fast the fast that God had chosen, delights in and accepts.

Reason Three. Because God takes pleasure in this fast and has a gracious respect to His people in it. After it, the service they render is acceptable to Him and ascends up as the offering of a sweet smelling sacrifice. It is a day that is accepted by the Lord wherein He takes pleasure in heaven. If, as Scripture teaches, there is joy in heaven when one sinner is converted, how much more when a whole congregation is turned to God. "To this man will I look," says God, "even to him that is poor and of a contrite spirit" (Isaiah 66:2). How much more is this so when it concerns an entire people!

Reason Four. Because God will, in His own time, make His gracious acceptation of His people's fast manifest to them. You feel that your prayers are not presently answered as you expected. This may be true but remember that your time is not His time. "Yet a little while, and He that shall come will come, and will not tarry" (Hebrews 10:37).

II. THE TESTIMONY GOD GIVES OF HIS ACCEPTANCE OF THE FAST WHICH HE CHOOSES.

We now consider what these spiritual or outward benefits are, whereby the Lord manifests His gracious acceptance of such a fast. In general, you may take it as a certain truth that when God is pleased to answer the prayers of His people, He testifies of His acceptance in particular ways.

1. When God gives them a praying and fasting frame of spirit. He requires just such a frame but it is not in man's power to bring himself into this frame of spirit. It is the gift of God's grace. When God prepares the heart of the humble, He also hears their cry (Psalm 10:17). When God causes your hearts and your tongues to pray, He will certainly cause His ears to hear, for He is the hearer of prayer. Prayer is a gift of God. "Likewise the Spirit also helpeth our infirmities: for we know not what we should pray for as we ought: but the Spirit Itself maketh intercession for us..." and God knows the meaning of the Spirit in us (Romans 8:26,27). When a man prays by His own spirit, his spirit is under his own command and, therefore, he is uniform in His prayer. He is not sometimes straightened and sometimes enlarged, unless it be through the upheavel of his emotional nature, but when a man prays by God's Spirit there are some strange out-goings of the heart in prayer which no mortal is able to command. There is such enlargedness of heart, such desire after Christ and His grace, such affliction for sin, such earnest longing for deliverance, as no man can possibly command in his own heart. When God gives such a spirit, it is evidence of His gracious acceptance. It is a day of humiliation when God gives you a humble spirit. It is a day of abstinence when God puts into your heart an earnest desire for divorcement from all sin, however pleasant and profitable. This is a pledge of God's gracious acceptance according to that promise, "Before they call, I will answer; and while they are yet speaking, I will hear" (Isaiah 65:24).

2. When God puts a determined spirit in His people. A God given heart after fasting and prayer puts into execution that which concerns ourselves in order to obtain our spiritual requests and supplications presented unto God. The presence of a reforming spirit, a purifying spirit, a watchful spirit against sin, when the soul sets itself with great watchfulness and industry to the work of the Lord, are testimonies of God's acceptance of a people. Consider how diligent in reform, purification and watchfulness against sin the people were after their humiliation in the days of Ezra (chapter 10) and Nehemiah (chapter 10). When church, court and commonwealth, all in their places, endeavor to remove sin and make up the breach between God and themselves, it is a certain demonstration that God is near at hand to answer them.

3. When God gives the promised blessings. It is a marvelous, gracious argument of our acceptance by God when He gives the spiritual or outward blessings mentioned in our text. There are eight glorious benefits enumerated here.

1) Light after darkness. "Then shall thy light break forth as the morning" (Isaiah 58:8). "Then shall thy light rise in obscurity, and thy darkness be as the noon day" (Isaiah 58:10). When God gives a poor soul light after darkness and light in obscurity breaking forth as the morning, this is a great benefit of an acceptable fast. Light signifies not only the enlightening of the understanding or quickening with spiritual light but all kinds of help, consolation and prosperity. Darkness signifies all kind of affliction, whether it be a sense of sin or other sorrows. There are four things to be observed in this.

First, it is light after darkness when you now see that darkness had covered your souls whereas you previously did not know what your state and condition were. There is also light after darkness when there has been distress upon a people and God causes light to spring forth so that you see that some glimpses of hope, some raising of your spirits, some expectations of good days, some comfortable changes of providence are on their way. Paul was comforted by the coming of Titus and ascribes this to God's comforting him. This is light after darkness.

Second, when this light that is promised is gradual, like the light of the morning that "shineth more and more unto the perfect day" (Proverbs 4:18). You must not say there is no light because it is not noon at dawn. If spiritually it is but the dawning of the day or the light of the morning star, you still have cause to acknowledge it is an answer to prayers. If it foreshows the beginning of your return from spiritual captivity or outward calamity you are to acknowledge it as a springing light which shall go on to the perfect day in full perfection of glory.

Third, it is a prevailing and overcoming light. It may be weak at first and obscured through clouds of darkness and temptation but it shall be victorious and overcoming at the last.

Fourth, this light is from the rising of the Sun of Righteousness. God will manifest His gracious acceptation to your souls when the Sun of Righteousness arises with healing in His wings (Malachi 4:2). Whether it be light in ordinances or light in providences it is still a light from the face of Jesus Christ for there is something of Christ in it. There are common refreshings that shine upon men which do not exalt Christ in the soul but the saving light that comes from Christ leads unto Christ and makes Christ most precious and most glorious unto the soul. This is the light God promises by which He will testify of His gracious acceptance of those that keep the fast which He has chosen.

2) Your health shall spring forth speedily when God is pleased to make fastings healings (Isaiah 58:6). This is His promise here: healing of your souls, of your families, of your churches, of your commonwealth, healing in your affairs both inward and outward, spiritual and worldly. There is still healing that God desires to give forth in the answer to the prayers of His poor people.

3) Your righteousness shall go before you (verse 8) and the Lord shall guide you continually (verse 11). If it is the fast that God has chosen, this will be the fruit of it. And what is this righteousness? The last expression of verse eight opens the first, Jehovah your righteousness shall be for you and the glory of the Lord shall be your rereward. It has reference to God's conduct of Israel through the wilderness. God went before them in the pillar of cloud by day and the pillar of fire by night. In time of danger the angel of God removed and went behind them as at the Red Sea (Exodus 14:19,20). Thus the righteousness of the Lord was in the cloud. They were a people full of all manner of iniquities, perversions and rebellion but it is said of God, "He hath not beheld iniquity in Jacob, neither hath He seen perverseness in Israel" (Numbers 23:21). Jehovah went before them as a God pardoning iniquity, transgression and sin (Exodus 34:5-7). He never led them through the wilderness but what, as their Righteousness, He went before them. When God accepts you graciously through the righteousness of His own Son Christ Jesus and so goes before you, this is a benefit whereby He manifests His gracious acceptance. The phrase signifies three things.

First, He goes before you to seek a place of rest for you. Thus our Lord Jesus Christ has gone before us into heaven as a forerunner (Hebrews 6:20), to prepare a place for us (John 14:2).

Second, He goes before you in His Word, guiding you in the way wherein you ought to follow Him that you also may attain to rest just as He did for Israel in the wilderness.

Third, He goes before you as the Captain of your Salvation to secure your way. He will lead you into your Canaan as He did Israel (Joshua 5:13-15). When you fast such a fast as He has chosen He will tread all your enemies under your feet including the Devil and the world. This will also be true of a commonwealth in time of war. If they fast sincerely He will go before them and make their way victorious and their end triumphant, just as Jehoshaphat's fast brought them to the valley of blessing (2 Chronicles 20:3-30).

4) He will be your rereward (Isaiah 58:8). This signifies the host that comes after the rest of the army that gathers up the weak, the feeble and those that are not able to secure themselves. In the march of Israel through the wilderness the tribe of Dan was the gathering host (Numbers 2:25-31). David refers to this in the words, "When my father and my mother forsake me, then the Lord will take me up" (Psalm 27:10). When your own heart fails and all succor from friends and expectations of creature helps are cut off, then the Lord will gather you up. You who are fatherless or widows, you who are under affliction or temptation that you cannot resist, you who cannot obtain help from any other source, know that when you fast the fast that God has chosen, God Himself will be your rereward and will come between you and the enemy (Exodus 14:19,20; Isaiah 59:15).

5) He will satisfy your souls in drought and make fat your bones and make you like a watered garden (Isaiah 58:11). A time of drought is a time of general want of rain and thereupon follows not only want of water, as in Ahab's day, but want of food also. In this time of drought God promises to satisfy your souls and to make you as a watered garden. Whatever wants and necessities have been or may be feared to come upon a person or people, when they fast the fast which God has chosen, He will satisfy their souls in drought and make fat their bones. This alludes to God's dealings with Israel in the wilderness where He gave them water out of the rock and manna from heaven which were not only food and water for their bodies but spiritual food and water for their souls. So also God will provide a sufficient supply of all that is good and needful for our souls and bodies in this present life. He promises "to deliver their soul from death, and to keep them alive in famine" Psalm 33:19).

6) He will make your souls as a watered garden and as a spring of water whose waters fail not (Isaiah 58:11). The expression, watered garden, signifies a garden that is enclosed and secured from them that might spoil the roots or fruits, or that might make any sad and woeful impression upon the plants. A fast which God has chosen is the way to all the fruitfulness that an enclosed garden suggests (Song of Solomon 4:12). And lest you should still fear barrenness, God adds, "like a spring of water, whose waters fail not." Jesus promises, "the water that I shall give him shall be in him a well of water springing up into everlasting life"

(John 4:14).

7) There will be a threefold blessing to your posterity and to yourselves (Isaiah 58:12).

First, they shall build the old waste. This wilderness, for all I know, had lain waste from the beginning and no civilized people lived here before. Fasting and prayer are the ways to build the old waste of Judah and Israel.

Second, you shall raise up the foundations of many generations, that is, you and your seed.

Third, you shall be called the repairer of the breach, the restorer of paths to dwell in. Many breaches are made in churches, commonwealths and upon men's souls. Who are those that shall repair such breaches? Those that observe such a fast as God has chosen. Many lose their way and do not know how to get right with God again. You that fast the fast which God has chosen, God will manifest His gracious acceptance of you by making you and your posterity instruments to hold forth the ways of God clearly so that poor souls may again walk with God and find peace in their souls.

8) Then you shall delight yourself in the Lord and He will cause you to ride upon the high places of the earth and will feed you with the heritage of Jacob (Isaiah 58:14). Consider these three things:

First, the sum of it all is that such a fast as God has chosen will be powerful and effectual in bringing you to the highest happiness, for you shall delight yourselves in the Lord, you shall have God for your chiefest good, and He will be your portion to all eternity.

Second, you will ride upon the high places of the earth. You that are trodden down will have a time of exaltation in a kingdom that cannot be shaken.

Third, you will be fed with the heritage of Jacob your father, for the mouth of the Lord hath spoken it. That is, after all your sorrows and troubles, you will still find that God is your feeder and that He does not feed with common food but with Jacob's heritage which was threefold: (1) The blessings necessary for this life. (2) The blessings necessary for the soul. (3) The external feeding which is promised at the glorious appearance of our Lord Jesus Christ, "The Lamb which is in the midst of the throne shall feed them, and shall lead them unto living fountains of waters: and God shall wipe away all tears from their eyes" (Revelation 7:17). Are not these glorious privileges and admirable advantages? These are the special favors of God whereby, in due time, He will manifest His gracious acceptance of His people in their fastings and prayers which have been such as He Himself has chosen.

III. THE SEASONS FOR THE FAST WHICH GOD CHOOSES.

There are seasons when God delights to give manifestation of His gracious acceptance of His people. It is true, God has reserved the seasons in His own power and therefore we cannot tell you the day, month or year, but still there are certain signs that are forerunners of God's gracious manifestations. Therefore, I will give you some general suggestions to help your faith raise up your expectations.

1. When the evil of afflictions has finished its work. God may hold you for a long time under some spiritual affliction or outward pressure. You may be as a sheaf upon the threshing floor, receiving stroke after stroke, hardly ever free from tribulation and yet content. When affliction has done its work God will call it back. This was the Centurion's conviction (Matthew 8:9). Afflictions come forth with a "Go!" from God, for they have their commission and a work to do. When their work is done, they will have their "Come!" and shall be called off again. As He afflicts you for your profit, when the end is attained, the affliction will be removed. Afflictions are to make us partakers of His holiness. See then that the work prospers in your souls under trials, temptations, and afflictions.

2. When your hearts are quickened to urgent importunity for the designed blessing on the affliction. You may try mightily for deliverance from evils that are felt or feared but are your souls wrestling with God importunately for the blessing as was Jacob, "I will not let Thee go, except Thou bless me" (Genesis 32:26). It is not the removal of the rod but the receiving of the blessing that will refresh you. Is it the blessing that your soul cries out for? Certainly God will answer such prayers just as He did for Jacob, who, after his earnest wrestling with God, saw the face of God in the face of his brother Esau (Genesis 33:10).

3. When your souls are ready to fail for thirst. In all the exercises and trials of God's people, He still has a tender care to prevent this sad inconvenience. "I will not contend forever, neither will I be always wroth: for the spirit should fail before Me, and the souls which I have made" (Isaiah 57:16). Hence David argues, "Hear me speedily, O Lord: my spirit faileth" (Psalm 143:7).

4. When the enemy is most insolent and violent. When the storm is high and terrible it can scarcely be endured. Unless the gusts soon blow over, great havoc will be wrought. "When the enemy shall come in like a flood, the Spirit of the Lord shall lift up a standard against him" (Isaiah

59:19). God Himself will interpose and engage for your souls. His Spirit will fight against your spiritual adversaries and the wonders of His providence against your outward enemies. When He saw that there was none to help, then His own arm brought salvation (Isaiah 59:16). When they seem to be under the power of the enemy, then it is time for God to work for their deliverance.

5. When you are come to a desperate stand. When you know you must have help or you will perish; when you know you have already suffered shipwreck and are in the midst of the flood; when you find yourself in the midst of the fiery furnace or in the lion's den, having received the sentence of death in yourselves; this is the time to trust in the living God who quickens the dead.

6. When you can struggle no longer. You can be certain deliverance is near when your soul is brought to a quiet and patient submission to the hand and dispensation of God, and committing yourselves to His sovereign pleasure, you wait patiently for His salvation. This is a great mystery, yet while a soul is struggling against providence and is displeased with God's dispensation toward it, there is cause to fear that deliverance is far off. But when that soul comes to submission, deliverance is near and pledges of God's favor are at hand. "I shall find favor in the eyes of the Lord," saith David, "He will bring me again... But if He thus say, I have no delight in thee; behold, here am I, let Him do to me as seemeth good unto Him" (2 Samuel 15:25-26). David is not far from deliverance when he is content that God should fulfill His own pleasure upon him, whatsoever it may be. This is the method that God normally observes in the way of His providence toward His people. The Apostle tells you, "Tribulation worketh patience; and patience, experience; and experience hope: and hope maketh not ashamed" (Romans 5:3-5). It is a mistake to look for an experience of mercy in divine deliverance before the work of patience in self-resignation to the will of God is achieved.

IV. THE EVIDENCE THAT THE FAST WHICH GOD CHOOSES BENEFITS AS HE INTENDS.

This may be hard to believe in times of temptation. Therefore, we need to bottom our faith well upon such a foundation that it cannot be overthrown. To this purpose I shall mention these points,

1. He has not commanded us to seek His face in vain. If God should fail to manifest His acceptance of His people upon this account, then those that are under the powerful command of God to seek His face would seek His face in vain. But God says, "I said not unto the seed of Jacob, seek ye Me in vain" (Isaiah 45:19).

2. He has promised to respond. The gracious promises that are before us are sufficient security that a fast that God has chosen will bring such gracious acceptance as these eight promises have described. God promised, "Call upon Me in the day of trouble: I will deliver thee, and thou shalt glorify Me" (Psalm 50:15). Christ Himself also promised, "If ye shall ask anything in My name, I will do it" (John 14:14).

3. He is a God of mercy. The manner of God's dealing with His servants establishes this truth unto us, "Be merciful unto me, as Thou usest to do unto those that love Thy name. Order my steps in Thy Word: and let not any iniquity have dominion over me (Psalm 119:132,133).

4. God rewards suitably. He does not suffer the fastings and the prayers of others, when they are hearty, even though not spiritual, to go without their reward. The young ravens do not cry unto Him but what He takes care of them. As already noted, God regarded the prayer and fasting of Ahab who sold himself to work wickedness: "Because he humbleth himself before Me, I will not bring the evil in his days" (1 Kings 21:29). When Ninevah humbled herself God saved the Ninevites from destruction though it was against the very grain of the soul of Jonah (Jonah 3:10).

5. Nothing prevents it. It must needs be so because there is nothing standing in the way to hinder it. A fast that God has chosen removes all impediments that stand in the way of mercy. The great obstruction is normally some sin committed or some habitual impenitence remaining. But when the heart is truly humbled and broken, the soul is prepared for some degrees of mercy wherein the acceptance of the suppliant may be made manifest.

V. THE REASONS GOD HAS FOR BENEFITING HIS PEOPLE WHEN THEY FAST THE FAST WHICH HE CHOOSES.

Negatively, not for any inherent excellency in their fasting and prayers or services, for what benefits does God get by our humbling ourselves, laying aside our ornaments, afflicting our bodies or by our diligent attention to external actions?

Positively, I will give you three reasons for it.

Reason One. Because it is a fast that God has chosen and therefore it is so successful. If the fast were chosen by men it could fail to benefit without dishonoring God. But God appoints the fast and therefore His own honor is at stake for a gracious answer.

Reason Two. Because the persons are accepted and therefore their offerings are accepted also. The petition of a favorite is not easily rejected by the prince, especially such a petition as his prince has chosen and appointed for him. They are in a state of favor with God and therefore their petitions must needs be successful. The spiritual sacrifices of this royal holy priesthood are acceptable to God by Jesus Christ (1 Peter 2:5).

Reason Three. Because there is an admirable, mysterious communion between God the Father, God the Son, and God the Holy Spirit and the right suppliant or that person who fasts the fast which God has chosen. There is not a holy prayer put up to God but its original is God the Father. That prayer of faith which proceeds from the heart of a Christian was first in the heart of God the Father. He, through the intercession and mediation of His Son, sends it down by His Holy Spirit into the heart of a poor sinner and so stamps His image of it upon the heart of the poor sinner that he believes. Then the Holy Spirit who stamped it there takes it from thence and presents it unto the Father through Christ. Then the Father's heart gives forth the answer through the intercession of the Son. Notice of this answer is given to the Christian by the Holy Spirit. When you receive the answer, the same Holy Spirit works in your heart to return praise and thanksgiving by the Son unto the Father. There is then marvelous spiritual and mysterious communion between God the Father, Son and Holy Spirit and the poor believer. Therefore such prayer and fasting cannot be in vain.

IMPROVEMENTS.

Of what concern then is all this to us? Truly it is of very great concern. We are the people that succeeded Israel. We are Jacob. We are the people described in the text that seek God daily and delight to know His ways (Isaiah 58:2). This is our commitment. We are a nation that seeks justice. We must do right and must not forsake the ordinances of our God. We believe that we are bound to hearken to God's will and enquire after His ordinances. We are the people that by our regular practice of appearing before God in Solemn Assemblies have professed that we delight to approach Him. Therefore we are those that need to take notice of this great and solemn truth, that the fast that is not of God's choosing will be ineffectual, but that which is of God's choosing will prevail.

IMPROVEMENT ONE. It will build us up in the knowledge that there are great mysteries contained in this truth. I shall touch upon those that are of present consideration.

1. It teaches that there is a vast difference between duty fulfilled in love and duty enacted as religious performance. That which is here said of fasting applies throughout the whole body of religious truth. There is a prayer that God has chosen and a prayer that God has not chosen. There is an ordinance and observation thereof which God will own and accept, and there is that which He will not countenance or bless. Our God is a God that will be worshipped in Spirit and in Truth. The manner and the end of our worship reveals what the nature of that service is or of that particular religious act which we put forth toward Him. Look then to your own spirits in your worship of God. As it is said of a person worshipping, so it is true of the worship, "For he is not a Jew, which is one outwardly... But he is a Jew which is one inwardly... whose praise is not of men, but of God" (Romans 2:28,29). You may be outwardly a Christian and inwardly a heathen in the sight of God. All these "are uncircumcised in heart" (Jeremiah 9:26), says the Prophet, when he reckons up the nations together with Judah. You may be a heathen in heart while you are in the outward man a Christian. Your circumcision may become uncircumcision before God. Alas, what is an outward baptism if your souls never reach after spiritual baptism. If you have the washing of water without the laver of regeneration and the renewing of the Holy Ghost, can you rest in that or will God take pleasure in it? What is the value for you to eat the Lord's Supper and not to eat the Lord who is that Supper? What is your prayer if it is not the prayer which God has chosen? It is then but the expression of a voice of lust that will not be accepted by God. "Ye ask, and receive not, because ye ask amiss, that ye may consume it upon your lusts" (James 4:3). There are many mock-services whereby mock-Christians mock God in their profession. It is a sad truth that there is a form of godliness without power. Those in this situation feed upon husks and deceive their own souls with shadows which will profit nothing. True believers are warned to turn away from such (2 Timothy 3:5).

2. We need to realize how hard it is to awaken a secure sinner that is covered under a form of powerless godliness. Speak to a profane person and the whole power of common light and common principles of humanity will join in convicting him of his miserable, lost condition. Tell a drunkard that he shall drink in hell for this, his conscience tells him so when he is sober. Even the adulterer, his conscience being awakened, knows he shall suffer eternal torment for his moment's pleasure. But a man under a form of godliness without the power thereof has a ready salve for every sore. He stops his ears with his tongue and becomes as the deaf adder. Hence God makes it plain that this is not the fast that He had chosen and calls upon the Prophet to "Cry aloud, spare not, lift up thy voice like a trumpet" (Isaiah 58:1) that you may awaken them to the consideration of their sin.

3. It concerns us to know that all our spiritual duties and services must be tried. God will not only call us to account for all our open wickedness and gross acts of transgression but will try every service we perform asking, "Is this the fast that I have chosen, saith God?" Was this My prayer? Was this participation in My ordinance? Is this My conference? Are these My holy meetings? Are these My Sabbaths? Thus God will ask you, and God will accept none of your services except those that pass His trial. Therefore we have need to examine our own services and our hearts in them. You are in your chamber meditating, but is this the meditation God has chosen? You are crying and praying, but is this the prayer that God has chosen? You are reproving, counselling, admonishing your children or others, but are these the words God has chosen? You are dealing with your neighbor or brother for some transgression, but is it such an admonition as God has chosen? Remember all your actions must come under this question. "I chose out their way" for them, says Job, of the time when he was as King among them (Job 29:25). Just so, if Christ is your King, He shall choose your way for you, and you will choose the things that please Him and will not be content in that which does not answer the Lord's expectation.

IMPROVEMENT TWO. To judge ourselves is the way to prevent God's judgment. Let us briefly examine ourselves concerning our present fast. Is it a fast which God has chosen? Did He choose our preparation for it? Have you had solemn and serious thoughts during the fast concerning the ways of God's providence, concerning your persons, your families and your relations? Have you considered your own transgressions before God and the great cause you have of deep humiliation before Him because of them? To fail here is to fail in God's expectation from the beginning. However you may have prepared, since the fast began have you been careful to abstain from natural, unnecessary comforts and refreshings and has your abstinence proceeded from inward self-abhorrence because of your sins? Extreme grief takes away the appetite for eating and drinking. All the self-denying acts that are required in a fast are to proceed from a deep affliction of heart, otherwise it is but a shallow performance and of no worth with God. It is therefore called the afflicting of the soul. If fasting does not come from soul-affliction it will be very unprofitable and unacceptable to Him.

Again, are we real? Are our hearts thorough with God in the solemn profession we make on such a day as this? Are you truly sensible of your sins whereby you have provoked the Lord—your particular sins, the sins of your families, towns, churches and the sins of this country? Do we sincerely look to God in Jesus Christ for the spirit of repentance? Is it His grace indeed that you look unto for help and succor? Where is that spiritual self-abhorrence that should carry us to the end of these holy services? Is there a forgiving spirit? When you come before God are not your hearts, many of yours, full of wrath and anger? Are you meek like lambs before the Lamb of God in your holy offerings? Do you present yourselves upon that altar which is the Lamb? Or do you fast for strife and debate, longing to be at it again, that you may maintain your displeasure when the time of fasting is over? Is there in you a spirit of compassion and the working of the bowels of mercy toward the poor and needy while you are seeking mercy from God? Do you oblige and engage your hearts to return to God and to reform what is amiss in your persons, families, churches and commonwealth?

IMPROVEMENT THREE. The Lord help us solemnly to examine ourselves, for if it be not thus it is not the fast which God has chosen but is sin. If it is sin it is like turning a holy ordinance into a loathsome idol. If it is sin it is is like taking God's name in vain and bringing extraordinary dishonor upon Him.

Consider what will be the woeful issue and evil consequence of such sin unless God gives you a repentance from your formality in your services; instead of softening it will harden you; instead of mortifying sin it will quicken it; instead of obtaining grace it will bring displeasure; it will drive the Spirit from you and bring Satan near to you; instead of the good you desire it will bring about a contrary evil; you will be the worse for it and not the better. Where can greater wickedness be effected than by heartless fasting and prayer? Consider the horrible wickedness in the case of Naboth as described in First Kings twenty-one. Was ever a woman more hardened than Jezebel? Who is there like Ahab that sold himself to work wickedness in the sight of the Lord, stirred up by that wicked woman?

The way to be sealed up under the tombstone of a hard heart is to celebrate a fast with a spirit, manner and purpose other than God has chosen. Woeful ill consequences commonly come upon persons and families upon this account after a fast or solemn ordinance that is not performed according to God's pleasure. Men, women and even children are the worse in their practice. "And this have ye done again, covering the altar of the Lord with tears, with weeping, and with crying out, insomuch that He regardeth not the offering any more, nor receiveth it with good will at your hand" (Malachi 2:13). When men will fast and pray and cover God's altar with tears and yet hold fast their carnal, corrupt and impenitent frame of heart, they will grow worse and worse. Alas, what outward miseries this can bring upon families. Consider that because they ate the Supper of the Lord unworthily, one was sick, another weak and another fallen asleep (1 Corinthians 11:29,30). Just so in fasting, if in fasting you do not fast, if in humbling your souls you do not humble your souls, if in praying you do not pray, if you perform not the services that God has chosen, it will bring sickness upon those that are well and weakness and death upon the sick. It is mercy when we are thus judged of the Lord that we may not be condemned with the world (1 Corinthians 11:31-33).

It concerns us to consider what evil consequences will come upon an entire people. From whence come wars, famines, earthquakes and plagues? These are judgments upon a professing people because their worship is not worship, their godliness is not godliness and their fasting and prayer is not such as God has chosen. Because there is not the life and power of godliness in what they offer up to God, He is provoked to deal dreadfully with them when lighter afflictions will not prevail. Desolation came upon Jerusalem because they fasted to themselves and not to the Lord. "Therefore it is come to pass that as he cried, and they would not hear; so they cried, and I would not hear, saith the Lord of Hosts: But I scattered them with a whirlwind among all the nations whom they knew not. Thus the land was desolate after them" (Zechariah 7:13,14).

IMPROVEMENT FOUR. It concerns those of us that are true observers of such a fast as God has chosen. Just as in the day of the Prophet Isaiah, God was pleased to set before them many precious hopes for themselves and their posterity, so God has set a like portion before all of us whom He has inclined to seek His face.

Objection One. But you will say, these promises are indeed very glorious but how can I take comfort in them since I find myself falling so exceeding short in the qualifications required thereto?

Answer. You must distinguish between falling short in degree and in the whole. If there is in you no degree of these spiritual qualifications, you must face the dreadful consequences thereof, but if there be any, though the least degree, I would not discourage you, for when we speak of evangelical duties we must understand the qualifications in a Gospel sense. God looks at sincerity and accepts the uprightness of the heart although it is accompanied with many infirmities.

Objection Two. Another may say, I have labored many a year and cannot find my prayers thus answered.

Answer. We ought not to judge ourselves by the issues of divine providence but by the operations of God's Spirit in us. If the work in your heart has been gracious, the issue will be glorious to your soul in the end, and He that shall come will come and will not tarry.

Objection Three. If these things be necessary for a fast to be acceptable, what benefit is there in a public fast wherein most fall short of what is required?

Answer. Despite whoever falls short, those that keep this fast that God has chosen will have the blessing thereof. Therefore look to your own heart and you will receive the testimony of His gracious acceptance. God knows how to save the good fig trees when He destroys a whole orchard of bad. He can find an ark for Noah and cull out eight persons from a whole world to show them His salvation. Besides, public fasts procure at least reprieves. God will wait to see the fruit of it and will not put a full end to His patience until there is no hope of answering humiliation by reformation.

IMPROVEMENT FIVE. It concerns every one of us to look diligently to our own souls, when we have any service to perform to the Lord our God, that we do it according to God's mind.

Is that really possible someone wonders? Yes, if now at last your soul truly repents of sin; if in humility you melt before God because of your carnality, unpreparedness for the day and unspiritualness in the day; if you look unto Christ's mediation for pardon and acceptance; if you trust His gracious help; if you resolve to return to God and to exercise mercy and lovingkindness among men and determine to do justice and judgment; if you walk righteously, holily and humbly with your God, this very fast day may be turned into a time of joy and in God's gracious acceptance may be esteemed such a fast as God has chosen.

I suggest a few things here for your consideration as the issue of this your fast:

1. Look into your own hearts. Get alone and consider what it is that has been amiss in your hearts and lives in times past. Set a narrow watch over your own soul for all time to come that you may not provoke God. Because you are weak and infirm, entreat God to set a watch over you by His Holy Spirit.

2. Take up a resolution to walk with God in your house in a perfect way. You need to do this so that neither you nor your relations may be the worse for your fastings and that judgment may not come upon you in your house because you have not glorified God in His house.

3. Use your utmost interest for public good. Determine that justice and judgment will have free passage among us and that righteousness and peace will prevail in the commonwealth and in our churches, and although you have no power of yourselves, wrestle with God for it that it may be so.

4. Take care that you hold fast the Word of God's patience in the time of your trial. Hold it fast in faith and practice. Remember that Word of God, "He that endureth to the end shall be saved" (Matthew 10:22). And again, "Hold that fast which thou hast, that no man take thy crown" (Revelation 3:11). It is a day of trial, but look to it that you may be found upright. Be open hearted and open handed to those that are in misery and affliction. "Blessed are the merciful: for they shall obtain mercy" (Matthew 5:7).

"Now unto Him that is able to do exceeding abundantly above all that we ask or think, according to the power that worketh in us, unto Him be glory in the Church by Christ Jesus throughout all ages, world without end. Amen" (Ephesians 3:20,21).

CHAPTER FIVE

The
Possibility
of
God Forsaking
a People

By
Joseph Rowlandson

Joseph Rowlandson, 1631-1678

Joseph Rowlandson was born about 1631, probably in England. He was the only Harvard graduate in the class of 1652. For some unknown reason, during his junior year, he posted a piece against the authorities on the meeting-house at Ipswich, his home. It was judged 'a scandalous lybell,' and in consequence he was sentenced to a public whipping and fines.

Upon graduation he studied theology for two years and in 1654 began preaching in Lancaster, Massachusetts. A church was legally organized there in 1660 and Rowlandson was ordained. He continued his labors in that place until the Philip's War. Eight persons were killed in the town in August of 1675. The following February, while he and two parishioners were "at Boston soliciting the Governor and Council for more soldiers for the protection of the place," fifteen hundred Indians under Philip assaulted the town which then consisted of about fifty families. A large portion of the inhabitants were killed, including Rowlandson's brother Thomas, and most of the others taken captive. His wife was wounded and made a prisoner along with their children. Joseph knew nothing of what had happened until his return to the smoldering ruins of what had been their home and the dead bodies of many of his parishioners. After eleven weeks and five days of dreadful suffering, his wife was redeemed and joined her husband in Boston where they were kindly cared for another eleven weeks in the home of Thomas Shepard of Charlestown. In time, their children joined them in a home provided for nine months in Boston by sympathetic friends who had also paid the ransoms.

In April of 1677 the Town of Weathersfield, Connecticut invited Rowlandson to settle among them as their Pastor. He served only briefly until his death in November 1678.

The preface of the sermon was addressed: "To the Courteous Reader, especially those inhabitants of the Town of Weathersfield and Lancaster in New-England." It states, "God's forsaking the people He has been near to is a thing of such weight and solemnity and has such bitter effects that it is a very difficult subject, especially in a dark and mourning day, for ministers to speak of and for people to listen to. But servants of God must warn of the danger and the people of God must act so as to avoid such a judgment. As God's presence is the greatest good His people can experience on this side of heaven, so His absence is the greatest misery they can know on this side of hell. This, therefore, must be a point of great concern to all such as are determined to please God in all that they do. The following sermon will appear as a solemn word if duly considered. The subject matter is very solemn and weighty for it treats of God being with or forsaking a people. The time when it was delivered was a solemn time—a day of fasting and humiliation throughout the Colonies. The Reverend Author that composed and preached it was himself solemn and serious above many others. That which adds even greater solemnity is the fact that it was the last word he spoke in the world, being delivered only two days before he left it. As it is solemn, so it is seasonable and pertinent. This is a time wherein we have given God just cause to forsake us. It is a time when God is in fact threatening to forsake us. It is a time where God has in some measure forsaken us already. What then can be more seasonable than to show the evils that befall a forsaken people that we may be awakened and return to the Lord before He forsakes us utterly."

First published as *The Possibility of God's Forsaking a People That Have Been Visibly Near and Dear to Him, Together With the Misery of a People Thus Forsaken, Set Forth in a Sermon, Preached at Weathersfield, November 21, 1678 Being a Day of Fast and Humiliation. By Mr. Joseph Rowlandson.* Boston, in New-England: Printed for John Ratcliffe & John Griffin, 1682.

The Possibility
of God Forsaking a People

**"And when this people, or the prophet, or a priest,
shall ask thee, saying, What is the burden of the Lord?
thou shalt then say unto them, What burden?
I will even forsake you, saith the Lord."
Jeremiah 23:33.**

In these words we find first, an indication concerning who the questioners are, "This people, or the prophet, or a priest."

Second, the question itself which they ask, "What is the burden of the Lord?"

Third, the answer, and it is a solemn answer too, which is put into his mouth by the Lord and which he is to return to the questioners as the Lord's answer, "Thou shalt then say unto them, What burden? I will even forsake you, saith the Lord."

In this answer there are three things to be observed:

1. An expression of indignation, "What burden?"

2. An assertion by way of answer to the question, "I will forsake you."

3. A seal of ratification, "Saith the Lord."

God had already spoken of the pastors that destroyed and scattered the flock in the beginning of the chapter, "Woe be unto the pastors that destroy and scatter the sheep of My pasture! saith the Lord!" (Jeremiah 23:1). "I will visit upon you the evil of your doings, saith the Lord" (verse 2). The false prophets were denounced in the words, "Mine heart within Me is broken because of the prophets" (verse 9), and "I am against them that prophesy false dreams, saith the Lord, and do tell them, and cause my people to err by their lies, and by their lightness; yet I sent them not, nor commanded them: therefore they shall not profit this people at all, saith the Lord" (verse 32). Indeed, it can be said of all false prophets, "I have not sent these prophets, yet they ran: I have not spoken to them, yet they prophesied" (verse 21).

Jeremiah deals not only with the wickedness of the pastors and prophets but with their effect upon the people that were seduced by them saying, "They strengthen also the hands of evildoers that none doth return from his wickedness" (verse 14). It was apparently a usual thing for a prophet of the Lord to begin his sermon with the phrase, "The burden of the Lord," but when this people, prophet or priest asked, "What is the burden of the Lord?" it is evident that they did not do so because they wished to know what was on God's heart but because they wished to mock both the prophet and the Lord.

Now let me briefly open up the words of the text.

"And" or "moreover" here indicates that the prophet, speaking under inspiration, is entering upon a new matter.

"This people" refers to the profane portion of them whom the false prophets had secured. Unto them he joins the prophet and the priest who were also profane. This is clearly indicated in the words, "For both prophet and priest are profane; yea, in my house have I found their wickedness, saith the Lord" (verse 11). It is terrible to have one or two false prophets, but how much worse to have an entire pack of them so that it must be said, "The prophets prophesy falsely, and the priests bear rule by their means; and my people love to have it so; and what will ye do in the end thereof?" (Jeremiah 5:31).

"Shall ask thee saying." This is not to be taken as a serious question but they ask in a deriding way and not out of a holy end or desire.

"What is the burden of the Lord?" Or what is the word from the Lord? This is how prophecies were styled that contained in them threatenings, judgments and plagues. It is as if they had said, "What further mischief do you have in your head to declare? What further woes and threatenings do you intend to pronounce? Have you nothing else to prophesy other than mischief and calamity? "What is the burden of the Lord?"

"Thou shalt then say unto them." The Lord knew what they would say to him and therefore tells the prophet what he should say by way of reply.

"What burden?" This is a retort by way of holy indignation. Do you dare to ask "What burden?" How can you speak to Me with such derision?

"I will even forsake you, saith the Lord." Here is a burden heavy enough indeed. They felt it then, and you are likely to feel it ere long. It is heavy enough to break your backs, to break your Church and your Commonwealth. It is heavy enough to sink your haughty spirits. When this burden shall come upon you, in its force and weight, you will not be able to escape it.

DOCTRINE: The Lord may even forsake a people that have been near to Him and that He has been near to, though for the Lord to do so is as fearful and loathsome a judgment as can be inflicted upon any

people.

The doctrine has two parts.

1. God may forsake a people that have been near to Him and that He may have been near to.

2. When God forsakes a people it is a very sad and heavy burden.

I. GOD MAY FORSAKE A PEOPLE THAT HAVE BEEN NEAR TO HIM AND THAT HE MAY HAVE BEEN NEAR TO.

This may be spoken of in this order:

1. What is meant by God forsaking a people?
2. How may it appear that God forsakes such a people?
3. Why does God forsake a people?
4. The application of this truth.

1. What is meant by God forsaking a people? What is intended thereby? It refers to God's withdrawing Himself, as the Prophet Hosea phrases it, "They shall go with their flocks and with their herds to seek the Lord; but they shall not find Him; He hath withdrawn Himself from them" (Hosea 5:6). They shall seek Him and not find Him and there is a good reason for this. He has withdrawn Himself, He is gone in respect to His gracious presence.

We must here distinguish between God's general presence and His precious presence.

In respect to His general presence, He is not far from any of us, "for in Him we live, and move, and have our being" (Acts 17:28). We have not only our beginning from Him but our being in Him, as the beam of light has its being in the sun. Of this general presence of God I must say that there is no place we can fly from it. The Psalmist asked, "Whither shall I go from Thy Spirit? or whither shall I flee from Thy presence?" (Psalm 139:7). In this sense God is everywhere, "If I ascend up into heaven, Thou art there: if I make my bed in hell [sheol], behold, Thou art there. If I take the wings of the morning, and dwell in the uttermost parts of the sea; Even there shall Thy hand lead me, and Thy right hand shall hold me" (verses 8-10). God fills heaven and earth and there is no hiding from Him. "'Can any hide himself in secret places that I shall not see him?' saith the Lord. 'Do not I fill heaven and earth?' saith the Lord" (Jeremiah 23:24). He has heaven for His throne and the earth for His footstool (Isaiah 66:1). This general presence of God, if believingly apprehended and strongly believed, might be of great use.

But it is not this general presence that is meant here but His special presence—His favorable, His gracious, His manifest presence—the removing of which is what is meant by the forsaking of which the text specifically speaks. God is said to forsake a wayward people both as to affection and action.

God forsakes a people as to affection, when He discontinues His love to them. When He takes away His love from a people, He takes His leave of them. The Lord said to Jeremiah, "My mind could not be toward this people: cast them out of My sight, and let them go forth" (Jeremiah 15:1). This is truly a very heavy judgment and a removal that is sad indeed. "Be thou instructed, O Jerusalem, lest my soul depart from Thee" (Jeremiah 6:8).

God forsakes a people as to action, when He takes away the signs of His presence, when He takes away merciful and gracious providences, when He no longer acts toward them as he was accustomed to do, but vexes them with all manner of adversity. "Then My anger shall be kindled against them in that day, and I will forsake them, and I will hide My face from them, and they shall be devoured, and many evils and troubles shall befall them; so that they will say in that day, Are not these evils come upon us, because our God is not among us? And I will surely hide My face in that day for all the evils which they shall have wrought" (Deuteronomy 31:17,18). A people must know that God has forsaken them when He ceases to protect them from their enemies as in times past and does not provide for them as He was generous in doing on earlier occasions. A people must know they are forsaken when God takes away His ordinances and deprives a people of the glorious things of His house, or takes away His Spirit from accompanying them so that the glory ceases and the ordinances are rendered ineffectual for the saving good of a people.

2. How may it appear that God forsakes such a people? God's forsaking a people may appear by what He has threatened, for whatever is threatened may be inflicted. Surely God has threatened to forsake His people when they are wayward. As noted already, "Then My anger shall be kindled against them in that day, and I will forsake them, and I will hide My face from them..." (Deuteronomy 31:17,18). Many threatenings like this are found in the Scripture against Israel, who are styled a people near unto Him.

It is the very ones who have been near to God and to whom He has been near that have complained of their being forsaken by God. "Thou hast forsaken us" is one of the bitterest moans on record that the Church of God has often had to make unto God.

What God has inflicted on such may be inflicted again. What God has done to some He may do to others in the same state and relation for He is unchangeable. Those that were once the only peculiar people of God, who were near to God and had God near to them, what is their condition today? Are they not in a forsaken condition? Is not the condition of the offspring of Abraham, God's friend, a seed which he had chosen and kept for above fifteen hundred years, forsaken? God has been angry with them and has forsaken them just as they were warned so long ago that He would do. How is it with the Churches of Asia—those once famous golden candlesticks? They had epistles of warning written to them. Are they not in a forsaken condition now? As far as we know there is not the trace of a Church to be found among them.

In that people are capable of doing that which may deserve a forsaking, they may, therefore, do that which will actually procure it. Any of God's people may do that which deserve God's judgment of forsaking them. They may, through the corruption and unbelief of their hearts, forsake God. If they do, God may in just judgment retaliate and thereupon forsake them. This very issue is spoken to in the before quoted place, They "will forsake Me, and break My covenant which I have made with them. Then My anger shall be kindled against them in that day, and I will forsake them, and I will hide My face from them" (Deuteronomy 31:16-17). So again, "But if ye forsake Him, He will forsake you" (2 Chronicles 15:2). The first is supposed, "if ye forsake Him," the latter is imposed, "He will forsake you."

3. Why does God forsake a people? The reasons are clear:

1) To show that He has no need of any. He has forsaken many and may forsake many more and would have the entire world take notice that although all men have need of Him, yet He has no need of any man.

2) To testify of His sanctity and His severity against sin. He will not spare them that have been near Him if they will not spare themselves from sin for His sake. He is a holy God, and if they will have their sins and their lusts and their own way, He will vindicate His holiness by inflicting this judgment upon them.

3) To be a warning to all that enjoy His gracious presence so that they value it highly and take heed that they do not sin against Him, forsaking Him and thus provoking Him to forsake them.

I must caution you that the point is to be understood of a people that are visibly and externally near and dear to God but who none the less may be totally and finally forsaken of God. Here it must be noted that God may exercise a great deal of patience and forbearance toward such as He is about to forsake. He did so with the old world. He did so with the Israelites of old. He did so with the Seven Churches of Asia. He is not apt to suddenly and all at once forsake a people that have been near and dear to Him. He is very likely to give them warning and in patience to bear a while with their frowardness, to wait and see if there be any returning to Him before He inflicts this heavy and sharp judgment.

4. The Application of This Truth. It serves to admonish us not to exalt ourselves too highly because of the blessings God gives us. It is a great privilege to have the Lord near us and to be near unto Him. Some lean upon this even though they abide in their sin. "They build up Zion with blood, and Jerusalem with iniquity. The heads thereof judge for reward, and the priests thereof teach for hire, and the prophets thereof divine for money: yet will they lean upon the Lord, and say, 'Is not the Lord among us? none evil can come upon us'" (Micah 3:10,11). If our deportment is not according to our privileges, if we do not conduct ourselves as becomes a humble, fruitful and holy people, the Lord will bring forth this heavy judgment against us and we shall be rejected and forsaken of the Lord, whatever our external privileges may be.

II. WHEN GOD FORSAKES A PEOPLE IT IS A VERY SAD AND HEAVY BURDEN.

This is the heaviest burden any people must bear for it is the sorest of all God's righteous judgments against a people.

There are two things that must be spoken of in the management of this truth. 1. The arguments that provide evidence of its truth. 2. The uses of this truth.

1. The arguments that provide evidence of its truth.

1) If God has threatened it as a very sore judgment then we may be sure it is so. When God has been angry with a people He has manifested the same by menacing them with His threatened judgments. When He has designed to do them a deep displeasure because of some high provocation, He is wont to threaten them, not by taking away this or that outward comfort from them, but by taking away Himself from them.

And that is a woe indeed, a woe of which the Scriptures speak, "Yea woe also to them when I depart from them!" (Hosea 9:12). Surely when God departs it is the most woeful day any people ever meet with.

2) God's forsaking a people is a sore judgment in that it exposes them to all the other judgments. Just as sin is a great evil in that it exposes the sinner to all other evils, so a great evil of the punishment of divine withdrawal is that it exposes the judged to all other punishments. If God is gone, our guard is gone, and we are as a city in the midst of enemies whose walls are broken down. With God gone, our strength to make

resistance is gone, for God is our strength. A forsaken people are left as a carcass without life and as a prey to beasts of prey. A people forsaken by their God are exposed to all their devouring enemies and to infernal and cursed spirits. They are exposed to the mischief and the malice of all their malignant enemies. When the Lord forsook Jerusalem, the Romans quickly made a prey of it. When they were destitute of God, their habitation became desolate also. There is no protection to a people whom the Lord has forsaken, but they are exposed to perplexity and destruction on every side.

3) The evils that fall on a God-forsaken people are only evils, that is to say, evils without any good in them. The prophet Ezekiel used the expression, "Thus saith the Lord God; An evil, an only evil, behold, is come" (Ezekiel 7:5). I speak of just such an evil, an evil which is only an evil. An evil which falls on a people when God is present may have much good in it. The Lord may sanctify it for abundance of blessing. There are always hopes of this while the Lord continues among a people. But if God is gone, an evil is only an evil, for such evils can have nothing but evil in them.

4) When God forsakes a people, no creature can then provide any help, for what can creatures do when God is departed. He makes the creatures useful and helpful but without Him they are unable to do us any good for they have no power of their own. They may say to you, as the King of Israel said to the woman that cried out, "Help, my lord, O king. If the Lord do not help thee, whence shall I help thee?" (2 Kings 6:26,27). All creatures may therefore say, if God is departed, "We cannot help." Even the Devil cannot help when God is gone. When God departed from Saul he sought help from the Witch of Endor. She supposedly brought forth dead Samuel who is credited with saying, "Wherefore then dost thou ask of me, seeing the Lord is departed from thee, and is become thine enemy?" (1 Samuel 28:16).

5) God's withdrawal of his gracious presence is seen as a sore judgment by the anguish and distress that men have been in who have been sensible that God has forsaken them. Sin has flown in the face of such and terrified them. Hear them groaning, "Oh, the blessed God is gone, and being gone, mercy is gone with Him! Oh the awful sins that lie upon me! What shall I do?" Hear the moan of saints of old who have found themselves in such a case, "My God, my God, why hast Thou forsaken me? why art Thou so far from helping me, and from the words of my roaring? O my God, I cry in the daytime, but Thou hearest not; and in the night season, and am not silent" (Psalm 22:1,2). Think of how Saul roared out his distress because God had departed from him. He

groaned not so much because the Philistines were upon him, for had God not been gone he could have dealt well enough with them, but the heart and the sting of his misery was that God had departed from him.

6) God's withdrawal is a sore punishment in that it is a great part of the punishment of Hell itself. Surely the fire of Hell that shall never be quenched is a dreadful punishment. Both the worm that never dies and the pain that never ceases are likewise indicators of most terrible punishment. But how can any of these sufferings compare with the awful fact that Hell is the place where God never visits.

2. The Uses of This Truth.

USE ONE. How foolish sinners are that even bid God depart from them, "Therefore they say unto God, 'Depart from us; for we desire not the knowledge of Thy ways'" (Job 21:14). But do they know what they say? Oh sinners is this your wish? If it is granted it will prove your woeful doom forever. Happily, God's presence is now your trouble but I tell you His absence will be your torment.

USE TWO. See here what an evil it is to forsake God. Is it a judgment of judgments to be forsaken of God? Surely then it is a sin of sins to forsake Him. The great evil of punishment is in being left by God. Just so, the great evil of sin is in leaving God. How could you even consider forsaking God who is your only good; God who made you and protected you from the beginning; God who has been the guard of your youth and has been good to you and fed you all your days? "Know therefore and see that it is an evil thing and bitter, that thou hast forsaken the Lord thy God" (Jeremiah 2:19). And in this passage there is an aggravation of this sin, "Thou hast forsaken the Lord thy God when He led thee by the way" (verse 17). To forsake a distant god who you do not know and have no relationship with would be one thing but when you forsake the very God who has been a guide to direct you, a staff to support you, a convoy to guard you, a Father to provide for you so that you have wanted nothing, then it must truly be said, "How evil and bitter a thing it is that thou hast forsaken the Lord." To this denouncement the prophet adds, "O generation!" (verse 31). Generation of what? Generation of whatever you want to add. God leaves a place that you may write what you please: "Generation of vipers," "Generation of backsliders," "Generation of mourners" or anything else you wish to add other than "Generation of God's people."

Do you hear the Word of the Lord, O sinner? Can you behold your face in that glass? Can you hear the Lord saying, "Because of your causeless apostasies, I have been a wilderness unto you O Israel? Have you wanted anything, Oh ye degenerating, crooked and wilful generation?" God may say to such sinners, as Pharaoh said to Hadad when he heard in Egypt that David was dead and desired to depart the country and go home, "But what hast thou lacked with me, that, behold, thou seekest to go to thine own country?" (1 Kings 11:21,22). What hast thou lacked sinner that thou seekest to be gone from the Lord? The sinner must answer with Hadad, "Nothing, howbeit let me go in any wise." He came to him in his distress and when it served his purpose he slipped away. Thus the very reason that sinners forsake God is because they will to forsake Him.

USE THREE. Do not wonder that God's saints have been so solicitous with Him not to forsake them. David cried, "O forsake me not utterly" (Psalm 119:8). If anybody had occasion to be solicitous in this matter it was David who understood very well what it was to be forsaken of the Lord, for he had experienced it after his horrible sin with Bathsheba (Psalm 32, 38). Those that truly know the Lord press Him hard that whatever He does, He will not leave them nor forsake them, crying, "Leave us not" (Jeremiah 14:9). Is it any wonder the saints moan when the Lord seems to have forsaken them?

USE FOUR. If God's forsaking is such a sore judgment, it should make us more cautious and wary lest we pull down this judgment on our own heads. Men should be vastly more afraid of this heaviest of all judgments than the child is of a whipping.

USE FIVE. Let God's dear ones take heed of concluding against themselves that they are under this judgment. They are the readiest to conclude against themselves and yet are really in the least danger. Thus we read, "But Zion said, The Lord hath forsaken me, and my Lord hath forgotten me" (Isaiah 49:14). But why did Zion say this? It was from diffidence, for saints do not take God for granted as others do. They are determined to be able to say, "I have not wickedly departed from my God" (Psalm 18:21). God will not forsake them as He forsakes others, and if He forsakes them at all He will not utterly forsake them. His forsaking of His own saints is but temporary and partial.

But here a question may be asked, "What is the difference between a sinner forsaken and a saint forsaken, for surely the Lord doth not forsake both alike?"

1. When God forsakes His own they cry after Him continually, whereas hardened sinners scarcely know and certainly do not care that God is gone. God sometimes withdraws Himself from His people that

they may cry after Him so that He may draw their hearts after Him just as a mother may hide away from her child that it may seek and cry the more earnestly after her.

2. When God forsakes the saints they retain good thoughts of Him in His withdrawal or absence from them just as the spouse in the Canticles did who called him her beloved still and as the faithful wife does who retains good thoughts of her husband and keeps up her respect though he is gone from her. But the wicked, when the Lord forsakes them, harbor hard thoughts against Him and are loath to serve the Lord and walk in His ways. "What good have I got by all that I have done," they ask. "See how He has served me," they complain bitterly.

3. When the Lord departs from His beloved, they seek Him until He returns again. When the Lord forsakes His Church she realizes that it is time to seek the Lord's presence afresh. God desires His people to seek after Him, and those who are really His own satisfy His desire. The true saint will be satisfied with nothing less that the Lord's return to him. Moreover, there is a great difference in God's forsaking the sinner and the saint. When He forsakes the wicked they remain in darkness, but when He withdraws from His own, He leaves some light whereby they may see which way He has gone, he leaves some glimmering light by which they may follow after him and find Him.

And again, when He leaves His own, His bowels are still toward them, "My bowels are troubled for him; I will surely have mercy upon Him, saith the Lord" (Jeremiah 31:20). God has an eye toward his own for much good even in forsaking them.

USE SIX. I exhort you to render thanksgiving to God in that He has not yet forsaken us. No matter what he has stripped us of, He has not yet stripped us of Himself for He has not yet forsaken us. He might have done this and done us no wrong, but He has not yet done it.

We need to entreat the Lord that He will not forsake us. Here let me add motives and means.

1. We need to consider that God is loath to forsake us. It is a blessed truth that God does not willingly afflict us with the rod of affliction or grieve us with His grievous strokes. God has shown Himself loath to depart from those that have departed from Him. He has warned us of His displeasure that we might stay by Him. It is contrary to God's heart desire to forsake a people that have been near to Him. I can almost hear Him saying, "How shall I ever give thee up, O New-England!" He speaks with great tenderness to warn us against forsaking Him, "Be thou instructed, O Jerusalem, lest My soul depart from thee; lest I make thee desolate, a land not inhabited" (Jeremiah 6:8). O New-England, you may easily stay Him. The matter is not so far gone but what you might stay Him yet. If we were but as loath that He should forsake us as He is to forsake us, He would never leave us. Even God's gradual movements away from a people argue His loathness and unwillingness to leave them.

2. We also need to consider what the Lord is to us or what relation He stands in to us while He is with us. He is our Friend. We have found Him to be so and that He is a special Friend indeed. Men in the world are not willing to lose a friend, especially a good friend. He is as faithful, skilful, powerful and tender-hearted a Friend as any people ever had. He stuck by us when our case was very woeful. "If it had not been the Lord who was on our side, when men rose up against us: then they had swallowed us up quick, when their wrath was kindled against us" (Psalm 124:2,3). Surely New-England may now say, "The Lord has been on our side." He has been a Father to us, a tender-hearted Father. We can say with the prophet, "Doubtless Thou art our Father, though Abraham be ignorant of us, and Israel acknowledge us not: Thou, O Lord, art our Father" (Isaiah 63:16). Can children be willing for their father to leave them? He has been our Husband, "For thy Maker is thine Husband" (Isaiah 54:5). He has been a loving, careful, tender Husband too. Can the wife be willing to part with her husband?

If the Lord forsakes us, we will be bereft of our Friend and left friendless indeed, for He is the only true Friend of New-England. If He leaves us, we shall be left as orphans, for he is related to us as our Father and what sad, poor orphans we will be. If He departs from us, we will be in a state of widowhood, and it will be a very sorrowful and solitary state, for He has been a faithful Husband to us.

God has been our Guide and our Pilot. What will become of the blind if their guide leaves them? What will become of the ship if the Pilot deserts it? Well may the Lord say to New-England, "O My people, what have I done unto thee? and wherein have I wearied thee? Testify against Me" (Micah 6:3).

3. We must consider that there are clear signs of God's intent to leave us unless something is done. If you inquire, "What?" I answer,

1) The sins for which God has forsaken others are rife among us. The very sins for which God forsook the Jews are our sins.

Horrid pride. "The pride of Israel doth testify to His face" (Hosea 5:5). We tolerate pride in parts and pride in hearts, pride in apparel and virtues, pride in gestures and in looks. "There is a generation that are pure in their own eyes, and yet is not washed from their filthiness. There is a generation, O how lofty are their eyes! and their eyelids are lifted up" (Proverbs 30:12,13). New-England is taken notice of abroad, and we are as proud a professing people as the world knows. When a people are humble the Lord will be with them, but if our fullness, which results from divine mercies, puffs us up, God will empty us, and He will blast that which we are proud of.

Deep and high ingratitude. "Do you thus requite the Lord, O foolish people and unwise? is not He thy Father that hath bought thee? hath He not made thee, and established thee?" (Deuteronomy 32:6). So the prophet upbraided the people, "For she did not know that I gave her corn, and wine, and oil, and multiplied her silver and gold, which they prepared for Baal" (Hosea 2:8). We have been blest but God has not gotten the glory for our blessings.

Oppression. "Hear this, O ye that swallow up the needy, even to make the poor of the land to fail" (Amos 8:4). These Jews were like the fish, the larger devouring the smaller. Some of us are like wild beasts that tear off the flesh of the sheep and destroy the flocks. There is more justice to be found in hell than among some men on earth, for no innocent persons are oppressed there!

Weariness of God's ordinances. Amos charged the people with asking, "When will the new moon be gone, that we may sell corn? And the sabbath, that we may set forth wheat, making the ephah small, and the shekel great, and falsifying the balances by deceit?" (Amos 8:5). They that are weary of the service of God and of the ordinances of God are weary of God Himself. Indeed, God has fed us to the full as to His ordinances, and we are glutted to the point where we have lost our esteem for them and for the God who gave them. When commodities are in low esteem they bear a small price. When Gospel ordinances are a cheap commodity it is because men have lost their sense of value and are weary of them. When this happens, God will let out His vineyard to another people. When His mercies become our burdens, God will ease us of them.

Dishonesty in trade. Many of our merchants and tradesmen are guilty of making the ephah small and the sheckel great and of selling the refuse of the wheat. They pick out the best of the grain for themselves and sell the worst to the poor for a vastly inflated price (Amos 8:5,6).

Idolatry. Have not material goods become our gods? Are there not many who are seeking to hold on to the world with one hand and God with the other? What is this but spiritual adultery?

Incorrigibleness or opposition to a spirit of reformation. When God calls a people to return by repentance but they go on in their sin, they are manifesting opposition to the spirit of reformation God sends. God calls to men by His judgments and by His rod, but many of them will not hear. "Thou hast stricken them, but they have not grieved; Thou hast consumed them, but they have refused to receive correction: they have made their faces harder than a rock; they have refused to return" (Jeremiah 5:3). When this is the case with a people, God will rise up and be gone just as Jeremiah warned, "Because ye have done all these works, saith the Lord, and I spake unto you, rising up early and speaking, but ye heard not; and I called you, but ye answered not; Therefore will I do unto this house... as I have done to Shiloh. And I will cast you out of My sight, as I have cast out all your brethren, even the whole seed of Ephraim" (Jeremiah 7:13-15). Why? "Go ye now unto My place which was in Shiloh, where I set My name at the first, and see what I did to it for the wickedness of my people Israel" (verse 12). Go and view it and you will see what He did. He left tokens of His wrath upon them and forsook them.

2) Another sign of God's intent to forsake us is that He is dealing with us as He is wont to deal with those that He is about to forsake. When He is about to forsake a people He may take away some of those that are near and dear to Him: He may remove His Watchmen, those that stand in the gap and bind His destructive hands with their prayer. When He has decided to pour out wrath upon a people He may remove the bright and shining lights that have held the evil in check.

3) Another sign that God may be getting ready to abandon us is our lukewarmness and insincerity in religion which is a usual forerunner of God's removal of Himself from His people. When a people do not care for God and the things pertaining to Himself which He has left them, He has in some measure already withdrawn, and if this spirit continues He will not tarry long with them.

USE SEVEN. Examine yourselves for all your departures from God and for your forsaking of Him. Humble yourselves for them. Confess with bitterness your evil therein. Weep before the Lord for the ways wherein you have grieved Him. May the Lord hear His people, from Dan to Beersheba, bemoaning themselves, Ephraim-like. Then the Lord will hear and have mercy and not leave us for His name's sake.

Judge yourselves worthy to be forsaken because you have forsaken God. If you judge yourselves worthy to be forsaken, God will not need to judge you that way, "For if we would judge ourselves, we should not be judged" (1 Corinthians 11:31).

Pray fervently that the Lord will not forsake us. The Lord is sometimes gracious in answering the prayers of a wayward people. Prayers have prevailed with His Majesty often before and may do so again.

Forsake your sin whereby you have forsaken Him. Nothing less than this will prevent the awful mischief of His final withdrawal from coming upon us. If there are any among us, whether they be father or mother, son or daughter, that will not leave their sins for God, God will leave them for their sins.

CHAPTER SIX

Returning unto God the Great Concern of a Covenant People

By
Increase Mather

Increase Mather, 1639-1723

The name Increase was given to the son of Rev. Richard and Catharine Mather, who was born on June 21, 1639 in appreciation for the great increase of every sort with which God was favoring New-England at the time. His father was pastor of the Congregational Church at Dorchester, Massachusetts. Increase was, without question, a very precocious child. He was admitted to Harvard College when twelve years of age. However, after only one year he was removed from the College because of poor health. He then studied for several years under Rev. John Norton and then re-enrolled at Harvard, graduating with the class of 1656. His parents had carefully schooled Increase in the things of Christ, and by the time of his great sickness he was fervently seeking God in fasting and prayer, deep lamentations over his personal sinfulness, and earnest endeavors after salvation. Immediately in connection with his conversion in his fourteenth year, he determined to devote himself to the ministry of the Gospel, and when he graduated from Harvard began preaching. His brother Samuel, who was pastoring in Dublin, Ireland, invited Increase to visit, and upon his brother's urging he enrolled in Trinity College. The Irish climate, however, appeared to disagree with his feeble health, and in consequence he soon went to England where he temporarily assumed the pastorate of John Howe's parish at Torrington in Devonshire. This was followed by a period of service on the Island of Guernsey. He returned to Boston in September of 1658 and aided his father in the work at Dorchester. Not long thereafter he began his ministry at the North Church in Boston.

In 1662 he married Maria, daughter of John Cotton. Between them they had ten children. The eldest son Cotton became one of the most distinguished men in the history of the American Church. Both his other sons, Nathaniel and Samuel, became useful ministers. Increase was a leading figure in the Synod of 1679. Perhaps more than any other individual he shaped its call to reformation and revival, writing its preface and contributing much to its heart-searching inquiries concerning the cause of God's judgments against New-England.

In 1681 Mather was asked to take the presidency of Harvard College. Because North Church was unwilling to part with him he declined the invitation to serve full-time but acted as President from 1681 to 1682 and again from 1684 to 1701. Harvard honored him with a Doctor of Divinity degree in 1692, the first such degree ever conferred in British America.

From April 1688 until May 1692 Dr. Mather was in England on behalf of the Colonies, meeting frequently with the King and endeavoring to secure greater liberties for the Colonists. Upon his return to Massachusetts he found the Colony embroiled in the witchcraft delusion and immediately wrote "Cases of Conscience Concerning Witchcraft" in an endeavor to arrest the error. His son Cotton had joined him as colleague at the Church in 1684, covering for his father during the English trip and his frequent duties at Harvard. This proved to be a remarkably fruitful relationship and continued until his death at the age of eighty-four, August 23, 1723. His last major service was rendered at the fast day of 1722 where he concluded the exercises with a prayer of remarkable pathos and power. Within two days he was taken with a serious illness from which he never recovered. The records indicate that his funeral was the most largely attended of any in the preceding history of the Colony.

Of his preaching the Rev. Benjamin Colman reported, "A most excellent preacher he was, using great plainness of speech, with much light and heat, force and power; for he taught as one having authority, commanding reverence from all that heard him; whilst he spake, (as becomes the oracles of God,) with the most awful reverence himself."

First published as *Returning unto God the Great Concern of A Covenant People or A Sermon Preached to the Second Church in Boston in New-England, March 17, 1680 when that Church did Solemnly and Explicitly Renew their Covenant with God and with One Another.* Boston: Printed by John Foster, 1680.

Returning Unto God the Great Concern of a Covenant People

**"Return unto the Lord Thy God;
for thou hast fallen by thine iniquity."
Hosea 14:1.**

These words are a gracious invitation from heaven unto a sinful, backsliding people. In this invitation there are contained four particulars:

1. The subject concerned is *Israel*, the Lord's Covenant people. The very name of *Israel* put them in mind of the Covenant that was between the Lord and them. They were descended from Israel, a holy man that was eminently interested in God's Covenant, and they themselves professed that they were the Lord's people.

2. The substance of the invitation is found in the word *return*, implying that they had not been duly mindful of that Covenant and engagement unto God which was upon them and that, therefore, it should have been their concern to repent and in that way to renew their Covenant.

3. The object unto which they should return was *the Lord*. In the Hebrew it means *even as far as unto the Lord* intimating that they had departed far from Him and that a continued and thorough conversion was necessary. It was requisite that they should not only begin to return but never quit turning until they were come quite over unto the Lord so as to become wholly subject unto Him in everything. They were to return "Even unto the Lord," who is here described from His relation unto them as "their God" or "thy God." This also respects the Covenant between God and them, whereby God became their God and they His people. Both expressions imply strong motives unto repentance. In other words, the Lord Jehovah is a universal good, the fountain of all mercies and good things, without whom there is no life and no happiness to be had or to be hoped for. Therefore return unto Him inasmuch as He is your God, and He is gracious and willing to accept you if you unfeignedly return unto Him.

4. This duty is urged from the necessity of it, "for thou hast fallen by

thine iniquity." This would be like saying, "You are fallen into a woeful pit of sin and misery, into a guile of destruction and are not able to save yourselves. Thus there is no way left but one, that of returning to your God."

DOCTRINE: When the Lord's Covenant people are fallen by iniquity it highly concerns them to return unto their God.

There are three things which need to be considered for a proper understanding of this doctrine.

1. What is this falling into iniquity which the Lord's people are subject unto?

2. What is implied in returning unto the Lord?

3. Why should the Lord's people return unto Him?

I. WHAT IS THIS FALLING INTO INIQUITY WHICH THE LORD'S PEOPLE ARE SUBJECT UNTO?

1. The Lord's own people are subject to decays of grace. Indeed, those that are sincere cannot fall totally and finally, yet they may be subject to partial apostasies from God and from His blessed ways. They may be, and too often are, on the losing hand as to the degrees and measures of grace. There may be sad intermissions as to the timely acting and exercise of grace. The spouse in the Canticles confesses that she was asleep. (Song of Solomon 5:2). All the virgins, wise as well as foolish, slumbered and slept (Matthew 25:5). It was said to the Church in Ephesus, "Thou hast left [though not wholly lost] thy first love" and, therefore, they needed to remember from whence they were fallen and do again the first works (Revelation 2:4,5), intimating that grace was not so lively in them nor were they so much in the practice of religion as they had sometimes been. It is noted concerning Solomon that in his old age, when one would have thought he would have walked most closely with God, "his heart was not perfect with the Lord his God," for he turned after other gods and he did evil in the sight of the Lord (1 Kings 11:4-6). Asa declined much in his latter time, which is what judicious interpreters take to be the true meaning and intention of that Scripture where, in the English translation, it is said "the Lord was with Jehoshaphat, because he walked in the first ways of his father David" (2 Chronicles 17:3), but which more literally means "He walked in the ways of David, of his father the first." Now Asa was Jehoshaphat's father whose first days were better than his last. His conduct in his latter days has no equal in any good man in Scripture. For this reason a judicious divine questions whether Asa was indeed a godly man and whether that statement of his heart being "perfect" intends any more than to indicate that he was not an idolater.[1] But suppose he did have the root of true faith in him—it was then a dreadful fall into iniquity to which he became subject.

2. The Lord's own servants may possibly fall into scandalous iniquity in both judgment and practice. A godly man may, for a time, be tainted with scandalous error, even with heresy in his judgment, albeit he cannot live and die in this condition without repentance and recovery. Hence the Apostle said to the Corinthians, "How say some among you that there is no resurrection of the dead?" (1 Corinthians 15:12). Certainly, the denial of the resurrection is a fundamental error. Moreover, a godly man may become guilty of scandalous practices both against the first table of the Law, as we see in Aaron who was sufficiently affected by the people to make and set up the golden calf in the wilderness, and in Peter who was once guilty of cursing and swearing falsely; as well as against the Second Table of the Law, as we see in David's adultery and subsequent act of murder, and in both Noah's and Lot's being guilty of the terrible intemperance the Scriptures mention concerning them.

3. They that are the Lord's people in respect to a visible Covenant interest only, may fall totally and finally. I say they may fall totally, for although special grace shall not, yet common grace may be wholly lost. Such professors may degenerate into mere formalists, even so as to become dead, sapless and lifeless altogether, even twice dead (Jude 12), having lost those quickenings and gracious illuminations which once they had experienced. Indeed, such professors of Christianity, once fallen away, may become bitter persecutors. This was the case with Saul for that which he had was taken from him, his gifts and common graces withered, the Spirit of the Lord departed from him, and an evil spirit took possession of him so that he became a most malignant persecutor of holy David whom once he had loved and honored. King Joash who, when a young man was very forward and zealous in the ways of God, after the death of Jehoiada under whom he had his education, persecuted his Jehoida's son Zechariah unto death for bearing witness against his and the people's apostasy (2 Chronicles 24:17-22). Alexander the coppersmith became a bitter and bloody enemy to Paul (2 Timothy 4:14), and yet some conceive[2] that this is the same Alexander who, when the time was right, stood up and showed himself willing to suffer with that holy Apostle (Acts

---

[1]Mr. Hocker on Acts 2:37, page 661.
[2]Hugo Grotius on the Second Timothy passage.

19:33).

Any professing Christians who are hypocrites in heart may fall finally as well as totally. The Apostle Paul said, "Demas hath forsaken me, having loved this present world" (2 Timothy 4:10). This is the very description which is given of an unregenerate man, "Love not the world, neither the things that are in the world. If any man love the world, the love of the Father is not in him" (1 John 2:15). Nor do the Scriptures say anything of the return of Demas, but in ecclesiastical tradition[3] he is reported to be one that lived and died an idolater. I must even say that such professing Christians may possibly become guilty of the sin against the Holy Ghost which is always attended with final impenitency. Those that have been enlightened and have had some taste of the heavenly gift may fall away so that it shall be impossible to renew them again to repentance (Hebrews 6:4-6). So true is that word of Christ, "whosoever hath not, from him shall be taken away even that he hath" (Matthew 13:12), that we can say he that does not have true grace is in danger of losing even the common grace which he has.

4. The Lord's people may fall under heavy judgments because of their iniquity. There is a falling into iniquity and a falling by, for, or because of iniquity. Doubtless both are intended in the text. Sore breaking judgments are expressed in the Scriptures by the expression "fall." "Israel and Ephraim fall in their iniquity; Judah also shall fall with them" (Hosea 5:5). Israel and Ephraim, two of the ten tribes, had the worse fall for they fell so as never to rise again; but Judah fell also, viz. under that judgment of the Babylonian captivity. The saddest of temporal judgments and desolations may possibly overtake the people of God, inasmuch as their sins are most dishonorable to His blessed name. We hear the church complaining, "Behold, and see if there be any sorrow like unto my sorrow, which is done unto me, wherewith the Lord hath afflicted me in the day of His fierce anger" (Lamentations 1:12). And the Prophet Daniel said, "Under the whole heaven hath not been done as hath been done upon Jerusalem" (Daniel 9:12). "Jerusalem is ruined, and Judah is fallen: because their tongue and their doings are against the Lord, to provoke the eyes of His glory" (Isaiah 3:8).

5. The Lord's people may fall from their visible church estate. This is what happened to Israel, for when backsliding Israel committed adulteries, God put them away and gave her a bill of divorce (Jeremiah

---

[3]Doronbeus in Synopsi.

3:8). As for the ten tribes, God has called them Lo-ammi, and written over them Lo-ruha-mah, saying, He would no more have mercy on them (Hosea 1:6,9). Some learned men have observed that those Israelites that were carried into captivity by the Assyrians were after many ages since swallowed up with Gentiles, being (as to the body of them) degenerated into mere heathen.[4] The Jews also are deprived of their church estate; the kingdom is taken from them and given to the Gentiles, for the Church of God which is His kingdom is not now to be found among them but among the Gentiles who are planted in their room.[5] Hence the apostle speaks of their fall (Romans 11:11,12), insomuch as they are fallen from their relation to God as His visible Covenant people. A like thing has happened unto many individual Gospel churches in these days of the New Testament.

To this end, consider the witness of all the churches in Asia. In some places in Asia Minor, where once glorious churches were seen, at this day there is not so much as one Christian. This is so in Ephesus and in Laodicea where not a house nor a man is to be seen. In Smyrna, Pergamos, Thyatira, Sardis and Philadelphia, there are no inhabitants except barbarous Turks and a few superstitious Greeks who call themselves Christians. One man that visited these desolate places within the last ten years professed that he could not look upon such amazing ruins without horror and admiration.[6] And there was once a famous church in Rome which the Lord has long since given a bill of divorce. Therefore, we now know Paul spoke like a prophet when he said to the Church of Rome, "Behold therefore the goodness and severity of God: on them which fell, severity; but toward thee, goodness, if thou continue in His goodness; otherwise thou also shalt be cut off" (Romans 11:22). Nor is there any individual church in the world but what this judgment may in time befall it. Never has any church enjoyed such a privilege as that of indestructibility or the impossibility of losing their church estate, no matter what some vain pretenders claim. Churches may degenerate so as to lose that which is the true substance of a church—visible saints. "How

---

[4]De Israelites qui per captivitatem Assyriam transportati funt, dicendum est, eos partim in Gentiles degenerasse, partim Judaicis Synagogis se adjunxisse, et cum iis coalluisse. Voet. Disput. de Convers. Judxor. p.133, 144, 149. Sic & Hornbeck, in Disput. contra Judxos. Prolog. p.4.

[5]Remember please that this sermon was preached in 1680.

[6]Mr. Thomas Smith in his "Remarks Upon the Manners, Religion and Government of the Turks. Together with a Survey of the Seven Churches of Asia as they Now Lye in their Ruins." London, 1678.

is the faithful city become an harlot! it was full of judgment; righteousness lodged in it; but now murderers" (Isaiah 1:21).

They may lose that which is the form of a church—the Covenant with God and with one another. Those two staves, Beauty and Bands, may be broken (Zechariah 11:10,14). Or if the churches should not degenerate as to their principles, they may be unchurched in other ways and by other means, including divisions. "If a house [or a church which is the house of God] be divided against itself, that house cannot stand" (Mark 3:25). Or the Lord may remove instruments whereby the affairs of His kingdom in this or that place are managed. Sometimes the plucking up of one pillar makes way for the whole house to fall speedily and irrecoverably. Or a storm of persecution may arise which shall blow the lights out of the candlesticks, yea, and tip them over too. The church came near being carried away with the flood of the Arian heresy and persecution (Revelation 12:15). In Augustine's time, while he was yet living, all the Churches in Africa (excepting three) were laid waste by the barbarous Goths and Vandals whom the Lord let loose upon them.[7] So it was with the old Church of Rome, they were (about 400 years after Christ) cut off by the sword of the Goths and Vandals and another people, viz. those whom we call the Italians, substituted in their room.[8] All these are like the ten tribes which fell into idolatry and were destroyed by the Assyrians and Samaritans.

II. WHAT IS IMPLIED IN RETURNING UNTO THE LORD?

It is the same as repentance. Sin is a departing from God but repentance is a returning unto Him again. Wherefore repentance is often expressed in the Scripture by "turning" and "returning" unto the Lord and by "conversion," the phrase being a metaphor taken from those that have gone out of the right way but return back again into the way wherein they should have gone. Repentance is nothing other than a turning from all sin unto God. It implies a change of the whole man.

The mind is renewed. As in returning, there is a change of the posture of the body, so where there is repentance, the mind is bent quite another way. It was looking sin-ward, earth-ward, hell-ward, but in repentance is fixed upon God and Christ in heaven. In returning, the further a man goes from a place, the less important do things seem that he has left behind him, so in returning to God, the more a man returns, the world

---

[7]Augustine's Life, pages 159,160.
[8]See Samuel Mather, "A Testimony from the Scripture against Idolatry and Superstition." Cambridge, 1670, page 13.

and the vanities of it seem as little and even as nothing to him.

Repentance implies a great turn in the heart and the affections so that those sins and corruptions which were most loved and delighted in are become the most hateful. We see this in returning Ephraim, "What have I to do any more with idols?" (Hosea 14:8). Before returning there was nothing so dear as idols, but after returning nothing could be more abominable.

Repentance implies also a change in a man's actions and conversation. The true penitent is turned into another way, "Let the wicked forsake his way, and the unrighteous man his thoughts: and let him return unto the Lord" (Isaiah 55:7). He was on the way to hell but is on the way to heaven. He was going on the broad way but is come about and has gotten onto the narrow way which leads to everlasting life.

III. WHY SHOULD THE LORD'S PEOPLE RETURN UNTO HIM?

I shall answer with only that reason implied in the text, namely, the consideration of the holy and gracious Covenant which they were under. "Return unto the Lord thy God, O Israel:" He is thy God and, therefore, thou art to return to Him. This consideration of the Covenant is often used in the Scripture as an argument to enforce repentance, "Turn, O backsliding children, saith the Lord; for I am married unto you" (Jeremiah 3:14), namely in respect to the Covenant which was between God and them. The Apostle Peter calls upon the Jews to repent and be converted and presses his exhortation by saying, "ye are the children of the prophets, and of the Covenant which God made with our fathers" (Acts 3:11).

Even the seals of the Covenant engage the subjects of them to repent and return unto the Lord more and more. Hence it is said of John the Baptist that he baptized "unto repentance" (Matthew 3:11), because those whom he baptized were thereby engaged to practice repentance. It is true that those who are in the Covenant with God are bound to walk closely with Him and to be careful that they do not violate the spirit of repentance. Nevertheless, in case they do fail and fall through temptation, the Covenant engages them to renew their repentance and to make haste to return unto the Lord again when they have backslidden from Him. Those that lie under their falls, refusing to rise again in repentance, continue breaking the everlasting Covenant. Moreover, the Lord, in the Covenant of Grace, declares unto men that He will pardon their sins if they unfeignedly return unto Him. The Gospel is sometimes called the Covenant. It was prophesied concerning Christ that "He shall confirm the Covenant with many for one week" (Daniel 9:27), that is for seven years which is a prophetical week. The Lord Christ Himself preached the

Gospel to the Jews for the space of three and one half years, and after that (as some observe) His Apostles offered the Gospel for another three years and some months before ever they preached to the Gentiles. Thus was the Covenant confirmed for one week. Now the Gospel commands men everywhere to repent and promises the remission of sins in case they do so. If those who are only under the external offer of the Covenant are bound to repent, how much more those that are indeed in Covenant relationship with God?

USE ONE. Let us be exhorted, persuaded and prevailed upon to return unto the Lord our God. Return unto thy God, O Israel, O New-England, for you have fallen by your iniquity.

Consider first, what cause we have, every one of us, to be returning unto the Lord our God.

Certainly we have need to be turning from sin and from the world yet more and more. Repentance is the work of a Christian as long as he lives in this world. There are many that are in a state of sin. A universal repentance is of absolute necessity to every such soul. There are others that are under the prevailing power of some special corruptions or temptation and they stand in need of a particular repentance. Therefore Christ said to His disciples, notwithstanding their being converted as to their state, "Except ye be converted... ye shall not enter into the kingdom of heaven" (Matthew 18:3), meaning that except they were converted from that particular sin of pride which was then too apparent in them they could not be saved. Are there not many individuals that are under woeful decays in their spiritual estate? Alas! They are not the same men that they were thirty or forty years ago. Oh, what great cause they have to be thinking of returning to the Lord from whom they have deeply revolted. In fact, is there not a general declension among the professed Christians of New-England? May we not confess, as the Lord's people sometimes did, "Our iniquities testify against us... for our backslidings are many" (Jeremiah 14:7).

Again, that which is spoken by Jeremiah may, in too sad a degree, be applied to New-England: "I had planted thee a noble vine, wholly a right seed: how then art thou turned into the degenerate plant of a strange vine unto Me?" (Jeremiah 2:21). Oh, how the power of godliness flourished in this land and in these churches during times past! But is it so at this day? Is there not a general decay as to the power of godliness? Oh, how Christians have left their first love. This was expressed in the sermon preached on the day when this church was gathered nearly thirty years ago: "It is too plain to be denied that there is a dying spirit in New-

England to the ways of God."⁹ If it were so then, how much more so now? Men have forgotten their errand into this wilderness. What came we unto this wilderness to see? It has often and truly been said that New-England differs from other places in our nation in that religion was the design of our Fathers in transporting themselves and families into this wasted and howling wilderness. But men are now pursuing a worldly interest with their whole hearts. The things of God and the great concerns of His holy kingdom are not sought after as a first priority. If the body of the present standing generation is compared with what was here some forty years ago, a very sad degeneracy is evident to the view of every man that has his heart exercised in discerning things of this nature.

Consider second, how solemnly God has been calling upon us to return, and that in more ways than one.

He is calling us by lesser and greater judgments. The Lord has come upon us as a moth and as a lion, in tearing wrath and furious judgments that have rent and borne down all before them. When lighter afflictions would not do, the Lord has made bare His arm against us, brandishing a glittering sword, making it bright for the slaughter, yea, and drunk with blood, and the voice of the Lord was in it, calling aloud from heaven, "return unto thy God, O New-England, for thou hast fallen by thine iniquity." The Lord has also sent the destroying angel among us with a broom of destruction whereby many hundreds have been swept away into the land of darkness. Ah! poor New-England! Ah! poor Boston! Will you not yet hear and turn and live?

Once more, the Lord has fallen upon us of late and rendered His rebukes in flames of fire. May we not call the name of this place Taberah because the fire of the Lord has burned among us? (Numbers 11:3). Come and behold the desolations which the Lord has made. Bewail the burning which the Lord has kindled. What is the Lord saying in all these solemn dispensations if it is not "Oh, New-England, and Boston especially, return unto the Lord your God for you have fallen by your iniquity?"

Oh, congregation, hear the Word of the Lord. We in this congregation, in a more particular manner, have been under solemn and awakening calls from heaven. When the vessel was blown up in the harbor five years ago and several desireable persons lost their lives, what a solemn blow that was. The Lord has made awful breaches among us. One of this church, a most desirable and useful man, died by the sword of the

---

⁹"By Mr. Samuel Mather, my most dear, and now blessed brother."

heathen;[10] some by the late mortal contagion[11] and divers have by other providences been taken away from us. God has thinned our glory. And do we not remember the dismal fire that was in this part of the town above three years ago, when this building was most desolate? The very house wherein we have been wont to praise the Lord was burned with fire and this candlestick was then under awful shaking.

Some observe that God used to move the candlesticks before He removed them.[12] Truly, God has been moving this candlestick, and I must solemnly declare that it looks like an ominous sign that the Lord intends at last to remove and break this candlestick if there is no returning to Him. Let us not be high-minded but fear. God can bring it to pass in one day, by one fatal stroke. Oh, then think what cause we have to say after the Lord's people, "Come, and let us return unto the Lord: for He hath torn, and He will heal us; He hath smitten, and He will bind us up" (Hosea 6:1).

Moreover the Lord has been calling upon His people in this wilderness, by His Word and faithful Ambassadors, by whose mouth He has threatened awful judgments unless we repent. The watchmen of Ephraim that have been with God have blown the trumpet and given the alarm. The alarm has been sounded not only by some who are still alive but by the former prophets who have finished their course and have gone to receive their crown. Through these the Lord has been speaking and solemnly warning this people. Oh, New-England, the day of your watchmen is come upon you, even the day which your watchmen told you was coming. How inexcusable then will we be if we do not return.

The Lord has very lately said that He would try one experiment more with a sinful people. It may be they will hear. He has, therefore, so ordered by His providence that the messengers of these churches met together here in His name to inquire into the causes of that dismal displeasure which has been written against us in fiery and bloody characters and to fix upon Scripture expedients for reformation.[13] If what comes in that way, and the voice of the Lord in it, is despised and rejected, we may justly fear that there is a woeful day not far off. It was a serious and weighty word which a faithful minister of Christ who lived in another colony expressed not long ago in a great assembly, "Your

---

[10]Captain Lake.
[11]Mr. Brackenbury and several other hopeful and desirable persons.
[12]See Mr. Fuller's Sermon on Revelation 2:5.
[13]Synod of Boston, "The Necessity of Reformation with the Expedients Subservient thereunto Asserted." Boston, 1679.

hearing the mind of God, declared by the Synod, will be a signal testimony of an humbled people; but if you will not hear what is so presented to you, I testify unto you in the name of the Lord, it may be written over your doors, 'They are not humbled unto this day.'"[14]

Consider third, there has not yet been that returning unto the Lord which ought to be and which He expects from this people.

The generality of men do not frame their affairs to return unto the Lord. If they return, it is not to the most High. It was a sad word which the Lord spoke against His people of old, "My people are bent to backsliding from Me: though they called them to the most High, none at all would exalt Him" (Hosea 11:7). Those that did return when called thereunto were so few that they seemed to be none at all. I do not doubt but that through grace there are many individuals among us to whom God has sanctified His awful dispensations in order to their effectual conversion and reformation; but our misery is that there is no general turning from sin and from the world unto God in Jesus Christ. Oh, the tragedy that it may be said of us as in the Book of Amos, "I have witholden the rain from you, when there were yet three months to the harvest: and I caused it to rain upon one city, and caused it not to rain upon another city: one piece was rained upon, and the piece whereupon it rained not withered... yet have ye not returned unto me, saith the Lord. I have smitten you with blasting and mildew... yet ye have not returned unto me, saith the Lord. I have sent among you the pestilence after the manner of Egypt... yet have ye not returned unto me, saith the Lord. I have overthrown some of you, as God overthrew Sodom and Gomorrah... yet have ye not returned unto me, saith the Lord... Prepare to meet thy God, O Israel" (Amos 4:7-12). He that was proud is proud still. He that was a worldling is one still. He that was a pot-companion and that haunted ale-houses does so still. That which is spoken of the Children of Israel is sadly true concerning most of the men among us: "For all this, they sinned still" (Psalm 78:32). Devouring plagues had been round about them: "For all this they sinned still." Most wonderful mercies and eminent deliverances were vouchsafed unto them by the Lord: "For all this they sinned still." And is it not so with us? War, mortalities, fires have been among us, yet men continue sinning still. The Lord has by a miracle of mercy restored peace and health to the land so that the inhabitants thereof are not sick, yet men still continue sinning.

---

[14]Mr. Nathaniel Collins, Pastor of the Church in Middletown, Connecticut.

Consider fourth, what blessed encouragement we have to be returning unto God.

He had a delight in our fathers and has chosen us, their children, to be His people. He is our God still. He has not written over us Lo-ammi and Lo-ruh-amah. As yet we have a day of grace. As particular persons, so also churches and congregations have their day of grace. Christ said unto Jerusalem, and He wept when He said it, "If thou hadst known, even thou, at least in this thy day, the things which belong unto thy peace!" (Luke 19:42). And oh, that in this New-England's day, we knew the things that belong unto our peace before they are hidden from our eyes. We will be happy if we have a heart to consider it. The Lord, we see, is loath to make us as Admah, to set us as Zeboim (Hosea 11:8). He is not willing to give up His interest here. He waits to be gracious. He waits to see if we will return unto Him so that we may be fit for mercy, and then we shall have it. Oh, let us return before the decree brings forth, before the day passes as the chaff, before the day of the Lord's anger comes upon us.

Consider fifth, the good that will follow in case we do return.

If we return to the Lord He will return to us with mercies and blessings more than ever. "Even from the days of your fathers ye are gone away from Mine ordinances, and have not kept them. Return unto Me, and I will return unto you, saith the Lord of Hosts" (Malachi 3:7). The Lord will then make it apparent that He is our God and that He is Jehovah, just as He was known unto His people in the years of ancient generations by His name Jehovah when He gave being to and fulfilled His gracious promises. Mark how the prophet Daniel speaks, "that we might turn from our iniquities, and understand Thy truth" (Daniel 9:13). The Lord has promised to save and bless those that turn from their iniquities, and if we had done this we would have known by gracious experience the truth of God's Word. So then, if we return, the benefits will be ours, good will come unto us thereby and to others also. We read it, "repent, and turn yourselves" (Ezekiel 18:30) but the Hebrew word signifies "to make to be converted," in other words, repent and make others to be converted. It is always the property of true repentance that it makes men endeavor that others too may repent. Usually if one repents another follows. Examples are very powerful. "Your zeal," says the Apostle, "hath provoked very many" (2 Corinthians 9:2). If one church sets a good example, it may be that many others will follow. And then, oh what glory will come to the blessed name of God! If a people should all become righteous, the Lord would be greatly glorified (Isaiah 60:21). Oh, the joy this causes in heaven! If there is joy in heaven when one sinner returns unto God, how much more when a whole church becomes zealous and repents and engages themselves in a more close and holy walk with God than ever before?

Consider sixth, we must of necessity return unto the Lord our God. As we always desire to escape destruction this concerns us greatly. What an awful Scripture it is that says, "I will destroy My people, since they return not from their ways" (Jeremiah 15:7). Being visibly the Lord's people and enjoying the external spiritual privileges cannot secure or save us unless we return. We have no other way left in heaven or on earth but this. We have many enemies, not only in hell but on earth, who are ready to swallow us up if the Lord is not on our side. If God is not our friend we are the most miserable people under heaven. And we have little reason to expect that the Lord will stand by us if we will not return unto Him. We shall have neither deliverance nor mercy if we do not return. It is true that God, to show His sovereignty, does sometimes save an apostate people as He did Israel in the days of Jehoahaz and of Jeroboam the Second (2 Kings 13:4-6; 14:27). But such deliverances leave men more inexcusable and usually end in the saddest possible destructions and desolations unless there is repentance.

Question. What shall we do that we may return unto the Lord our God?

Answer One. Let us now up and be doing. The longer a person or a people shall defer their repentance, the harder work will they have in it. "Can the Ethiopian change his skin, or the leopard his spots? then may ye also do good, that are accustomed to do evil?" (Jeremiah 13:23). Therefore the Lord urges men unto present obedience. "The Lord has sent unto you all His servants the prophets, rising early and sending them... They said, Turn ye again now every one from his evil way, and from the evil of your doings" (Jeremiah 25:4,5). Ephraim is an unwise son when he stays long in the birth. Is not repentance a good work and are not the expedients in order thereunto good to be attended? Then the sooner we do it the better. The elders of Israel were sometimes asked, "Why are ye the last to bring the king back to his house?" (2 Samuel 19:11). Every church is a house of David, that is, Christ the true David. Why should any of us, especially why should any churches, seek to be the last that, by renewing their repentance and solemn engagements unto the Lord, endeavor to establish Christ's throne among us?

Answer Two. Let us pray and promise better obedience. Oh, cry to heaven as Ephraim did, "Turn Thou me, and I shall be turned" (Jeremiah

31:18). Men say they cannot turn themselves. Must they sit still then and do nothing under pretence that God must do it all? No! But they must stir up themselves and call upon God. It is a precious truth that the Lord has, in His gracious Covenant, promised that His people shall return unto Him. Nevertheless he says, "I will yet for this be enquired of by the house of Israel, to do it for them" (Ezekiel 36:37). Nor is it enough for us to pray. We must, though not in our own strength, promise better obedience. This particular not only suits the solemn work which we are now to attend and which has occasioned our being thus before the Lord this day, but it is the very direction which God Himself gives unto His Israel in this context so that they might become a returned, reformed people. "Take with you words, and turn to the Lord." What words? Even words of prayer; therefore, it is added, "Say unto Him, take away all iniquity, and receive us graciously." And words of promise too: "So will we render the calves of our lips" (Hosea 14:2). The Lord prompts them to promise that they would live more to His praise and glory for the time to come than ever they had done before. Accordingly, we see them renewing their Covenant, "Asshur shall not save us; we will not ride upon horses: neither will we say any more to the work of our hands, ye are our gods." So they commit themselves against the special reigning sin of the times of which they had been guilty and promise for the future that they will endeavor to love God more and serve Him better.

That this renewing of Covenant is a duty incumbent upon these churches, I have formerly shown[15] so shall not now insist much upon it, especially considering that there is a great voice out of the temple calling us to it. I speak in respect to what the Messengers of the Churches have lately and unanimously declared to be the mind of Christ concerning the matter. The truth is that if there were no visible apostasy among us, yet it might be good to renew our Covenant with God so that we may be better able to stand our ground if a temptation to forsake the truth should overtake us.[16] The children of Israel served the Lord all the days of Joshua, yet he required them to renew their Covenant so that they might be kept from apostasy in the future (Joshua 24:27).

There seems to be an hour of temptation coming upon all the churches of Christ dispersed throughout the world. If so, these New-England churches must expect a day of trial ere long, though what the

---

[15]"Renewal of Covenant the Great Duty Incumbent on Decaying or Distressed Churches." Boston, 1677. A sermon on Nehemiah 9:38.

[16]See Mr. Samuel Willard's Sermon on John 14:22, "The Duty of a People that Have Renewed their Covenant with God." Boston, 1680.

particular temptation will be is with God. Now for us, in the most solemn manner, to renew our engagements to the Lord and to one another is the way, by the grace of Christ, to stand fast in the profession of the faith and order of the Gospel. There is miserable self-sufficiency in the revolting hearts of men. Upon this account all existing bonds are expedient and necessary.[17] Yet I perceive that there are needless scruples and objections in the minds of men against so good and holy a work.

Objection One. What need is there for any particular sins to be mentioned? Must we tell the world our particular sins?

Answer. As for the secret sins of which only God knows, men ought not to declare them before the world; but such evils as are public ought to be publicly and particularly engaged against. Thus, when the Lord's people renewed their Covenant in Nehemiah's time, they engaged particularly against those evils of unlawful marriages, oppression, Sabbath breaking and neglect of divine institutions which were the special prevailing iniquities of that time and place (Nehemiah 10:30-39). A general confession of sin is not true repentance unless particular sins are bewailed before the Lord, nor are general promises for reformation sufficient.

Objection Two. Some say our fathers, forty years ago, did not practice any such renewing of Covenant as that which is now urged, nor did they approve of it.

Answer. If when Asa called upon the Lord's people to attend this work, they should have put it off by saying, "In the days of David, your great grandfather, there was no such thing practiced, therefore, why should we do it now?" It would have easy to answer, "The state of things then and now greatly differs. There is more cause and greater call to attend such a duty now than there was then." The same answer may be given in this case. There were not such pride, intemperance, formality in religion and other evils among professed Christians then as are now to be seen and, therefore, there was not so much need to engage against those sins formerly as at this day.

Nor can it truly be said that this is a new practice or not approved of by those who were instruments in the hands of Christ in planting these churches. They proceeded much upon the principle that renovation of Covenant was an expedient for church reformation.[18] And their practice

---

[17]See Edward Reynolds, "Seven Sermons on Hosea 14," page 71.

[18]John Norton in Resp. ad Appol. c. 2; William Ames, "The Marrow of Theology," 1.1, Cap.

was accordingly. They were in Covenant with God even before they knew this land and therefore what they did here was a renewing of that Covenant.

Objection Three. But what shall become of the old Covenant?

Answer. If when Moses called upon the Children of Israel to renew their Covenant in the plains of Moab (Deuteronomy 29:1) it should have been said, "but what shall become of the old Covenant which we entered into at Horeb forty years ago?" Would not the reply have been, "That Covenant is not hereby nullified but confirmed." The Covenant by which we are now engaging ourselves unto the Lord is a Covenant in confirmation of what has been formerly done by us. There is not one particular mentioned in this Covenant which is a new duty or not required in the everlasting Covenant, nor indeed is there anything in it but what was contained in the former Covenant. We promise to cleave unto the Lord as our God and to Him only and to the Lord Jesus Christ as our only Priest, Prophet and King. He that observes the first and great commandment cannot but keep all the rest. So if this general and comprehensive Covenant be duly remembered and observed, no more is required. The particulars which this Covenant specifies explain and confirm our former engagements. It is of great advantage to have the Covenant thus particularly expressed and explained so that any one may see what they are bound unto.

Objection Four. Although the Old Testament speaks much about renewing Covenant, yet we read nothing of that matter in the New Testament.

Answer. Is the Old Testament become Apocrypha in these days? Men fail to consider that by this objection they strike at the foundation of all these churches and introduce a principle that is destructive to the very form and being of our New-England Churches. Where does the New Testament, in so many express words, speak of any explicit church Covenant? The New Testament is sparing in mentioning things abundantly insisted upon in the Old Testament. When the anabaptists object that the New Testament says nothing of children's rights to the seal of the Covenant, do we not rightly answer them that their right thereunto is plainly asserted in the Old Testament and nowhere repealed in the New? Even so, we have examples for renewal of Covenant in the Old Testament which are nowhere condemned in the New. As the judgments which befell

---

32 and Robert Parker, "De Politeia Ecclesiastica Christi," Cap. 3, pp. 172, 173.

the Lord's people of old were recorded for our admonition, so the course which they took in bringing about reformation is written for our instruction and imitation (1 Corinthians 10:11). It is a great truth that practices mentioned in the Old Testament, not peculiar to that pedagogy but of moral and perpetual equity, do bind men in the days of the Gospel. The necessity of the renewal of the Covenant with the Lord our God is of this sort of truth.

Nor must it be granted that the New Testament is a stranger to any such practice. The Jews that we read of in the second chapter of the Acts were in Covenant with God before the time of the reformation came, as the Apostle says (Hebrews 9:10), yet it is past doubt that when three thousand were added to them, that is to the Church at Jerusalem, they renewed their Covenant with God and with the Lord Jesus Christ. I desire those that make this objection to give us an instance of any Gospel church which, being under spiritual declensions, was recovered from their backslidings without renewing their Covenant. When some of the churches in Asia had fallen by their iniquity, the Lord Jesus called upon them to repent and return, and that implied that they ought to attend Scripture expedients for reformation, of which this renewal of Covenant is not one of the least.

Objection Five. Some say the Covenant is so strict we shall make men afraid to join the church.

Answer. The Covenant is no stricter than God Himself has made it. He says to everyone that hates to be reformed, "What hast thou to do... that thou shouldest take my Covenant in thy mouth?" (Psalm 50:16). In the Covenant which we are about to renew, there is nothing expressed but plain, clear duties required in the Gospel. Those that are sincere will not be afraid of church membership because they are already under obligation to practice according to the Scriptures. As for those that are not sincere, they are better out of the church than in it. It was a mercy to the Primitive church[19] when it could be said of those that were not true believers, "and of the rest durst no man join himself to them... And believers were the more added to the Lord" (Acts 5:13,14). The fewer hypocrites (those who are loath to come up to the practice and power of godliness) in a church, the better. Though such will creep in unawares (Jude 4), yet we should not let them in if we know them to be such. Sincere professors are golden members and, therefore, to have churches consist of such, as much as may be, is the way to have the churches

---

[19]Read Mr. Cotton on the holiness of church membership.

continue as golden candlesticks.

Objection Six. This Covenant is either of grace or of works: if of works, we dare not meddle with it; if of grace, why should we renew it?

Answer. How is it possible for any understanding Christian to imagine that a Covenant made with God through Jesus Christ is a Covenant of works or that a Covenant, wherein men profess themselves unable to do anything of themselves and that wherein they fail in their obedience they look for pardoning mercy through the Mediator, is a Covenant of Works? All that I have just said is true in reference to the Covenant before us. And whereas it is said that men under the Covenant of Grace need not to renew their covenanting with God, nothing can be spoken which is more contrary to Scripture or to the practice of saints. Was not Jacob under the Covenant of Grace? Was he in a state of salvation by virtue of any other Covenant than that of Grace? Yet in the time of his distress he renewed his Covenant in giving himself up to God and promising to cleave unto the Lord as his God (Genesis 28:20-22). Does not faith in Christ give men an interest in the Covenant of Grace? Then as often as believers renew their closing with Christ, they do, on their part, renew their Covenant. Those that already believe may, and should, again and again give themselves up to the Lord Jesus. Christians, every time they worship the Lord Jesus Christ, especially in the ordinance of the Lord's Supper, implicitly renew their consent to the Covenant of Grace. If an implicit renewal of Covenant is necessary, then sometimes to do it after the most solemn and express manner possible will certainly tend to the glory of God and to the good of souls.

Objection Seven. Some object, why should we renew the Covenant if we shall not keep Covenant when we have finished?

Answer. That is not a good objection. It makes me think of the man who Mr. Luther speaks of that had made many vows to God but had broken them all and therefore resolved that for the future he would live at loose ends and covenant no more so that he might be at more liberty to sin. Is it so with any of your souls? Then in the name of God, how can you dare approach the table of the Lord? I solemnly declare unto you, in the name of the Lord Jesus Christ, that if any man or woman among you is secretly in league with sin and therefore unwilling to be further engaged to the holy and glorious God, you will eat and drink judgment to yourselves, and the oftener you come to that sacred ordinance, the greater will be your damnation in the last day. Let everyone of us be sincere and watchful;, then we shall keep Covenant.

1. Be sincere. Let us not give up our names only but our hearts unto God in Jesus Christ. It is recorded concerning the Lord's people in the days of Asa that they entered into a Covenant to seek the Lord God of their fathers with all their hearts and with all their souls (2 Chronicles 15:12). Let us be sure that our hearts are in this work, then we shall be likely to keep Covenant. Good King Josiah, when he renewed Covenant, did it with all his heart (2 Chronicles 34:31). Hence he performed what he promised. But the people too generally did what they did out of compliance to him for their hearts were not in it (Jeremiah 3:10). Therefore, they quickly broke their Covenant with God. Oh, then let us be sincere in this matter.

2. Be watchful. A sincere, godly man may be guilty of great violations of the Covenant and by his iniquity in that respect be still under the heavy judging hand of God, and all this for want of due watchfulness. How have the Lord's servant come to fall after such a fearful manner as some of them have done and that so soon upon the most solemn engagements unto God? Because they do not duly watch and take heed to their spirits lest they deal treacherously. Peter renewed his Covenant with the Lord Jesus when he promised never to forsake Him but to die rather than to do so, yet he quickly acted contrary to that engagement because he depended too much upon his own strength and was not humbly watchful as he ought to have been.

3. Look up to Christ. Oh, look unto Jesus! Let us look unto Him for pardoning mercy. He has offered sacrifice whereby atonement is made for the whole congregation. Look to Him for all supplies of grace continually. He has grace enough for us all. "Of His fullness have all we received, and grace for grace" (John 1:16). And what is all that can be done or thought of without Christ? What are vows and covenants except Christ be in them? Alas, many poor souls, when outward and inward distress and anguish is upon them, will vow and swear to God that they will never commit such and such sins any more; yet when strong temptations come, they break all bonds and their corruptions are as much unmortified as ever. Why? Because they promise in their own strength and do not know what it is by faith to fetch supplies of grace and strength from the blood and from the Spirit of the Lord Jesus. We say in the Covenant, which we have met before the Lord this day to renew, that we will do this and all the other things which God requires, by the help of Christ. Oh, remember that it must be by the help of Christ that we do anything. Therefore, let us depend upon God in Jesus Christ to do all our works in us and for us.

Amen, Lord Jesus!

The Covenant Which Was Unanimously Consented Unto Is As Follows.

We who through the exceeding riches of the grace and patience of God do yet continue members of this church, being now assembled in the holy presence of God and in the name of our Lord Jesus Christ; after humble confession of our manifold breaches of Covenant before the Lord our God and earnest supplications for pardoning mercy through the blood of Christ and deep acknowledgement of our great unworthiness to be owned as the Lord's Covenant people; also acknowledging our inability to keep Covenant with God or to perform any spiritual duty unless the Lord Jesus do enable us thereunto by His Spirit dwelling in us; and being awfully sensible that it is a dreadful thing for sinful dust and ashes personally to transact with the infinitely glorious Majesty of heaven and earth, we do in humble confidence of His gracious assistance and acceptance through Christ, each one of us, for ourselves, and jointly, as a church of the living God, explicitly renew our Covenant with God and one with another in manner and form following. That is to say,

We do give up ourselves unto that God whose name alone is Jehovah, Father, Son, and Holy Spirit, as the only true and living God and unto our blessed Lord Jesus Christ as our only Saviour, Prophet, Priest and King over our souls and only Mediator of the Covenant of Grace; promising (by the help of His Spirit and grace) to cleave unto God as our chief good and unto the Lord Jesus Christ by faith in a way of Gospel obedience as becometh His Covenant people for ever. We do also give up our offspring unto God in Jesus Christ, avouching the Lord to be our God and the God of our children and ourselves with our children to be His people; humbly adjuring this grace of God, that we and our offspring with us may be looked upon as the Lord's.

We do also give up ourselves one unto another, in the Lord according to the will of God, freely covenanting and binding ourselves to walk together as a right ordered congregation and Church of Christ; in all the ways of His worship, according to the holy rules of the Word of God; promising, in brotherly love, faithfully to watch over one another's souls and to submit ourselves unto the discipline and government of Christ and His church and duly to attend the seals, censures or whatever ordinances Christ has commanded to be observed by His people, according to the order of the Gospel, so far as the Lord hath or shall reveal more unto us by His Word and Spirit.

And whereas the Messengers of these Churches, who have met together in the name of Christ to enquire into the reason of the Lord's controversy with this His people, have taken notice of many provoking evils as the procuring cause of the judgments of God upon New-England; so far as we, or any of us, have been guilty of sin in respect to any of them, we desire from our hearts to bewail it before the Lord and humbly to entreat for pardoning mercy for the sake of the blood of the everlasting Covenant.

And as an expedient unto reformation of those or whatever evils have provoked the eyes of God's glory among us, we do subjoin unto our church Covenant a further engagement, whereby we do, as in the presence of God, promise,

1. That we will (by the help of Christ) labor, every one of us, to reform his own heart and life by seeking to mortify all our sin and endeavouring to walk more closely with God than ever we have done and to uphold the power of godliness; and that we will continue to worship God in public, private, secret, and this (as God shall help us) without formality and hypocrisy; and more fully and faithfully than heretofore, to discharge all Covenant duties one towards another in a way of church communion.

2. We promise (by the help of Christ) that we will endeavour to walk before God in our houses with a perfect heart and that we will uphold the worship of God therein continually, according as He in His Word doth require, both in respect of prayer and reading the Scriptures, so that the Word of Christ may dwell richly in us; and that we will do what in us lyeth, to bring up our children for Christ, that they may become such, as they that have the Lord's name put upon them by a solemn dedication to God in Christ, ought to be; and that therefore we will (so far as there shall be need of it) catechize them, and exhort and charge them to fear and serve the Lord, and endeavour to set an holy example before them, and be much in prayer for their conversion and salvation.

3. We do further engage (the Lord helping us) to do what in us is, that we may be pure from the sins of the times, even those provoking evils that have brought the judgment of God upon New-England; and in our places to endeavour the suppression thereof; and that we will make conscience to walk so, as that we may not give occasion to others to sin or to speak evil of our holy profession.

Now, that we may observe and keep this sacred Covenant and all the branches of it inviolable for ever, we desire to deny ourselves, to depend wholly upon the power of the eternal Spirit of Grace, and upon the free mercy of God, and upon the merit of Jesus Christ, and where we shall fail, there to wait upon the Lord Jesus for pardon, and for acceptance, and for healing, for his name's sake.

CHAPTER SEVEN

The Danger
of Not Reforming
Known Evils

By
William Williams

William Williams, 1665-1741

William Williams was born at Newtown, Massachusetts, February 2, 1665. His grandfather, Robert Williams of Roxbury, was the first of the Williams name to settle in the new world. His father, Isaac, was a man of substance, serving his town in the Massachusetts General Court and commanding a military company. William graduated from Harvard in 1683. The total class consisted of three scholars and included his cousin, John Williams of Deerfield, whose history was memorialized as the result of his capture by hostile Indians.

Not unlike many Pastors of his day, William Williams assumed the pastorate of the Congregational Church at Hatfield, Massachusetts in the year 1685 and continued there until his death on August 29, 1741, a total of fifty-six years. His first wife, Elizabeth, daughter of Rev. Seaborn Cotton of Hampton, New Hampshire, bore him two sons: William, pastor at Weston, Massachusetts and Elisha, Rector of Yale College, and one daughter. His second marriage was to a daughter of the Rev. Solomon Stoddard of Northampton. This union produced five children, one of whom, Solomon, became the distinguished Pastor of the Congregational Church in Lebanon, Connecticut. In a letter to President Stiles, Charles Chauncy wrote, "I have read all Mr. Stoddard's writings, but have never been able to see in them that strength of genius some have attributed to them. Mr. Williams of Hatfield, his son-in-law, I believe to have been the greater man, and I am ready to think greater than any of his sons, though they were all men of more than common understanding."

Jonathan Edwards preached the funeral sermon for Williams on Matthew 14:12. In this message he said, "God has now taken away from you an able and faithful minister of the New Testament, one that has long been a father to you and a father in our Israel; a person of uncommon natural abilities and distinguished learning, a great divine, of very comprehensive knowledge, and of a solid, accurate judgment. Judiciousness and wisdom were eminently his character. He was one of eminent gifts, qualifying him for all parts of the work of the ministry; and there appeared a savour of holiness in his exercise of these gifts, both in public and in private; so that he improved them as a servant of Christ and a man of God. He was not negligent of the talents which his Lord had committed to him; you need not be told with what constant diligence he improved them, how studious at home, and how laborious in his public work... You know his manner of addressing heaven in public prayers with you and for you; with what sanctity, humility, faith and fervency, he seemed to apply himself to the Father of Lights, from time to time, when he stood in this desk, as your mouth to God; and interceding for you, pleading with God through the grace and the merits of a glorious Mediator. And you know his manner of applying himself to you, when he came to you, from time to time, in the name of the Lord. In his public ministry, he mainly insisted on the most weighty and important things of religion; he was eminently an evangelical preacher; evangelical subjects seemed to be his delight. Christ was the great subject of his preaching; and he much insisted on those things that... concern the essence and power of religion; and had a peculiar faculty of judiciously and clearly handling the doctrines he insisted on, and treating properly whatever subject he took in hand; and of selecting the most weighty arguments and motives to enforce, and set home those things which concern Christian experience and practice. His subjects were always weighty, and his manner of treating them peculiarly happy, showing the strength and accuracy of his judgment, and ever breathing forth the spirit of piety, and a deep sense of the things he delivered, on his heart. His sermons were none of them mean, but were all wise, solid compositions. His words were none of them vain, but were all weighty."

First published as *The Danger of Not Reforming Known Evils Or The Inexcusableness of a Knowing People Refusing to be Reformed, as it Was Set Forth on a Day of Public Fasting, April 16, 1707, at Hatfield. By William Williams, Pastor of the Church there.* Boston: Printed by B. Green, 1707.

The Danger of Not Reforming Known Evils

"For I have told him that I will judge his
house for ever for the iniquity which he knoweth;
because his sons made themselves vile,
and he restrained them not."
First Samuel 3:13.

God's own visible people are not exempt from judgments. Even those among them who are truly godly and dear to God may, by their sinful carriages, cast dishonor upon God and upon religion and expose themselves to many humbling and afflictive rebukes from God in this world. Although their sin is pardoned and shall not condemn them in the world to come, yet God sees it necessary for the vindication of His own name and the promoting of their good, to give some public testimony of His displeasure against sin. It is not only those who are of a profane and vicious spirit, whose carriages are an open defiance to heaven, that help to bring public rebukes and judgments upon themselves and others, but many times it is the sins of those who are upright and sincere. God was so displeased with the impatience and dissidence of Moses and Aaron that He excluded them from Canaan (Deuteronomy 32:51,52). God was so offended with David in the matter of Uriah that He brought a great deal of sorrow upon his family and kingdom (2 Samuel 6; 1 Chronicles 13-18). He was so provoked with Solomon for his connivance at and encouragement of the idolatry of his wives that He tore away ten parts of the Kingdom of Israel out of the hand of his son (1 Kings 11:31). And in the context before us God pronounces an awful threatening against the House of Eli for his undue toleration and connivance at the wickedness of his sons. Such examples should instruct us not to be high-minded but to fear. They should teach us not to think ourselves secure because of any visible relation to God but to carry a holy awe and trembling upon our hearts because of His holiness and jealousy, who is of purer eyes than to look upon sin (Habakkuk 1:13).

In the words of the text we take notice of three things.

1. A severe threatening denounced against the house of Eli: "I have told him." This was done by the message which had earlier been sent to him, "I will judge." The word signifies either to condemn, punish, or destroy. Here it seems to speak of intended punishment. "His house": that is, his family or posterity which is often called a man's house. "For ever": that is, either until they are utterly wasted and consumed or rather for a long time, as the phrase forever is often used. This was fulfilled in part when his two sons were slain by the Philistines (1 Samuel 4:11) and in part when Saul slew Abimileck and his family (1 Samuel 22:18) and finally when the priesthood was transferred from the House of Eli and Abiathar to that of Eliazar by Solomon about eighty years later (1 Kings 2:27).

2. The reason for this threatening: "Because his sons made themselves vile, and he restrained them not." Their sins were very horrid and prodigious as is reported in the preceding chapter. Their sins were such as rendered them abominable to God and contemptible to the people. They brought their sacred offices and God's holy ordinances into contempt. Yet their father did not use that authority which God had given him as a high priest, as a judge, and as chief magistrate in punishing them as he was obliged to do by the Law of God, but contented himself with an easy and gentle reproof.

3. The aggravation of this sin: This is especially taken notice of as the immediate, procuring cause of the judgment: "For the iniquity which he knoweth." Eli could not pretend ignorance or want of evidence. The crimes of his sons were certain for the cry of their wickedness had gotten abroad among all Israel. God had even given Eli a particular warning by sending a man of God unto him (1 Samuel 2:27). Although the matter was notorious, yet his parental fondness and indulgence seems to have bribed his judgment so that he did not attend to his duty to God and to his sons in punishing them suitably for their horrid sins.

"For the iniquity which he knoweth" is the clause in the text that I desire to particularly notice at this time. From it we may deduce this

DOCTRINE: It is highly offensive to God and shows men to be very faulty when they will not reform what they know must be amiss.

This is what aggravated Eli's sin. He knew his sons were vile and yet did not do what he could or what he should to restrain them. Sometimes a particular person or an entire people sin through ignorance. Perhaps they are under the disadvantage of not knowing the mind of God on specific cases, or perhaps the matter is subject to dispute and they do not know whether or not the thing is a sin. Although ignorance does not wholly excuse sin, it lessens it in that it is not aggravated by sinning against knowledge. But when men have so much light shine forth that a particular sin is know to be sin, God Himself plainly testifying against it and they themselves often confessing it, and yet do not set themselves to reform but still persist in committing the sin, this makes them very guilty before God and shows their offence to be very great. Hence it is that God threatens in a peculiar manner to punish His own people, "You only have I known of all the families of the earth: therefore I will punish you for all your iniquities" (Amos 3:2). Why is this? Surely not because God loves them less than He does other people. No, but because His name and honor suffer more by their sins than by the sins of the world. Likewise their sins are committed against more light than the sins of others and are therefore more inexcusable. "If I had not come and spoken unto them, they had not had sin: but now they have no cloak for their sin" (John 15:22). "Therefore to him that knoweth to do good, and doeth it not, to him it is sin" (James 4:17), that is, it is sin with peculiar aggravation.

I must first give you the confirmation of this doctrine and then make some application of it.

I. THE CONFIRMATION OF THIS DOCTRINE.

1. Those who wilfully sin against knowledge reveal a prevailing love to sin. When one knowingly sins it shows that sin has gotten a great deal of power in his heart. The more light that is resisted in sinning, the stronger and deeper must be man's love for sin. Their pleas and excuses for it, their willingness to justify it, their readiness to roll it as a sweet morsel under their tongues—all show that their hearts are too much set upon it, that sin occupies a great position in their affections and that it has much power to corrupt and blind their judgments. If they had such hatred and abhorrence of sin as they ought, they would be watchful against it, resist it with great care, shun temptations when offered and put forth major endeavors to mortify it. Men's eagerness in serving sin despite light and conviction is a sign it has gotten a great deal of power in their hearts. This is the very reason the Apostle gives us why Baalam was so set to curse Israel: he "loved the wages of unrighteousness" (2 Peter 2:15).

To love sin is always a bad sign. Where the love of sin reigns a man is shown to be in a very bad state. The Psalmist indicates the character of the wicked man by saying, "Thou lovest evil more than good; and lying rather than to speak righteousness" (Psalm 52:3). When men prefer sin before holiness in their ordinary, habitual course, it shows their state is bad, it shows their hearts are in a bad frame and very much wanting in the exercise of grace which ought to be maintained. Love of sin very much aggravates the heinousness of sin. "This is the condemnation, that light is come into the world, and men loved darkness rather than light, because their deeds were evil" (John 3:19).

2. Those who wilfully sin against knowledge show their lack of love to God and regard for God's honor. Sin is loathsome and abominable to God. He looks upon it with displeasure and abhorrence. This is the very way it should be looked upon by us. It should be the object of our hatred and displeasure. Where a spirit of love to God is kept in exercise it will be so. Those that love the Lord will hate evil. The Psalmist expresses his indignation against sin by saying, "I hate the work of them that turn aside; it shall not cleave to me" (Psalm 101:3) and "I hate every false way" (Psalm 119:104). If persons have a tender respect for God's glory, His name and honor will be dear to them. This will make them afraid of provoking Him or doing anything that will lessen and obscure it. It will make them watchful against all encroachments of sin and enable them to be ready to say, as did Joseph, "How then can I do this great wickedness, and sin against God?" (Genesis 39:9).

When, therefore, persons persevere in the practice of known evils (though they see sin they are not willing to forsake it) it shows either the want of love to God or the want of the exercise of that love. When love to God is being exercised, sin becomes a burden and a grief to the soul and holiness is desired and endeavored after by the use of every possible means. Jesus said, "If a man love Me, he will keep My words" (John 14:23). We must readily grant that men are very much to blame either when they lack a spirit of love to God or when they do not maintain it in all its lively exercises and activities. God is worthy of our love. Our best affections are due to Him, both on account of His infinite and amiable perfections and His innumerable and repeated benefits and also because love to God is the great principle of all evangelical obedience; nothing is well done in religion without it.

3. Those who wilfully sin against knowledge demonstrate much deadness, stupidity and sleepiness of conscience. That sin can be let alone and suffered to lie quietly in the heart is an indicator of serious soul difficulties. A tender conscience may sometimes be clouded with ignorance and through mistakes may pass a wrong judgment in particular cases and thus allow a man to lie for a time in some sin without repentance; but otherwise a wakeful and tender conscience will smite and condemn him for his sin. The conscience is God's deputy in the soul. It will take His part and witness for Him when His honor is treated with contempt and His law violated. Although David had only cut off the skirt of Saul's robe, his heart soon smote him (1 Samuel 24:5). Peter denied

Christ with curses, but when he remembered the words of Christ he went out and wept bitterly (Matthew 26:75). A sensible conscience will fill the soul with disquieting accusations. It will make it uneasy under the burden of its own guilt and restless to be delivered both from it and from the burdensome and distressing effects and consequences of it. A tender conscience will drive a man to use the proper means to ease it. When the Apostle Paul had stirred up the consciences of the Corinthians to reflect upon their sinful connivance with the incestuous person among them and of their pride and unhumbled spirit in not mourning for and over him, they were made sorrowful after a godly sort and with great carefulness and zeal sought to make right the wrong (2 Corinthians 7:11). They could not rest until they were thoroughly clear of the guilt and had by unfeigned repentance testified of their displeasures against the sin.

It is everyone's unquestionable duty to get and keep a tender conscience. When sin prevails and men give way to security and sleepiness of conscience, it shows a careless, unwatchful, unthinking heart as well as the lack of a due sense of God's unspotted holiness and purity. It is evident such sinners lack the certainty of God's righteous judgments and the care they need to please God and approve their hearts to Him in holy conversation. Yea, if conscience is allowed to fall asleep, the soul will lie like a town unguarded. It will be a ready prey to an approaching enemy. Satan easily gets an advantage over such, many sad breaches are made in the peace of their souls, and many defilements are contracted to their unspeakable prejudice.

4. Those who wilfully sin against knowledge fall into a greater voluntariness and freedom in sinning. Such persons do not sin through inadvertency or from the sudden surprise of temptation but with more deliberation. The more freely men commit sin and the more of the content of the will there is in it, the more vile it is. Wilful sin reveals a very bad state or frame of heart. It indicates that men have lost, in a great measure, the sense of God's authority and the awe of His judgment, and therefore, such sins are the more heinous and offensive to God. As Christ explained, "If I had not come and spoken unto them, they had not had sin: but now they have no cloak for their sin" (John 15:22). The coming in of so much light made their sin inexcusable and took away all pleas and pretenses that they had to excuse or cover it before. They can no longer say they did not know it was sin or that it was a thing so offensive to God or that it would have such a dangerous tendency in themselves. The coming in of light reveals these things to them. Hence Christ tells us that such sins expose to greater judgment, "The servant which knew his

Lord's will and prepared not himself,neither did according to His will, shall be beaten with many stripes" (Luke 12:47). Just as hereafter it exposes to a sorer condemnation, so at present, whenever the conscience of a sinner comes to be awakened, the remembrance of the light that has been resisted and the warning and convictions that have been slighted makes deep wounds in the conscience and procures many heart-piercing fears and agonies of spirit. It is a great folly for anyone to expose themself to these disquiets of conscience by giving way to such wilful, wasting sins.

5. Those who wilfully sin against knowledge show that there is but little dread upon their hearts of God's judgments, either felt or threatened. Sin exposes men to the just displeasure of a holy and righteous God. Many times in His providences He reveals His wrath against the ungodliness and unrighteousness of men and expects that these things should strike awe upon their hearts and be a means to restrain them from adventuring any longer in their impenitency. Even when His wrath is not made visible in the punishment of sin it is always discovered in His threatenings against it and hangs like a flaming sword over the head of sinners. These threatenings should produce an awe in persons and make them afraid of exposing themselves to divine justice. They have worked this way in some. David said, "My flesh trembleth for fear of Thee; and I am afraid of Thy judgments" (Psalm 119:120). Job said, "Destruction from God was a terror to me, and by reason of His highness I could not endure" (Job 31:23). This is how it should be with all of us for God requires men to "stand in awe, and sin not" (Psalm 4:4). He Himself has declared that when His judgments are abroad in the earth the inhabitants of the world will learn righteousness (Isaiah 26:9). Corrections should be instructive. We should learn the evil of sin by them and be afraid of continuing in it. It would be so if there were any suitable awe of the justice or truth of God upon their hearts, any sense of the terribleness of His displeasure and what a fearful thing it is to be the sorrowful subject of His threatenings or judgments. Those, therefore, are very much to blame whose hearts are glued so fast to their lusts and idols that rather than part with them they will fight their own mercies and expose themselves to the wrath and jealousy of a sin-revenging God and, though knowing the judgment of God in His threatenings or providences, will not be checked or restrained by it.

II. SOME APPLICATIONS OF THIS DOCTRINE.

USE ONE. This doctrine shows us that a people under a prevailing unreformed spirit are many times more culpable in the sight of God than they are aware. Not only are the evils that prevail among them very offensive to God, but their not improving the light held forth to them for their conversion and reformation renders their sin very culpable and highly aggravated in the sight of God. When a people corrupt themselves and grow degenerate they are to be blamed, but it is much worse when they continue in this condition and will not be reclaimed. Thus they are to be blamed upon a double account.

1. Unreformed people manifest unthankfulness for the light that is held forth to them. Their not improving it and submitting to it shows their low esteem of it. In not doing what they ought, they refuse to acknowledge the mercy of God in it. There is great evidence of God's frown upon a people when He lets them alone in their sins and does not use the means that are necessary to convince, reform and convert them and bring them back to their duty. When God suffers people to walk in their own ways, as He did the Gentile world (Acts 14:16), when He lets them alone to be joined to idols (Hosea 4:17), when He leaves them in their blindness and darkness and will not guarantee to use those means with them that he normally uses with His people, when He does not discover their sin or danger to them nor call them to repentance, it is a sign God has marked them out for His vengeance and displeasure.

It is, on the other hand, a great mercy and blessing when God takes pains with men to bring them to a sight of sin and a conviction of their duty, reveals His will to them, shows them how they should govern themselves and order their conversations, testifies against their evils, warns them of the danger of sin and encourages them to obedience by promises of mercy. These are fit means to work upon a heart and gain men to their duty. God granted great indulgence to Israel in that "He showeth His Word unto Jacob, His statutes and His judgments unto Israel. He hath not dealt so with any [other] nation (Psalm 147:19,20). God justly takes it ill when such mercies are not duly received: "I have written to him the great things of My law, but they were counted as a strange thing" (Hosea 8:12). Israel treated God's special mercies as a foreign thing or as a thing they had no concern with, a thing not belonging to them, a thing they did not desire to be governed by. Whatever pretenses men make of thankfulness for the Word of God, however they speak of it as a privilege to have light and the means of grace, if they do not yield obedience to the light and conform themselves to the commands of it, they are practically unthankful and do in effect cast it behind their backs (Nehemiah 9:26).

2. An unwillingness to be reformed argues much of an incorrigible spirit. It shows their hearts are set upon their evil ways. "My people are bent to backsliding from Me" (Hosea 11:7). Although the prophets called them to the most High, none would exalt Him. The inveterateness of a disease is shown when it resists and overcomes healing medicines. Just so, when suitable means are used to bring a people to repentance and all prove frustrated and ineffectual, it shows their incorrigibility and irreclaimability. When they say, either in words or practice, as they did in Jeremiah's day, "As for the Word that thou hast spoken unto us in the name of the Lord, we will not hearken unto thee" (Jeremiah 44:16), or when it can be said of a people as it was said of King Uzziah, "His name spread far abroad; for he was marvelously helped, till he was strong. But when he was strong, his heart was lifted up to his destruction: for he transgressed against the Lord his God" (2 Chronicles 26:15,16). When this comes to the height, judgments come on irremediably and there is no resisting or escaping.

Ordinarily, this spirit does not come to the height at once but grows upon a people gradually. The heart is hardened some degrees by withstanding the means of conviction. It is hardened further by refusing to hearken to the voice of God's warnings or judgments when they appear against sin. The hardness becomes greater still when an unwillingness to repent, reform and unfeignedly turn to God is manifested. To allow such a spirit that will slight reproofs and scorn reprovers is to be in a very bad estate. It is bad enough when the hearts of a people are gone off from God and set upon their lusts, but it is much worse when they will not return to Him but persevere in their evil ways.

USE TWO. This doctrine is to warn you not to resist the light that will reveal your sin and bring you to your duty. It is a dangerous thing to neglect to reform what you know to be amiss. There is a great deal of sin in it and it exposes those who are guilty of it to many judgments. Eli had earlier been warned of the wickedness of his sons, but his sinful indulgence toward them blinded him and so God must here tell him that "He will judge his house for ever." Thus the prophet declared against Amaziah, "I know that God hath determined to destroy thee, because thou hast done this, and hast not hearkened unto my counsel" (2 Chronicles 25:16). Notwithstanding clear cut testimonies from God, men sometimes harden their hearts and by persisting in sin expose themselves to spiritual, temporal and eternal judgments. I will remind you of some of the ways whereby persons sometimes do this in order that you may be cautioned against them.

THE DANGER OF NOT REFORMING 129

1. By pleading the example of others. Bad examples are very pernicious and provide a great occasion of hardening men in sin. Jereboam's idolatry had a fatal influence upon all the succeeding Kings of Israel. In Jeremiah you find the people justifying themselves in their idolatrous practices by using the examples of their kings, princes and fathers before them (Jeremiah 44:17). So it is now. Some vindicate themselves by insisting that they are not alone in what they do. They claim they know many who act as they act, wise and good men too. But this is an insufficient vindication. If the thing is in its nature or under such circumstances evil, the practice of others will not make it good no matter how many are doing it. You know that good men have their failings and many good things carry corruption. Besides, all are not good men that are taken to be, for many that the world calls wise, knowing men are and will be found fools at the last. But even if they are ever so good and wise you must follow none of them any farther than they follow Christ (1 Corinthians 11:1). Precepts must be your rule, not examples. There is hardly any duty but some fail in it or any sin but some have fallen into it, especially in a degenerate time such as this when there is a great laxness both as to principles and practices prevailing among people. Thus, if you make it a rule to excuse yourself whenever you find someone else doing a thing, you will find very little that needs to be reformed and a great part of your Bible will be laid aside as useless and unnecessary.

2. By entertaining prejudices against those that warn and reprove you as if they acted not out of faithfulness to you but from some ill design. This was one reason why Israel rejected the Word God sent them by the Prophets, "The Lord our God hath not sent thee... but Baruch the Son of Neriah setteth thee on against us" (Jeremiah 43:2,3). Thus the prophet asked, "To whom shall I speak, and give warning, that they may hear? behold, their ear is uncircumcised, and they cannot hearken: behold the word of the Lord is unto them a reproach; they have no delight in it" (Jeremiah 6:10). They interpreted faithful reproofs to be reproaches. They said they were railed upon. Ahab was prejudiced against Elijah and Micaiah, as if their reproofs were only from want of love to his person. He counted them his enemies and thus took nothing kindly (I Kings 22; 2 Chronicles 18).

Sometimes persons pretend that others seek to restrain them from their just liberties or that they do not know the circumstances of their condition. On another occasion they may accuse reprovers of aiming at their own particular interest. It must be understood that these pretenses are ordinarily from the deceitfulness of sin or the result of the efficacy of

Satan in hardening the heart. In short, there is no just reason for them. Our duty, when reproved, is to seriously examine the case. If the Word of God condemns the practice, that must be sufficient to deter us from it, for it is by this that God will justify or condemn us.

3. By trusting in their religious privileges or seeming goodness in other cases. The carnal Jews, when reproved for their oppression, injustice, idolatry and called to amend their ways, boasted of their privileges, saying, "The temple of the Lord, The temple of the Lord, are these" (Jeremiah 7:4), as if their visible relationship to God and their external observations of religion would secure them from judgments. Israel makes this a cloak for her wickedness saying, "I have peace offerings with me; this day have I payed my vows" (Proverbs 7:14). In the same way carnal Christians rest upon their external show of devotions. Because they attend the public worship of God, pray in their families, and make other outward shows of devotion, they expect God will excuse their immoralities. They trust in their own righteousness and commit iniquity, not knowing that their righteousness shall not be remembered by God (Ezekiel 33:13). Alas, these things aggravate rather than excuse sin and clearly prove that men do not know their duty.

God calls for universal obedience. The doing of one duty will not compensate for the neglect of another (James 2:10,11). Herod did many things and heard John gladly but he would not part with his Herodias (Luke 3:19,20). The Pharisee could boast that he was no extortioner, no adulterer, but he could not say he was not proud and self-confident (Luke 18:9-14). The God that calls you to pray, to hear, and to meditate upon His Word, calls you also to live soberly and righteously and to walk humbly with God. Partiality in religion spoils it and utterly frustrates men receiving the glad rewards of it. "If any man among you seem to be religious, and bridleth not his tongue, but deceiveth his own heart, this man's religion is vain" (James 1:26). If the heart is upright, all duty will be chosen and all sin avoided. Then the person will be able to say, "Then shall I not be ashamed, when I have respect unto all Thy commandments" (Psalm 119:6).

4. By presuming upon the mercy of God, hoping it shall secure them from the strokes of justice. They sin freely and cry, "God is merciful!" They don't think God will be as severe as He threatens or as men would have them believe. "And it come to pass, when he heareth the words of this curse, that he bless himself in his heart, saying, I shall have peace, though I walk in the imagination of mine heart..." (Deuteronomy 29:19). This awful error hardens the hearts of many. They take up wrong conceptions of God's mercy as if He were of so pitiful and tender a nature that He could not bear to see men suffer the very thing He threatens. But you must know that God is just as well as merciful! It is not unmerciful for God to punish men according to His threatenings. Yea, His truth and faithfulness oblige Him to do it. God Himself has determined the way and the time for the exercise of His mercy. If these are neglected, no mercy will be shown. The very devils may as well hope for mercy as impenitent unbelievers who neglect the day of salvation and do not seek for mercy in a Gospel way. You cannot take a more direct and dangerous route to turning away the heart of a merciful God from you than by abusing His goodness in strengthening yourselves in rebellion against Him. This is both a most vile abuse of it and an a most unreasonable inference from it. Paul asks, "Shall we continue in sin, that grace may abound?" and answers emphatically, "God forbid!" (Romans 6:1). Such a thought is to be abhorred.

5. By entertaining purposes of future repentance. Men know their course is evil and such as God condemns. They know that this and that and the other practices which they indulge in are sinful. They dare not justify them, but they still their consciences with the thought that they intend to repent later. They reckon upon no great difficulty in this, assuming the repenting is theirs, under their control, and all will be well. They do not seem to realize that these purposes to repent in the future abundantly harden and make them bold to continue in sin against all counsel and reproof. But alas, repentance is not so easy a work. The heart that is now so much in love with sin and so full of enmity against holiness will not be easily changed. A deceitful heart will find other excuses when the present ones are answered. The old man will struggle hard before it is subdued. Perhaps they do not know that repentance is a grace of God's giving. The heart of stone is too hard for any created power to break. Repentance is a gift that only God can give and fortunately when He gives it He does so freely. Because men can only repent when God enables, Paul said to Timothy, "God peradventure will give them repentance" (2 Timothy 2:25). Many that presume upon having repentance at leisure find themselves disappointed. Either a sudden death arrests them or a hard heart and a sleepy conscience seizes upon them. It is a very bold adventure to reject God's gracious offers, presuming upon future time or grace.

USE THREE. This doctrine is designed to examine you and expostulate with you whether or not you are faulty in this matter. Are there not several things which you know to be duties neglected and several things that you know to be sins practiced? We live in a land of light. We have the great advantage of knowing the mind of God. We know how we should adorn the Gospel and what our profession of it should be like. The grace of God toward us, both as to light and peace under Gospel privileges, is very peculiar and distinguishing. Although there may be errors in practice that arise through ignorance and inadvertency and some points even that are disputable that persons are not so well satisfied about, yet, surely, the evils of this country are, for the most part, in such things as are known, even such things as have been often acknowledged, sometimes in a more public manner both by civil and ecclesiastical rulers and often in a general way upon such days as this. It is not the want of light that retards the reformation which has been so long called for, but the failure to improve and submit to the light that we have. Let me prosecute this expostulation in the following particulars.

1. As to the great duty of improving seasons and means of grace unto a repentance from dead works, faith in the Lord Jesus Christ and getting into a converted and pardoned estate while the patience and longsuffering of God is continued. Is not this a thing abundantly known and confessed? Certainly persons that have been raised under the calls of the Gospel and have had the duties of it so frequently inculcated upon them, cannot be ignorant of these things. The Word is plain and positive concerning them, presenting a present repentance and conversion to God. "Seek ye the Lord while He may be found, call ye upon Him while He is near: Let the wicked forsake his way, and the unrighteous man his thoughts: and let him return unto the Lord..." (Isaiah 55:6,7). "Behold, now is the accepted time; behold, now is the day of salvation" (2 Corinthians 6:2). "Wherefore as the Holy Ghost saith, Today if ye will hear His voice, Harden not your hearts..." (Hebrews 3:7,8). Think how plainly the Scriptures warn of the dangers of neglecting it, "How shall we escape, if we neglect so great salvation?" (Hebrews 2:3). For those who neglect salvation there will be no escaping or avoiding the sorest condemnation.

God shows the riches of His grace in affording the seasons of grace unto men. These are not to be slighted and trifled away but seriously, seasonably and faithfully improved. Men cast great dishonor upon Christ and show contempt for the love of God in the work of redemption, when peace and reconciliation with Him are not regarded and when the fruits of redeeming love in sanctification and holiness are counted a misery rather that a privilege. It is a daring presumption as well as positive disobedience, when God calls for present repentance and conversion, to defer the matter to future care.

Surely men know it is their duty to honor the Lord Jesus Christ and to acknowledge Him in His office of Redeemer. Surely it is fit that He, who at the expense of His precious blood has undergone such abasement and sufferings, should be glorious in the eyes of those to whom He is offered and the fruits of His redeeming love received with all thankfulness. This is plainly required. The Saviour Himself said, "The Father judgeth no man, but hath committed all judgment unto the Son: That all men should honour the Son, even as they honour the Father" (John 5:22,23). How is Christ honored if it is not by believing Him and obeying Him? (John 3; Hebrews 5:9). Do not all professed Christians confess that there is no other way of salvation but this which God has consecrated through faith in His blood? Yet alas, how many there are who neglect these great duties; live in impenitency and unbelief; are very little concerned to obtain a real union with Christ and communion in the benefits of redemption; make no great matter of letting slip the seasons of grace; feel no misery in estrangement from God and captivity to sin and Satan; do not groan after redemption; are more intent upon securing the world than obtaining heaven; are more inquisitive what they shall eat and drink and wherewith they shall be clothed than how they may glorify God, adorn the Gospel, and secure the happiness of their souls in Christ and an unfailing title to that glory which He has purchased.

2. As to the means of worship which God has appointed, whether public, private or secret. Certainly the omissions of those that are among us are not through ignorance. Men know and confess that God is the supreme and first being, the fountain of goodness and thence the proper object of worship. They acknowledge that all our mercies flow from Him and should be asked for in prayer and acknowledged with praise. As to the secret duties of worship, how plain is the precept, "When thou prayest, enter into thy closet, and when thou hast shut thy door, pray to thy Father which is in secret" (Matthew 6:6). Every man has personal wants, his sins and temptations, his many concerns that are most fit to be transacted in secret between God and his own soul; therefore to omit it is but an act of disobedience to God and a great prejudice to yourselves. Yet are there not many who are strangers to this duty? There are those who can seldom find time to converse with God in secret, who can often sin in secret, be wanton, unjust, intemperate in secret, and yet do not pray in secret?

As to the public worship of God, how plainly God has enjoined the several parts of it and particularly that very much neglected ordinance of the Lord's Supper. He has obliged all His disciples to observe it in remembrance of Him (Luke 22:19), that they might keep up a thankful memorial of the death of Christ and the great ends of it and testify of their dependence upon Him for the blessings purchased by it. Love to Christ and hatred of sin is excited, increased and inflamed by the lively representation of His painful sufferings and bitter death. Though these things are very plain, many live from year to year in the neglect of this ordinance. While they may pretend a want of preparation for it and a fear of polluting it by unworthy participation, it is really from a slight and low view of God's authority enjoining it that they dare to absent themselves from His table. If they possessed a real tenderness toward the Lord they would set themselves faithfully to meet Him at His table and would bewail their ignorance, reform their lives, cry day and night to God for His sanctifying grace to purify their hearts and fit them for communion with God. But alas, how this table is neglected! Such neglecters will be very inexcusable in the day of Christ. Some of you pretend a zeal for Christ's institutions and commend your fore-fathers that ventured their blood to refuse the ordinance from Popish corruptions, and yet when you may attend it in Gospel purity, you turn your backs upon it!

3. As to families, do not men know that it is their duty to educate and influence them in religion and virtue and restrain them from impieties and immoralities? This is plain, "Train up a child in the way he should go..." (Proverbs 22:6). "Bring them up in the nurture and admonition of the Lord" (Ephesians 6:4). For this Abraham is honored and commended by God, "For I know him, that he will command his children and household after him, and they shall keep the way of the Lord, to do justice and judgment" (Genesis 18:19). It is the way for parents to convey the best blessings to their children. Not only do the ties of religion and conscience require it but nature also obliges it. To neglect it would be to be worse than the ostriches of the wilderness. Have you not solemnly dedicated your children to God and professed a desire that they may be the Lords? Then it will be gross hypocrisy to be negligent of their education as well as great unfaithfulness to God and to their souls. Have you not been the immediate instruments of propagating original sin to them? Should not this oblige you to do the best you can for them that they may be delivered from the guilt of it? Besides, you have a special interest in them. You are always with them. You know their tempers and dispositions. You have a peculiar advantage in teaching the principles of piety and virtue and accustoming them to the practice of religion, civility and industry.

The great concern of upholding religion and propagating it to succeeding generations should be a pressing encouragement hereunto. The work of Christ in our towns and churches will soon languish if this is neglected. Our children will be like unpolished stones, unfit to be laid in any building, if a virtuous and pious education is neglected. The present sorrowful state of many of our children, snatched from us and exposed to a popish and heathenish education, should awaken us to serious reflections whether, among other just reasons for it, God may not be pointing at this neglect. It is certain from our text that Eli's posterity smarted for his indulgence. So did David's, although he was a very holy man. Those, therefore, who know all these things and yet neglect the godly education of their families, who indulge them in ignorance of things fundamental to their conversion and salvation, who connive at their irreligiousness, rudeness, disorders, neglect of family worship and misuse of the Lord's day, who allow irreverent, clownish carriages, are greatly to blame. Despite the excuses the heathen make for such things, they are certainly inexcusable among those that profess themselves Christian, who know their duty and have many encouragements to do it.

4. Do not men know that an inordinate affection for the things of this world is very unbecoming to those that profess Christianity and most frequently forbidden in the Word of God? "Ye adulterers and adulteresses, know ye not that the friendship of the world is enmity with God? Whosoever therefore will be a friend of the world is the enemy of God" (James 4:4). "Let your conversation be without covetousness; and be content with such things as ye have" (Hebrews 13:5). "No man can serve two masters: for either he will hate the one, and love the other; or else he will hold to the one, and despise the other. Ye cannot serve God and mammon" (Matthew 6:24). Yea, God has told you that this is idolatry (Colossians 3:5). When that esteem, love, contentment, and desire which is due to God is set upon the world, this is idolatry as real as men's bowing down to a stock or a stone.

God has plainly declared that this inordinancy of heart discovers itself in anxious, perplexing, disquieting cares, neglecting dependence upon God or satisfaction with the disposals of His providence and in greedy, violent desires. "They that will be rich fall into temptation and a snare, and into many foolish and hurtful lusts, which drown men in destruction and perdition. For the love of money is the root of all evil: which while some coveted after, they have erred from the faith, and pierced themselves through with many sorrows" (1 Timothy 6:9,10). We are told, "He that maketh haste to be rich shall not be innocent" (Proverbs 28:20). Men wrong their souls, wound their consciences and blast their reputations when they take unrighteous ways of gain, defraud others, oppress and overreach in their dealings, do not act truly and honestly, neglect paying just debts, avoid necessary acts of charity, fear to depend upon divine providence and the encouragements of the promises of God but withhold more than is meet, begrudging God His due and the poor what is rightfully theirs, counting themselves losers in all that they give in supposed works of mercy and charity.

The same effect is had when their worldly cares encroach upon their time and thoughts, choke convictions, hinder the duties of religion or occasion formality and slightness in them, when the care for the body crowds out care for the soul, and things of the world make them neglect the realities of heaven. Such a spirit prevails altogether too much among us, notwithstanding convictions and professions to the contrary. Is it not perfectly obvious that the abatement of love to Christ and the increase of love to the world is a main root of the degeneracy that has grown upon us? We have great reason to think that God's impoverishing providences point to this evil and give us special reason to lament our too great aversion to reform it!

5. Do we not all know that intemperance is an evil? The very light of nature condemns it. Civilized heathen have abhorred it and borne witness against it. The Word of God speaks strongly against it, witnessing against the grosser acts of it in notorious drunkenness and shameful spewing and denouncing all that tends that way. God denounces men who tarry long at the wine and forbids looking upon the wine "when it is red, when it giveth his colour in the cup, when it moveth itself aright" (Proverbs 23:30,31). God pronounces a woe against those that are mighty to drink wine and men of strength who mingle strong drink (Isaiah 5:22), that pour down cup after cup before being intoxicated and bereft of the exercise of reason. The Gospel requires men to live soberly (Titus 2:12,13) and to govern their appetites as to meat and drink. If any act contrary to this teaching, needlessly wasting away their time and estates in indulging a tippling humor and gratifying the inordinacy of their appetites to the wounding of their consciences, quenching their convictions, dishonoring their profession, impoverishing their families, and refusing to be reformed, they will certainly be found very culpable before God and altogether inexcusable. These things, with others of like nature that might have been named, are the sad evidences of a great abuse of the light that God has afforded us.

USE FOUR. This doctrine should persuade you to reform those things that you know to be amiss and are plainly revealed to be sins. If you neglect this, there will be just cause to fear that God's displeasure will be continued and increased. God is as angry today with men's pride and stubbornness in contempt of His warnings as He has been in former times. It is a dangerous thing for a people against whom God has a controversy to delay their repentance and to continue the causes of His anger. For as it is with particular persons, so it is with a people; God limits the time of His patience. How long will He wait before the warning period is past and His wrath breaks out until there is no remedy? It would be wisdom on our part to take up the matter quickly, following the example of Moses who said to Aaron, "Take a censer, and put fire therein from off the altar, and put on incense, and go quickly unto the congregation, and make an atonement for them: for there is wrath gone out from the Lord; the plague is begun" (Numbers 16:46-50). We ought immediately to remove what we know to be evil and to search out what we know not. In particular, I would make these suggestions.

1. Reform such things as your own consciences tell you are amiss and for which they often smite and condemn you. The conscience is God's monitor in your breasts. You should listen to it as you would a messenger from heaven when it warns you of evil committed or of duty neglected. Is not conscience often smiting you? Does it not smite you when you hear sin reproved, when a day of distress and affliction comes, when you think death and judgment are near? Are there not many inward disquitments and perplexing thoughts arising in your hearts? Are there not secret resolutions to avoid those evils or to do those duties that conscience deals with you about? Oh, then, obey the voice of conscience in these things. Whatever it witnesses to, don't slight it or smother it. Do not withstand its checks. If you do not act kindly toward it as a friend you must expect that it will shortly act toward you as an enraged enemy and will dreadfully upbraid you for the violence done to it. "A wounded spirit who can bear?" (Proverbs 18:14).

2. Reform what you often confess to be amiss. Doubtless, besides public prayers and solemn confessions that are made on such days as this, wherein we are uttering many things against ourselves for the vindication of the righteousness of God in the things He has brought upon us, God has your particular and personal confessions in the daily prayers that you make. How often are you bewailing the misspending of time, abuse of the seasons and means of grace, unthankfulness for Gospel mercies, barrenness and unprofitableness under divine cultivations, the neglect of government over your spirits and passions, inordinate affection for the things of the world and a too great indifference and coldness to the things of God and your own salvation? Now will you not be self-condemned if, notwithstanding these confessions, these things are still continued? How sad it is when a man's prayers serve only for a testimony of his hypocrisy and prove the deceitfulness of his heart in the religious shows that he makes. When there is a hearty sorrow for such evils and a due sense of them, it is manifested in a serious endeavour both to reform and mortify them.

3. Reform those things that are plainly witnessed against by the Word of God. You all confess the Word of God to be the rule according to which our lives and actions should be ordered. You acknowledge that it is to be our guide in matters of institution, moral duties, truth, justice, temperance, charity, modesty and the like. Whenever the Word of God convinces your conscience in a matter, be careful you don't withstand such counsel or message from God to you. David said, "My heart standeth in awe of Thy word" (Psalm 119:161). God looks graciously on those that tremble at His word (Isaiah 66:2). When any duty is enforced by it or sin condemned, we should submit to it with reverence and thankfulness. It is not a matter of liberty whether you will receive or reject the commands of God. Whatever God requires must be cheerfully submitted to. Indeed, where matters are disputable or dark to them, it is men's duty to enquire and to labor to have their doubts resolved. Where matters are plain and unquestionable as in duties of love to God and man, especially in moral precepts and in such things as all agree to be duties, if in such cases men do not hearken to the voice of God, He will surely require it of them. To enforce this exhortation, I shall add these following considerations.

1) Neglecting to reform what you know to be amiss will prove you to be guilty of great hypocrisy in your solemn transactions with God on such days as these. Days of humiliation without reformation are not acceptable to God but are rather days of provocation (Isaiah 58:5-7). When there is not that humiliation, repentance, brokenness of heart for sin and humble waiting upon God for mercy that ought to be present, but when men put off God with empty shows and external devotions, they heighten rather than moderate His anger. When there is a serious desire and commitment of heart to be reconciled to God, men are willing to remove what lies as a bar in the way to it. When men count sin to be as bad as they profess it to be, they certainly are willing to let it go. What is it but hypocrisy when men pretend to desire peace and atonement with God and yet neglect the terms upon which He offers it? To cry for favor and pardoning mercy while perpetrating the grounds of God's controversy, what is this but to mock God, to flatter Him with your lips while your hearts are

far from Him? The carnality and selfishness of men's hearts are clearly shown in such prayers. "They have not cried unto me with their heart, when they howled upon their beds: they assemble themselves for corn and wine, and they rebel against me" (Hosea 7:14).

2) Consider what losers you have been and are still likely to be by not reforming the evils God has witnessed against. It is a fact that the sins of God's professing people are the provoking causes of their calamities, "For the transgression of Jacob is all this, and for the sins of the house of Israel" (Micah 1:5). Idolatry, oppression and neglect of God's worship prevailed, and that brought on abundance of misery. It is the abounding of iniquities among us that has made way for the many rebukes of heaven that we have been under. It is neglecting to reform that has forced God to continue them. Our own experience should convince us what losers we have been hereby. We have forsaken God to our loss. Is not much of the presence of God lost from among us? Where is His gracious spiritual presence in His ordinances and His protecting presence in His providences? Consider the losses in your outward comforts, in your liberties, estates and families.

Men have been violent to serve their lusts and have smarted sorely for it. And is it likely to be otherwise still? Can we expect that God will change the methods of His providence if there is no change for the better in us? "If ye thoroughly amend your ways and your doings; if ye thoroughly execute judgment between a man and his neighbor; If ye oppress not the stranger, the fatherless, and the widow, and shed not innocent blood in this place: neither walk after other gods to your hurt: Then I will cause you to dwell in this place, in the land that I gave to your fathers, for ever and ever" (Jeremiah 7:5-7). God is immutably just and holy. If our behavior is changed, then we become meet subjects for His mercy to be showered upon. Surely then, the bitter fruits of sin should make every one willing to forsake it. Surely it is time to grow wiser, to say, "I will go and return to my first husband; for then was it better with me than now" (Hosea 2:7). Some men think to advance themselves by sin, to get estates and raise their families by injustice, oppression, and a violent pursuit of the world, but in reality they bring shame to their houses. What are men likely to get by greediness, intemperance, sottish neglect of their souls and of the great salvation provided for them through Christ but sorrow here and eternal ruin at the last?

3) If you reform what you know to be amiss it will give ground for hope that God will show you what you do not know. Some are asking, "Wherein shall we return?" If this question is serious, those that ask it will reform what they know to be evil. If they do otherwise, they act like those

denounced by the prophet, who set up their idols in their hearts and put the stumblingblock of their iniquity before their face (Ezekiel 14:3,4,7). In doing so they expose themselves by their mocking of God to greater judgments. But God is ready to teach those that are willing to do their duty. Christ assured us, "If any man will do His will, he shall know of the doctrine, whether it be of God, or whether I speak of Myself" (John 7:17).[1] Job prayed that God would teach him what he knew not, while he resolved that wherein he had done iniquity, he would do so no more (Job 34:32).

4) To do this will give hope that God will have a gracious respect to our prayers this day. God does not begrudge mercies to His people when they are obedient. "If ye be willing and obedient, ye shall eat the good of the land" (Isaiah 1:19). We have very great and weighty requests to present before God this day. We must pray that God will bless our Sovereign and our nation, smile upon their war-like preparations, honor them with success and victory, give enlargement to His Church and a revival to the oppressed, persecuted members of it, preserve our land from the incursions of adversaries, bless, guide and prosper our military forces, and remember and restore our distressed captives. Surely there is no thoughtful person here but would count it a singular mercy if our prayers for these things are accepted at the Throne of Grace. And will you not be prevailed upon so far as to part with your sins, that you may obtain these mercies? Oh, that you would consider it! Is it not better to part with the dearest lust than to be an Achan to trouble our Israel at such a time as this?

How reasonable God's demands are! When He calls men to deny ungodliness and worldly lusts, to live soberly, righteously and godly in this present world, to love God and to love one another, especially to love their own souls by being thoroughly careful to redeem time and make good use of all the help hHe has provided, to secure the happiness of them in Christ while the day of salvation is continued, to turn to Him by a thorough repentance and acknowledgement of all offenses and a humble application to the blood of the Covenant that God will pardon our sins and heal our land, He asks nothing but what is perfectly just. God requires no compensation for the wrongs we have done Him. He demands no requitals for His injured name and glory which has suffered so much by us. If you will return to Him with all your hearts, accept His redeeming grace, and resign yourselves to His service in sincerity, He will

---

[1] See also Philippians 3:15,16.

be gracious and present us with blessings of goodness. "Turn ye unto me, saith the Lord of hosts, and I will turn unto you, saith the Lord of hosts" (Zechariah 1:3). Can any be unwilling to do this? Many are ready to say they would be willing to part with large portions of their estates and even to venture their lives that they might enjoy peaceable days again. And will you not part with your lusts for the return of God's blessings upon us? Will you not renounce all unlawful liberties, humble yourselves before God and seek His holiness in order that you may obtain it? "To him that ordereth his conversation aright will I show the salvation of God" (Psalm 50:23).

CHAPTER EIGHT

Our
Fathers' Sins
and Ours

By
Benjamin Colman

Benjamin Colman, 1673-1747

Benjamin Colman was born in Boston on October 19, 1673. His father Benjamin and his mother Elizabeth, an eminently spiritual woman, had emigrated from England, settling in Boston just shortly before his birth. From about the time he was five years of age, he manifested considerable spiritual concern and commitment and throughout life, appeared to walk in the fear and love of God. Apparently he was dedicated to the Lord and the Gospel ministry by his parents and never considered any other course. Benjamin joined the Second Church in Boston prior to entering Harvard in 1688. He graduated with high honors in 1692, studying there during the time of Increase Mather's presidency. After a brief theological course, he began his preaching ministry in Medford, remaining there a few months before returning to Harvard to gain an M.A. in 1695. He then determined to visit England, which he reached only after an amazing experience of capture by a French privateer and imprisonment in a French prison, where he was graciously received by many of the leading dissenting ministers. Of the between three and four years that Colman spent in England, two were devoted to a ministry at Bath.

In 1699 he returned to Boston to pastor the newly organized Brattle Street Church. Because of differences with the other Boston churches, the founders of Brattle Street urged Colman to seek ordination by the London Presbytery. He began his ministry in Boston in November. The new church was firm in its adherence to the Westminster Standards but somewhat at odds with the Congregational structures of New-England. Within months a partial reconciliation had occurred, and Colman became one of the most prominent and dearly loved spiritual leaders of the Colony.

Colman was a fellow of Harvard College from 1717 to 1728, and an Overseer until his death. Principally through his efforts large donations were received from foreign patrons, not the least of which were the Hollis and Holden benefactions. In 1724 he was offered the presidency of the College, but the General Court prevented his acceptance. Colman also had a strong interest in Yale College and was especially useful there in the enlarging the library. A man of charitable heart and spirit, Colman was deeply interested in the mission to the Housatonic Indians and other evangelistic and social agencies. As the result of his few years in England he had established friendships with a number of evangelicals, including Isaac Watts, with whom he kept up correspondence throughout most of his life. Glasgow University conferred a degree of D.D. upon him in 1731.

From 1715 to 1743 Colman was assisted in the ministry at Brattle Street Church by William Cooper, and upon Cooper's death by his son Samuel. Despite frail health, Colman continued his ministry almost unabated, preaching on the Sabbath before his death, August 29, 1747.

At the time of the Great Awakening Dr. Colman was one of the most prominent supporters of George Whitefield and of the revival. Yet he as obviously disturbed by its excesses and errors and gently but firmly opposed anything which he believed robbed God of His glory or destroyed the great work which was occurring.

As a preacher, Colman was a man of extraordinary grace and usefulness. Dozens of his sermons were published between 1702 and 1746. They cover a wide range of biblical issues. Many were sermons preached at the funerals of colleagues like Solomon Stoddard, Samuel Willard, Cotton Mather and William Cooper. Others were preached at ordinations and installations. Among the most interesting are those on the 1727 earthquake and the Great Awakening. For an extensive bibliography on Colman see "Whitefield In Print."

First published as *A Brief Enquiry Into the Reasons Why the People of God Have Been Wont to Bring into Their Penitential Confessions the Sins of their Fathers and Ancestors In Times Long Since Past, Preached on a Day of General Prayer and Fasting, March 22, 1716. By Benjamin Colman.* Boston: Printed by T. Fleet and T. Crump for Samuel Gerrish, 1716.

Our Fathers' Sins
and Ours

**"We have sinned with our fathers, we have
committed iniquity, we have done wickedly."
Psalm 106:6.**

This Psalm is a history or rather a penitential confession of the
rebellions and provocations of the Children of Israel from the day of their
departure out of Egypt through all their travels and long sojourning in the
wilderness. In the text, the psalmist, in the name of the people of his own
generation, confesses their interest and share in the sins of their fathers
and ancestors.

"We have sinned with our fathers." The critics render it by "sieut" and
"aque" as expressing the similitude of one unto the other or the aggravation of the one from the other. It is like saying "We have done as our
fathers did before us, with equal perverseness and rebellion. We have
added to the stock of hereditary guilt and filled up the measure of their
iniquity. Not only have we sinned in their loins, being the children and
posterity of wicked ancestors, but we ourselves have been a disobedient,
impenitent, and sometimes idolatrous people after the similitude of their
transgressions. We have sinned like them, whereas by their example of
sins and sufferings, we should have taken warning."

This seems to be the meaning of the confession in the text. By it we
see that the psalmist leads the people in confession in deep humiliation
by calling to remembrance the aggravation of their own iniquities in the
sins of their ancestors. Nor is it barely the sins of their immediate
progenitors which they here confess, but they look back unto the first
times of their being a free and distinct people, as you may see at large
through the Psalm.

Moreover, I would observe the repetition of the confession which is
doubled and tripled to express the mighty sense they had of the greatness
of their own guilt, "We have sinned with our fathers, we have committed
iniquity, we have done wickedly." The same thing is repeated over and
over in other words, yet here it is no tautology or vain repetition. Out of
the abundance of the heart, the mouth pours out its confessions, the more

to express the reality and certainty of the thing and the shame and sorrow felt on that account, the more to affect themselves with the thing and to aggravate it upon themselves. I observe the following doctrine drawn from this text.

DOCTRINE: It becomes the professing people of God in their humiliations and confessions of their own sins and the sins of their own times and generation to remember, mention and bewail also the sins of their fathers and ancestors, even in times long since past.

That we should mourn for our own personal sins in the first place, you will easily acknowledge. These should always lie nearest to and heaviest upon our hearts. The prophet Jeremiah laments, "I hearkened and heard, but they spake not aright: no man repented him of his wickedness, saying, What have I done?" (Jeremiah 8:6).

But we must mourn for the sins of others together with our own. Sin ought to grieve us wherever we see it. "I beheld the transgressors, and was grieved" (Psalm 119:158). In particular, we should be affected with and afflicted for the sins of the times, the people and places wherein our lot is cast. "Go through the midst of the city, through the midst of Jerusalem, and set a mark upon the foreheads of the men that sigh and that cry for all the abominations that be done in the midst thereof" (Ezekiel 9:4).

It is probable that the teaching in my text has been less thought of than that in the others which I have named: that is, that we should bring into our humiliations and confessions of the sins of our people now living, the sins of the generations before us, even the sins of those who are long since dead and were so before we were born. I lay before you,

1. **What God Demands of Us in this Doctrine.**
2. **The Reasons for this Duty.**
3. **The Application.**

I. WHAT GOD DEMANDS OF US IN THIS DOCTRINE.

It is the will of God that we, in our penitential and solemn confessions, should remember and mourn for the sins of those that are gone before us and who may have been long since dead. God prescribes this to Israel by the hand of Moses in the after-confessions of future generations, and in particular, in the captivities which their sins would bring upon them. "And they that are left of you shall pine away in their iniquity in your enemies' lands; and also in the iniquities of their fathers shall they pine away with them. If they shall confess their iniquity, and the iniquity of their fathers, with their trespasses which they trespassed against Me, and that also they have walked contrary unto Me... Then will I remember my covenant..." (Leviticus 26:39-41).

In obedience to this direction and command of God, the faithful and penitent in Israel made this kind of confession on every solemn occasion. The Psalm before us is a copious illustration of this. This was especially the burden of the Church's confession during and after the Babylonish captivity, to which some believe this Psalm refers. Jeremiah, Ezra, and Nehemiah all made their confessions along these lines: "We lie down in our shame, and our confusion covereth us: for we have sinned against the Lord our God, we and our fathers, from our youth even unto this day, and have not obeyed the voice of the Lord our God" (Jeremiah 3:25). "Our fathers have sinned, and are not; and we have borne their iniquities" (Lamentations 5:7). "Since the days of our fathers have we been in a great trespass unto this day; and for our iniquities have we, our kings, and our priests, been delivered into the hand of the kings of the lands, to the sword, to captivity, and to a spoil, and to confusion of face, as it is this day" (Ezra 9:7). "Let Thine ear now be attentive, and Thine eyes open, that Thou mayest hear the prayer of Thy servant, which I pray before Thee now, day and night, for the children of Israel Thy servants, and confess the sins of the children of Israel, which we have sinned against Thee: both I and my father's house have sinned. We have dealt very corruptly against Thee, and have not kept the commandments, nor the statutes, nor the judgments, which Thou commandedst Thy servant Moses" (Nehemiah 1:6,7). Even more particularly, in the ninth chapter we have a major account of a day of prayer solemnized by Nehemiah and the remnant of Judah, the very design of which solemn day is thus declared, "The seed of Israel separated themselves from all strangers, and stood and confessed their sins, and the iniquities of their fathers" (verse 2). They were at that time smarting for both together and could not very well separate them. "They and our fathers dealt proudly,and hardened their necks, and hearkened not to Thy commandments" (verse 16), "Neither have our kings, our princes, our priests, nor our fathers, kept Thy law, nor hearkened unto Thy commandments and Thy testimonies..." (verse 34).

Thus the practice is established in Scripture by precept and by example. We find the holy men of God, under the inspiration of the Holy Ghost and the special influence of His grace, bringing the sins of their ancestors and of the generations before them into their confessions before God. This occurred in their private confessions as well as in their more public humiliations.

II. THE REASONS FOR THIS DUTY.

This doctrine seems liable to two objections: 1. It implies want of reverence to our ancestors. 2. It suggests irreverence toward God. Let me premise the reasons for this duty with answers to these difficulties.

1. It implies no want of reverence to our ancestors, nor is it to be charged with the spirit of graceless Ham, who was condemned for not covering his father's nakedness (Genesis 9:22). We cannot uncover the shame of our fathers before God, to whose eye all things are naked and open (Hebrews 4:13). If we remember our ancestors sins with abasement before God as we prostrate ourselves in the dust, we do so before our Father in heaven that His name and holiness may be glorified whose honor should be infinitely dearer to us than even the name of our earthly parents.

2. On the other hand, it is far from implying any irreverence toward God. In this doctrine I am not speaking of God punishing us for our fathers' sins, nor am I suggesting we should take up the foolish and profane proverb which was sometimes used by the wicked Israelites, "The fathers have eaten sour grapes, and the children's teeth are set on edge" (Ezekiel 18:2). No! What I am arguing for is just the reverse of this blasphemy. The wicked object to the doctrine as if it is against the justice of Providence, we on the contrary, confess God's righteousness herein. They sneer and jest at it as if it were an absurdity; we in solemn manner adore the sovereign God in his dispensations and abase ourselves before Him in profound humiliation. They cast reflections upon the divine government; we justify God's administration and acknowledge there is no hardship done us for we know that we shall never be punished for our fathers' sins if we do not walk in their steps. Then too, we know that the suffering a believer endures because of sins is only in temporal matters, not in the eternal state, and whatever punishment is experienced will always be less than our many iniquities deserve.

Having premised these two things for the guarding and stating the truth before us, I shall now offer three or four more direct reasons why we should confess the iniquity of our fathers together with our own in our solemn humiliations.

1. We should confess the sins of our fathers as well as our own in order to better repair, if it is possible, the dishonor done unto the name of God and His holy law. As the only avenue of restoration of the glory of God open to us has to do with the explicit humiliation of our own souls, we will, therefore, render the greater glory to the name of God if, while in our confessions, we look back to the sins of our ancestors as well as recollecting our own. If our parents, in their lifetime, had injured a neighbor, I am sure that it would be accounted a very worthy action among men if we, after their death, should do what we could to right that wrong. Doubtless the great God will accept such an act of piety and duty from us toward Himself.

If we have suffered because our fathers have sinned against God, and who has not, should we not say so before Him? What better reverence can we show unto our Father in heaven while we go backward, like the blushing sons of Noah, drawing a covering over our earthly parents' nakedness? And while we will not look upon that nakedness, yet we know and are concerned that it lies exposed. To whom do we publish it? To God! And why? That He may be glorified! Where then is the trespass on filial piety by this act of devotion and worship? Even if this is hard on the names of the deceased, what is their honor in comparison with the honor of the eternal God?

In confessing the sins of our Fathers we adore the God of our Fathers and in effect we do but give Him the glory of that relationship. If He is our fathers' God, it is our duty to exalt Him, and we do as truly exalt Him in our penitent confessions as in our thankful praises. It was Ezra the priest who said, "Ye have transgressed, and have taken strange wives, to increase the trespass of Israel. Now therefore make confession unto the Lord God of your fathers..." (Ezra 10:10,11). Can we remember Him as our Fathers' God in our confessions and never bring our fathers' sins into those confessions? Where then is His honor, and where is His fear as the Lord God of our fathers?

2. It becomes us to confess the sins of our fathers with our own, to show our impartiality in the hatred of sin, that we grieve and mourn for it because it is sin, because it is contrary to God and abhorred by Him, and that without any respect of persons. Sin is the same in itself and the same in the sight of God, no matter who the sinner is. Therefore, whether it be our sin or their sin, it is equally to be repented of by us as being against God. "Do not I hate them, O Lord, that hate Thee? and am not I grieved with those that rise up against thee?" (Psalm 139:21). Such a sincere and upright detestation of sin ought to characterize all of us equally.

Some can freely enough fault sin in those that are not related to them, but oh, how they cover and excuse it when it occurs in their own household. Such duplicity of conduct brings the most vocal protestations against sin under a just suspicion in anyone. The hatred of sin which God requires in us must be impartial because it is based on the honor of God. Those that justify sin in relatives and close friends which they condemn in others demonstrate their great distance from a right understanding and practice of this doctrine.

   3. It is just for a wicked posterity to join the sins of their ancestors with their own in their confessions because they are actually partakers with them in their iniquity. Indeed, this is too much the course of this world in the several generations of it. Posterity learns and retains the vices of their ancestors. As one generation corrupts itself, it is a pretty sure way to make the next generation even worse. It is only with great difficulty that a people are brought to reform the errors of their predecessors which they are educated in and suck in with their mother's milk. So Israel's apostasy grew on with each succeeding generation after the death of Joshua, and again after the reigns of David and Solomon. "All that generation were gathered unto their fathers: and there arose another generation after them, which knew not the Lord, nor yet the works which He had done for Israel" (Judges 2:10). And the next generation after them "returned, and corrupted themselves more than their fathers..." (verse 19).

   Fortunately it is possible for the prophet to describe the happy case of a particular son that "seeth all his father's sins which he hath done, and considereth, and doeth not such like" (Ezekiel 18:14). By God's grace this is sometimes the case, and to God be the praise whenever it is so. But the contrary is usually the case with a degenerate people. Posterity inherits their fathers' manners and are often fixed in evil customs by the practice and examples of ancestors. They sometimes even receive their errors with reverence.

   Now if the people of our age retain the evils of the last generation and carry impiety to a greater length than it was carried before our time, have we not made our fathers' sins our own, and does not our conduct prove this? It is as our Saviour said to the Jews in His time, "Truly ye bear witness that ye allow the deeds of your fathers: for they indeed killed them, and ye build their sepulchers" (Luke 11:48). That is, they treated the prophets in their day just as their fathers had done long before; they were impenitent and obstinate in sin just as their fathers had been under the ministry of former prophets; they were of the same persecuting spirit as their fathers; thus their fathers' sin was theirs, and both were to be confessed in the same breath.

   It was part of the folly of the Pharisees and an evidence of their hypocrisy that they could confess their fathers' persecution of the prophets and not discern their own. The error of sin may seem less if we confess it as our own fault and not as the fault of our ancestors, but if our confessions are to be perfect we must omit neither. I remind you that the martyr Stephen made confession for the Jewish rulers, since they would not do it for themselves, "Ye stiffnecked and uncircumcised in heart and ears, ye do always resist the Holy Ghost: as your fathers did, so do ye. Which of the prophets have not your fathers persecuted? and they have slain them which shewed before of the coming of the Just One; of whom ye have been now the betrayers and murderers" (Acts 7:51,52).

4. Confessing the sins of our fathers with our own may have special influence in keeping us from them or in convincing us of them and it may make us more zealous in reforming and amending them, that the wrath of God may be turned away from us.

Confessing the sins of our fathers may keep us from them. If we have not fallen into their sins already we may not, for there is scarcely a more effectual way to prevent sin than to maintain a sincere penitential confession of it which binds the soul not to do it. "And be not ye like your fathers, and like your brethren, which trespassed against the Lord God of their fathers, who therefore gave them up to desolation, as ye see. Now be ye not stiffnecked, as your fathers were, but yield yourselves unto the Lord..." (2 Chronicles 30:7,8).

Confessing the sins of our fathers must surely all the more convince us of and humble us for our own sins, especially if we have sinned after the similitude of the sins of our fathers which we confess. It must leave us self-judged and condemned. Our own lips do then fall upon us and our own tongue rises in judgment. The guilt of a people is greatly aggravated, and the offence of God rises exceedingly, when the sins of ancestors are retained. People may not be ready to apprehend this, but God desires all of us to be convinced of it. "And it shall come to pass, when thou shalt shew this people all these words, and they shall say unto thee, Wherefore hath the Lord pronounced all this great evil against us? or what is our iniquity? or what is our sin that we have committed against the Lord our God? Then shalt thou say unto them, Because your fathers have forsaken Me, saith the Lord, and have walked after other gods, and have served them, and have worshiped them, and have forsaken Me, and have not kept My law; And ye have done worse than your fathers; for, behold, ye walk every one after the imagination of his evil heart..." (Jeremiah 16:10-12). If this will not convince a people, what can? "Even from the days of your fathers ye are gone away from mine ordinances, and have not kept them" (Malachi 3:7). Antiquity, usage, and long custom is so far from extenuating the apostasy that it aggravates it. "Fill ye up then the measure of your fathers" (Matthew 23:32).

If we are convinced of and humbled for the sins of our fathers found among ourselves, we shall reform and forsake them as well as confess them. It was for this purpose that Hezekiah gathered the priests and Levites together and said unto them, "Our fathers have trespassed, and done that which was evil in the eyes of the Lord our God, and have forsaken Him, and have turned away their faces from the habitation of the Lord, and turned their backs... Now it is in mine heart to make a covenant with the Lord God of Israel, that His fierce wrath may turn away from us" (2 Chronicles 29:6,10).

Thankfully, God will turn away His wrath from and mercifully pardon a people who penitently confess and reform their own and their fathers' sins. But on the other hand, it is absolutely certain that a people that persists impenitently in their fathers' sins heaps up guilt and treasures up wrath from generation to generation until at last they bring down fearful destructions on themselves. "I will not keep silence, but will recompense, even recompense into their bosom, your iniquities, and the iniquities of your fathers together, saith the Lord, which have burned incense upon the mountains, and blasphemed Me upon the hills: therefore will I measure their former work into their bosom" (Isaiah 65:6,7). Very pathetic are the biblical expostulations to this purpose, "Therefore now thus saith the Lord, the God of hosts, the God of Israel; Wherefore commit ye this great evil against your souls, to cut off from you man and woman, child and suckling, out of Judah, to leave you none to remain?" (Jeremiah 44:7). "Have ye forgotten the wickedness of your fathers, and the wicked-ness of the kings of Judah, and the wickedness of their wives, and your own wickedness, and the wickedness of your wives, which they have committed in the land of Judah, and in the streets of Jerusalem? They are not humbled even unto this day, neither have they feared, nor walked in My law, nor in My statutes, that I set before you and before your fathers" (verses 9,10). And again, "Are ye polluted after the manner of your fathers? And commit ye whoredoms after their abominations?.... As I live, saith the Lord God, surely with a mighty hand, and with a stretched out arm, and with fury poured out, will I rule over you.... Like as I pleaded with your fathers in the wilderness of the land of Egypt, so will I plead with you, saith the Lord God" (Ezekiel 20:30,33,36).

The entail of wrath is certainly cut off if a people repents of and reforms concerning the sins of their fathers and do not relapse into them or allow any like provocations of their own. King Josiah would have saved Judah from ruin, despite all their earlier apostasies and impenitence, if his people would have done and been like him. He rent his clothes when he heard the words of the Book of the Law and cried out,"Great is the wrath of the Lord that is kindled against us, because our fathers have not hearkened unto the words of this book, to do according unto all that which is written concerning us" (2 Kings 22:13). Whereupon he sent and gathered unto him all the elders of Judah and of Jerusalem and went with them in a Solemn Assembly into the House of the Lord and there caused to be read in their hearing all the words of the Book of the Covenant. The King then and there publicly covenanted before the Lord to walk after God and to keep His commandments and His testimonies and His statutes with all their hearts and with all their souls. And all the people stood in ratification of the Covenant, declaring their consent to it and binding themselves to keep it. Had they actually kept this Covenant, Jerusalem's destruction would not have come so soon thereafter (2 Kings 23:1-3).

These are some of the great reasons why a people, in confessing their own iniquity, should confess also the sins of their fathers. I will conclude with a few proper inferences from the premises advanced.

III. THE APPLICATION.

USE ONE. Hence I infer that in our conduct and actions we should always consider that we act for posterity. The influence of our principles and practices reaches to them. Therefore, when we are regulating our own behavior, we should by no means limit our thoughts merely to ourselves and our own times. If we of this age are wicked, we hurt not only the present but ages to come. Not only will those who are now alive see our ill example, but those too who are not yet born may be much prejudiced against holiness by our ill conduct. On the other hand, if we are virtuous and religious, we serve not only our own generation but those that come after us and perhaps many generations to come. For this reason and in view of this, let us desire so to live that posterity may not be the worse because of us but the better, that they may not be miserable through our fault and come to curse us, but that our memory may be dear and precious, venerable and blessed to them. Let us not live so that our children's children are ashamed of us and remember us only in their confessions and abasements, but in such a way that at times they acknowledge us with reverence and esteem, to the glory of God. Let us live so that our posterity is able to join the Psalmist in saying, "Our fathers trusted in Thee: they trusted, and Thou didst deliver them. They cried unto Thee, and were delivered: they trusted in Thee, and were not confounded" (Psalm 22:4-5).

USE TWO. If we ought to confess the sins of our fathers, then pious fathers should bewail the sins and degeneracy of their children and be afflicted and abased before God in the prospect and fear thereof. This is a very natural grief to holy hearts, and alas, too commonly there is occasion given for it. The fear of this gives a very painful concern to those that bear us, and if they live to see it, it brings down their grey hairs with sorrow to the grave. Like Eli of old, they sit trembling for the Ark of God in the hands of their ungodly offspring. They tremble for their sons, to think what will become of them, but they tremble much more for the name and honor of God that suffers by them and which is infinitely more precious to them than the lives of their own children.

In this spirit, faithful Moses took sorrowful leave of Israel, knowing of their past sins and foreseeing those to come. He even confessed and bewailed them before those were born that committed them saying, "For I know thy rebellion, and thy stiff neck: behold, while I am yet alive with you this day, ye have been rebellious against the Lord; and how much more after my death? Gather unto me all the elders of your tribes, and your officers, that I may speak these words in their ears, and call heaven and earth to record against them. For I know that after my death ye will utterly corrupt yourselves, and turn aside from the way which I have commanded you; and evil will befall you in the latter days; because ye will do evil in the sight of the Lord, to provoke Him to anger through the work of your hands" (Deuteronomy 31:27-29).

USE THREE. If we should confess the sins of those who have gone before us, then whatever has been amiss in our fathers we should reform. I have no particular accusation to bring against the fathers of our country whose memory is blessed with us even though they themselves were far from pretending to perfection. They were, however, men subject to passions and errors like us. While we venerate their devotion and ought to imitate their virtues, we should take care not to be misled by their example in anything in which they were amiss, receiving it by tradition from them. We would do well to compare ourselves with them, however, for the generation that has risen in their place is a more mixed people who act more on worldly views, maxims, and customs than they did.

If in the beginning of the country they founded their churches in any place on too narrow a bottom and in too much independence one from another, their posterity has done well to enlarge the foundations. Any who call this apostasy are to be pitied. Certainly at the present moment we have too many unbaptized persons among us who grieve us deeply by neglecting so frequently the Lord's Table. If there are any customs in our churches which are derived from our ancestors whereby terms of admission of persons to the Lord's Table are imposed which Christ has not imposed in the New Testament, such impositions ought to be laid aside. They are justly to be condemned, especially in us, because we are the very people who complain of impositions in other communions, and our fathers fled their native lands because of these very impositions.

There was a custom among us whereby communion in our churches was made a test for the enjoyment of civil privileges in the state. This was in violation of the natural rights of men and the legal rights of English men whose rights exist without respect to one Church state and communion or another. We did well long ago to abolish such corrupt and persecuting maxims which are a mischief to any free people and would have been a scandal for any communion of Christians to retain.

There were laws enacted of old among our fathers which carried too much of the spirit of cruelty and persecution. Judgments were given, and executions were accomplished according to these harsh laws. We ought to be greatly humbled for any such errors of our fathers and confess them to have been sinful in these things. Blessed be God, a more catholic spirit of charity now distinguishes us.

If there ever was any grounds among our fathers for that gross accusation which has been made by some against them, which I am ready to believe was a slander and calumny unjustly cast upon their memory because I have heard the same accusations made most unjustly in some particular cases against our judges now alive, if there has been even partiality in doing justice and judgment out of respect to persons because of our own communion or way of worship, God forbid that the least of this leaven or tincture should be found among us now.

If any of our fathers ever dealt proudly in censuring and judging others that differed from them in modes of worship, let us, their posterity, the rather be clothed with humility, meekness, and charity, preserving truth and holiness with the laudable zeal of our predecessors.

If we and our fathers before us have been guilty of negligence in evangelizing the heathen as we might have done, or if the funds for that service might have been more faithfully and wisely applied than they sometimes have been, (which also has been often said to our dishonor), I am sure that those concerned in that affair, as well as all of us in our several stations, should be quickened to consider what the honor of God and compassion for souls calls for at our hands.

Finally, if any of our fathers may have sometimes seemed too strict in judging others for lawful liberties, we must confess this sin. But at the same time we must realize that the easy pardon and license to evil of our own day is the graver sin. They instructed us better both by precept and example, and to their praise be it spoken. We never received the immoral practices of the present generation from them. They never taught us to be profane, disobedient to parents, dishonest in our dealings, unclean, false, selfish, covetous, and worldly.

USE FOUR. If we should be ready to confess the sins of our fathers, then whatever was good and worthy in them should also be remembered, appreciated, praised, and imitated by us. Our reverence to God and man commands this of us, and it is one instance of our obedience to the first commandment with promise, "Honor thy father and thy mother: that thy days may be long upon the land which the Lord thy God giveth thee" (Exodus 20:12). "If there be any virtue, and if there be any praise, think on these things" (Philippians 4:8).

Our fathers had their infirmities no doubt, but they had their virtues and integrity. They were a company of brave and honest men. Not many wise men after the flesh, not many mighty and noble were among them, but neither were there many of base and vile outward estate or character. They were, as a body, serious and godly Christians. They were men who were rich in faith and heirs of a better world. For that better country they left their pleasant native land, and in removing into a wilderness, mostly for religion's sake, they declared plainly that they sought it.

They came over on a most worthy design, with the noblest motives, and with the best intentions. Pure and undefiled religion was their proposed end and their support in all their undertakings. Their first care was to plant churches rather than towns. As soon as they saw towns increase, they established schools and colleges in order that they might leave a learned ministry and a religion of power to their posterity. Government and good order was as much their care as liberty of conscience. They did not use liberty for an occasion of the flesh but stood fast in that liberty wherewith Christ had made them free.

They have left us their testimony for the purity of God's worship according to the institution of Scriptures and without the additions of men. They stood against will-worship, superstition, formality, and hypocrisy. They have instructed us in the strict observation of the Sabbath which has been the honor of these churches. Its decay is a distinct mark of our real apostasy from vital religion. They commended to us strict family government and the good education of our children which was for our happiness under their wise and faithful care. They taught us by word and life that the grace of God which brings us salvation demands that we deny ungodliness and worldly lusts and live soberly, righteously, and godly in this present world (Titus 2:12). They sought to teach us how to honor all men, to love the brotherhood, to fear God, and to honor the king (1 Peter 2:17). They have left us the noble example of a public spirit to love our country, to act for posterity, and to seek the good of all future generations.

Such a sort of men were the founders and fathers of our country. They were men of whom the world was not worthy. Though they were plain men, they were not wanting in wisdom, learning, prudence, integrity, and true devotion. I must also mention the great stock of prayers they laid up for us, which have brought down many blessings on us already, and we hope will bring yet many more in the generations yet to come.

Nor may I omit to mention how much humanity and a truly Christian zeal they had at heart and with which they labored for the civilizing, the instruction, and the conversion of the natives. The names of Eliot and Mayhew are made immortal among us on this account and their eternal rest is glorious. They served the part of apostles and evangelists with a truly primitive spirit. The government treated the barbarous people with many courtesies and obligations. Unknown labors were used and pains taken with them to acquaint them with the ways of God. The Bible was translated into the Indian tongues with vast pains and diligence and printed for their use and distributed among them. They were preached to, they were argued with and entreated. An Indian college was built and some of their children, with much difficulty, were put in school. One or two of their number have been brought up at the college but tragically died there.

Although the success of their labors among the Indians has not answered the pious hopes, intentions, and prayers of our fathers, their piety is nevertheless conspicuous, and their reward is with God even though but few of the savages have been gathered. Although some may think they might have utilized wiser methods, they did what appeared to them best for the Indian people and what probably cost them more expense and fatigue than the other proposed methods would have. Although some parts were neglected and some of our own plantations were settled in too heathenish a manner, nevertheless if much of the Spirit and presence of God had not been with our fathers, they would never have done half the great and good things they did.

I have given here but a small tribute to their memory with the hope it will excite our emulation.

USE FIVE. If we should consider the faults of our ancestors to confess them, how much more ought we to bewail our own sins and the sins of our own day.

1. We ought to lament our own personal transgressions and guilt. Without these, the sins of others gone before us, would not hurt us much.

The soul that sins shall die: the son shall not bear the iniquity of his father if he considereth and doeth not the like (Ezekiel 18:14ff).

Lay your hand then upon your heart and smite there for your own abominations. For these God will judge you in the last day. The thing He looks for from you today is that you feel the plague of your own heart and so spread forth your hands in supplications for mercy toward His house. What right would any of us have to confess the sins of others if we are not first affected with our own? "Thou hypocrite, first cast out the beam out of thine own eye; and then shalt thou see clearly to cast out the mote out of thy brother's eye" (Matthew 7:5). Repent of your own wickedness and say, "What have I done? When I speak of sinners, am I not the chief? Where is my own repentance this day before the Lord? Am I humbled for my own sins? Am I bewailing the awful things I have done? Have I reformed? Do I keep myself from my own iniquity? Do I fervently pray, "Wash me thoroughly from my iniquity, and cleanse me from my sin. For I acknowledge my transgressions: and my sin is ever before me" (Psalm 51:2,3).

2. Let us lay to heart the sins of our day and time, whether they are those of our own New-England or of our nation. The sins of New-England must concern us gravely. We are sadly on the decay as to serious piety and vital religion. We have lost our first love, life, and zeal. Where is the Christian affection of our fathers? Where is their spirit of devotion? Where is their sobriety and temperance? Where is their godliness and honesty? Sensuality, worldliness and pride are grown up in the place of these virtues. Profaneness, lukewarmness, hypocrisy, selfishness, and unrighteousness hold the land in their grip. Our fathers would be ready to disown us on these accounts, and we ought to realize how they will rise up in the judgment against us and condemn us for our backslidings. Let us consider from whence we have fallen and repent.

Our work today is to bewail the present degeneracy and corruption of our hearts. We must show the people their transgressions and the house of Jacob their sins (Isaiah 58:1). Let us, therefore, bring our peace-offerings just as repenting Judah did and make confession to the Lord God of our fathers (2 Chronicles 30:22). Let us lay to heart the sins of our nation, the place of our fathers' sepulchers. Here a dismal scene opens to our view of such iniquity as I hope is not yet known among us here in this section of the nation. However it will threaten us soon if it is not reformed there. For besides formality of religion, sensuality, pro-faneness, injustice, worldliness, pride, covetousness whereof we have our share there are yet greater, glaring abominations there such as atheism, infidelity, and open contempt of all that is not sacred, not only expressed in dissoluteness of life but also in public conversation and in writings.

The venerable name of religion and of the church is made a pretence for the worst of villainies, for all manner of uncharitableness and unnatural oppression of the pious and peaceable, for slanderous lies and falsehoods, for divisive hatred and animosities, for bribery and perjury, for disloyalty and perfidy, for tumults, mutinies and rebellions, for all kinds of ingratitude to God and therefore against the king and our country.

The perilous times have arrived when men have become "lovers of their own selves," sacrificing the public to their own private gains and ambition, "covetous, boasters, proud, blasphemers, disobedient to parents, unthankful, unholy, without natural affection, trucebreakers, false accusers, incontinent, fierce, despisers of those that are good, traitors, heady, highminded, lovers of pleasures more than lovers of God; having a form of godliness, but denying the power thereof" (2 Timothy 3:1-5). And here I am speaking not of an occasional individual but of multitudes of persons. "From such turn away," commands the Apostle Paul. I pray God that He will purge the court, nobility, and magistracy of this leprous-like plague and not the court only but also the Church and the clergy, the universities and academies, as well as the camp and the fleet; that the spirit of parties and factions may not increase unto more ungodliness and to all barbarities.

Ah, calamitous day whereunto we are fallen and into which the sins of an infatuated age has brought us. "Here this, ye old men, and give ear, all ye inhabitants of the land. Hath this been in your days, or even in the days of your fathers?" (Joel 1:2). "For they are a nation void of counsel, neither is there any understanding in them!" (Deuteronomy 32:28). They are as if "their Rock had sold them, and the Lord had shut them up" (verse 30). "O that they were wise, that they understood this, that they would consider their latter end!" (verse 29). Oh, that at least when their judge comes, there might be some faith and charity found in the land.

Doubtless there is some faith among professing Christians of every denomination but oh, how wanting it is among men in every part of the nation. However, I am very glad that I can do our brethren in Great Britain and this country the honor and the justice of saying that in this time of public treacheries, perjuries, rebellions and treasons, not a dog can wag his tongue to charge us with disloyalty, unresponsiveness to duty, disrespect to government, or want of zeal and fidelity to the protestant succession, the peaceful reign of the King, and the true interests of the nation as to its civil and religious rights.

Indeed, it is an amazing thing, and one would think incredible, that any

Protestant or member of the Church of England should have joined the late rebellions against his present Majesty, to set up a Popish pretender whom they have so often and justly abjured. It is as the Right Reverend, the Bishops excellently say in their late pious and loyal declaration, it is "so vile and detestable a thing as may justly make them odious to God and man. And at the same time to pretend a zeal for the Church of England is such an imposition on the common sense of mankind, that nothing even in Popery itself can be more absurd. And nothing but an infatuation from God, justly inflicted for our sins can suffer it to pass upon the nation." Wherefore, in the name of God, those most Reverend persons call upon the nation to "humble themselves before God for the great and crying sins of the nation; for that spirit of infidelity and libertinism; of unthankfulness for the mercies of the Gospel; of formality and hypocrisy, of strife and envy, of hatred and animosity, which are so rife in it, and generally the forerunners of the destruction of any people."

Blessed be God for this seasonable and true testimony of these fathers in the Church. They have said what the body of the dissenting ministers have long thought and said, often weeping, but in vain. The atheistical and immoral part of the nation are the source of its miseries and dangers. God heal its sins and breaches! God make the Bishops of the Church its healers! And God grant that we may see the things of our peace before they are hid from our eyes.

I pray God that the day may come when we may no longer hate to be reformed and that the King may live to be the glorious instrument in the hand of God of our reformation in every respect. So may he be blessed and his throne established before the Lord for ever.

CHAPTER NINE

God's Face
Set Against an
Incorrigible People

By
Thomas Foxcroft

Thomas Foxcroft, 1696-1769

Thomas Foxcroft was born at Cambridge, Massachusetts, in 1696. His father was Colonel Francis Foxcroft. By 1714 Thomas had graduated from Harvard College. His father desired him to enter the Episcopal ministry, but after study and consultation, Thomas was brought to the conviction that he was best suited as a Congregationalist. He pursued theological studies and was licensed to preach in the Congregational Churches. He received a call from the First Church in Boston in 1717 and was ordained as a colleague with Rev. Benjamin Wadsworth.

Harvard called Wadsworth to its Presidency in 1725, and Foxcroft was sole pastor until joined by Charles Chauncy in 1727. Foxcroft was a man of deep piety, a warm friend of revival, and a man of decided Reformed convictions, while Chauncy was a man with an almost violent anti-revival spirit who in later life was an avowed Universalist. Despite the wide differences between them, the two colleagues appear to have remained on cordial terms, working together with a surprising degree of harmony. Having come to his Congregational convictions after much thought and consideration, Foxcroft took a strong anti-Episcopal position during the Episcopalian controversy that divided New-England and wrote a vigorous pamphlet on "The Ruling and Ordaining Power of Congregational Bishops, or Presbyters, Defended," which was published in 1724, the same year in which this fast day sermon was preached.

During the days of the Great Awakening, Foxcroft was one of its most able supporters. A warm friend of Whitefield's, he published two pamphlets in his defence: "Some Seasonable Thoughts on Evangelic Preaching; Its Nature, Usefulness and Obligation. A Sermon Deliver'd (in Part) at the Old-Church-Lecture in Boston, Thursday, Oct. 23, 1740. To a Numerous Audience. Occasion'd by the Late Visit, and Uncommon Labours, in Daily and Powerful Preaching, of the Rev. Mr. Whitefield, Whose Praise is in the Gospel, Throughout all the Churches," and "An Apology in Behalf of the Rev. Mr. Whitefield; Offering a Fair Solution of Certain Difficulties, Objected Against Some Parts of His Publick Conduct, in Point of Moral Honesty, and Uniformity with His Own Subscriptions and Ordination Vows: as the Said Exceptions are Set Forth in a Late Pamphlet, Intitled, A Letter to the Rev. Mr. George Whitefield, Publickly Calling Upon Him to Vindicate His Conduct or Confess His Faults."

Foxcroft suffered a paralytic shock in 1736. As the years advanced it became increasingly difficult for him to minister effectively. For several years before his death in 1769, he was scarcely able to serve at all. In Foxcroft's funeral sermon Chauncy said, "He was a real good Christian; a partaker of the Holy Ghost; uniform in his walk with God in the way of His commandments, though, instead of trusting that he was righteous in the eye of a strict law, he accounted himself an unprofitable servant; fixing his dependence not on his own worthiness, not on any work of righteousness which he had done, but on the mercy of God and the atoning blood and perfect righteousness of Jesus Christ. His writings evince a clearness of perception, copiousness of invention, liveliness of imagination, and soundness of judgment. They bear testimony also of his unfeigned piety."

One additional publication of Foxcroft, published in Boston in 1747, is worthy of notice; "A Seasonable Memento for New Year's Day. A Sermon Preached at the Old Church Lecture in Boston, on Thursday, January 1, 1746. Wherein the Most Important Duty of Remembering the Years of the Right Hand of the Most High, and Commemorating God's Wonderful Works of Creation, Redemption, and Providence, Is Inculcated; and Recommended as Good Employment for the First Day of the Year in Particular."

First published as *God's Face Set Against an Incorrigible People, A Sermon Preached at the Public Lecture in Boston, Thursday, July 30, 1724 By Thomas Foxcroft One of the Pastors of the Old Church in Boston, With a Preface by the Reverend Mr. Cooper.* Boston: Printed by B. Green, for John Eliot, at his Shop at the South End of the Town, 1724.

God's Face Set Against An Incorrigible People

"They are not humbled even unto this day, neither have they feared, nor walked in My law, nor in My statutes, that I set before you and before your fathers. Therefore thus saith the Lord of hosts, the God of Israel; Behold, I will set My face against you for evil, and to cut off all Judah."
Jeremiah 44:10,11.

Jeremiah was called early to be a teacher in Israel and an inspired prophet. He continued in his work for a long time, from the days of good Josiah through all the succeeding wicked reigns down to the Jewish captivity and even for some time after that. He is commonly styled "The Weeping Prophet." He was a mournful spectator of the sins and sorrows of the Jewish nation, then the only professing people of God. In his Book of Prophecies we have many melancholy chapters concerning them. We have also Jeremiah's Book of Lamentations which one writer has called "An Elegy upon Jerusalem's Funeral." He was sent to warn backsliding Israel of the desolating judgments that were coming on them unless they repented. Tragically, he lived to see a great part of his sad predictions fulfilled, for the people did not turn at his reproof.

As became a faithful prophet, a lover of Zion, and one jealous for the Lord, Jeremiah set himself to bear testimony against the growing degeneracies of that unhappy day and to reform the corruptions of the times. How painful were his endeavors! How fervent his applications to conscience! How impartial his rebukes! How loud and plain his warnings! How pathetic and moving his exhortations! He was a wise, zealous, and powerful preacher. And yet, oh sorrowful thought, he seems to have had but very little success in his ministry. He lived among a people that hated to be reformed and that would not be healed. Nevertheless the prophet, in preaching the Word, was instant in season and out of season. He rebuked, reproved, and exhorted with all longsuffering and doctrine (2 Timothy 4:2). After Jerusalem was made desolate and the body of the nation carried captive to Babylon, he remained prophesying to the small remnant that were still allowed to abide in the land. When this ungrateful, wicked remnant deserted their own land and compelled Jeremiah to go down with them into Egypt, he still attended the duties of a prophet and did the best service he could for his countrymen there.

This forty-fourth chapter of his book, out of which I have taken my text, begins with an awakening sermon which Jeremiah preached to the Jews in Egypt wherein the prophet first reminds them of those desolating judgments that were brought upon Jerusalem and upon themselves. He then observes to them the procuring cause of their miseries—their own wickedness. In the next place, he puts them in mind of the warnings they had been given and the pains that God had taken with them to bring them to repentance; he upbraids them with their former obstinacy in their own land and with the fatal consequences of it; he reproves them for their continued impenitence and repeated idolatries now in Egypt and expostulates with them concerning the unreasonableness and madness of their conduct; he finally threatens them with a total destruction for their incurable stubbornness and impenitence.

My text takes in part of the last two issues, for in it we have a charge and a threat.

First, there is a charge against the Jews: "They are not humbled, even unto this day, neither have they feared nor walked in My Law." They were not humbled for their sins as they ought to have been and as God expected. They were not afraid of His judgments neither did they turn from their evil ways unto God's testimonies, notwithstanding all the methods used with them to that end. This is the charge advanced against them, the complaint sighed over them.

Then a threatening follows: "Therefore thus saith the Lord of Hosts, the God of Israel: Behold I will set My face against you for evil." They had set their faces to go into the land of Egypt in a daring contradiction to the revealed will of God and had hardened their faces against God in ways of rebellion and wickedness. God, therefore, will also set His face against them in ways of judgment, to punish them for all their iniquities.

Whatever may be further needed for the explanation of the words of the text may be given in speaking of the doctrines that I design to speak upon, which are:

1. God expects a people under His corrective hand to humble themselves, fear, and turn their feet unto His testimonies and to walk in His Law.

2. It is sometimes the sad case of a people under divine rebukes that they continue, notwithstanding all, unhumbled and unreformed.

3. God observes a people's conduct under His judgments and marks against them all their obstinacy and impenitence.

4. When a people are finally irreclaimable, God will set His face against them for evil.

I. GOD EXPECTS A PEOPLE UNDER HIS CORRECTIVE HAND TO HUMBLE THEMSELVES, FEAR, AND TURN THEIR FEET UNTO HIS TESTIMONIES AND TO WALK IN HIS LAW.

Here there are three comprehensive articles of duty which may all be profitably expounded.

1. A people under God's judgments should humble themselves.

The complaint in our text, "They have not humbled themselves," shows God's expectation of it from them and this must be founded upon the strongest reasons and the demands of His own Law. The call of God to an afflicted people runs in such languages as, "Be afflicted, and mourn, and weep: let your laughter be turned to mourning, and your joy to heaviness. Humble yourselves in the sight of the Lord" (James 4:9,10). It is expressly required by many divine precepts that we humble ourselves under God's judgments. This is described as our indispensable duty. The very nature and reason of things requires this at our hands. The calamities we are groaning under loudly preach to us of the power of God, of His holiness and justice, His displeasure at us for our sins, all of which are grounds and motives for humiliation. Hence it is but our reasonable service and justly complies with our state and circumstances. Moreover, humbling ourselves will be for our own safety and interest. If we are humbled, it will dispose us to seek God and to engage in a saving, thorough, and lasting work of reformation and so will give us ground to hope for and prepare to receive the salvation which God has promised to a reforming and repenting people. God will not forget the humble. The poor of the flock shall trust in Him. They shall trust in Him and lie down in safety. They shall rejoice in the Holy One of Israel and shall tread down the haughty under their feet.

When once a people are brought to humble themselves under God's judgments, it bodes deliverance and presages the return of good times. This accords with that word of the Apostle, "Be clothed with humility: for God resisteth the proud, and giveth grace to the humble. Humble yourselves therefore under the mighty hand of God, that He may exalt you in due time: Casting all your care upon Him; for He careth for you" (1 Peter 5:5-7).

But here the inquiry arises, "What is that humbling of themselves which God expects from a people under the rebukes of His providence?" To this I answer, it implies something inward in the heart and something external in the life.

First, it may be considered as internal in the heart and so it implies many gracious dispositions and actings of the soul.

Indeed, it is this inward humiliation that is principally intended, for God looks chiefly at the heart. "The sacrifices of God are a broken spirit: a broken and a contrite heart..."(Psalm 51:17). "To this man will I look," saith the Lord, "even to him that is poor and of a contrite spirit, and trembleth at My word." (Isaiah 66:2). "The Lord seeth not as man seeth; for man looketh on the outward appearance, but the Lord looketh on the heart" (1 Samuel 16:7). If we are not of a humble spirit then we have not truly humbled ourselves in the sight of God. To humble ourselves outwardly and in the sight of men only will not suffice; we must humble ourselves in the sight of God also. The heart must be humbled, and this includes a variety of religious frames and devout affections which I shall endeavour to sum up in the following statements:

It implies, as the foundation of it, a deep conviction of guilt, the fruit of a thorough self-examination and impartial self-judging. Under the judgments of God it becomes a people to judge themselves. We should search our hearts and try our ways to find out the provoking evils that are the unhappy grounds of God's controversy with us. God expects to hear every one of us inquiring, "What have I done?" (Jeremiah 8:6). We must be very accurate, impartial, and thorough in this inquiry, willing to know the worst about ourselves and the totality of our guilt. Wherein we have done iniquity, our hearts must condemn us, and our consciences must accuses us, charging upon us our sins and reading our doom to us from the Law of God.

Being thus convinced and condemned in ourselves, there must be a deep self-abasement, shame, remorse of conscience, and holy indignation at ourselves and a humble submission to the will of God.

There must be a godly shame and self-abasement under the sense of our guilt and vileness. As becomes self-condemned malefactors, we must be filled with shame and confusion at the remembrance of our faults. When we remember our evil ways and our doings that have not been good, we must loathe ourselves in our own sight for our iniquities and for our abominations and be ashamed, yea even confounded for our own ways (Ezekiel 36:31,32). We must not rest in the visible signs and outward expressions of shame, but the inner man must be suitably affected and abased, the heart must blush, pride within must be mortified, and every self-exalting thought subdued. Knowing every man the plague of his own heart, we must be vile in our own eyes. We must join Job in saying, "I abhor myself, and repent in dust and ashes" (Job 42:6). Like Asaph we must say, "So foolish was I, and ignorant: I was as a beast before Thee"

(Psalm 73:22). With Ezra, we must fall down on our knees and say, "O my God, I am ashamed and blush to lift up my face to Thee, my God: for our iniquities are increased over our head, and our trespass is grown up unto the heavens" (Ezra 9:5,6).

Moreover, there must also be a godly sorrow and remorse of conscience with a spirit of holy mourning and true contrition of heart. This is required! "Know therefore and see that it is an evil thing and bitter, that thou hast forsaken the Lord thy God" (Jeremiah 2:19). And as naturally follows, we should "make... mourning, as for an only son, most bitter lamentation" (Jeremiah 6:26). The Apostle Peter, after the denial of his Lord, is an illustration of this. Of him it is said, "He went out, and wept bitterly" (Matthew 26:75). The call of God to every one of us is, in the words of our Saviour, "Go, and do thou likewise" (Luke 10:37). It was prophesied of some, "They... shall be... like doves of the valleys, all of them mourning, everyone for his iniquity" (Ezekiel 7:16). In describing the Corinthians the Apostle said, "I rejoice, not that ye were made sorry, but that ye sorrowed to repentance: for ye were made sorry after a godly manner... For godly sorrow worketh repentance to salvation not to be repented of" (2 Corinthians 7:8-10).

Such penitent mourners must we be if we would prove ourselves truly humbled. Our sorrow must be inward and unfeigned. We must be pricked at the heart, our spirits wounded, our souls melted into penitential tears. "Now saith the Lord, turn ye even to Me with all your heart, and with fasting, and with weeping, and with mourning; and rend your heart and not your garments" (Joel 2:12,13). We must afflict our souls. Our hearts must be rent and broken with a mighty sense of sin and we must be ground, as it were, to pieces with a prevailing sorrow. This should happen especially at a time when we are bewailing not only our own personal sins, but also the sins of others and of the land. Our hearts must be full indeed at a time like this. A great and deep sorrow becomes us proportionable to the grounds and occasions of grief that are before us and which are, alas, at this day very large and plentiful. Yet the mournful penitent must keep his resentments and passions within due bounds, remembering the Apostle's caution, "Lest perhaps such a one should be swallowed up with overmuch sorrow" (2 Corinthians 2:7).

As our sorrow must be hearty and deep, so it must be universal and impartial. Indeed, if it has the former qualification, it will have the latter. We must mourn after this godly sort for all our sins. We must not flatter any favorite vices while we pretend to humble ourselves for our sins. If we have grown weary of one sin or its evil effects have become grievous and irksome to us, we must not then rejoice in another that is more agreeable to our humor or appears to be more to our worldly advantage. This seems to be the manner of some. No! We must repent of all our sins without any exception. Our hearts must be broken for and broken off from our most beloved lusts. As there must be no partiality with reference to our own sins, so neither can there be any toward the sins of others. "Each," says one writer, "must mourn the sins common to all and the gross trespasses of each sort must be bewailed by every sort." "Set a mark upon the foreheads of the men that sigh and that cry for all the abominations that be done in the midst thereof" (Ezekiel 9:4).

We must bewail all the sins of our families, all the sins of the town and of the region in which we live, and all the sins of the nation to which we belong. No consideration whatsoever may bias us to tenderness in any point, or to the sparing of any particular sin and excepting it out of our lamentations. No pretended reverence to our forefathers or to the character of rulers or ministers, no regard to the interest of any sort of men or to the fashion and custom of the multitude and no fondness for a party ought to have any influence in the matter. We must not cover the sins of others any more than our own. No sinister views, no private affections, may lessen our resentment of their miscarriages or dispose us to palliate, excuse, or extenuate them. Hear in what strains the prophet Daniel bewails the public guilt, "O Lord, righteousness belongeth unto Thee, but unto us confusion of faces, as at this day; to the men of Judah, and to the inhabitants of Jerusalem, and unto all Israel that are near, and that are far off, through all the countries whither Thou hast driven them, because of their trespass that they have trespassed against Thee... to our Kings, to our princes, and to our fathers, because we have sinned against Thee" (Daniel 9:7,8).

Now in consequence of this shame and sorrow for sin, there must be an holy indignation at ourselves. We must conceive a displeasure at ourselves like the Corinthian penitents in whom the Apostle commends this self-indignation as a fruit and argument of their godly sorrow, "Behold this selfsame thing, that ye sorrowed after a godly sort, what carefulness it wrought in you, yea, what clearing of yourselves, yea, what indignation, yea, what fear, yea, what vehement desire, yea, what zeal, yea, what revenge" (2 Corinthians 7:11). If we are truly penitent, our hearts will be hot within us in resentment of our follies; a holy anger at ourselves will kindle in our breasts; and conscience will stir itself up to scourge and smite us.

Furthermore, where there is a true humiliation under God's hand, there will be a cheerful submission to His will in all the afflictive dispensations that befall us. This is made one sign and character of a true humiliation, "If then their uncircumcised hearts be humbled, and they then accept of the punishment of their iniquity: Then will I remember My covenant with Jacob..." (Leviticus 26:41,42). "It is good for a man that he bear the yoke in his youth. He sitteth alone and keepeth silence, because he hath borne it upon him. He putteth his mouth in the dust; if so be there may be hope" (Lamentations 3:27-30). "That thou mayest remember, and be confounded, and never open thy mouth any more because of thy shame, when I am pacified toward thee for all that thou hast done, saith the Lord God" (Ezekiel 16:63). We must never open our mouths in any way of murmuring or complaint. We must not harden our necks and resist God. We must not exalt ourselves against the Lord and despise His chastening or strive with our Maker as those of old of whom we read that they "say in the pride and stoutness of heart, The bricks are fallen down, but we will build with hewn stones: the sycamores are cut down, but we will change them into cedars" (Isaiah 9:9,10). May such a spirit and carriage be far from us. The temper and conduct of holy Job becomes us in all our afflictions, "Behold, I am vile; what shall I answer Thee? I will lay mine hand upon my mouth" (Job 40:4). In the same vein the Psalmist said, "I was dumb, I opened not my mouth; because Thou didst it" (Psalm 39:9).

As there must be a meek and patient submission to God under all His dealings with us, so where this is there will be a thankful notice taken of the mercies that are mixed with divine judgments and a due sense of our own unworthiness of these mercies. The humble disposition and language of our souls will be, "After all that is come upon us for our evil deeds... Thou our God hast punished us less than our iniquities deserve" (Ezra 9:13), and "I am not worthy of the least of all the mercies, and of all the truth, which Thou has showed unto Thy servant" (Genesis 32:10).

In a word, there will also be the exercise of faith and hope in God through Jesus Christ for the pardon of sin, the removal of the grounds of God's controversy with us and putting a happy end to it. The humble centurion had great faith, "Lord, I am not worthy that Thou shouldest come under my roof: but speak the word only, and my servant shall be healed" (Matthew 8:8). So did holy Job who said, "Though He slay me, yet will I trust in Him; but I will maintain my own ways before Him. He also shall be my salvation: for an hypocrite shall not come before Him" (Job 13:15,16). We read of some who said, "We have trespassed against our God, and have taken strange wives of the people of the land: yet now there is hope in Israel concerning this thing" (Ezra 10:2). We must not mourn, in any case, as those that have no hope; although we are perplexed, we are not in despair (2 Corinthians 4:8). "It is good that a man should both hope and quietly wait for the salvation of the Lord" (Lamentations 3:26). "Trust in Him at all times; ye people, pour out your heart before Him" (Psalm 62:8). God is a refuge for us through Jesus Christ. Fly for refuge to lay hold of the hope set before you. "Who is among you that feareth the Lord, that obeyeth the voice of His servant, that walketh in darkness, and hath no light? Let him trust in the name of the Lord, and stay upon his God" (Isaiah 50:10). The church of old said, "In the way of Thy judgments, O Lord, have we waited for Thee" (Isaiah 26:8). The prophet Micah wrote in the church's name, "Therefore, I will look unto the Lord; I will wait for the God of my salvation: my God will hear me. Rejoice not against me, O mine enemy: when I fall, I shall arise; when I sit in darkness, the Lord shall be a light unto me. I will bear the indignation of the Lord, because I have sinned against Him, until He plead my cause and execute judgment for me: He will bring me forth to the light, and I shall behold His righteousness" (Micah 7:7-9).

Thus I have mentioned some of those inward affections and graces which are implied in the humiliation required. We must, therefore, put on humbleness of mind. Our souls must be humbled within us. Unless we have such gracious tempers reigning in us, it may be complained of us as of him of old, "Thou... hast not humbled thine heart, though thou knewest all this... and the God in whose hand thy breath is, and whose are all thy ways, hast thou not glorified" (Daniel 5:22,23).

Second, it implies something external in the life and actions: outward expressions agreeable to our inward impressions.

Thus it implies proper acts of mortification and self-denial. There must be a kind of pious self-revenge and self-affliction for sin. We must inflict proper severities upon ourselves in a way of just correction for our follies. I do not mean here any such absurd discipline as Popish penances, the going on a pilgrimage, the macerating our flesh unreasonably or the mutilating, wounding, or whipping of our bodies. I mean treating our bodies, the instruments of sin, with something of austerity, as well as afflicting our souls by a more spiritual and rational discipline. We must labor to crucify the flesh, to mortify the members that are upon the earth, that the body of sin may be destroyed, that henceforth we may not serve sin. We must endeavor to pluck out the right eye and to cut off the right hand that offend us. We must deny ourselves and take up our cross and follow Him. We must deprive ourselves of many lawful gratifications as well as of all sinful extravagances. The Apostle commends such a conduct in the Corinthians as a fruit and argument of their true repentance, "Behold this selfsame thing, that ye sorrowed after a godly sort, what carefulness it wrought in you, yea, what clearing of yourselves, yea, what indignation, yea, what fear, yea, what vehement desire, yea, what zeal, yea, what revenge!" (2 Corinthians 7:11). They took a holy revenge on themselves for their sins by agreeable acts of discipline. We should follow their example in solemn fastings and watchings, by a daily course of abstinence in self denials and mortifications.

In a time of public judgments, if a people would humble themselves aright, it becomes them to observe many solemn days of fasting and humiliation. That is the call of God to them, "Sanctify ye a fast, call a solemn assembly, gather the elders and all the inhabitants of the land into the house of the Lord your God, and cry unto the Lord" (Joel 1:14). "Turn ye even to Me with all your heart, and with fasting, and with weeping, and with mourning" (Joel 2:12). Thus Josiah humbled himself, "Thine heart was tender, and thou didst humble thyself before God... and didst rend thy clothes, and weep before Me" (2 Chronicles 34:27). So we read of the Ninevites, "The people of Ninevah believed God, and proclaimed a fast, and put on sackcloth, from the greatest of them even to the least of them. For word came unto the King of Ninevah, and he arose from his throne, and he laid his robe from him, and covered him with sackcloth, and sat in ashes" (Jonah 3:5,6).

Besides these extraordinary mortifications, there should be more common and continued self-denials in general practice among such a people. In the day of trouble we should deny ourselves in the use of many lawful liberties, retrench our unnecessary expenses, lay aside our gallantry, clothe ourselves with humility, and be modest and lowly in our whole appearance. Surely it ill becomes a poor and afflicted people to affect gaiety and pomp in their apparel, luxury at their tables, mirth and jollity and great delicacy of living. Hear how the prophet complains of and rebukes this in God's people of old, "In that day did the Lord God of Hosts call to weeping, and to mourning, and to baldness, and to girding with sackcloth; and behold joy and gladness, slaying oxen and killing sheep, eating flesh and drinking wine" (Isaiah 22:12,13). Consider that solemn woe announced by Amos, "Woe to them that are at ease in Zion... That lie upon beds of ivory, and stretch themselves upon their couches, and eat the lambs out of the flock, and the calves out of the midst of the stall; that chant to the sound of the viol... that drink wine in bowls, and anoint themselves with the chief ornaments: but they are not grieved for the affliction of Joseph" (Amos 6:1-6).

Furthermore, the humiliation required implies a due confession of our sins to God. There must be a most hearty confession of sin, in all the instances and in all the aggravations of it. It must be an open and full acknowledgement of our offenses unto God. This is everywhere in Scripture represented as the duty of an afflicted people and the property of self-judging penitents. "If they shall confess their iniquity, and the iniquity of their fathers, with their trespass which they trespassed against Me... if then their uncircumcised hearts be humbled, and they then accept of the punishment of their iniquity: then will I remember My covenant..." (Leviticus 26:40,42). Ezra confessed, "weeping and casting himself down before the house of God" (Ezra 10:1). Daniel made confession of his sin and of the sin of his people, when he set himself to seek by prayer with fasting, for the holy mountain of his God (Daniel 9:20). We read that the children of Israel, when they assembled themselves with fasting, stood and confessed their sins and the iniquities of their fathers (Nehemiah 9:2). Thus should we confess our sins to God, and we should do it with the deepest humility and bent of mind.

Again, there must be an express justifying of God's providence in all that befalls us. Thus we read, "The princes of Israel and the king humbled themselves; and they said, The Lord is righteous" (2 Chronicles 12:6). We must acknowledge to God our utter unworthiness of the least mercy at His hands and subscribe to the justice of His proceedings with us in any punishments already inflicted or that He may see fit to bring upon us. Our humble language must be like that of people of old who said, "If Thou, Lord, shouldest mark iniquities, O Lord, who shall stand?" (Psalm 130:3). "Thou art just in all that is brought upon us; for Thou hast done right, but we have done wickedly" (Nehemiah 9:33). "O Lord God of Israel, Thou art righteous... behold, we are before Thee in our trespasses: for we cannot stand before Thee because of this" (Ezra 9:15). "O Lord, righteousness belongeth unto Thee, but unto us confusion of faces, as at this day" (Daniel 9:7).

Moreover, there must be much fervent prayer. This is the natural effect of true humiliation. We read of Manasseh, "When he was in affliction, he besought the Lord his God, and humbled himself greatly before the God of His fathers" (2 Chronicles 33:12). The Psalmist said, "I humbled my soul with fasting; and my prayer returned into mine own bosom" (Psalm 35:13). When we humble ourselves to God, we should seek His face, grieve over the continuance of His frowns, and entreat the return of His favors. We must seek reconciliation with God, casting ourselves down at His feet, crying to Him for pardoning mercy and deliverance. The direction given to us by Hosea is, "Take with you words, and turn to the Lord: say unto Him, Take away all iniquity, and receive us graciously" (Hosea 14:2). We must pray as the church of old did, "O Lord, be gracious unto us; we have waited for Thee: be Thou their arm every morning, our salvation also in the time of trouble" (Isaiah 33:2). "Look down from heaven, and behold from the habitation of Thy holiness and of Thy glory: where is Thy zeal and Thy strength, the sounding of Thy bowels, and of Thy mercies towards me? Are they restrained?" (Isaiah 63:15). "Behold, Thou art wroth; for we have sinned" (Isaiah 64:5). "But now, O Lord, Thou art our Father; we are the clay, and Thou our potter; and we all are the work of Thy hand. Be not wroth very sore, O Lord, neither remember iniquity for ever" (Isaiah 64:8,9). "O Lord God, destroy not Thy people and Thine inheritance, which Thou hast redeemed through Thy greatness... look not unto the stubbornness of this people, nor to their wickedness, nor to their sin" (Deuteronomy 9:26,27). "O Lord, though our iniquities testify against us, do Thou it for Thy name's sake: for our backslidings are many; we have sinned against Thee. O the hope of Israel, the Saviour thereof in time of trouble, why shouldest Thou be a stranger in the land, and as a wayfaring man that turneth aside to tarry for a night? Why shouldest Thou be as a man astonied, as a mighty man that cannot save? Yet Thou, O Lord, art in the midst of us, and we are called by Thy name; leave us not" (Jeremiah 14:7-9). "Hast Thou utterly rejected Judah? Hath Thy soul loathed Zion? Why hast Thou smitten us, and there is no healing for us? ... We acknowledge, O Lord, our wickedness, and the iniquity of our fathers: for we have sinned against Thee. Do not abhor us, for Thy name's sake, do not disgrace the throne of Thy glory: remember, break not Thy covenant with us. Are there any among the vanities of the Gentiles that can cause rain? ... Art not Thou He, O Lord our God? Therefore we will wait upon Thee: for Thou hast made all these things" (Jeremiah 14:19-22).

In such strains as these did the most devout and fervent of the prophets and people of God in old times call upon Him in their days of trouble. These prayers were put on record for the use and intimation of succeeding ages. "Take, my brethren, the prophets, who have spoken in the name of the Lord, for an example... Is any among you afflicted? let him pray" (James 5:10,13). "Call upon Me in the day of trouble: I will deliver thee" (Psalm 50:15).

When we humble ourselves before God, we must call upon Him with a holy confidence in the name of Christ. We must include the Mediator in all our addresses to heaven and bring Him in the arms of our faith; holding Him up as the expiatory sacrifice and pleading the atonement of His blood which is sufficient both for the priesthood and for the congregation. "Let us therefore come boldly unto the throne of grace, that we may obtain mercy, and find grace to help in time of need" (Hebrews 4:16). Let us continue in prayer knowing we are instructed, "Ye that make mention of the Lord, keep not silence, and give Him no rest, till he establish, and till He make Jerusalem a praise in the earth" (Isaiah 62:6,7).

In short, the humiliation required implies a sincere consecration of ourselves to God and solemn vows of reformation and obedience for the future. Surely it is appropriate to say unto God, "I will not offend any more... if I have done iniquity, I will do no more" (Job 34:31,32). That is exactly what Ephraim meant as, bemoaning himself, he said, "What have I to do any more with idols?" (Hosea 14:8). This is the proper language of backsliding children humbling themselves, "Behold we come unto Thee; for Thou art the Lord our God" (Jeremiah 3:22). "O Lord our God, other lords besides Thee have had dominion over us: but by Thee only will we make mention of Thy name" (Isaiah 26:13). "For the Lord is our judge, the Lord is our lawgiver, the Lord is our king; He will save us" (Isaiah 33:22). "So will not we go back from Thee: quicken us, and we will call upon Thy name" (Psalm 80:18).

Thus there must be a resolute renouncing of sin and devoting ourselves to God. We must cast away every idol of jealousy and allow no competitor with God nor seek any other Saviour nor own any other Lord. We must yield ourselves to God and join ourselves to Him in a perpetual Covenant. Thus we read how the people of Judah in Asa's time, when humbling themselves for their sins, "Entered into a covenant to seek the Lord God of their fathers with all their heart and with all their soul... And they sware unto the Lord with a loud voice, and with shouting, and with trumpets, and with cornets. And all Judah rejoiced at the oath: for they had sworn with all their heart, and sought Him with their whole desire" (2 Chronicles 15:12-15). In Nehemiah's time we read that the people and the priests and the nobles entered into a curse, and into an oath, to walk in God's law and to observe all the commandments of the Lord their God (Nehemiah 10:29).

Thus I have considered the nature and manner of a people's humbling themselves under the judgment of God, which was the first thing proposed.

2. A people under divine judgments should fear. They should fear God and tremble at His judgments. They should be afraid of sin, the procuring cause. Sometimes in Scripture fear is put for religious worship and sometimes for the whole of religion, but as it stands in the text, I think it is to be taken for that passion of the mind called fear. There should be a holy fear of God and of His wrath, a trembling at His judgments, and a solicitous care to obtain His favor. We read, "They also that dwell in the uttermost parts are afraid at Thy tokens" (Psalm 65:8). The Psalmist said, "My flesh trembleth for fear of Thee; and I am afraid of Thy judgments" (Psalm 119:120). The prophet declared, "When I heard, my belly trembled; my lips quivered at the voice... and I trembled in myself, that I might rest in the day of trouble" (Habakkuk 3:16). We should stand trembling before God under the apprehensions of present and impending dispensations of His wrath and even more importantly, under the sense of whatever provoking evils have kindled the Lord's displeasure and made Him threaten to depart from us. "Then were assembled unto me every one that trembled at the words of the God of Israel, because of the transgression of those that had been carried away; and I sat astonied until the evening sacrifice" (Ezra 9:4). "All the people sat in the street of the house of God, trembling because of this matter" (Ezra 10:9).

In the New Testament Scriptures this fear is mentioned by the Apostle as one of the evidences of the Corinthian repentance already cited, "Yea, what fear" (2 Corinthians 7:11), what an awe of God, what a reverence of His majesty and dread of His wrath.

Such a fear is one cause and fruit of humiliation. In the prophet's description of the true penitent, these two characteristics are joined, "To this man will I look," says the Lord, "even to him that is poor and of a contrite spirit, and trembleth at My word" (Isaiah 66:2). If there is in us a humbling sense of our provocations, there will also be an awakened sense and trembling apprehension of the dreadful wrath of God hanging over our guilty heads. Moreover, there will be a fear of sin, a caution and self-jealousy, a distrust of our own hearts, a sense of their treachery, and a dread of turning again unto folly, of relapsing into those sins which have already been the occasion of so much sorrow and anguish to us.

There ought to be such a fear in us all and particularly when under divine judgments. "Sanctify the Lord of hosts Himself; and let Him be your fear, and let Him be your dread" (Isaiah 8:13). Where there is a due humiliation, there will be this godly fear; where there is such a humiliation and fear, there will be the last thing in the text, as the effect thereof— reformation and obedience.

3. A people under divine judgments should turn their feet unto God's testimonies, to walk in His laws. In the day of adversity we should consider God and be afraid; we should consider ourselves and be ashamed; we should consider our ways and repent; we should consider God's statues and turn our feet unto His testimonies; we should consider our professed humiliation and bring forth fruit worthy of repentance, forsaking the sins we pretend a shame and sorrow for; we should consider the vows we make in the time of our distresses and set ourselves daily to perform them; we should consider the calls of providence and heed the rod and turn at God's reproof, who chastens us for our profit that we might be made partakers of His holiness and who expects that we will be reformed by these things.

If we are indeed humbled, this will be one speedy and visible effect. Where there is a broken heart, there will be a reformed life. "Reformation and obedience are the first fruits of true humiliation. God accounts those not humbled but hardened, who are not reformed and do not become obedient to His will; let their pretended attrition or contrition be in outward appearance what it will."[1] This is the repentance God calls for, even a thorough and universal change of heart and life. This is the fast which He has chosen, "To loose the bands of wickedness..." (Isaiah 58:6). to turn from our evil ways, to make our doings good, and to walk in His Law. We are instructed to "fear the Lord, and depart from evil" (Proverbs 3:7). We only truly love God when we keep His commandments. "And now Israel, what doth the Lord Thy God require of Thee, but to fear the Lord Thy God, to walk in all His ways, and to love Him, and to serve the Lord thy God with all thy heart, and with all thy soul?" (Deuteronomy 10:12). "He hath shewed thee, O man, what is good; and what doth the Lord require of thee, but to do justly, and to love mercy, and to walk humbly with Thy God?" (Micah 6:8). This is what God calls us to by His judgments. The promise of salvation is suspended on this condition. "If My people, which are called by My name, shall humble themselves, and pray, and seek my face, and turn from their wicked ways; then I will hear from heaven, and will forgive their sin, and will heal their land" (2 Chronicles 7:14).

We see then what is the duty and business of the present day. We in this place and land are an afflicted people, groaning under a variety of awful judgments. From what I have already set before you may be learned what tempers and deportment become our condition. Surely it becomes us to be a self-humbling, a trembling, and a reforming people. Oh, that we may be found such! Let us, every one personally, humble ourselves and fear and reform and be obedient. Then in our several places let us lay ourselves out to promote such a disposition and conduct in all those about us. If we do this it will be a sure token for good and will afford the most desirable sign of a happy change of times approaching.

---

[1]Matthew Pool's Commentary on the text.

Blessed be God, the God of all grace, that there are found among us a number of people who tremble at His Word and at His judgments, men of humble and contrite spirits, men of prayer, and men of holy conversation. These surely are the strength and security, the riches and beauty of the land. The Lord add to them daily and make them a thousand times more than they now are! The Lord revive His work! Help, Lord, for the faithful fail! It is to be feared that such persons are but thinly sown among us, that the number of them is continually lessening, and that this people in general have the complaint in our text too deservedly lying against them—"Ye have not humbled your selves, even to this day, neither have ye feared, nor walked in God's law." This leads me to another observation from the text.

II. IT IS SOMETIMES THE SAD CASE OF A PEOPLE UNDER DIVINE REBUKES THAT THEY CONTINUE, NOTWITHSTANDING ALL, UNHUMBLED AND UNREFORMED.

The Jews in our text had met with a long train of very desolating judgments, all of which were too little to make them weary of sin and willing to turn to God. They would not be reformed by these things but still went on in their trespasses and walked contrary to God. This is the sad state and case of many others in the world besides the Jews. In a very real way it can be said of people now just the same as then that they do not humble themselves and fear and walk in God's Law, although He visits their iniquities upon them and brings them low by one judgment after another—judgments hardening rather than melting them. All the methods of discipline have been used upon them, yet they will not receive correction, they will not be instructed, they will not hear the reproof, but stop their ears and refuse to return to the Lord.

Sometimes they are stupid under the tokens of God's displeasure and remain insensible under all the means used to awaken them out of their spiritual slumber. "Ephraim is a cake not turned. Strangers have devoured his strength, and he knoweth it not: yea, gray hairs are here and there upon him, yet he knoweth not" (Hosea 7:8,9). "The stork in the heaven knoweth her appointed times; and the turtle [dove] and the crane and the swallow observe the time of their coming; but My people know not the judgment of the Lord" (Jeremiah 8:7). God pours on them the fury of His anger and the strength of battle; and it sets them on fire round about, yet they know it not; and it burns them, yet they lay it not to heart (Isaiah 42:25). His hand is lifted up but they will not see. They are a foolish people and without understanding. They have eyes and see not and ears which hear not. A revolting and rebellious heart have they, even a heart of stone that will not relent. They harden their faces as a rock. Are they ashamed when they commit abominations? No, they are not at all ashamed, neither can they blush (Jeremiah 6:15). They are like brass and iron, as hard as an adamant stone, harder than flint.

If they are not altogether insensible, they are unsubdued and inflexible, being very resolute and madly in love with their lusts. They are as the untamed horse or unbroken mule that has no understanding. They reject the council of God against themselves and say in the pride of their hearts, like those in our context said to Jeremiah, "As for the word that thou hast spoken unto us in the name of the Lord, we will not hearken unto thee. But we will certainly do whatsoever thing goeth forth out of our own mouth" (Jeremiah 44:16,17). Either that, or they say in their despair, "There is no hope: but we will walk after our own devices, and we will every one do the imagination of his evil heart" (Jeremiah 18:12).

Many times they proudly assert their own innocence in the face of all the convictions offered them. They will not see and own their iniquity. They call evil good and good evil. The put darkness for light and light for darkness. They deny the charge of guilt and stand upon their own vindication. Thus our Lord reproved the Pharisees saying, "Ye are they which justify yourselves before men; but God knoweth your hearts: for that which is highly esteemed among men is abomination in the sight of God" (Luke 16:15). All too commonly it is the unhappy case of a people that every individual shifts the blame off from himself, imputing the cause of divine judgments to the sins of others, so looking on himself as unconcerned in the calls to repentance.

Many times the most needy will scoff at God's messengers, laugh at their solemn rebukes and warnings and turn all into banter and ridicule. We read of scornful men that ruled in Jerusalem, who made lies their refuge (Isaiah 28:15,17). The Jews in Zedekiah's days, "Mocked the messengers of God, and despised His words, and misused His prophets" (2 Chronicles 36:16). When Hezekiah sent messengers to summon the Israelites to a Solemn Assembly, "They laughed them to scorn, and mocked them" (2 Chronicles 30:10). In the same way, the Pharisees repeatedly derided our Saviour's councils and admonitions. Just so, the Athenians mocked when Paul rebuked their superstition and warned them of a future judgment (Acts 17:32).

Today many people murmur at the providences of God, are enraged at their reprovers, and cannot bear the means that are used to bring them to repentance. Under the divine chastening they charge God foolishly and complain that His ways are not equal. Their hearts rise against God and are hot within them. They rage and fret themselves, as bullocks unaccustomed to the yoke (Jeremiah 31:18). They hate him that rebukes and "lay a snare for him that reproveth in the gate" (Isaiah 29:21). They cannot endure to be told of their sins. They spurn reproof and fly in the face of those who deal plainly with them, abhorring him that speaks uprightly. "This is a rebellious people, lying children, children that will not hear the Law of the Lord: which say to the seers, See not; and to the prophets, Prophesy not unto us right things, speak unto us smooth things, prophecy deceits" (Isaiah 30:9,10). It is as if they say, "Leave off your present course of preaching; trouble us no more with harsh rebukes and terrible threatenings." Is not this often the language of sinners? They would fain stop the mouths of their faithful monitors and put out the eyes of their watchful seers. They love darkness rather than light because their deeds are evil (John 3:19). Their hearts are fully set in them to do evil and they go on forwardly in the ways of their own eyes.

If any one stand in their way, to check them in their wild career, they take it heinously. They say to their reprovers, "Get out of the way and let us alone." Sometimes they jeer and scorn and deride them. Sometimes they brow-beat and hector and revile them. They lift their horn on high and speak with a stiff neck. They swell and rage; they huff and threaten. Amaziah is an illustration of this. The Lord was angry with him and sent a prophet to ask, "Why hast thou sought after the gods of the people, which could not deliver their own people out of thine hand?" As he talked with him, the king said, "Art thou made of the king's counsel? forbear; why shouldest thou be smitten?" (2 Chronicles 25:15,16). Sometimes they proceed to persecution and violence. Thus wicked Ahab took Micaiah who had prophesied evil of him and put him in prison, there to be fed with the bread of affliction and with water of affliction (2 Chronicles 18:26). Good King Asa himself was once so angry with Hanani the seer for reproving him that he put him in a prison house, for he was in a rage with him because of what he said (2 Chronicles 15:10). In the same way the Jews devised devices against Jeremiah and smote him with the tongue, dug a pit for his soul, and hid snares for his feet (Jeremiah 18:22,23).

These are some of the signs and fruits of an unhumbled spirit and rebellious heart which are too often visible among a people under divine judgments. Sometimes such evil and malignant tempers reign among them and are almost epidemical. This shows the greatest defiance of authority and incorrigibleness. Where this is the case, they are truly and emphatically a stiffnecked generation, a crooked and perverse nation.

But this is not always the case even where a people may be said to be unhumbled. Sometimes there may not appear such a proud, passionate, impatient, inflexible spirit among a people under divine judgments, and yet they may be unsubdued and impenitent. Sometimes sinners are pretty patient of reproofs from men. They do not mock or rage and brave it as others do, but they listen modestly and calmly and yet go on still in their own way. Sometimes they patiently bear divine rebukes. Under afflictive providences they are quiet and silent and seemingly penitent, but still nothing is reformed. Or possibly some reformation is produced and humiliation pretended, yet notwithstanding, it may be truly said of them, "They are not humbled even unto this day, neither have they feared" (Jeremiah 44:10).

They may be said to humble themselves in no better sense than is affirmed of Ahab who fasted and lay in sackcloth and went softly, and yet the statutes of Omri were still kept and none of the sins forsaken for which all that mourning was pretended (1 Kings 16:28-34). Perhaps in their affliction they keep days of fasting and prayer and call Solemn Assemblies to seek God and to humble themselves in His sight, but still they are not humbled. They do not fast aright for they do not fast to God. God is near their mouths but far from their hearts. They inquire after Him in insincerity, and all their humiliations are but pageantry and pretence. They make a grand show of self-abasement, mortification, and devotion, but reality is wanting. They put on a demure countenance, disfigure their faces, and hang down their heads as a bulrush for a day (Isaiah 58:5). They lie down in their shame and spread sackcloth and ashes under themselves. They make a show of affections and cover the altar with tears, pouring out their prayers with seeming ardor, causing their voice to be heard on high. They make heavy complaints of the wickedness of the times and very plentiful confessions of their own sins together with very solemn protestations of repentance. They plight their vows to God and make resolutions of amendment for time to come. They ask of Him the ordinances of justice as a nation that loved righteousness and forsook not the ordinance of their God. And yet after all this, there is nothing but the thin shadow of a fast, nothing but the empty appearance of humiliations, nothing but the bare promise of reformation. Their profuse tears dry up and all their seeming devotion soon expires as a vapor. They forget their vows and turn from the holy commandments. Sin revives, unmortified lusts awake in them by which they are enticed and overcome.

Thus it happens to them according to the true proverb, "The dog is turned to his own vomit again; and the sow that was washed to her wallowing in the mire" (2 Peter 2:22). So the Apostle complains of some among the primitive Christians, and thus God often complained of the Jews of old, "When He slew them, then they sought Him: and they returned and inquired early after God. And they remembered that God was their rock, and the high God their redeemer. Nevertheless they did flatter Him with their mouth, and they lied unto Him with their tongues. For their heart was not right with Him, neither were they steadfast in His covenant" (Psalm 78:34-37). "Why then is this people of Jerusalem slidden back by a perpetual backsliding? They hold fast deceit, they refuse to return. I hearkened and heard, but they spake not aright: no man repented him of his wickedness, saying, What have I done? Every one turned to his course, as the horse rusheth into the battle" (Jeremiah 8:5,6). "O Ephraim, what shall I do unto thee? O Judah, what shall I do unto thee? for your goodness is as a morning cloud, and as the early dew it goeth away... But they like men have transgressed the covenant: there have they dealt treacherously against me" (Hosea 6:4,7). "And they have not cried unto Me with their heart, when they howled upon their beds: they assemble themselves for corn and wine, and they rebel against me... They return, but not to the most High: they are like a deceitful bow" (Hosea 7:14-16).

Is this sometimes the case of a people now under God's judgments? Let it then put us to inquiring into our own case. We have been and are today under the rod of divine providence. But what is our frame and deportment? Are we truly humbled? Do we fear God? Do we walk in His Laws? Or are we secure, impenitent, and unreformed? Let us inquire into these things. It is an inquiry of vast concern to us and therefore we should earnestly examine ourselves. If we think we are something when indeed we are nothing we deceive ourselves (Galatians 6:3). If we deceive ourselves, iniquity will be our ruin.

III. GOD OBSERVES A PEOPLE'S CONDUCT UNDER HIS JUDGMENTS AND MARKS AGAINST THEM ALL THEIR OBSTINACY AND IMPENITENCE.

This is implied in the complaint which God makes in our text: "They have not humbled themselves, neither have they feared." This note may be confirmed from another passage in the same prophecy, "I hearkened and heard, but they spake not aright: no man repented him of his wickedness" (Jeremiah 8:6). Likewise, God looks upon men when they have done amiss and are under His chastening to hear if any say, "I have sinned" (Job 32:27). He diligently observes all mankind, especially in affliction and distress. "The eyes of the Lord are in every place, beholding the evil and the good" (Proverbs 15:3). His eyes are open to all the ways of man. He compasses our path. He tries our hearts and weighs our actions. He observes men's conduct at all times, in all places, and under all His dealings with them. Particularly, He observes how they carry it under His rod; what their tempers and deportments are; whether they are duly humbled for their sins; whether they are afraid of His judgments; whether they turn from their evil doings. He takes notice if they neglect these things. If they are impenitent, obstinate, and irreclaimable, He marks it against them. He critically observes this misconduct in a people in general and in every person in particular. His eye is upon every one of whatever rank, age, or condition, taking an exact notice of their thoughts, words, and actions under His afflicting hand and noting it all down in His Book of Remembrance.

This kind of careful observation is necessary in order to rightly judge their conduct and suit further dispensations to their case. He does not act therein as a careless, indifferent spectator of human affairs but as the Lord and Judge of the world. Hence we read, "I the Lord search the heart, I try the reins, even to give to every man according to his ways, and according to the fruit of his doings" (Jeremiah 17:10). The Lord is a God of judgment. He is righteous in all His ways and all His works are done in wisdom. He contrives the best methods for managing His providential government, and He ordinarily observes a rule in His dispensations towards a people. Infinite wisdom and justice proportions the punishment to the provocation, so that commonly a people's sufferings are greater or lesser according to the kind and degree of their sins. In order to accomplish this, a right judgment must be passed on men and, therefore, an accurate inspection of them is necessary. Hence God is represented as taking the most critical observations of us, "His eyes behold, His eyelids try, the children of men" (Psalm 11:4).

In the light of this, think how watchful we should be over ourselves at all times. Particularly in a day of adversity, we ought to consider our ways, ponder the path of our feet and take heed to ourselves; giving diligence lest any man fail of the grace of God. "See then that ye walk circumspectly, not as fools, but as wise, Redeeming the time, because the days are evil" (Ephesians 5:15,16). Lay to heart the judgments of God and study to improve them to your repentance and reformation, fearing further judgments to which impenitence will expose us.

This leads me to the last observation from the text.

IV. WHEN A PEOPLE ARE FINALLY IRRECLAIMABLE, GOD WILL SET HIS FACE AGAINST THEM FOR EVIL.

This is the threat in the our text, "They are not humbled, even to this day; therefore saith the Lord, Behold I will set My face against you for evil."

1. God will set His face against them. This implies resentment and displeasure in the superlative degree. God will turn away His favor from such a people and His jealousy will burn against them. His soul will depart from them and will loathe them, neither will He spare, neither will He repent. He that made them will have no mercy upon them and He that formed them will show them no favor. He will cast them off; He will cast them out of His presence. He will withdraw His directing and protecting presence and will no longer be their Guide or Guard. He will remove His sanctifying presence and will take away His Holy Spirit from them. In the end, He will take away His kingdom from among them, remove their candlestick out of its place and put out their light in obscure darkness.

He will loathe their persons and turn to be their adversary (Isaiah 63:10). He will reject all their pretended services and will cast them back as filth in their faces. Their new moons and their Sabbaths His soul will hate. When they spread forth their hands, He will hide His eyes from them. Yea, when they make many prayers, He will not hear (Isaiah 1:13-15). When they fast, He will not reward them, and when they offer an oblation, He will not accept them, for He remembers their iniquity, that they loved to wander and would not return from their evil ways. "They refused to hearken, and pulled away the shoulder, and stopped their ears, that they should not hear. Yea, they made their hearts as an adamant stone, lest they should hear the law... Therefore it is come to pass, that as He cried, and they would not hear; so they cried, and I would not hear them saith the Lord of hosts" (Zechariah 7:11-13). He will cover Himself with a cloud, that their prayer should not pass through. He will not regard their affliction but in answer will shut up His tender mercies and be favorable no more. Oh tragedy of tragedies, He will laugh at their calamity and mock when their fear comes (Proverbs 1:26).

2. He will set His face against them for evil. He will not only withdraw His favor from them, but will pour out His indignation upon them. He will not only reject their prayers and deny them an answer of peace but will answer them in terrible things by righteousness. His heart is turned from them and His presence gone, which is their only safety and happiness, the strength and glory of a people. His face is set against them and woe to them that are in such a circumstance. Who knows the power of His anger? "It is a fearful thing to fall into the hands of the living God" (Hebrews 10:31). When God is angry with a people and causes His fury to rest on them, all kinds of evil will break in upon them as a flood or as a consuming fire. When God sets His face against a people and forsakes them, iniquity will abound more and more until wrath comes upon them to the uttermost. Their misery will be great upon them and the very blessings that may be spared to them for a while will be turned into curses and become a snare to them.

If a people are finally impenitent, God will thus set His face against them for evil. He may bear long with them but He will not bear always. He is a gracious and longsuffering God, but if His patience is abused and His grace turned into wantonness, it will kindle His anger and He will punish at the last. If a professing people forsake the Lord, then He will turn and will do them hurt, after that He had done them good. If they finally forsake God, He will be angry with them until He consumes them utterly.

That God will thus set His face against a people for evil if they be obstinately impenitent, appears from many awful threatenings in the Word of Truth. "The Lord is with you, while ye be with Him; and if ye seek Him, He will be found of you; but if ye forsake Him, He will forsake you" (2 Chronicles 15:2). How plain, decisive, and solemn are those menaces in the book of Leviticus where God says to His people, "If ye will not hearken unto Me, but will break My Covenant, I also will do this unto you, I will appoint over you terror, consumption, and the burning ague: and I will set My face against you and ye shall be slain before your enemies. And if ye will not yet for all this hearken to Me, then will I punish you seven times more for your sins: and I will break the pride of your power; and I will make your heaven as iron, and your earth as brass, and your land shall not yield her increase. And if ye walk contrary unto Me, and will not hearken to Me, I will bring seven times more plagues upon you, according to your sins, and will send wild beasts among you, which shall rob you of your children. And if you will not be reformed by Me by these things, but will walk contrary unto Me, then will I also walk contrary unto you, and will punish you yet seven times for your sins, and I will bring the sword upon you, that shall avenge the quarrel of My Covenant: I will send the pestilence among you. And if ye will not for all this hearken unto me, but walk contrary unto me, then I also will walk contrary unto you in fury, and I, even I, will chastise you seven times for your sins. And My soul shall abhor you, and I will make your cities waste, and bring your sanctuaries into desolation, and I will not smell the savour of your sweet odors."[2]

---

[2]A paraphrase of selected portions of Leviticus 26.

Thus God threatened the Jewish Nation of old. In like manner He threatened Israel's evil neighbors, the heathen nations bordering upon Judea, "If they will diligently learn the ways of My people, to swear by My name, The Lord liveth; as they taught My people to swear by Baal; then shall they be built in the midst of my people. But if they will not obey, I will utterly pluck up and destroy that nation, saith the Lord" (Jeremiah 12:16,17).

It seems to be a standing law of God's providential government that "At what instant I shall speak concerning a nation, and concerning a kingdom, to build and to plant it; If it do evil in My sight, that it obey not My voice, then I will repent of the good, wherewith I said I would benefit them" (Jeremiah 18:9,10). We have a similar text relating to Gospel times, "The nation and kingdom that will not serve Thee [or will not submit to Christ's scepter] shall perish; yea, those nations shall be utterly wasted" (Isaiah 60:12). The God who threatens is the God of truth, "Hath He said it, and will He not do it?" Although the sentence may not be speedily executed, it shall not always be delayed. Although He may be slow to anger, He will be true to His threatenings, and not one iota of them shall fail.

We may confirm this argument from the many known examples of divine vengeance. There have been many sad and lamentable instances of peoples being ruined by their iniquity and provoking God to anger until He has set His face against them to destroy them. Many cities and countries that were once lifted up to heaven have long since been brought into desolation for their sins. Great Babylon, which in its day was the wonder of the world, the glory of kingdoms, has long since been totally and irrecoverably destroyed, as when God overthrew Sodom and Gomorrah. Jerusalem was the beauty of Judea and the joy of the whole earth. She was the place God once chose for His habitation, where He had His temple, and whither the tribes of Israel went up. There was set the throne of the House of David. Within her walls were peace and prosperity in all her palaces. If there was any place in the world that was lifted up to heaven it was Jerusalem, yet even this place was destroyed utterly. For crucifying the Lord of Glory, the Jewish nation was rejected by God from being any more His people, and their land was made an utter desolation. A similar fate has befallen many places since, that in the early ages of Christianity were flourishing and populous. Many famous churches that were once the beauty and glory of the Christian world have long since been reduced to shame and ruin for their apostasy and impenitence and have become habitations of cruelty, the seats of barbarity and idolatry. These examples are like loud lectures to us on our text. They provide clear evidence of the truth of the doctrine before us.

We may expect that God will deal alike with those that share the same guilt. God seems to have one rule of dealing with a professing people, the measures of providence being usually the same. He does, however, reserve a sovereign liberty to Himself as to the circumstances of His dispensations in which there is often a variety. Some have gentler discipline than others. Some have a longer space to repent than others. However, in general, there is one stated rule according to which God in His providence impartially proceeds, especially with a professing people. Hence He sends backsliding Jerusalem to self-ruined Shiloh to view His judgments there upon His rebellious people and reminds them of the ruin of the Ten Tribes so that, by comparing cases, they might draw proper conclusions for their own instruction and conviction. It is written, "Go ye now unto My place which was in Shiloh, where I set My name at the first, and see what I did to it for the wickedness of My people Israel. And now, because ye have done all these works, saith the Lord... Therefore will I do unto this house... as I have done to Shiloh. And I will cast you out of my sight, as I have cast out all your brethren, even the whole seed of Ephraim" (Jeremiah 7:12-15).

All these judgments happened to them for examples and the record of them was made for our learning and admonition upon whom the ends of the world are come. As one writer said, "God writes His severe truths with the blood of His disobedient subjects, and makes their ruinous heaps to proclaim knowledge and council to the rest of the world. Sodom's ashes, Shiloh's fire, Jerusalem's desolation, are uses of instruction and warning to all the inhabitants of the earth." They fell by their iniquity, and those who tread in their wicked steps may expect to fall by the same judgments. God is uniform and of a single mind with Himself in His judicial proceedings. It is a rule of justice that the equally guilty should be punished alike. "Except ye repent, ye shall all likewise perish" (Luke 13:3,5).

The reasons and foundations of God's judicial proceedings with any people, especially a professing people, seem to be very clear and obvious. The honor of His own name calls for such conduct toward an impenitent people. His glory is especially concerned in the matter, the glory of His holiness, faithfulness and wisdom. He seems bound in honor to these attributes, to witness against the apostasies of His people by inflicting judgments upon them. Otherwise His name will peculiarly suffer by their wickedness and impenitence. Hence He tells Israel of old, "You only have

I known of all the families of the earth: therefore I will punish you for all your iniquities" (Amos 3:2).

In a word, the honor of divine justice requires the punishing of a sinful people and the destroying of them if they are finally impenitent. Will not the judge of all the earth do right? Is there any iniquity with God? Will He not render to every man according to His work and to every people according to the fruit of their doings? Verily, He will render a reward to the proud. There is no unrighteousness in Him. As He is obliged in justice, He will not let a rebellious people go unpunished.

Indeed, as to particular individuals, there may possibly be some exceptions during the present state; some sinners may have almost all their punishment reserved for the future world. But if we consider men as united in society and making up distinct provinces, kingdoms, and nations, we shall find the conduct of God's providence toward them vastly different in this particular. National guilt infers national judgments. God exercises a government over men as they coalesce into distinct communities. "For the kingdom is the Lord's: and He is the governor among the nations" (Psalm 22:28). His government is infinitely wise, good, just, and holy. He governs by law and rule and judges them according to their doings. We must have very odd notions of things if we imagine that human societies as such will have any place in the future state or that they will be judged in another world. Hence, if ever God punishes them, it must be in the present state. Divine justice, then, seems more concerned to punish the nations in the life that now is than individual persons.

God can punish whole nations as easily as He can particular persons, and for this purpose God has many national judgments which he can utilize. If a people sin, they lay themselves open to such judgments. If they are finally impenitent, divine justice calls aloud for their utter destruction. When a people are obstinate and irreclaimable, after a long time of trial and much waiting upon them, God represents Himself as weary with repenting and obliged to proceed to their destruction, "Who shall have pity upon thee, O Jerusalem? or who shall bemoan thee? or who shall go aside to ask how thou doest? Thou hast forsaken Me, saith the Lord, thou art gone backward: therefore will I stretch out My hand against thee and destroy thee; I am weary with repenting" (Jeremiah 15:5,6). He may justly do so, for exceedingly aggravated is the provocation that such a people offer unto God. The affronts they put upon Him are very great. It is the highest instance of stubbornness and rebellion against God to be incorrigible and unhumbled under very humbling dispensations and not afraid of the consequence. It is, in effect, bidding defiance to God and challenging His vengeance to do its utmost. It is the highest insolence and contempt of God and must be extremely provoking to Him. He may well, therefore, set His face against such a rebellious people. Shall not God visit such a nation as this?

Moreover, it defeats the design of providence in afflictive dispensations. Their great end ordinarily is to bring a people to repentance, and for this purpose, divine judgments are usually tempered with much mercy for a long time, that by the goodness of God we may be led to repentance (Romans 2:4). It is God's method to try a people by less and lighter judgments at first, and if these are ineffectual, He brings greater and heavier. If after all this they walk contrary to God and will not be reformed by these things but defeat His gracious design by a persevering impenitence, how reasonably, how justly may His abused patience turn into flaming indignation? His anger may well burn against them, and His fury be poured out like a fire to consume them utterly.

When a people have withstood all the methods of reformation, they are completely ripe for ruin. They have filled up the measure of their iniquity; they have provoked God to the last degree. Why should He not set His face against them for evil, to cut them off and to end their rebellion? "Shall not My soul be avenged on such a nation as this" (Jeremiah 5:9), saith the Lord. "Behold, I am against Thee... I will make thee vile, and will set thee as a gazingstock" (Nahum 3:5,6). "I am weary with repenting" (Jeremiah 15:6). I will surely destroy thee; neither will I repent any more, nor shall mine eyes spare thee, saith the Lord.

I must now apply this doctrine.

USE ONE. This doctrine provides a sad prospect to a people that have long continued impenitent under a course of afflictive dispensations.

It tells us they are likely to have the blessed God set His face against them. If they are resolved upon sinning, He is resolved upon punishing. God is jealous and the Lord revenges. The Lord will take vengeance on his adversaries, for He reserves wrath for His enemies. Though He is slow to anger, He will never acquit the wicked. Oh, consider how miserable a people are certain to be in the end, who are secure and stupid under many judgments. They must expect the continuance and aggravation of all their calamities, for there is no prospect of any end to their troubles unless God is pleased to cease striving with them. If He does that, it is the most formidable judgment in the world.

Thankfully, sometimes sovereign divine grace is exalted and triumphs in the conversion of a person or a people after they have long stood against all means. Isaiah describes a case like this, "I was wroth, and smote him: I hid Me, and was wroth; and he went on frowardly in the way of his heart. I have seen His ways and will heal Him" (Isaiah 57:17,18). But this is extraordinary. If we consider the common course of providence and the constant tenor of the Covenant, they both with united voices speak sadly to such a people.

From hence we may learn what we have to fear if we do not repent and turn to God. We have sinned and God has a controversy with us, although hitherto He has dealt very tenderly and compassionately with us, in wrath remembering mercy. But if we go on still in our trespasses, we must expect that God will heap on us more severe and heavy judgments than any we have yet felt. We may expect fearful tragedies to be acted on the stage before God has performed His work, whether they be of mercy or of vengeance.

USE TWO. What has been said may help to account for those dark appearances of providence wherein God seems to be setting His face against this people today.

We are fallen by our iniquity. God has visited our sins upon us from time to time by scarcity, by epidemics, by war in our borders and by piracies in our seas. By various judgments we have been brought low many times. Consider how our common calamities have grown and aggravated at this day! This is, in many respects, a time of Jacob's trouble. It is particularly a day of battle and war. We are frequently made to bleed by the sword. It is a scorching season wherein God is withholding the rain of heaven and making our land like powder and dust. Our distresses and perplexities are great on these accounts as well as others, and God seems to be threatening us with still greater calamities. At the present time providence seems to be frowning upon us in our most important interests. Above all, the withdrawal of the Spirit of God from among us affords the most awful evidence that God is setting His face against us.

And what is the ground of all? Why because we are not humbled, even to this day. The people do not turn to Him that smites them, and therefore His anger is not turned away but His hand is stretched out still, notwithstanding the many days of humiliation we have solemnized. I must be the first to lay my hand on my own breast and acknowledge my guilt in these things, but allow me to say that we have, in general, far too many reasons to condemn ourselves as the very cause of our own distresses. It is because we are still unreformed that God will not put an end to His controversy with us.

USE THREE. Let us see and admire the patience of God toward us in this land.

Oh, the riches of the patience and forbearance of God who, although He has not suffered us to go unpunished, has yet mingled a great many mercies with His judgments. He has not rewarded us according to our iniquities. He has not in anger shut up His compassions toward us but has been longsuffering, not willing that we should perish, but that we should all come to repentance. Indeed, He is contending with us awfully by various judgments, avenging the quarrel of His violated Covenant and is making progress in His controversy with us, yet He takes but very slow steps, making many pauses, giving us space to repent, and waiting to be gracious. Surely He is a God who is slow to anger, longsuffering, and abundant in goodness and mercy. Surely it is of the Lord's mercy that we are not consumed. Oh, let us realize the divine leniency and forbearance toward us and give God the glory for His infinite patience.

USE FOUR. What has been said warns us to beware of continued impenitence and calls upon us to humble ourselves in the sight of God, lest He be provoked to abandon us utterly.

"Return, thou backsliding Israel, saith the Lord; and I will not cause my anger to fall upon you: for I am merciful, saith the Lord, and I will not keep anger for ever... Turn, O backsliding children, saith the Lord; for I am married unto you!" (Jeremiah 3:12,14). "Circumcise yourselves to the Lord, and take away the foreskins of your heart... lest My fury come forth like fire, and burn that none can quench it, because of the evil of your doings" (Jeremiah 4:4). Be not stiffnecked but yield yourselves unto God, that the fierceness of His wrath may turn away from you. He will not turn away His face, if you return unto Him. He will not hide Himself forever. "O Jerusalem, wash thine heart from wickedness, that thou mayest be saved. How long shall thy vain thoughts lodge within Thee?" (Jeremiah 4:14). How long will you refuse to humble yourself before Me, saith the Lord. How long will this people provoke Me? "Do they provoke Me to anger? saith the Lord: do they not provoke themselves to the confusion of their own faces?" (Jeremiah 7:19). Do you provoke the Lord to jealousy? Are you stronger than He?

O foolish people, and unwise! Shall briars and thorns be set in array against devouring fire? Verily, He is a jealous God with whom we have to do, and He is a strong Lord. Who knows the power of His wrath? Who can stand before Him when once He is angry? Why then should we incense Him yet more by a persevering impenitence? He is jealous of His great name, which is particularly concerned in our conduct and in the manner of His dealings with us. He will have honor from us, either in our repentance or in our ruin. For many years He has been witnessing against our apostasies and seeking to turn us by more mild exercises of His rod. But if we continue unhumbled, we must expect more severe and terrible dispensations of His wrath.

Oh, why then should we harden our hearts any longer? Have we not smarted enough already? Why should we oblige Him to inflict heavier judgments upon us? Oh, let us not be so egregiously foolish. Remember, divine corrections are ordinarily progressive and commonly rise in proportion to a people's guilt. Should we not tremble then to think of going on still in our provocations? Verily, God is not done with us. He has not yet shot all His arrows. The worst are still in His quiver, and there seems to be a sharp and terrible one upon the string at this moment.

Oh, let us then fall down at God's feet and humble ourselves and cry mightily to Him and turn every one from his evil way. Who can tell if God will repent and turn away from His fierce anger that we perish not? Oh, let us not dare God and force Him to take more rigorous methods with us. It is high time for us to awake out of our carnal sleep, to look about us and see if there is any way to escape, that we be not consumed. Oh, let us make haste and not delay, but as the Holy Ghost says, "Today if ye will hear His voice, harden not your hearts" (Hebrews 3:7,15). "Be thou instructed, O Jerusalem, lest My soul depart from thee; lest I make thee desolate, a land not inhabited" (Jeremiah 6:8). "He that will love life, and see good days, let him refrain his tongue from evil, and his lips that they speak no guile: Let him eschew evil, and do good... For the eyes of the Lord are over the righteous, and His ears are open unto their prayers: but the face of the Lord is against them that do evil" (1 Peter 3:10-12).

CHAPTER TEN

A
Holy Fear of God
and His
Judgments

By
John Cotton

With an appendix containing a remarkable
account of the extraordinary impressions made
on the inhabitants of Haverhill

John Cotton, 1693-1757

The author of this sermon was the great grandson of the justly famous Puritan leader, John Cotton, 1585-1652, who was, doubtless, one of the foremost preachers in all American history. Young John was born July 15, 1693. His father was the Reverend Rowland Cotton of Sandwich, Massachusetts. His mother was a member of the prominent Saltonstall family. John Cotton studied Latin under the tutelege of his Uncle Josiah Cotton before attending Harvard College. Beginning in 1711, he taught school at Beverly, Massachusetts, where he also joined the local Congregational church. After receiving a number of pressing invitations to pastor, John accepted a call as the third minister of the church at Newton, having been recommended to that congregation by his relative, Cotton Mather. He succeeded Nehemiah Hobart who had pastored there most of his long life. John was ordained as a Congregational minister in November of 1714. Peter Thatcher, John Danforth, Cotton Mather, and Rowland Cotton, John's father, all participated in the ceremony. In 1719 he and Mary Gibbs, daughter of a Boston merchant, were married. They lived in the Hobart parsonage where John had been keeping house with his sister Joanna since assuming the pastorate, but after only a year of bliss, the home was destroyed by fire along with their books and household goods.

In the early days of the Great Awakening, Mr. Cotton appears to have eagerly welcomed George Whitefield to his pulpit, rejoicing in the conversions that occurred among his congregation. In 1743 he publically endorsed "the late Happy Revival," but for reasons that are not at all clear at this time, by 1745 he appears to have changed his views, joining a group of other clergy in voting not to admit Mr. Whitefield to their pulpits. Despite this vote, Whitefield preached in Newton again three years later. Cotton himself saw something of the extraordinary power of Holy Spirit conviction in a case recorded by Thomas Prince in volume one of The Christian History. *When preaching in 1742 at the first parish of Wrentham on Matthew 11:28, a man of mature years cried out in the midst of the sermon in deep soul concern. "Soon after the discourse was dismissed he went to...Mr. Cotton; who asking the reason of his crying out in the assembly, in the manner he had done, the man reply'd, that he could not avoid his doing so; tho' he had often spoke against other people crying out and had said that they might, if they would, refrain from it, and not disturb the congregation in hearing." He acknowledged that he had come to the meeting supposing himself a righteous man, but in the midst of the sermon he was brought to see his sin, misery, and danger, and his need of Christ to help and save him, and saw that if a saving change was not wrought by the Spirit of God upon his heart, he should be undone forever. An enduring conversion followed.*

Cotton's ministry was received with great joy by those who saw in him "the name and spirit" of his great-grandfather. Unlike many in his day, he was usually unwilling to have his messages printed. This earthquake sermon was his first published work. A second earthquake sermon was preached on February 8, 1728. It bore the title God's Awful Determination Against a People That Will Not Obey His Voice, by His Word, and Judgments. *It was published in Boston in 1728 and is also worthy of reading. Benjamin Colman wrote the preface to the second sermon which was based on Zephaniah 3:2,7,8. Cotton's faithful and fruitful labors for Jesus Christ ended on May 17, 1757, when he died of a very violent fever.*

First published as *A Holy Fear of God, and His Judgments, Exhorted to in a Sermon Preached at Newton, November 3, 1727, On a Day of Fasting and Prayer, Occasioned by the Terrible Earthquake that Shook New-England, on the Lord's Day Night Before. By John Cotton, Pastor of the Church of Christ There. With an Appendix Containing a Remarkable Account of the Extraordinary Impressions Made on the Inhabitants of Haverhill, &c.* Boston: Printed by B. Green, Jun. for S. Gerrish, at the lower end of Cornhill, 1727.

A Holy Fear of God
and His Judgments

**"My flesh trembleth for fear of Thee;
and I am afraid of Thy judgments."**
Psalm 119:120

I persuade myself that this text has so often employed the thoughts of many of us since we felt the awful shaking and trembling of the earth under us that we have been and are now ready to cry out, "My flesh trembleth for fear of Thee; and I am afraid of Thy judgments." It is a day of no little distress, concern, and fear, and it may well be so, for what a holy and provoked God may be about ready to do with us, He alone knows. One thing is certain, our transgressions have been multiplied, and our iniquities testify against us. In past years the Lord has been, in various awful ways, testifying to His anger and displeasure against us, and we may be wisely afraid He will do yet more awful and terrible things. I am convinced that this is the great fear of every one that truly fears the great God today. Would to God that we did not have such solid reasons to fear that the Lord will yet dispense more terrible things in righteousness to a sinful, unreformed people. Yet I am sure the spirits of all flesh in the midst of us have reason enough to tremble for fear of what God may further bring upon us.

I shall improve the words of the text then, on this solemn occasion, by applying it not only to particular persons but more especially to a backsliding and sinful people. Accordingly, I propose this doctrine for our present instruction and improvement:

DOCTRINE. The condition and circumstances of a people may be such that their flesh may well tremble for fear of God, and they may wisely be afraid of His judgments.

In the prosecution of this doctrine I will show:

I. What is meant by the judgments of God and what judgments we are exposed to that we ought to be afraid of.

II. What is meant by trembling for fear of God and being afraid of His judgments.

III. That our condition and circumstance are such that we have abundant reasons and occasions to tremble and be afraid.

I. WHAT IS MEANT BY THE JUDGMENTS OF GOD AND WHAT JUDGMENTS WE ARE EXPOSED TO THAT WE OUGHT TO BE AFRAID OF.

The judgments of God are those manifestations of His vindictive or corrective justice whereby He lets the world know what a sin-hating God He is.

These judgments are temporal, spiritual, and eternal. God can arm the whole creation against us and make everything we enjoy destructive to us. God does not willingly afflict or grieve the children of men but when, by their sins, they provoke Him, He sends down His judgments upon them. The judgments of God ought to be the object of a natural man's fear, for hereby God reveals His just displeasure against sin. "The Lord is known by the judgment which He executeth" (Psalm 9:16). Godly men are afraid of God's judgments. This was the case of the Psalmist in the text, "I am afraid of Thy judgments." This was so of holy Job, "Destruction from God was a terror to me" (Job 31:23).

The judgments of God and the rebukes of heaven that we lie exposed to and are often suffering and groaning under are various. The great God, who is holy in all His ways and righteous in all His works, is sometimes provoked to come out in judgment and to write bitter things against us in the way of His Providence. It is sometimes the sovereign and holy pleasure of God to lay us under some sore judgments and to threaten the infliction of yet more and greater ones. There are the judgments of sword, pestilence, and sickness that the Lord often brings upon us. He sometimes sends cleanness of teeth or a great scarcity of the necessities of life. He sometimes withholds the rain which makes the earth fruitful, causing the heavens over us to be as brass and the earth under us as iron and the rain of the land powder and dust (Deuteronomy 28:23,24). We have sometimes had sad occasions to say with the prophet, "The fire hath devoured the pastures of the wilderness, and the flame hath burned all the trees of the field. The beasts of the field cry also unto Thee: for the rivers of water are dried up, and fire hath devoured the pastures of the wilderness" (Joel 1:19,20). God sometimes visits His people with scorching droughts so that the fruits of the earth are diminished, the trees do not yield their fruit nor the land its usual increase. Sometimes God sends surplus of rain so that the crops drown or rot. Sometimes He sends infectious epididemic sickness that proves mortal and sweeps away multitudes. There is also the judgment of the sword, when God lets loose the enemy upon us, to waste our substance and destroy the lives of many of our people. The sovereign and righteous God has dreadfully punished us in years past by long and bloody wars, when we have seen garments rolled in blood, our young men slain, and many carried into miserable captivity and there poisoned with the Romish religion. There are also judgments of storms and tempests of wind, of thunder and lightening which we have seen and felt to an uncommon degree in the weeks and months that are past. Only a very few weeks ago, upon the evening before the Sabbath, the Lord brought down upon us a violent storm and awful were its effects on our orchards and among the trees of the woods, while some in the city were sorely wounded and one slain.

Now, upon the evening after the Sabbath, the Lord has brought upon us the unusual and terrible judgment of an earthquake. We have thus seen those awful words fulfilled, "Thou shalt be visited of the Lord of hosts with thunder, and with earthquake, and great noise, with storm and tempest, and the flame of devouring fire" (Isaiah 29:6), and "The earth shook and trembled; the foundations also of the hills moved and were shaken, because He was wroth" (Psalm 18:7). Among the awful judgments of God, that of the earthquake is much described. It is very particularly and most awfully detailed in the twenty-fourth chapter of Isaiah which you will do well to read this day with very great attention. I will single out a few verses and read them to you now. "Behold, the Lord maketh the earth empty, and maketh it waste, and turneth it upside down, and scattereth abroad the inhabitants thereof... The land shall be utterly emptied, and utterly spoiled: for the Lord hath spoken this word. The earth mourneth and fadeth away, the world languisheth and fadeth away, the haughty people of the earth do languish. The earth also is defiled under the inhabitants thereof; because they have transgressed the laws, changed the ordinance, broken the everlasting covenant. Therefore hath the curse devoured the earth, and they that dwell therein are desolate: therefore the inhabitants of the earth are burned, and few men left... All the merry-hearted do sigh... The noise of them that rejoice endeth, the joy of the harp ceaseth. They shall not drink wine with a song; strong drink shall be bitter to them that drink it... All joy is darkened, the mirth of the land is gone. In the city is left desolation... Fear, and the pit, and the snare, are upon thee, O inhabitant of the earth. And it shall come to pass, that he who fleeth from the noise of the fear shall fall into the pit; and he that cometh up out of the midst of the pit shall be taken in the snare: for the windows from on high are open, and the foundations of the earth do shake... The earth is moved exceedingly. The earth shall reel to and fro like a drunkard... and the transgression thereof shall be heavy upon it; and it shall fall, and not rise again" (verses 1,3-12,17-20).

The Prophet predicted that in that day "they shall go into the holes of the rocks, and into the caves of the earth, for fear of the Lord, and for the glory of His majesty, when He ariseth to shake terribly the earth" (Isaiah 2:19). The Lord said, "Therefore I will shake the heavens, and the earth shall remove out of her place" (Isaiah 13:13). The Prophet Ezekiel also spoke of earthquakes saying, "Surely in that day there shall be a great shaking in the land of Israel; so that the fishes of the sea, and the fowls of the heaven, and the beasts of the field, and all creeping things that creep upon the earth, and all men that are upon the face of the earth, shall shake at My presence, and the mountains shall be thrown down, and the steep places shall fall, and every wall shall fall to the ground" (Ezekiel 38:19,20)). Joel wrote, "The Lord also shall roar out of Zion, and utter His voice from Jerusalem; and the heavens and the earth shall shake" (Joel 3:16). The prophet Haggai recorded, "For thus saith the Lord of hosts; Yet once, it is a little while, and I will shake the heavens, and the earth, and the sea and the dry land; and I will shake all nations..." (Haggai 2:6,7). Malachi also spoke of this day of the Lord, "For behold, the day cometh, that shall burn as an oven; and all the proud, yea, and all that do wickedly, shall be stubble: and the day that cometh shall burn them up, saith the Lord of hosts, that it shall leave them neither root nor branch" (Malachi 4:1).

In the Gospel we read of earthquakes as forerunners of our Saviour coming to judgment, "There shall be famines, and pestilences, and earthquakes, in divers places. All these are the beginning of sorrows" (Matthew 24:7,8). Matthew speaks here of the Son of Man's coming in the clouds of heaven with power and great glory and of the same signs preceding it that the prophets I have just mentioned spoke of. The Apostle Peter also speaks remarkably of our hastening unto the coming of the day of God and of its coming most suddenly and unexpectedly upon a secure, unprepared world, when "the heavens shall pass away with a great noise, and the elements shall melt with fervent heat, the earth also and the works that are therein shall be burned up" (2 Peter 3:10).

Thus we see that we may wisely look for such awful shaking dispensations as we have been under this week. They are very terrible indeed and God only knows what will be the outcome. It certainly looks as if God is very angry with us and that we are ripe for His terrible judgments. When God threatens to bring judgments in general and earthquakes in particular, He says, "I will shake the heavens, and the earth shall remove out of her place, in the wrath of the Lord of hosts, and in the day of His fierce anger"(Isaiah 13:13); "For in My jealousy and in the fire of My wrath have I spoken, Surely in that day there shall be a great shaking in the land" (Ezekiel 38:19). Our flesh, therefore, trembles for fear of what God may be about to do in a still more special manner by this judicial dispensation.

I must also speak of spiritual plagues and judgments we lie exposed to and, doubtless in many instances, are bringing down upon ourselves. These are the worst of God's judgments. How can any temporal judgment be compared with being given up to blindness of mind and hardness of heart, to being cast away from the presence of God and having His Holy Spirit cease striving with us, in having the Word and the means of grace made a savor of death unto death instead of life unto life, having a blinding and hardening effect on the hearts of men. Oh, dreadful judgments! These above all others are to be feared, for if these judgments are inflicted on any, they will ripen rapidly for eternal destruction. If persons under such judgments are allowed to continue longer upon the earth, it will only be to fill up the measure of their iniquities and to permit them to treasure up to themselves wrath against the day of wrath and revelation of the righteous judgments of God which will be revealed against them and forever inflicted on them in the world to which they are going.

This, I trust, will suffice to answer the first question, "What is meant by the judgments of God and what judgments are we exposed to that we ought to be afraid of."

II. WHAT IS MEANT BY TREMBLING FOR FEAR OF GOD AND BEING AFRAID OF HIS JUDGMENTS?

1. Trembling for fear of God implies our solemn and awful apprehensions of the great God, who brings such judgments upon us.

We are to adore God's infinite wisdom and almighty power. We are to love Him who is wise in heart and mighty in strength. Who has ever hardened themselves against Him and prospered? He removes the mountains and they know not. He overturns them in His anger. He shakes the earth out of her place and the pillars thereof tremble (Job 9:4-6). We must sanctify this Lord of Hosts Himself and make Him our fear and our dread. To fear God means that we adore His sovereignty and righteousness even in His awful dispensations and that we employ our serious, devout, and solemn thoughts on these and other glorious excellencies and perfections of Almighty God displayed in His judgments. They must be the subject of our frequent and solemn meditations so that we may always maintain in our hearts suitable apprehensions of the great

God who sends His judgments upon us.

2. Trembling for fear of God means that we are sensibly touched and affected with the consideration of the judgments that are or may yet be brought upon us.

It suggests that we so abhor them that they make deep impressions upon our hearts; that our spirits are so sorrowfully affected with the tokens of the divine anger visible therein that we weep bitterly in secret places in the consideration thereof. Indeed, they have the power to make us cry out, "Oh that my head were waters, and mine eyes a fountain of tears, that I might weep day and night" (Jeremiah 9:1). Our hearts then should be deeply and sorrowfully affected with the judgments of heaven inflicted or threatened to the point that we are grieved and concerned continually. This may be very much what is meant by "trembling for fear of God and being afraid of His judgments."

3. Trembling for fear of God means our humbling ourselves exceedingly before Him who is thus visiting and threatening us.

We can wisely lay our hands on our mouths and our mouths in the dust before Him and there repent and abhor ourselves. We ought, while trembling before Him, to judge and condemn ourselves, acknowledging that we are guilty before God, that He is justly angry with us, and that He could, in righteousness, afflict us until we are so consumed that not even a remnant escapes. We need to humbly acknowledge and declare that the Lord is just in whatever He is pleased to lay upon us; that He does right but we have done wickedly; that He punishes us much less than our iniquities deserve and, therefore, He is justified when He speaks and clear when He judges. We need to humbly accept the punishment of our sins and bear the indignation of the Lord because we have sinned against Him. We have every reason to continue sighing and crying for the abominations that are committed among us and for the many provoking evils that are to be found in the midst of us, to the infinite dishonor of the holy God and the wounding of many precious souls.

4. Trembling for fear of God implies in it the greatness of our fear and distress.

In the text it appears that the apprehensions of God's judgments frightened the Psalmist as nothing else could. It is doubtless expressed this way to set forth the greatness of his fear and to show how deeply he regarded the hand of God therein. We see how profoundly Moses felt the judgments of God, "Who knoweth the power of Thine anger? even according to Thy fear, so is Thy wrath" (Psalm 90:11). We too must receive the judgments of God in such a way as to prove they are no light and trivial thing to us. This was the attitude of David when he prayed, "O Lord, rebuke me not in Thine anger, neither chasten me in Thy hot displeasure" (Psalm 6:1). When men are very much frightened, their countenances change and their bodies tremble. Nothing can cause this trembling more than the sense of God's anger manifested in His judgments, if we are rightly sensible of them. Belshazzar's knees shook and trembled at the judgment threatened in the writing on the wall (Daniel 5:6). The holy prophet Habakkuk quaked for fear of God saying, "When I heard, my belly trembled: my lips quivered at the voice: rottenness entered into my bones, and I trembled in myself" (Habakkuk 3:16). Just so the Psalmist, in these words of our text, expresses the greatness of his fear at the apprehension of God's displeasure in His judgments. Is it not clear that these words imply our fearing nothing so much as the Lord's anger in His judicial dispensations? Surely the consideration thereof fills us with the greatest fear and concern of spirit that God has been so provoked that He has had to come out against us in His anger and to threaten our utter ruin and desolation.

5. This fear and trembling implies in it a conscientiousness and diligent care to avoid and forsake every provoking evil and to rush to God in Christ as our only refuge and safety.

Our fear of God must excite us to depart from all evil and to abstain from all appearances of it and approaches toward it. We must stand in such awe of God that we dread to allow ourselves to commit any known evil, realizing that sins are the procuring causes of the divine anger. Out of holy fear and concern of soul we will, in times of distress and danger or when under judgments indicated or feared, make haste to Christ to get under the shadow of His wings. At such times we will, in fear and trembling, say, "Be merciful unto me, O God, be merciful unto me: for my soul trusteth in Thee: yea, in the shadow of Thy wings will I make my refuge, until these calamities be overpast" (Psalm 57:1).

Such things as these are implied in our trembling for fear of God and being afraid of His judgments. I now proceed to the third and last head propounded.

III. THAT OUR CONDITION AND CIRCUMSTANCES ARE SUCH THAT WE HAVE ABUNDANT REASONS AND OCCASIONS TO TREMBLE AND BE AFRAID.

A professing people may be left to fall into sad degeneracy. They may forsake the Lord God of their fathers, depart from the blessed truths of His Word, abandon Him in respect to His holy institutions, worship, and ordinances, disregard Him in their conversation by walking in the way of pride, sensuality, and unrighteousness and by being unholy and profane. The fear of God can be so evidently wanting in men that their conduct becomes scandalous, and they sin against great light, love, and grace. Our apostasies from the good ways of the Lord may even be such that He says to us, "I had planted thee a noble vine, wholly a right seed: how then art thou turned into the degenerate plant of a strange vine unto Me?" (Jeremiah 2:21).

It is recorded concerning the children of Israel, "They turned quickly out of the way which their fathers walked in, obeying the commandments of the Lord; but they did not so" (Judges 2:17). The fathers endeavoured to uphold religion in its power, but their children did not do so. Notice how Moses once spoke to them, "Behold, ye are risen up in your fathers' stead, an increase of sinful men, to augment yet the fierce anger of the Lord toward Israel" (Numbers 32:14).

Alas! How this very thing is true in this day. The first generation of Christians has gone off the stage and in a manner the second, and is there not another, and a more sinful, risen up in their stead? We read, "Hear this, ye old men, and give ear, all ye inhabitants of the land. Hath this been in your days, or even in the days of your fathers?" (Joel 1:2). Were there such judgments formerly in New-England as there are now? You may, therefore, conclude that you have departed from God and by your sins have provoked Him so to punish you. Must not this very thing be said with reference to our state and circumstances and the late dispensations of God toward us? Alas! For us!

Did we ever have more reason to stand trembling before God under fearful apprehensions of impending vengeance when we consider the many scandalous, provoking evils abounding among us including oppression, injustice, fraud, deceit, falsehood, evil speaking, pride, contention, intemperance, drunkenness, unchastity, excessive and inordinate love of the world, and may I add, the rudeness and profaneness of young people? God Himself, and our duty to Him, is evidently neglected and forgotten by many, and a form of godliness is maintained and kept up without the life and power of it. The sacred and dreadful name of God is dishonored and blasphemed by profane cursing and swearing. His holy Sabbaths, instead of being strictly observed and sanctified, are very much profaned by idle, vain, trifling and unsuitable conduct. Some forsake the house of the Lord, frequently neglecting and needlessly staying away from the public worship of God. Has not manifold contempt been put upon the Lord's holy ordinances and institutions? Are there not many who disregard coming to them in a serious and worthy manner? Must we not acknowledge that mutual Christian love and charity grow cold? Are not both the love of men to God and the love of men to their neighbors treated with a visible coldness and indifference that clearly mark the lack of the power of godliness? Alas, for this people!

Are not the iniquities I have just described, and many more, prevailing among us and testifying against us, loudly proclaiming our impiety and great degeneracy, declaring that we are an impenitent, incorrigible, and unreformed people still, ripening rapidly for a destruction without remedy? Surely then, if this is the case with us, we have reason to tremble for fear of God and to be greatly afraid of His judgments. We might wisely be afraid of temporal plagues and judgments of a far heavier and sorer nature than we have yet been visited with, for the transgressions of God's covenant people are exceedingly provoking to Him and richly deserve to be severely punished. I beg of you, do not forget that our sins are the more offensive and provoking to God for we are a people in covenant with Him.

We are not altogether unlike those of old of whom it was said, "You only have I known of all the families of the earth: therefore I will punish you for all your iniquities" (Amos 3:2). See how God once solemnly threatened Israel, "But if ye will not hearken unto me, and will not do all these commandments; and if ye shall despise My statutes, or if your soul abhor my judgments, so that ye will not do all my commandments, but that ye break My covenant: I also will do this unto you, I will even appoint over you terror, consumption, and the burning ague, that shall consume the eyes, and cause sorrow of heart: and ye shall sow your seed in vain, for your enemies shall eat it. And I will set My face against you, and ye shall be slain before your enemies: they that hate you shall reign over you; and ye shall flee when none pursueth you. And if ye will not yet for all this hearken unto Me, then I will punish you seven times more for your sins. And I will break the pride of your power; and I will make your heaven as iron, and your earth as brass: and your strength shall be spent in vain; for your land shall not yield her increase, neither shall the trees of the land yield their fruits. And if ye walk contrary unto me, and will not hearken unto me; I will bring seven times more plagues upon you according to your sins. I will also send wild beasts among you, which shall rob you of your children, and destroy your cattle, and make you few in number; and your high ways shall be desolate. And if ye will not be reformed by Me by these things, but will walk contrary unto Me; then will I also walk contrary unto you, and will punish you yet seven times for your sins. And I will bring a sword upon you, that shall avenge the quarrel of My covenant: and when ye are gathered together within your cities, I will send the pestilence among you; and ye shall be delivered into the hand of the enemy. And when I have broken the staff of your bread, ten women shall bake your bread in one oven, and they shall deliver you your bread again by weight: and ye shall eat and not be satisfied. And if ye will not for all this hearken unto Me, but walk contrary unto Me; Then I will walk contrary unto you also in fury; and I, even I, will chastise you seven times for your sins. And ye shall eat the flesh of your sons, and the flesh of your daughters shall ye eat. And I will destroy your high places, and cut down your images, and cast your carcasses upon the carcasses of your idols, and my soul shall abhor you. And I will make your cities waste, and bring your sanctuaries unto desolation, and I will not smell the savour of your sweet odors" (Leviticus 26:14-31).

Do not we in this day need to be justly afraid of the fulfillment of these terrible threatenings? Indeed, some of them have been awfully inflicted already. When we consider our many and grievous provocations of the great God, have we not reason to fear we shall be laid utterly waste and desolate? Or if the Lord shall yet spare us, have we not reason to be greatly afraid of having brought on ourselves that fearful judgment denounced against Israel after the Lord had sworn He would not forget any of their sins and that the land should tremble for them? "Behold, the days come, saith the Lord God, that I will send a famine in the land, not a famine of bread, nor a thirst for water, but of hearing the words of the Lord: and they shall wander from sea to sea, and from the north even to the east, they shall run to and fro to seek the word of the Lord, and shall not find it" (Amos 8:11,12).

And even if our eyes shall yet see our teachers, and our ears yet hear the Word of Life dispensed to us, have we not reason to fear that the Lord's Ambassadors shall be sent on that same doleful errand the Prophet Isaiah was when one of the seraphim touched his mouth with a live coal from off the altar and told him, "Go and tell this people, Hear ye indeed, but understand not; and see ye indeed, but perceive not. Make the heart of this people fat, and make their ears heavy, and shut their eyes; lest they see with their eyes, and hear with their ears, and understand with their heart, and convert, and be healed" (Isaiah 6:9,10).

I say, when we reflect on our past unprofitableness and unfruitfulness under the precious means and advantages enjoyed by us, may we not fear the Lord thus judicially coming out against us and causing the means of grace to have a blinding and hardening efficacy upon us? May we not fear that some are already and more shall be, under such a judicial dispensation that they have not been nor are likely to be reformed, either by signal mercies or terrible judgments? May not the Lord say unto this people, as He once said unto Jerusalem when He wept over it, oh that "thou hadst known, even thou, at least in this thy day, the things which belong unto thy peace! but now they are hid from thine eyes" (Luke 19:42).

What awful symptoms there are of blindness and hardness of heart right in our midst. Ought we not to fear that men are dreadfully blinded and hardened in their sins when there is not so much as external reformation in connection with such an awful judgment of God as this earthquake? Are not the very iniquities that have been frequently and solemnly testified against by the Lord's ambassadors prevailing now as much as ever before? It was once said by an eminent divine of our own, in a sermon on a very public and solemn occasion, "That there was not a general reformation in respect of so much as any one evil found amongst us." If this is still so, and we continue going on incorrigibly in our evil ways, we must look for a continuation of temporal judgments and of shaking dispensations to be trembled at. "The Lord hath sworn by the excellency of Jacob, Surely I will never forget any of their works. Shall not the land tremble for this, and every one mourn that dwelleth therein?" (Amos 8:7,8).

Hopefully, these truths will suffice for the confirmation of the doctrine I have set before you, that the condition and circumstances of a people may be such that they have abundant reasons to tremble for fear of God and to be afraid of His judgments. If I am not greatly mistaken, we are in such a condition, and the circumstances of this day should give us sad occasion for such reflections.

I proceed to make some application of these truths.

USE ONE. We learn from the text considered, the astonishing stupidity, madness, and folly of those who do not fear the Lord and are not afraid of His judgments.

Sinners usually mock at God's judgments and put the evil day far from them, but if they would just consider that God's omniscient eye can find them out and His omnipotent arm can punish them, they may justly fear and tremble as the godly Psalmist does here in our text. I am inclined to hope that there is not a man, woman, or child who is able to reflect upon the providential dispensation of God toward us but who has had, and especially since that awful night after the last Sabbath, some concern of spirit awakened in them about working out their own salvation with fear and trembling and thereby preparing for the coming of the Lord. Verily, if you cannot say that it has been so, you have been exceedingly stupid! If you cherish such a frame, you are guilty of the greatest madness and folly. Indeed, if you don't fall down before Him and give glory to that God who has made the earth to tremble and so make confession of your sins and seek earnestly for peace with Him, He may not give you any further warning before He executes the fierceness of His anger upon you. "Hear now this, O foolish people, and without understanding; which have eyes, and see not; which have ears, and hear not: Fear ye not Me? saith the Lord: will ye not tremble at My presence?" (Jeremiah 5:21,22).

USE TWO. We learn from this text what is the best frame with which to entertain God's judgments.

We are to adore the perfections of the glorious God who is displayed in them. We are to be afraid of them, deeply abhoring the divine displeasure and humbling ourselves under His mighty hand. We are to stand in such awe of Him that we renounce and abandon every evil way and rush to the Lord Jesus Christ as our only place of refuge. "Kiss the Son, lest He be angry , and ye perish from the way, when His wrath is kindled but a little. Blessed are all they that put their trust in Him." (Psalm 2:12).

USE THREE. We learn from this text that it is not cowardly to be afraid of God's judgments but very agreeable to true Christian courage.

God is no fit match for us to contend with. No one has ever hardened himself against Him and prospered (Job 9:4). He is our Creator, we are His creatures. We are as clay in the hands of the potter. He is the King of Kings and the Lord of Lords. God cannot err on His end, as the princes of this world may in the execution of their displeasure through impotency or want of knowledge, for He is infinite in knowledge, wisdom, and power, and there is no comparison between infinite and finite. It is not cowardly then to fear God. Our Saviour advises us, "Fear not them which kill the body, but are not able to kill the soul; but rather fear Him which is able to destroy both soul and body in hell" (Matthew 10:28). Such wise fear is agreeable to true Christian courage. This should be expressed in our lives by maintaining a reverential fear of God upon our minds, in fighting against the enemies of our salvation; in mortifying our lusts; in steadfastly persevering in all the duties of our holy religion; in not disobeying His commands, despising His judgments, scorning His rod or setting ourselves in opposition to His threatenings, which is the most daring and prodigious folly and madness and will be found so in the end.

USE FOUR. We learn from what we have heard the reason for the Lord's awful threatening us as He does at this day.

Our many provoking iniquities have been the procuring cause. Our evil ways and doings have brought these rebukes from heaven upon us. We are not humbled even unto this day, neither have we feared or walked in His statues which He set before us and before our fathers. Therefore the Lord of hosts, the God of Israel, has set His face against us for evil (Jeremiah 44:10,11).

USE FIVE. Let our flesh now tremble for fear of God. Let us be afraid of His judgments. Let us at last hearken immediately to the exhortation to reform and amend our ways and doings. This we most certainly must do if we are to expect or even hope to be saved from destroying judgments.

My dear neighbors, are you trembling this day for fear of God? Are you now afraid of His judgments? Are you sensibly touched and deeply affected with the threatening tokens of the divine anger? I am sure you ought to be, and if you are not, you are stupid indeed! I hope there are few or none before the Lord now but who are in this day of fear and aprehension, serious and thoughtful concerning what may be God's meaning in this terrible dispensation. Surely the great God is very wroth. Therefore, He has been shaking the earth so terribly. In this week before us we may expect to feel yet more terrible shocks, if a thorough repentance and reformation do not prevent additional judgment. This very repentance you have been, oh how often, exhorted and urged to, and the Lord, who alone knows and searches hearts, knows how many of you there are who have never yet complied with this exhortation and have, therefore, been greatly instrumental in bringing down this unusual judgment of God upon us.

Unto such I would now address myself and with bowels of pity and concern entreat and beseech you not to go on any longer in your unrepentant state. I advise such not to be deaf to God's voice unto them this week but to be searching their hearts and trying their ways. I beseech you to no longer delay taking some suitable time to look within yourselves and to reflect with all possible seriousness and solemnity of spirit upon all your past evil ways and doings. You are also to bring to your remembrance and to especially mourn for the carnality, the corruptions, and great wickedness of your evil hearts, realizing that carnal mind and heart within you is enmity against God. Oh, be persuaded to bring your hard, corrupt, and depraved hearts to God for softening, renewing, cleansing, and healing. Plead with Him that He will take away your hearts of stone and give you hearts of flesh! Oh, plead with God the gracious promises He has made to do so for those who will seek Him for it.

And as you bring unto the Lord your corrupt and wicked hearts, so come to Him also with the wickedness of your lives lying heavy upon your hearts; wickedness by which you have dishonored God, squelched the Spirit of God and wounded your own souls. Oh, come with the utmost grief, distress, and anguish. Know and see the evil and bitterness of such ways and doings which your consciences must tell you have not been right. Abhor yourselves before God in the very remembrance of them. Judge and condemn yourselves before Him as utterly unworthy of any mercy or salvation from Him, and having thus mourned for your provocations of God, earnestly implore divine pity and pardoning mercy through the merits of Christ for His sake alone. Resolve, by the help of divine grace, that you will cast away from you all your transgressions. Then you will have reason to hope to be saved from the judgments of God or hid under the shadow of His wings until the heat of His indignation is past. By such a repentance and reformation you may answer the Lord's design and end the threatening dispensation we have been experiencing. You might then have reason to hope that the Lord will turn from the evil which he had thought yet further to have brought upon you. "Therefore now amend your ways and your doings, and obey the voice of the Lord your God; and the Lord will repent Him of the evil that He hath pronounced against you" (Jeremiah 26:13).

Oh, what encouragement have we then to be humbling ourselves before God as we do this day. But what will all our confessions avail if we will not forsake as well as confess our sins. Let each one of us then, from this day onward, set himself to reform and amend everything that is amiss. Let every one ask, "What have I done?" And "have not I done a great deal to bring down this new and tremendous judgment on the land?" If we do not, with the greatest possible concern of soul, do so, this will not be an acceptable day unto the Lord. I trust God has a remnant of His reformed and faithful people here, a number of such that tremble at His Word and at His judgments, men of humble and contrite spirits, men of prayer and of holy conversation, men who are burdened over the sins of the times and of the place in which they live, who are daily interceding with God for sparing mercy to a sinful land. And how many such are there in other towns and places, doing as we are doing here and have been in a very solemn manner all this week,[1] who are this day[2] pleading with God for mercy to a sinful people. But whether their intercessions

---

[1] The day before, all the churches in Boston kept a day of fasting and prayer.
[2] Churches in Charlestown and Roxbury and other places were fasting and praying at the time this sermon was preached.

shall prevail, God only knows.

Oh, that this might be a day of atonement to us and to our houses. Oh, that God would hear and answer our supplications to Him in this time of distress, while we are trembling before Him and greatly afraid of further terrible manifestations of His holy displeasure. Let us beg the Lord to show us what he would have us learn and do by this awful voice by which He has spoken to us. I hope, my neighbors, this is your great concern this day. I dare not any longer delay calling you thus together that we might once more unite in humbling ourselves before God and seeking His face and favor.

We do not know what a day or a night may bring forth. We are told that the day of the Lord will come as a thief in the night (2 Peter 3:10), which intimates how unexpected it will be and how surprising to a secure and wicked world. How frequent and solemn are the exhortations given us in the Gospels to "Watch and Pray" and how awakening are the motives used to excite us to do so. "Take ye heed, watch and pray: for ye know not when the time is... Watch ye therefore: for ye know not when the Master of the house cometh, at even, or at midnight, or at the cockcrowing, or in the morning: Lest coming suddenly He find you sleeping. And what I say unto you, I say unto all, Watch!" (Mark 13:33,35,36).

Oh, what cause we have had to think much upon this exhortation and the call of God to us since the last Lord's day night? How very surprising and amazing was the first sudden shock and convulsion we felt! Our houses and beds were shaking, and the earth was trembling and reeling under us like, I suppose, none ever felt in this part of the world before. And how many times has the awful noise been repeated, though not to so fearful a degree? Well may the people in this city and in the country round about be filled with the surprise and consternation of which we see and hear. Multitudes seem to be under great conviction, distress, and concern about their souls and eternity. Oh, that the impressions might abide until conversion to God is accomplished and the great work of their salvation is completed.

But it may be that up until now many of us have not been duly affected with God's awful providence. I trust many of you are now become more thoughtful about death, judgment, eternity and the speedy coming of the Lord Jesus Christ. Oh, that the Spirit of God might now fix in your hearts His convictions and never leave you until you are savingly brought to God.

You ought surely to be afraid of delaying your repentance and reformation any longer. Be thankful for the time God has given you to repent. You might have been swallowed up in the deep vaults and caverns of the earth the very first night the earth shook. But the mighty God has stayed His hand and has spared you to this hour. Will you not now do as you were exhorted to do the last Lord's day? Come trembling and abased to your Saviour and say, "Lord, what wilt Thou have me to do?" Remember the Philippian jailor came trembling to Paul and Silas after the earthquake crying out, "Sirs, what must I do to be saved?" (Acts 16:25-34). Will you not do the same? "Give glory to the Lord your God," I beseech you, "before He cause darkness, and before your feet stumble upon the dark mountains, and, while ye look for light, He turn it into the shadow of death, and make it gross darkness" (Jeremiah 13:16). "Seeing then that all these things shall be dissolved, what manner of persons ought ye to be in all holy conversation and godliness" (2 Peter 3:11). "Watch ye therefore, and pray always, that ye may be accounted worthy to escape all these things that shall come to pass, and to stand before the Son of man" (Luke 21:36). "Wherefore, beloved, seeing that ye look for such things, be diligent that ye may be found of Him in peace, without spot, and blameless" (2 Peter 3:14).

If you have an interest in God through Jesus Christ as the portion of your soul, He will be your hope and your strength. "The day of the Lord is near in the valley of decision... The Lord also shall roar out of Zion, and utter His voice from Jerusalem; and the heavens and the earth shall shake: but the Lord will be the hope of His people, and the strength of the children of Israel" (Joel 3:14,16). Such of you may say and sing with the holy Psalmist, "God is our refuge and strength, a very present help in trouble. Therefore will not we fear, though the earth be removed, and though the mountains be carried into the midst of the sea; Though the waters thereof roar and be troubled, though the mountains shake with the swelling thereof... The Lord of hosts is with us; the God of Jacob is our refuge" (Psalm 46:1-3,7). We may say with the prophet Jeremiah, "We have heard a voice of trembling, of fear, and not of peace... and all faces are turned into paleness. Alas! for that day is great, so that none is like it: it is even the time of Jacob's trouble, but he shall be saved out of it" (Jeremiah 30:5-7). The Lord will set a mark upon such as are sighing and crying for their own sins and the sins of others (Ezekiel 9:4), and He will be their protection and give them a part and portion of His kingdom that cannot be shaken when multitudes about them shall cry to the shaking rocks and mountains to fall on them and hide them from the presence of Him that sits upon the throne and from the wrath of the Lamb (Revelation 6:16,17).

Oh, that we could realize these things more! Let us cry unto God with whom is the residue of the Spirit, that He will now pour Him out upon us and our families, that our houses may be sprinkled with the blood of the great sacrifice. Let us all resolve that we will, by the help of God, walk before Him in our houses with a perfect heart; that we will put away all iniquity far from our churches; that family religion, family prayer, instruction and government shall be maintained and kept up in them; that we will be more diligent and faithful in our Master's work; that we will be consciencious about sanctifying His holy Sabbaths; that we will be no longer slothful in the business of religion but fervent in Spirit, serving the Lord; that we will work out our salvation with fear and trembling.

Make haste to Christ and so get on good terms with heaven. Give not sleep to your eyes nor slumber to your eyelids until you have sought earnestly a reconciliation to God. He may not suffer you to rest quietly if you neglect it. Oh, how comfortable it would be to be able to say with holy David, "I will both lay me down in peace, and sleep: for Thou, Lord, only makest me dwell in safety" (Psalm 4:8).

I will only add that I am greatly afraid that notwithstanding the surprise and consternation many have been and are yet in because of these terrible earthquakes, that if they should quickly and wholly cease, many in every place will return to their carnal, secure frames again. Oh, what need we have then to cry mightily unto God that He will make the impressions lasting on the souls of parents, children, young, old, rich, poor, bond and free! We have done it already. We will continue to do it, and we hope the Lord will not turn away our prayers nor His mercy from us.

Appendix

Just as the foregoing sermon was committed to the press, I received the following letter from my worthy brother, the minister of Haverhill. I believe it is well worthy of being read and will be a grateful entertainment to many and especially to all who, after their sincere humiliations and fervent supplications, are waiting and hoping to see and hear of gracious answers to prayer. When that God with whom is the residue of the Spirit shall pour it out upon the inhabitants of any place, it is certainly a just cause of great rejoicing.

While we behold or hear of such grace of God manifested towards such numbers and are glad and are giving to God the glory of His free and sovereign grace in such remarkable effects, let us earnestly pray that their goodness may not be as the morning cloud and early dew that soon goes away but that they may with purpose of heart cleave unto the Lord. Let us hope that as they have received Christ Jesus the Lord so they may walk in Him and be stabilized in the faith and standing fast in the Lord. Let us pray that the Spirit of God will fasten the convictions and impressions made upon their hearts and make them a people ready and prepared for the Lord and that there may be joy in heaven and upon earth at seeing hopeful symptoms of a true repentance and thorough reformation upon yet many more there and in other places.

Would to God we might have reason to call upon others as they do on us, to glorify God for remarkable convictions and deep impressions on the hearts of parents and children among us and in our neighborhood. Oh, that we might have in consequence thereof, a flocking of many to the Lord Jesus Christ, as of doves to their windows, asking the way to Zion with their faces thitherward and saying, "Come and let us join ourselves to the Lord in a perpetual covenant that shall never be forgotten and to the church and people of God and by due approaches to Christ at His table, prepare for His coming." Let the grace of God shown to others encourage even the chief of sinners under their convictions to cry mightily to God that the like free and sovereign grace may be glorified towards them.

If the impressions should wear off and such should return to and go on in their foolish and hurtful ways again, there will be less hope than ever of their reformation and conversion. If the late terrible earthquake doesn't stir men up to amend their ways and doings and return unto the Lord; if after this shaking they settle upon their lees again, I also say, the Lord have mercy on them.

The Letter

Haverhill
November 20, 1727

Reverend and Dear Brother,

I have wanted very much to write to you and hear from you ever since the first earthquake but I have scarcely had time to do so. The earthquakes, as far as I can hear, were much more terrible hereabouts than with you. I think there has not been a twenty-four hour period since the first quake that we have not heard them.

As to the damage done, I suppose you may have already had a better account than I can give. They say it has broken the ground in many places in Newbury. In our town, I think, no such thing has been observed but only the shaking down of tops of chimneys, the shattering of some brick houses, the shaking others so as to throw pewter off the shelves and make andirons jump off the hearth and the throwing down of stone walls, &c. In our house it stopped our clock just half an hour past ten p.m. We were in bed and I need not tell you how much we were surprised, as were indeed almost all the good people as well as bad in the town. But something of the deep and, I hope, good impressions it has made on us, I think myself concerned, in honor to our Saviour, to relate.

The next day after the first quake, October 30, we kept a public fast and had an extraordinarily full meeting from all parts of the town, six miles distance, with only two or three hours warning. I preached from Isaiah 26:21, "For, behold, the Lord cometh out of His place to punish the inhabitants of the earth for their iniquity: the earth also shall disclose her blood, and shall no more cover her slain." We were very earnest and enlarged in prayer, which seemed to be a token for good. The next Wednesday, the earthquakes still continuing, we kept another fast and had a meeting very full, with notice only given in the morning. Mr. Parsons of Bradford preached in the forenoon from Isaiah 27:9, "By this therefore shall the iniquity of Jacob be purged; and this is all the fruit to take away his sin," which I hope will be fulfilled. I preached in the afternoon from Isaiah 26:9, "With my soul have I desired Thee in the night; yea, with my spirit within me will I seek Thee early: for when Thy judgments are in the earth, the inhabitants of the world will learn righteousness." We were again very much afflicted and enlarged and the congregation the most affected that I ever saw. On Thursday we met and prayed at Bradford. From then to Saturday night I was fully employed in discoursing with people about their souls by night and day. On the Lord's day, November 5, I preached on Hosea 11:8ff, "How shall I give thee up, Ephraim? How shall I deliver thee, Israel? How shall I make thee as Admah? How shall I set thee as Zeboim? Mine heart is turned within Me, My repentings are kindled together. I will not execute the fierceness of Mine anger..." My purpose was not any further to alarm but to melt our hearts into repentance. The same day some persons that stood propounded[3] to own the Covenant, were now forthwith admitted to full communion and above thirty persons more were propounded.[4]

All the week before and after Thanksgiving I was still so busy with inquirers, rain or shine, some days from morning until eight o'clock at night, that I hardly had so much as time to take any bodily refreshments and I had but a few hours intermission for making my Thanksgiving sermon from Psalm 65:1, "Praise waiteth for Thee, O God, in Sion: and unto Thee shall the vow be performed." The next Sabbath, November 12, we propounded eighty-four persons; and again yesterday, November 19 (for my hands were full the third week) thirty-nine. People are still coming to me, so that now, since the earthquakes, I have admitted and propounded one hundred fifty-four persons; eighty-seven for the Lord's table, the rest for baptism or the renewing of their baptismal covenant. The number of men and women is pretty nearly equal, mostly younger people from fifteen to thirty, some upwards. The larger portion of those that own the Covenant are unmarried persons.

Besides these, we have a great many people that do not have enough knowledge to make any profession, yet now gladly come to enquire, "What shall I do to be saved?"

I never saw better symptoms of conversion—persons so deeply affected and seemingly humbled for their sins. Although many of them were thoughtful and, I trust, somewhat experienced in piety before, yet I cannot but think some have been immediately converted in this time of the earthquakes. Some that were the worst of drunkards, swearers, often blaspheming God, others living the worst possible kinds of lives, have been brought to their knees, humbled to the dust, melted into tears, and have seemingly made the profoundest resolutions for a new life. There seems to be in the town a general reformation. Profaneness is restrained, family worship is set up even in the most unlikely houses, the public worship is attended with earnestness, young men's meetings multiply and

---

[3]Persons who had been previously named as candidates for admission into the church.
[4]Named as candidates.

increase, family meetings are set up and Christians are generally awakened and seem to have quite another view of this and the other world.

It has looked, in short, as if we were going into a new world. These things have occasioned in me various thoughts which have been as surprising as the earthquakes themselves. I have just now been looking over the additions made to our church heretofore, and I find of one hundred nine persons that have owned the Covenant since my ministry began, fifty-four of them have done so just since last May. More than twenty young unmarried persons have been added just this summer. Of one hundred thirty persons admitted to the Lord's Table from 1719 until these earthquakes, thirty of them have been admitted within a year past, which is three times as many as in any one year before, except the first year of my ministry in which I admitted thirty-two. The evidence is that we have for some time past been growing and ripening for this harvest.

I need not make any reflections to you on these things. I want very much to hear what effects the awful visitation has had near and about you and what are the thoughts of the most judicious about the signs of the times. I beg you to send me the best accounts and to communicate this letter where you think proper, that they may glorify God for our professed subjection to the Gospel of Christ and by their prayers for such a miserable, sinful people as in general we have been.

The account I have given is in a degree proportionably true, as far as I can learn, of the towns hereabouts, considering how much less reason they have had to be humbled and reformed than we.

At Exeter, I heard a week ago, there had been forty persons baptized since the earthquake. At Almsbury, as one informed me, they seem as if they are willing to spend their whole time in the worship of God although they were too remarkably backward and slothful in duty before.

I have been so busy at home that I have heard but little from abroad. I must add, however, that the impression among us is not so general but that some, alas too many, remaining in appearance just where they were in their former security, a generation in their declining age, settled on their lees, is proof of the sovereign grace of God in effecting these things among us. The Lord have mercy on them. I beg your prayers that the impressions and convictions made on so many may issue in a repentance unto salvation not to be repented of and that we may be prepared for all future events of Providence, yea, and for the coming of the Day of God.

I subscribe, your Loving Brother,
John Brown.

CHAPTER ELEVEN

The Duty of a Degenerate People to Pray for the Reviving of God's Work

By
John Webb

John Webb, 1686-1750

John Webb was born at Braintree, Massachusetts in 1686. He graduated from Harvard College in 1708. Following this he was in charge of a school at Reading where he was very effective in impressing on the students the urgency of remembering their Creator in the days of their youth. Webb reported long afterward that this year spent keeping school afforded him more satisfaction than almost any other year of his life. Webb's great purpose in life was to serve God in the Gospel of His Son and so he entered the preaching ministry. In the course of time he was recommended by Increase Mather to the newly gathered congregation known as New North Church, Boston and in October of 1714 was ordained as their first pastor. Some years later Mather publicly declared, "I have not seen cause to repent (nor ever shall) of my commending to them a person qualified with such ministerial accomplishments, and that does lay himself out in sedulous [zealous] endeavors for the good of their children as well as of themselves." Peter Thacher was his colleague between 1720 and Thacher's death in 1738. In 1742, Andrew Eliot was ordained as his colleague. They worked together until Webb's death on April 16, 1750. Whitefield ministered at the New North Church with Webb and reported an extraordinary move of the Holy Spirit, especially among children and youth.

In Eliot's funeral address on the text, "He was a burning and a shining light," Webb was cautiously compared with the great John the Baptist of whom the words were originally spoken. "When I consider the whole of his character, I cannot but think him one of the best of Christians and one of the best ministers....It was evidently, his great concern, that he might be instrumental to build up the Redeemer's Kingdom among you; and he was for ever contriving methods in which he might serve your best interests. In his composures for the pulpit, he labored to be plain and close, that he might inform the understanding and awaken the conscience at the same time. He studied the sense more than the language, and had rather lead his hearers into right sentiments and practice, than tickle their ears with smooth and well turned periods. Nor yet was he wholly negligent of style. There was nothing in his discourses groveling or indecent; on the contrary, you will find in them a considerable correctness of language, especially in those which were composed before that paralytic shock, which he received some years since; by which (as I am told) his powers both of body and mind were greatly enfeebled. But his great ambition was, as he said several times in his sickness, to be a Gospel preacher; to dispense the Gospel of Christ in its native purity and simplicity; to bring his hearers to know God and Christ and to walk in conformity to the rules of our holy religion. And his public discourses were admirably calculated to answer these blessed purposes... He uttered his sermons with a becoming earnestness; as one that, having an inward vital sense of religion and an ardent love to God and holiness, was desirous others might be animated with the same passions which he felt in himself... His discourses were always studied, nor did I ever know him to enter the pulpit without a sermon written at length; and he herein acted upon principle, because he would not serve God with that which cost him nothing. But sometimes his heart was so warmed with the divine truths he was delivering that his notes seemed a confinement and he would, as it were, break loose and give way to those devout sentiments which crowded almost too fast into his mind, so as to render him, to use the figurative language of Elihu, 'like a bottle ready to burst.' In his public prayers, he breathed the spirit of true devotion. With what humility and lowly reverence, and yet with what ardor and earnestness did he besiege the throne of grace? Like Jacob, he wrestled with God, not knowing how to let Him go without the blessing. In him we had an example of that in-wrought fervent prayer

First published as *The Duty Of a Degenerate People To Pray For The Reviving of God's Work. A Sermon Preached June 18, 1734, Being a Day of Prayer With Fasting Observed By the New North Church in Boston. By John Webb, A. B. A Pastor of the Said Church.* Boston: Printed and sold by S. Kneeland and T. Green, 1734.

The Duty of
a Degenerate People
to Pray for the Reviving
of God's Work

**"O Lord, I have heard Thy speech, and was afraid:
O Lord, revive Thy work in the midst of the years,
in the midst of the years make known;
in wrath remember mercy."
Habakkuk 3:2**

The prophet Habakkuk lived and prophesied during one of the most degenerate times of the Jewish church state. His ministry probably occurred under the reign of Manassah, King of Judah. Vital religion was almost wholly banished from the land. The most horrid impieties against God and the greatest injustices among men were the distinguishing characteristics of the age. For these reasons the Lord revealed to this prophet His just indignation against the Jews and His holy resolution to punish them for their sins with a distressing captivity by the Chaldeans. We have a particular account of this judgment in the beginning of the first chapter. Upon hearing this, the prophet humbly complained to God of the miseries that were coming upon His people by their enemies, from the twelfth verse to the end of the chapter. It seems, by the manner of the complaint, as though the prophet was at some loss, as David before him had been, to vindicate the justice of God in punishing His sinful people by a nation at least as vile and wicked as themselves. God's gracious condescension in clearing up this difficulty for him is described in the second chapter. As a result, the prophet was encouraged to offer up that excellent prayer of faith which we find recorded in the third and last chapter.

Having given this short and general account of the scope and design of the prophecy, I now come to consider the words of my text which are the first petition in this admirable address to heaven, "Lord, revive Thy work in the midst of the years." For the understanding of this prayer we may observe two things in the verse:

First, we have here the awful impression which the above mentioned prediction and foresight of the Jewish calamities that were nigh at hand brought upon the prophet. They filled him with a holy fear and trembling, and this he confessed to God in these words, "O Lord, I have heard Thy speech and was afraid." By speech we are to understand those terrible threatenings of wrath which God had denounced against the sinful Jews and which are recorded in the preceding chapters. These threatenings God first revealed to his prophet by the Spirit of prophecy and made him the messenger of them to His sinful people. The nature of this message was such that it filled the prophet with the utmost concern as to what the events would be. He was afraid the approaching calamities would be so many, so great, and of such long continuance that the spirit of his people would fail and that the interest of religion would lose ground rather than gain by them.

Second, we may observe also the use the prophet made of these awful predictions of divine wrath against his sinful people. They constrained him to fall on his knees and pour out his heart in this prayer to God, "O Lord, revive Thy work in the midst of the years, in the midst of the years make known, in wrath remember mercy." Here you see the several articles of address to God. But it is only the first of them to which I shall confine my meditation at this time, it being more immediately adapted to the solemn occasion of this day, and that is, "O Lord, revive Thy work in the midst of the years." In these words we have the prophet's earnest request to God that He would revive His work among the apostate Jews.

As the present state and circumstances of this sinful people do too visibly and sadly resemble those of the degenerate Jews in the great decay of vital Christianity and in the growth of open profaneness and wickedness among us, I need only observe this to convince all that it is our duty and in our interest on this day to adopt this prayer of the prophet to our own case. I do not doubt that everyone of us who has the glory of God and the interest of religion at heart will humbly and earnestly join in uttering this important petition, "O Lord, revive Thy work among us."

Now, that I may in the most effectual manner excite and assist you in this affair which is the proper business of the day, I shall take up the following points:

I. What We Are to Understand by the Work of God.

II. What Is Meant by the Reviving of that Work.

III. How We Are Severally and Jointly to Make This Address to Heaven.

IV. How These Prayers Are to Be Qualified and What We Must Do That They May Be Heard and Answered by God.

I. WHAT WE ARE TO UNDERSTAND BY THE WORK OF GOD.

By the work of God, we may, in this text, understand either:

First, the Church of God among the Jews, which is sometimes called the work of His hands. In this case, the meaning of the petition is that God would revive and comfort His people and keep them from fainting in the midst of those years of affliction that were coming upon them.

Or second, by this work of God, we may understand the work of grace in and upon the hearts of His people. Then the meaning may be that God would sanctify all the dispensations of providence towards His sinful people, more particularly their approaching troubles, and make them a happy means of spiritual and saving good to them. This is the sense in which I shall consider the words and the application of them to ourselves in this day of degeneracy.

II. WHAT IS MEANT BY THE REVIVING OF THAT WORK.

I come now to observe what this petition in general implies in it so that we may better know what or how to make use of it with respect to ourselves. To this purpose, as we are now uniting in this address to heaven, I shall observe that there are three things evidently implied in it:

1. That There Was Once a Very Distinguishing Work of God's Grace in the Midst of Us, That is Either Among Our People in General or in Our Own Hearts in Particular, or in Both of Them.

For to revive anything is to renew or recover the life that once was in it. Therefore, no people in general, nor any person in particular, can properly use the prayer in this text for themselves unless God had once been graciously at work among them, unless He has heretofore set up the kingdom of His grace in the midst of them and in the administrations of this kingdom wrought many gracious effects by His Holy Spirit, either among that people in general or in the hearts of some particular persons among them. Of necessity then, this supposition comes right into the very foundation of this petition and must have been our own case if we are to use the petition with any propriety.

2. It Supposes That This Work of Divine Grace, Whatever It May be, is Fallen Into a Languishing State for the Present.

Nothing can be said properly to revive which has not lost something at least of the life and vigour it once had. Therefore, as these words in the text, "O Lord, revive Thy work in the midst of the years," had respect to the state of religion among the Jews, they suppose that it had lost much of the life and power of it and had scarcely any more than the bare form of it left. Of this, no doubt, the Prophet had an affecting sight, and like the true son of Zion who ever has the interest of religion nearest to his heart, he breathed out this pathetic prayer to heaven on his people's behalf. Consequently, this is a petition which everyone should make whenever he observes the work of God's grace in decline, either in his own heart or in the place where he lives. We shall see the reasonableness and necessity of this in what I am to observe in the next place.

3. In This Petition We Pray That the Work of God's Grace May Recover the Ground It has Lost and Come Again to Be in as Flourishing a State as Ever It Was in.

A thing never begins to revive until it begins to recover the life and strength and beauty it once had, nor can it be fully revived until it is fully restored to itself in these respects. Therefore, when we pray that God would revive His work among us, we pray that He would recover us from our own declensions in religion and that He would make the life and power of godliness to grow and prevail as much as ever. Just as vital religion never arrived to that pitch of perfection in any place or in any particular persons in this world but what there was still room for further improvements, so when we pray that God would revive His work among us, we may and ought to pray that He would enable us to daily grow in grace and abound more and more in the fruits of righteousness which are by Jesus Christ to the praise and glory of God. These are the things principally intended when we pray that God would revive His work among us.

III. HOW WE ARE SEVERALLY AND JOINTLY TO MAKE THIS ADDRESS TO HEAVEN.

Here, as the decay of vital Christianity is almost universal and there is scarce any one person or society among us but what must confess that we need the reviving influences of God's Holy Spirit at this time, I shall observe under this head that in making this address to heaven, we must pray that God would revive the work of His grace:

1. In our own hearts.
2. In our houses.
3. In our churches.
4. In our land or among our people in general.

1. We Must Pray That God Will Revive the Work of His Grace in Our Own Hearts and That This Discourse May be Universally Serviceable and by the Blessing of God Prove a Means to Convince Everyone That He is Someway or Other Concerned in it.

I shall direct myself here to two sorts of persons; first, to the unconverted and second, to the converted; and show each one how he ought to pray for the reviving of God's work in him.

1) I shall direct myself to those of you that are in an unconverted state and who, upon the least reflection, cannot fail to realize that you are so by the profane and irreligious lives which you lead.
It is your duty to pray to God that He would revive the work of conviction in you and carry it on to a thorough and saving conversion. That you may not be at a loss to know what I intend here by this reviving of conviction, I shall pursue this point in a close address to your own conscience, and I pray that, in compassion to your own souls, you will seriously attend to me for a few minutes.

In the first place, can't each of you call to mind that in some time past, perhaps in your early childhood, while you were under the care and instruction of pious parents or tutors, your heart was very much affected at the serious and solemn counsel they gave you to forsake the sins and vanities of childhood and youth and to remember your great Creator and Redeemer in your early days? When they gave you to understand what the evil and accursed nature of sin is, what the wrath of God and the torments of hell due to you for them are, did not such discourses create in you some kind of horror at sin and make you afraid to commit many sins which your heart was otherwise much inclined toward? When they went on to exhort you in the name and fear of God to give up yourself to God through Jesus Christ, in your early childhood, and represented the sweet delights and advantages of a religious life, did you not find a seeming love of religion and think and resolve many times that you would devote yourself to God as soon as you could and that you would love and serve a glorious God and Saviour all your days? As you grew to riper years, can't you remember the time when you could scarcely read the Bible or any other spiritual book or hear an awakening sermon but what your heart was affected with what you read and heard? Did you not engage conscienciously at that time in secret prayer and did you not govern carefully your thoughts, words, and actions? Were you not then afraid of many sins and afraid to live in the neglect of the most important duties of Christianity?

I am persuaded there is scarcely any person in the world born in a land of Gospel light, and more especially in this land and town, who had any due care taken of him in his childhood, but can call to mind something of this nature in his past experience. Now whatever you have had of experience of this kind in your past childhood and youth was the work of God's Spirit in and upon your hearts. The blessed Holy Spirit made use of your parents, instructors of His Word, ministers, and the like to work these convictions and awakenings in you and to excite all those good resolutions and endeavors that were consequent upon them. These are what I mean by the work of His grace in you. Although that work fell short of what we usually call saving conversion, yet then you were in a fair way to this conviction and not far from the kingdom of God.

But now let me inquire further. How is it with you at the present? Have you not lost many of the awakening impressions of your childhood and youth? Have you not broken the many solemn vows and promises you formerly made to forsake sin and to lead a holy and godly life? Have you not so long resisted and grieved the Holy Spirit that at length He has been provoked to forsake you in a great measure? And in consequence of this, do you not now live in a course of known sin and in a shameful neglect of obvious duty without any considerable remorse of conscience? Have you not at length cast off the restraints you were once under with respect to sin and taken greater delight in it than formerly you did or could? Don't you now run greedily into bad company and take a great deal of pleasure in their profane conversation? Nay, don't you readily bear a part with them in it? Can't you now curse and swear and game and drink to excess as much as the worst of them? And besides, are you not become as irreligious as any or all of them? Have you not, in a high degree, cast off the fear of God? Don't you now live in the neglect of secret prayer? Don't you despise and neglect your Bible? Don't you frequently hear the most awakening and heart searching truths delivered by ministers of Christ with an unrelenting and hard heart? In the long run, are you not growing to that point where you despise the most serious and solemn warnings and counsels that are given you in the name and fear of God and are not some of you arrived at that pitch of wickedness where you even despise your reprovers and make banter of all serious and strict religion?

Now as far as this appears to be the case with any of you that were once under the good impressions that were before mentioned, so far has the work of conviction, which was the work of God, lost ground in you. Therefore, if any in the world are bound to pray for the reviving of God's work in themselves, there is an infinite necessity that you should do so. For let me speak freely in this case and say until this work is revived you are in a most abandoned state and can have no hope at all of eternal salvation. For since by your boldness and obstinacy in sin you have already provoked the Holy Spirit to depart from you, if he never returns you will certainly be ruined forever. I plead with you, hear what the God of truth, who is certainly the best judge, has pronounced in your case:

"Woe also to them when I depart from them" (Hosea 9:12). That is simply to say "they are forever undone when I take My everlasting leave of them." That you may understand the reason for this I shall briefly observe that the Holy Spirit of God is the great author and effectual cause of a sinner's conversion and salvation. Therefore, when the Holy Spirit takes His final leave of a sinner it will not be within the power of all the angels of heaven or men on earth to convert that sinner from the error of his ways. That sinner will certainly walk on in the ways of his own heart and in the sight of his own eyes without control, just as we read of some who did so in the like case, "But My people would not hearken to My voice; and Israel would none of me. So I gave them up unto their own heart's lusts: and they walked in their own counsels" (Psalm 81:11,12). This indeed is what many a graceless and profane sinner would gladly come to for the present, for there is nothing in the world so troublesome to him now as the stings of an accusing conscience awakened by the Spirit of God. These stings do terribly embitter the pleasure of sin and make his life uncomfortable to Him. Therefore, the profane sinner favors getting rid of those convictions as fast as he can and thinks he shall never enjoy a happy moment until he has wholly suppressed them and is able to pursue his sinful lusts and pleasures without any restraint or remorse.

But alas, poor wretch, you are under the most fatal delusion in the world. Although it is according to your desire that the Holy Spirit of God should entirely forsake you and suffer you to go on in sin without any resistance, you would have but a very short race to run in sin for you would quickly fill up the measure of your iniquities and when this is once filled up it will be impossible to save you one moment longer from the dreadful damnation of hell (1 Thessalonians 2:16). Indeed, sinner, in the case you are now in, you have brought yourself near, yea, very near to the brink of endless perdition. You have no way to escape the infinite hazard but to take all the pains you can to prevail with the blessed Spirit to return and to revive the work of conviction in you. For this end you must earnestly pray to God, as in our text, "O Lord, revive Thy work in me." That is, you must go aside in some secret place and fall on your knees and there in prayer to God confess your aggravated sin and guilt in resisting and grieving His Holy Spirit so long as to provoke His withdrawal from you. Although you have forfeited God's favor and can never deserve the return of it, yet you may and must pray humbly and earnestly that God will graciously grant the return of His Spirit to you. And when you have done this, you must go on to plead that God will give you an ear more open then ever to hearken to the admonitions and counsels of the blessed Spirit of grace and an heart more soft than ever to receive all suitable impressions from them. But then, as the bare convictions of the Spirit fall short of saving conversion and the ordinary dispensations of divine grace are to be considered only as something preparatory to so great and blessed a change, you must by no means rest contented in the bare reviving of your convictions. But you must still proceed in your requests to heaven and come at length to the grand article on which the salvation of a soul depends, and with all possible importunity, you must plead that the Holy Spirit will carry on your convictions until they end in a thorough and saving conversion to God.

This is the sum of what the unconverted are to pray for when they pray that God will revive His work in them in their unconverted state and condition. Therefore, if any such sinner, who has heard or may read these seasonable truths, should be so far awakened by the Spirit of grace as to accept and make it his great concern to pursue this necessary direction, God will be glorified in that sinner and the sinner himself brought in a fair way to enjoy the presence and comfort of the Holy Ghost while he lives. He will come at length to the full and everlasting enjoyment of God through Jesus Christ in His eternal kingdom.

2) And having gone at length in my address to the unconverted, I come in the next place to direct this discourse to those of you who are in a converted state.

The sum of your duty is to pray earnestly to God that He will revive and carry on the work of His special grace in you until He has perfected your grace in eternal glory. That you may see the reasonableness and necessity of this duty, let me beseech you to enquire into your spiritual state and to see whether the good work of God has graciously begun in you. If it has begun, is it in a flourishing or a languishing condition? I fear, upon inquiry, too many of you will find in these declining years a great many reasons to complain of the decaying state of grace in your own hearts.

Do but ask yourselves these serious questions, and let each of you answer them uprightly in your own conscience: Am I as studious and diligent as I once was, to examine into my state, to determine how the case stands between God and my own soul? Am I as watchful against sin now and as careful as I once was to do my duty towards God and my neighbor? Do I take the pains I formerly took to grow and increase in grace? Do I give the same diligence to make my calling and election sure? Do I pray with as much frequency and fervency as ever? Do I carefully improve all opportunities to read and attend upon the Word of God in His house and at His table? Do I take the same pleasure and delight I once did in these duties? And do I, by these and such like means, make the same progress in grace and holiness?

When you have seriously asked yourself these questions and come to give an impartial answer to them, must not many of you be forced to bring in this heavy charge against yourselves: alas, I have made no sensible progress in grace for a great while passed but have reason to fear I have for a long time gone behind in this important concern. I am sensibly fallen into a dead, dull, and slothful frame. I am not so careful to watch over my heart and ways as once I was. I find a great indisposition to duty growing upon me. I am not so constant and lively in it as at the time of my first conviction and awakening. As the fruit of this, I find that I have lost much of my first love and have not those holy ardors of affection for God and Christ, for heaven and heavenly objects, that were once active in my soul. Neither is my faith as lively and vigorous nor my hope so strong and steadfast as in times past. In a word, I perceive all the graces of the Holy Spirit are in a very languishing condition in me. Nay, the work of God has for so long a time been losing ground in me that I am now brought to a stand and question whether I ever had even the least spark of saving grace in me. And by this means, I have lost those comforts of the blessed Spirit which once were the support and delight of my soul. I now spend my days in darkness and sorrow and fear what will become of me forever.

For all of you who are forced to subscribe to such a heavy charge against yourselves, and alas how few of us in this day of declension have been able to steer clear of it, your immediate duty is to beg God earnestly that He will strengthen the things that remain and are ready to die and that He will revive the work of grace in your hearts. You must confess and bewail your late slothfulness and negligence in duty and own that the languishing state your graces are fallen into is owing to this guilty cause. You must then fly to the blood of Jesus for a new and sealed pardon. When you have done this you must humbly and earnestly plead with God that He will not forsake the work of His grace in you, but as He has mercifully begun this good work by His Holy Spirit, you must pray for further measures of the same Spirit to enable you to arise from your bed of sloth and shake off your spiritual slumber and put on new resolution and strength in your Christian race. In particular, you must plead that the Holy Spirit will rekindle the flames of divine love in you, that He will increase your faith and strengthen your hope and every other saving grace in you. Not being content with barely regaining the ground which you have lost, you must plead that God will enlarge your heart and thereby enable you to double your diligence and make the most quick and sensible advances toward the perfection of grace and holiness. Since there is nothing that does so wonderfully strengthen and encourage the child of God in His Christian race as the light of his Father's countenance and the comforts of the Holy Ghost, you must also pray with David, "Restore unto me the joy of Thy salvation; and uphold me with Thy free Spirit" (Psalm 51:12). This is the sum of what the children of God should pray for when they are called upon to pray that God will revive His work among them.

Oh, where is the lively Christian who has made such swift advances in holiness from the day of his conversion to God to this moment that he does not find the necessity of putting up some such petition to the throne of grace on his own behalf? I am sure I dare not pretend to it myself. Although I do not doubt there are many fruitful Christians among us, yet I question whether the best of you would venture to excuse yourself in this matter.

Hence it is the duty of every child of God here to pray that God will revive and carry on the work of grace in his own soul. If the Spirit of grace that dwells in you enlarges your hearts in these supplications, you will find your account in them rich indeed, for then the same Spirit will be also a Spirit of consolation in you and will fill you with joy unspeakable and full of glory.

And thus we have considered the first article proposed. I have shown both sinners and saints how they ought to pray that God will revive His own work in them. Sinners must pray that God will revive the work of conviction in them and carry it on until they are savingly converted to Himself. The children of God must pray to their heavenly Father that He will revive and carry on the work of His special grace in them until He has perfected their grace in eternal glory. I have gone to this length on the first point because, if ever there is to be a reviving of God's work among us, it must first begin with particular persons and then extend to the several communities to which we belong. This leads me now to the next article.

2. We Must, in This Day of Declension, Pray That God Will Revive the Work of His Grace in Our Own Houses.

As every man is bound, in the first place, to have an immediate respect to himself, so next to himself, every man ought to be immediately concerned for the welfare of his own household or family. For these, of all others, are in the nearest relationship to him and claim the next share in his affectionate regard for their good. Hence, all heads of families are strictly required in the Gospels to provide for their own, especially for those in their own houses (1 Timothy 5:8). He that neglects to take this care of them is said in the same place to have denied the faith and is pronounced worse than an infidel. Clearly, the provision here intended by the Apostle is financial support; but if the command for support is binding, it is much more binding with regard to the spiritual and eternal welfare of those whom God in His providence has committed to our charge. Our souls are certainly more precious than our bodies, and by consequence, the souls of those in our families are even in a more special manner to be taken care of by us. In expressing this care for those we are so immediately concerned for, we ought particularly to pray that God would revive the work of His grace in their hearts.

That you may know how to time this duty aright and when to use the greatest importunity in it, you that are heads of the families and have the instruction and government of others committed to you by our common Lord and Master must carefully observe the state of religion in the house and inquire how it is with every particular person in it. Then you may have the greater influence and success in this matter. You must begin yourselves and with the tenderest affection observe each other. If either of you discerns the least decay of that vital piety or any neglect of duty growing on the other, you ought in this case, first, in the most affectionate manner to admonish one another of what you have seen amiss. Then in your secret address to heaven, the husband must plead with God for the wife as for his own soul that He would revive His work in her, and the wife in her turn must beg the same mercy for him and with the same importunity. When the heads of the family are thus faithful to one another, they will have surer grounds to hope for the success of their prayers to God for their household.

When you have done your duty toward each other, you must unite in observing what is the state of religion among your dear children and others in your household. As pious parents are accustomed to begin to instruct their little ones in the fear and service of God and for the most part to see the reward of their care and pains and prayers in the early impressions that are made on their tender minds and consciences, so as your children and youth grow in years and are more exposed to bad company and evil examples abroad, you must diligently observe what impressions the manner of the world makes upon them. If you perceive they are gradually falling away from the hopeful beginnings that were earlier discernable in them, you must instantly carry their case to the God of all grace and beg earnestly of Him that He would not forsake such a child nor suffer the good impressions of early childhood to wear away and to come to nothing. Beseech Him to still remember covenant mercies and to revive the work of His grace in that child so as it grows in years it may grow in grace and in the knowledge of our Lord and Saviour Jesus Christ and be furnished with all those gifts and graces that are necessary for the serving of God and it's generation according to the will of God. This duty is certainly comprehended in that general charge which the Apostle has given to parents and heads of families to bring up their children in the nurture and admonition of the Lord (Ephesians 6:4). Without it we can never resolve to any purpose that as for us and our houses we will serve the Lord. From hence it appears that this duty is in a peculiar manner incumbent on the heads of families.

However, the duty is not to be confined to heads of families in such a way as to excuse all the other branches and members of it. In many of our houses there are children and youth who are grown to years of understanding who are capable of observation and prayer. Where there are such children, their near relationship to the family and their interest in it is so united with the whole that God expects them to pray for their parents and for one another that whatever may be wanting of the grace of God in them may be richly supplied by the Spirit of our Lord Jesus Christ and that everyone in the house may abound everyday more and more in the fruits of righteousness.

To close this point, we may observe, for our encouragement to duty, that when families are made up of such religious members, their houses are the dwelling places of Jacob, and the God of Jacob will be in the midst of them to revive and to carry on His own work in them and to shower down all the blessings of goodness upon them.

3. While Religion is Losing Ground Among Us We Must Pray That God Will Revive His Work in Our Churches.

In order that we may know how to form our petitions aright on this head, let us consider that when God first planted these churches, He planted them a noble vine and a ripe seed. From the several accounts our fathers have left, we have reason to think that there was as great a purity in doctrine and worship, as much of vital Christianity, and as many evidences of the gracious presence and glory of Christ in them as in any of the churches in these latter days. But now, though we still retain to a good degree the purity of Christian doctrine and worship, yet as God has increased our numbers and blessed us more abundantly in outward respects, the Spirit of this world has eaten out much of the life and power of godliness, and with the Ephesians of old, we have lost much of our first love. We must acknowledge that we do not have nearly as much of that zeal for the honor of God and of that indignation against sin as was once the glory of these churches. To speak freely in the case, have we not altogether too much reason to fear that those of us in the ministry are not universally so full of tender concern for the glory of our Redeemer and the salvation of precious souls nor nearly so lively and searching in our preaching as our fathers that have gone to glory?

When we take a careful survey of our dear people, how do we find the case with them? Is it any breach of charity for me to say that I fear they do not so generally prize and improve their opportunities for hearing the Word as the generations did that are past? Of this I think we have the most convincing proof in the scandalously thin attendance we have on lecture days which in late remembrance used to be met with crowded assemblies. But even more distressing is the shameful neglect of public worship on the Lord's day of which many are guilty and which has often been lamented as a growing sin in the town and land. When we go into a Christian assembly, how little we have of that religious attention, love, and delight which were once to be seen in the countenances of God's people, and how few of the hearers now make it a matter of conscience to water the seed of the Word with their prayers to God. As a direct result of this neglect of means, thorough and saving conversions are comparatively rare in our churches. Of this small number is there not still a lesser number, in proportion, that are bright ornaments of Christianity and who show forth the life and power of godliness in their whole conversation? Besides this, have we not just cause to fear that the reins of church discipline have been let loose to an unreasonable length in many of our churches and that we are grown too careless in our admissions to the holy table of the Lord, too negligent in our watch over those who are admitted, and too indulgent to too many whose lives are a scandal to their holy profession? For these and like reasons, are not our churches falling rapidly into a most detestable lukewarmness and indifference in religion?

Indeed, God has now and then, by His Word and providence, somewhat revived His work among us. In particular, between six and seven years ago, there was, I believe, as great and general a concern awakened in our people about the state of their souls and another world, when the heavens were blazing over our heads and the earth trembling under our feet, as there has ever been at any time from our beginning to this day. I cannot but hope there were many saving conversions wrought in our churches at that time. But alas, as though nothing of the most amazing thunders and lightnings and the most terrible earthquakes could awaken us, we are at this time fallen into as deep a sleep as ever. Indeed, there is scarcely anything of the working of God's Spirit to be seen among us now. For now it is seldom indeed that any sinner is so far awakened by the Word as to go to His minister and enquire of him what he must do to be saved. It is a rare thing to see someone come and give up his name to God in public and so renew his covenant at the table of the Lord. This is certainly one of the darkest signs we have of the Holy Spirit's withdrawal from us. We of this church have sad reason to lament after a departing God in this respect. From the mournful complaints I have heard from many others, I fear it is too universally so throughout the land.

From the observation of these things it is easy to learn how we are to form our petitions when we pray that God will revive His work in our churches. We must pray that He will abundantly pour forth His Spirit from on high and recover these declining churches to their first love and to their first works. We must pray that a double portion of that good Spirit which rested upon our Fathers in the ministry may descend upon the existing and upcoming ministry at this day to enable them to preach the Gospel of Christ in the greatest plainness and purity and to make them burning and shining lights both in their doctrine and conversation. Again, we must pray that the administration of divine ordinances in our churches may be attended and made successful by the Spirit of our Redeemer. We must pray that saving conversions may be multiplied in them and converts filled with righteousness. In particular, we must pray for the children of God's covenanting people that God will revive His work among them and sanctify their souls in their young and tender years and make them a seed to serve the Lord. If we can once see the success of these prayers, God's work will gloriously revive in our churches, and our blessed Redeemer will delight to dwell in the midst of them to defend them from their enemies and to refresh them with the presence and communion of His Holy Spirit. As an excellent means to this end, I observe in the last place that,

4. We Must, in These Declining Years, Pray That God Will Revive His Work in Our Land and Among Our People in General.

If we will only consider what a people we once were and what we are now become, we shall soon see the necessity of making this address to heaven. If we look back to that generation of our forefathers who first came into this wilderness, we shall find they were a generation of wise and conscientious men who came hither purely on the score of religion that they and their posterity might enjoy the ordinances of Christ in the purity of them. Consequently, as soon as they gained footing here, they not only set up churches according to the Scripture pattern but formed the civil government and all the societies among them in the best manner to serve the great ends of Christianity. Agreeably, there was a most religious and commendable zeal in all orders to suppress every vice and immorality at the very first appearance of it and to promote the honor of God.

But alas! How we are fallen from our first purity! Are we not at this day become the degenerate plants of a strange vine? Is it not visible to every eye that irreligion and profaneness abound in every part of the land? Have you not, many times, had a black catalogue set before you of the most barefaced and horrid impieties that are reigning among us? Where is the zeal and courage, in any order of men, that are necessary to stem this torrent of iniquity which threatens us with swift destruction? And what can we do less in this day of degeneracy than to cry earnestly to God that He would revive His work in this whole land? Accordingly, we are indispensably bound to pray that God would pour down His Holy Spirit on all orders and ages among us. First, upon our rulers that they may be inspired with zeal and strength to make headway against the growing iniquities of the time and, by their authority and example, to beat all immortality and irreligion quite out of countenance. Then, upon our people in general to restrain their unruly lusts and to inspire them with principles of sobriety, righteousness, and godliness. In a word, we must pray that the several orders and societies of men among us, whether greater or lesser, may happily unite in promoting the glory of God, the interest of religion, and the welfare of the whole, so that as the prophet says, "Let judgment run down as waters, and righteousness as a mighty stream" (Amos 5:24). If we live to see such happy days as these, we shall live to see the work of God gloriously revived among us. Thus I have largely considered the third general point in this discourse and have shown how we are to severally and jointly make our address to God that He would revive His work among us. And, therefore, I come now in the last place to consider

IV. HOW THESE PRAYERS ARE TO BE QUALIFIED AND WHAT WE MUST DO THAT THEY MAY BE HEARD AND ANSWERED BY GOD.

Here let me provide the following particulars,

1. We Must Humbly Offer up These Prayers to God in the Name of the Lord Jesus.

There is but one only living and true God who is the proper object of prayer and but one Mediator between God and men, the man Christ Jesus (1 Timothy 2:5). We have no other way of access to the Father, in our fallen state, but in and through Him. Out of Christ, God is a consuming fire. In and through Him, He is a prayer-hearing God. For this reason Christ Himself said "I am the way, the truth, and the life: no man cometh unto the Father, but by Me" (John 14:6). His Apostle tells us that believers have boldness to enter into the holiest by the blood of Jesus by a new and living way which He has consecrated for us through the veil, that is to say His flesh (Hebrews 10:19,20). Just as through Christ we offer up our prayers to God on every other occasion so on the present occasion we must make use of the merits and mediation of our dear Saviour for audience and acceptance. And agreeably, Christ Himself has directed us to this and given His word that such prayers, when the matter of them is according to the will of God, shall obtain an answer of peace: "Verily, verily, I say unto you, Whatsoever ye shall ask the Father in My name, He will give it you... Ask, and ye shall receive, that your joy may be full" (John 16:23-24).

2. We Must Pray by the Help and Assistance of the Holy Spirit of God.

Although God has made it our duty to pray to Him and although we have continual dependence upon Him for all we need, yet we ourselves do not know what to pray for or how to order our speech before Him. We even have, by nature, a great indisposition to this duty. For the most part, a sinner would rather do most anything than engage in serious and solemn prayer. When he is driven to it in any extremity, he finds more of a burden in it than any true pleasure or delight. We must therefore obtain direction and assistance from on high before we can perform the duty to any advantage. This truth is confirmed to us in that remarkable passage of the Apostle Paul, "Likewise the Spirit also helpeth our infirmities: for we know not what we should pray for as we ought: but the Spirit Himself maketh intercession for us with groanings which cannot be uttered. And He that searcheth the hearts knoweth what is the mind of the Spirit, because He maketh intercession for the saints according to the will of God" (Romans 8:26,27). Therefore, when we pray to God in any case, if we desire to be heard and accepted of Him, we must offer up our prayer not only in the name of Christ but by the special assistance of the Holy Spirit. And to this purpose, whenever we go into the presence of God on any occasion, we must first of all be concerned to obtain the presence of the blessed Spirit with us and beg this gift from God who has given us encouragement to ask saying, "If ye then, being evil, know how to give good gifts unto your children: how much more shall your heavenly Father give the Holy Spirit to them that ask Him?" (Luke 11:13). Then, under the influence of this Spirit of grace and prayer, we must spread our requests before God as He shall direct and enable us in the name of our Lord Jesus Christ. Having such a prevailing Mediator in heaven as Christ and such a powerful assistant on earth as the Holy Spirit,

3. We Must in the Next Place Offer Up Our Prayers to God in Faith.
That is, we must firmly believe that whatever we ask of God according to His will, in the name of Christ and by the help of the Holy Spirit, shall be graciously heard and answered. We have the surest foundation for such a faith in the Word of God. For therein God is not only styled a prayer-hearing God, "O Thou that hearest prayer" (Psalm 65:2), but a prayer-answering God as our blessed Redeemer has promised in the foresighted sixteenth chapter of John, "Verily, verily I say unto you, whatsoever ye shall ask the Father in My name, He will give it you" (verse 23) And this is the ground of that holy assurance which the Apostle John expresses, "This is the confidence that we have in Him, that, if we ask anything according to His will, He heareth us" (1 John 5:14). But lest this faith should prove but a bold presumption, I come to say,

4. We Must Be Very Earnest and Importunate in Our Prayers to God and Persevere in Them Until We Obtain the Mercy We Pray For.
To be cold and formal in any prayer to God is to invite a denial from Him. Therefore, in such a case, to hope for an answer of peace is the most daring presumption. For this reason fervency is made an essential qualification of such prayers as are acceptable to God through Jesus Christ: "The effectual fervent prayer of a righteous man availeth much" (James 5:16). Indeed, when we consider with whom we have to do in prayer, of how great importance it is that we should obtain the answer of our requests, especially when we pray for such a comprehensive blessing as the reviving of God's work, we may easily be convinced that we can never be too much in earnest in our supplications to God on this occasion. Agreeably, when we look into the Holy Scriptures and meet with any account of the saints praying to God, we shall find either in the prayer itself, if it be recorded there, or in the general account that is given of it that they were in a flame of devotion and offered up their petitions to heaven with the greatest ardency of soul. This you may easily see by turning to the prayers of Moses, Samuel, David, Ezra, Daniel, and many more that are recorded at length in the sacred pages. But I shall only observe to my purpose that the language which the Holy Ghost frequently makes use of to express the prayers of the saints denotes the greatest fervor of spirit in them. Thus the prayers of Moses and Samuel for the people of Israel in the times of their distress are expressed by

their crying to the Lord.[1] The same language is often used in regard to the prayers of David in the Book of Psalms and in many other instances besides those I have named.

Therefore, if we would succeed in our supplications to God for so important a blessing as the reviving of the work of God, we must be frequent and fervent in our prayers to God for it. If we do not presently see the success of these prayers, we must not be discouraged and give over the duty, but we must humbly resolve, with holy Jacob in his wrestling with the angel of the Lord, that we will not let Him alone until He blesses us (Genesis 32:24-26). We must persevere in the duty and cry to God with all possible importunity until we find the Holy Spirit reviving His own work both in ourselves and in others. If God does but once open and enlarge our hearts to pray to Him with this persevering importunity, we need not doubt the success of our prayers. God can as soon deny Himself as deny an answer to the fervent prayers of His people. Thus you see how our prayers must be qualified if we desire to obtain a gracious answer to them.

I shall observe one thing more which will be the result of such prayers and which, if we could suppose the want of, would hinder the efficacy of the best of our prayers, and that is,

5. We Must With Our Prayers to God for This Mercy, Unite Our Best Endeavors to Obtain What We Pray For.

To help you understand the reason for this I shall just observe that although it is God alone who performs all things for us by His almighty efficacy, yet as He has made us reasonable creatures and furnished us with noble powers fit for important service, He justly expects we should be workers together with Him in accomplishing our peace and happiness. This is evident from those passages of the Apostle which have respect to the greatest concern which we have in the world, namely the securing of our eternal salvation: "Work out your own salvation with fear and trembling. For it is God which worketh in you both to will and to do of His good pleasure" (Philippians 2:12,13). There is no man in the exercise of reason but thinks it his duty, when he prays to God for any temporal good, to do the best he can in the use of lawful means for the obtaining of it. And, therefore, if we should pray to God for any spiritual blessing and take no further care or pains to obtain what we pray for, it would be vain presumption in us to ever expect the answer of such prayers of mercy. From hence it appears very evident that we must not only pray to

---

[1]See Exodus 15:25, First Samuel 7:9.

God for the mercies we need, but we must at the same time use all other means that are proper and necessary to obtain them. Now let me apply this to the case at hand.

1) Do we pray that God will graciously revive His work in our own hearts?

We must take the greatest pains we can in the use of all proper means to revive His work in us. Therefore, I shall say first to the unconverted, when God has brought you to pray that He will revive the work of conviction in you and carry it on to a thorough conversion, you must at the same time sit down and think first how great your sin and guilt has been in stifling your past convictions and what a dreadful case you will quickly be in should the blessed Spirit of grace wholly forsake you and leave you to perish forever in your sins. Then you must take all the pains you can, not only in prayer but also by meditation, self examination, reading, hearing the Word of God, Christian conversation, and the like, to get and preserve a tender conscience in yourself. In particular, you must strive to break off your sins by righteousness and your iniquities by turning unto God. You must cast off all your old companions in sin and do what you can to forsake those evil courses whereby you have hardened your heart in rebellion against God. Then apply yourself with care and diligence to all the above-mentioned duties of religion which have a tendency to bring a sinner into a state of salvation by the Redeemer. If ever God should have mercy upon you and revive His work in you to any saving advantage, it will doubtless be in this way.

With respect to such of you as are in a converted state, you cannot but see the need in which you stand of the revival of God's work in you in these degenerate years. Although God, of His free and sovereign grace, has already brought you into a state of salvation, yet are not your graces so weak and languishing as to require the reviving of them, and must they not be carried on many degrees farther toward the perfection of grace before you can think yourselves meet for eternal glory? Therefore, you must not only pray to God for this invaluable mercy but you must stir yourself up to a more diligent use and improvement of all those means which God has appointed for our growth in grace and in the knowledge of our Lord and Saviour Jesus Christ. These in general are the same that God has ordained for the getting of grace in the hearts of the unconverted, except the feeling ordinances of the new covenant which are more peculiarly adapted to the state of the converted and have a singular tendency in the right use of them to strengthen the graces of the Holy

Spirit in the hearts of God's children. Shall not the sensible need you stand in of the comforting presence of God, while you want His reviving influences, be as a thousand motives to quicken you to all diligence in your duty? For can you enjoy any comfort while a heavenly Father frowns upon you? Can you ever expect to rejoice in the light of His countenance until you receive the word of exhortation from Peter, "Wherefore the rather, brethren, give diligence to make your calling and election sure" (2 Peter 1:10).

2) Do we pray that God will revive His work in our houses?

These prayers must be accompanied with all proper endeavors by those in the family, especially by the heads of it, to make religion thrive and flourish in it. Therefore, we that are parents and heads of families must set ourselves to reform all family disorders and to keep up family instruction and worship and government after the example of Abraham concerning whom God gave this honorable testimony, "For I know him, that he will command his children and his household after him, and they shall keep the way of the Lord, to do justice and judgment" (Genesis 18:19), and after the example of Joshua who came to that resolution which no doubt he made good to the day of his death, "But as for me and my house, we will serve the Lord" (Joshua 24:15). For this purpose we must first set a holy example before our houses. Each of us must say with David, "I will walk within my house with a perfect heart" (Psalm 101:2) and so by a heavenly conversation recommend vital religion to all whom God has placed under our charge. Again, we must daily and seasonably keep up family worship such as reading the Word of God and prayer and show the warmth of our devotion both in our morning and evening sacrifices. Once more, we must carefully improve all proper seasons for the instruction of our dear children and other householders in the principles of holy religion. That these instructions may answer the great end for which they were given, we must often set before them both the awakening and alluring motives of the Gospel. We must on the one hand represent sin to them, in all its frightful colors, and show them the accursed nature and dreadful tendencies of it. On the other hand, we must exhibit true religion to them in all its attractive charms, as it is accomplished with the most substantial peace in this world and leads to everlasting blessedness in the world to come, and see if by these means we can't bring them quickly to know and serve the God of their fathers with a perfect heart and a willing mind. But if these endeavors prove unsuccessful and we find necessity for it, we must in the last place, lay the restraints of reproof and correction upon them. For in this case the wise man tells us, "The rod and reproof give wisdom: but a child left to himself bringeth his mother to shame" (Proverbs 29:15), and "Correct thy son, and he shall give thee rest; yea, he shall give delight unto thy soul" (verse 17). And to show how consistent this is with the most tender paternal affection, he tells us in another place, "He that spareth his rod hateth his son: but he that loveth him chasteneth him betimes" (Proverbs 13:24).

3) Do we pray that God will revive His work in our churches?

We must with our prayers unite heart and hand in recovering and promoting the power of godliness in them. Ministers must take all possible care and pains in the course of their ministry to revive the work of conviction and conversion among the unconverted and to promote the work of edification and comfort among the converted in their flocks. The people under their charge must make conscientious effort to give the most diligent and careful attendance to all the administrations of divine ordinances among them and both together, that is both ministers and people, must unite in maintaining the purity of worship and the discipline in the churches of our Lord Jesus Christ. I cannot forebear, on this occasion, putting you in mind that as we are perhaps the most explicit of any in the world in our covenanting one with another when first forming ourselves into the church state and in our admission of members afterwards to the special privileges of church communion, so I verily believe the scandalous neglect of the duties of this covenant, which are no other than what the Gospel expressly requires of all the disciples of Christ, is one of the most fatal causes of that sad degeneracy we are experiencing. For while those who are under the most solemn covenant ties one to another do, contrary to their engagements, neglect to watch over and reprove each other as the matter may require, and afterwards refuse to inform and to give in their testimony against those whom they know to be scandalous in their lives, all the care and vigilance of the overseer proves many times to be ineffectual in bringing such offenders under the discipline of the church and wiping off the reproach that is too often cast on our churches by this means. Therefore, I must press it as indispensable duty on all that are in the communion of our churches to remember the solemn vows we are under to God and to one another to maintain the purity of Christian morals in our religious combinations. As we would not be partakers of other men's sins, nor run the hazard of God's displeasure by a criminal indifference when His holy name and religion are reproached among us, we must be faithful to God, faithful to His church and people, and faithful to each minister of the church society to which we belong in bearing a testimony against sin both private and public as the particular case may call for it. If to this we add the reviving of Christian conversation, which too many professors are growing great strangers unto, and improve proper times and seasons to quicken and encourage one another by this means in the ways of virtue and religion, I am persuaded these things would go a great length toward reviving the work of God among us at this day. Now in the last place,

4) Do we pray that God would revive His work in our land?

These prayers must be accompanied with the united endeavors of both magistrates and peoples, in their respective places, to put a stop to that flood of iniquity which so amazingly threatens our ruin at this day and to encourage virtue and religion wherever it appears. Accordingly, all those that are clothed with any civil authority should, in their several stations, exert themselves with the greatest zeal and diligence in this matter. For this is the very end for which they are ordained of God. The Apostle Paul observes, "Rulers are not a terror to good works, but to the evil... He is the minister of God to thee for good... a revenger to execute wrath upon him that doeth evil" (Romans 13:3,4). With this the Apostle Peter agrees, for he says rulers are ordained for the punishment of evil doers and for the praise of them that do well (1 Peter 2:14). Therefore, if they would answer the great end of their institution, they must, in this degenerate age, first lead the way to a reformation by their own exemplary conversation which can scarce fail of having a good influence when it is conspicuous to the world. Then they must exert their superior power to keep up good order among the people and to maintain the authority of the good and wholesome laws we have for the support of religion, for the protection and encouragement of those who do well, and for the restraint of evil doers. Since these last are the men to whom all our miseries are owing, since they are greatly increased through the land and do daily strengthen one another's hand in wickedness and many times bid defiance to all opposition, civil rulers should make it a great part of their business to curb the unruly lusts of these bold and daring transgressors and bear a due and faithful testimony against them by a zealous and impartial execution of the laws against all open profaneness and irreligion.

And as they will need all the assistance they can obtain in this affair, all persons in a private station, who have the interest of religion and the welfare of their people at heart, must zealously unite with them in the same good cause. For though you have no coercive power in your hands to restrain and chastise the open profaneness and insolence of others, yet you may do a great deal to promote a general reformation. You may and must condemn the ungodly lives of sinners by a good conversation in

Christ Jesus and hereby endeavor to shame them out of their evil courses in keeping with that direction our Saviour gave to His disciples, "Let your light so shine before men, that they may see your good works, and glorify your Father which is in heaven" (Matthew 5:16).

Again, where there is any hope of reclaiming such as walk disorderly, you must act the part of faithful and friendly reprovers of them. This is a duty (notwithstanding the too general neglect of it) which God indispensably requires of us, "Thou shalt not hate thy brother in thine heart: thou shalt in any wise rebuke thy neighbor, and not suffer sin upon him" (Leviticus 19:17). If there be anything of ingenuity in the sinner he will receive such reproofs in a friendly manner and say with David, "Let the righteous smite me; it shall be a kindness: and let him reprove me; it shall be an excellent oil, which shall not break my head" (Psalm 141:5).

But where all other means prove unsuccessful and sinners appear bold and incorrigible in their transgressions, you must in good conscience inform the civil magistrates against them. They have power to call them to an account and to punish them for their open profaneness and irreligion. When you are required by lawful authority, you must be sure to give a plain and faithful testimony against them in order that they may receive the just punishment due evil doers and be made public examples for a warning to others. In this way you will certainly deliver your own souls and may be a means also, by the grace of God, to save the souls of others from eternal death. Thus I have briefly considered the means we must use, with our prayers to God, for the revival of His work among us.

And now to conclude. If by such prayers and endeavors as these we can once prevail with the Lord to revive His work in these declining years, Oh, what a happy prospect we shall have. Then may we hope to see the fulfillment of those gracious promises in Isaiah, "For I will pour water upon him that is thirsty, and floods upon the dry ground: I will pour My Spirit upon thy seed, and My blessing upon thine offspring: And they shall spring up as among the grass, as willows by the water courses. One shall say, I am the Lord's; and another shall call himself by the name of Jacob; and another shall subscribe with his hand unto the Lord, and surname himself by the name of Israel" (Isaiah 44:3,5). In a word, then may we hope that the great Emmanuel will own us for His land and people and that the name of this place from hence forward will be Jehovah-Shammah, the Lord is here. Amen.

CHAPTER TWELVE

God's People Must Enquire of Him to Bestow the Blessings Promised in His Word

By
Joseph Sewall

Joseph Sewall, 1688-1769

Joseph Sewall was born in the city of Boston, in a very distinguished home, on August 15, 1688. His father, the Honorable Samuel Sewall, was a long-time judge and for several years the Chief Justice of the Superior Court of Massachusetts. His mother's father was John Hull, one of the founders of the Old South Church and one-time Treasurer of the Province.

As a youth he came under deep spiritual impressions, was converted, and determined to enter the ministry. He graduated from Harvard in 1707. In 1713 he was invited to share the ministry at Old South Church with Ebenezer Pemberton and was ordained there on September 16, with both Pemberton and Increase Mather participating. That same year he married Elizabeth Walley, a widow. Only one of his children survived him, a son Samuel. During his years at Old South, he shared the ministry not only with Pemberton but with Thomas Prince, Alexander Cumming, and John Blair. Sewall was on excellent terms with each of these colleagues but particularly intimate with Prince with whom he shared regular seasons of united prayer as these extracts from his diary indicate: "1721,2, January 5. Mr. Prince and I prayed together, as is usual before the sacrament of the Lord's Supper. Lord hear our prayers...1722, Nov. 2. Mr. Prince and I met together and prayed to God for direction and assistance relating to the fast to be kept by the church we stand related to."

In 1724 Harvard chose him as President, but he declined because his church was unwilling to release him. He did become a Fellow of the Corporation in 1728 and served the in that capacity until 1765. Upon the death of his parents, he received a considerable inheritance,.much of which was used to support godly students who would have otherwise been unable to attend college. The University of Glasgow honored him with a Doctor of Divinity degree in 1731. He served as a corresponding member of the S.P.C.K. in Scotland and was a Commissioners "For the Propagation of the Gospel in New England..." Dr. Sewall enjoyed physical, mental, and spiritual health, preaching on the completion of his eightieth year. The next Sabbath he was taken ill and after months of suffering died victoriously June 27, 1769. According to Sprague, Sewall "was distinguished above almost any other man of his time for devotional fervor, and simple and earnest engagedness in his work. He was familiarly known as 'the good Dr. Sewall,' and sometimes as 'the weeping prophet.' Into the revival of 1740 he entered with his whole heart, and without endorsing all Whitefield's extravagances, he cordially welcomed him to his pulpit, cooperated with him in his measures, and gave him the full influence of his general approval." Dr. John Eliot said, "He was a man who seemed to breathe the air of heaven, while he was here upon earth; he delighted in the work of the ministry; and when he grew venerable for his age as well as for his piety, he was regarded as the father of the clergy. The rising generation looked upon him with reverence, and all classes of people felt a respect for his name. He was a genuine disciple of the famous John Calvin. He dwelt upon the great articles of the Christian faith in preaching and conversation; and dreaded the propagation of any opinions in this country, which were contrary to the principles of our fathers. Hence he was no friend of free inquiries, or to any discussion of theological opinions, which were held by the first Reformers... His sermons were pathetic; and the pious strains of his prayers, as well as preaching, excited serious attention, and made a devout assembly. His character was uniform; and the observation has often been made, if he entered into company, something serious or good dropped from his lips. His very presence banished away everything of levity, and solemnized the minds of all those who were with him."

First published as *God's People Must Enquire of Him To Bestow the Blessings Promised In His Word. A sermon Preached February 16, 1741-1742 on a Day of Prayer Observed by the South Church...in Boston, to Seek of God the More Plentiful Effusion of His Holy Spirit upon Them and His People.* Boston: Printed by D. Fowle for D. Henchman in Cornhill, 1742.

God's People Must Enquire of Him to Bestow the Blessings Promised in His Word

**"Thus saith the Lord God;
I will yet for this be enquired of
by the house of Israel, to do it for them."
Ezekiel 36:37**

The prophecies contained in this chapter may relate to the deliverance of God's ancient people out of the Babylonish captivity. Doubtless, they also look further and may refer to the calling of the Jews, even to the flourishing state of the whole Israel of God. Temporal blessings are promised here, but the promise of spiritual blessings is even more apparent. It is said that God will do these great things for them in answer to prayer. God had earlier put His people in mind of their own great unworthiness and declared that He would not do these things for their sakes but for His holy name's sake. However, He desired the House of Israel to enquire of Him for these benefits. The words may imply a command that God required His people to seek Him for the accomplishment of these precious promises. They may also embrace in them a further promise that God will put it into their hearts and incline them thus to enquire after Him. The words here used should be seen as signifying their seeking and inquiring with all diligence. The words may also imply that God will manifest Himself so that He can readily be found of them.

DOCTRINE. God will be enquired of and sought unto by His people, to bestow the blessings which He hath promised to them in His Word.

I. God has in His Word promised to bestow all needed blessings upon His people.

II. God will be enquired of and sought by His people that He may bestow these blessings upon them.

I. GOD HAS IN HIS WORD PROMISED TO BESTOW ALL

NEEDED BLESSINGS UPON HIS PEOPLE.

In the Bible we have the great charter of God's Covenant People. It contains and confirms to the faithful all those blessings which God is pleased of His free grace, through the merits of Christ, to confer upon them. "According as His divine power hath given unto us all things that pertain unto life and godliness, through the knowledge of Him that hath called us to glory and virtue: Whereby are given unto us exceeding great and precious promises: that by these ye might be partakers of the divine nature, having escaped the corruption that is in the world through lust" (2 Peter 1:3,4). That goodness which is taught and pressed upon us in the Word is profitable to all things, having promise of the life that now is and of that which is to come. But the design of our present meeting leads me to speak of spiritual blessings, which if we obtain, other things shall be added, so far as God shall see these to be truly good for His people.

Let us consider some of the spiritual blessings which are promised to God's people in this chapter, for which God declares He will be enquired of. "Then will I sprinkle clean water upon you, and ye shall be clean" (verse 25). God here assures His people that by His Word and Spirit He will apply the virtues of the blood of Jesus, that blood of sprinkling, to wash them from the guilt and defilement of sin. The blood of Christ, the then promised Messiah, is the blood of atonement, and it cleanses from all sin: "A new heart also will I give you, and a new spirit will I put within you: and I will take away the stony heart out of your flesh, and I will give you an heart of flesh" (verse 26). God here promises that He will savingly convert them and form in them a new frame and excellent disposition in spiritual qualities. He promises to renew His image upon them in knowledge, righteousness, and holiness. Thus they will be made new creatures in a spiritual sense, old things will pass away, and all things will become new. God promises also to take away the stony heart which was hard and insensible and which refused to yield to good impressions. In opposition to that evil heart God promises to give a soft and tender heart which, like living flesh, is quick and sensible and ready to yield to the living soul that animates it. In like manner God's people, being quickened and governed by the Spirit, should be ready to receive impressions from Him. Agreeably it follows, "And I will put my Spirit within you, and cause you to walk in My statutes, and ye shall keep My judgments, and do them" (verse 27). God will not only send His Spirit to strive with them but He will effectually bestow Him upon them and send Him to dwell in their hearts by His saving operations as a renewing, sanctifying and comforting Spirit by whom God communicates all spiritual blessings to His people. And to crown it all, God says, "And ye shall dwell in the land that I gave to your fathers; and ye shall be my people, and I will be your God" (verse 28). God will enable them to discharge the duties of their covenant relation to Him, and He will fulfill His part in giving them the sure mercies of the new covenant. He promises to bless them as their covenant God with all spiritual blessings in heavenly places in Christ Jesus. This then is all our salvation and should be all our desire, even to inherit the great and good things contained in the promises of God.

II. GOD WILL BE ENQUIRED OF AND SOUGHT BY HIS PEOPLE THAT HE MAY BESTOW THESE BLESSINGS UPON THEM.
We may, under this head, speak to the following things:
A. What is implied in our enquiring of God and seeking Him for the blessings promised in His Word?
B. How and after what manner should we attend this duty?
C. What are our obligations thus to enquire of the Lord.

A. What Is Implied in Our Inquiring of God to Bestow These Promised Blessings Upon Us? In general, that we seek these blessings in the ways of God's appointment and that God alone is able to bestow them.

1. It supposes a realized apprehension of our need of these blessings and that God alone is able to bestow them.
Men will not be solicitous to enquire after that which they imagine they have in hand or do not need. When, therefore, the Laodiceans presumed that they were rich and had need of nothing, our Saviour first declared to them that they were, upon spiritual accounts, wretched and miserable and poor and blind and naked, and then He counseled them to come to Him for gold tried in the fire (Revelation 3:17,18). If we are not sensible of our spiritual maladies, we shall not seek after God to cleanse and heal our souls. If we are not sensible that we have become guilty before God and obnoxious to Him and are under His wrath and curse as transgressors of the law, we shall not, with any due concern, enquire after Christ and seek an interest in Him as the Lord our righteousness. If we are not sensible of being empty of grace and of our need of it, we shall never go to God by Jesus Christ, that of His fullness we may receive grace for grace. Unless we see and feel our need of the gracious influences of the Spirit to renew us and change our hearts we shall not, in a due manner, ask this great gift of God. In a word, we must behold God as the God of all grace and Father of mercies in Christ Jesus, or we shall not leave our broken cisterns to go to Him as the Fountain of Living

Waters for all needed supplies. Agreeably, when God was about to invite His people to return to Him as their only Saviour, He said to them, "O Israel, thou hast destroyed thyself: but in Me is thine help" (Hosea 13:9).

2. It intends that we value and desire these blessings as the best things.

Before we will search after any blessing we must have placed a due value on it and have desires after it excited in us. "Through desire a man, having separated himself, seeketh and intermeddleth with all wisdom" (Proverbs 18:1). Will we then enquire of God concerning spiritual blessings? We must count them to be the most excellent things and, accordingly, search for them as for hidden treasures. We must esteem the promises to be exceeding great and precious and earnestly desire the good contained in them. We must open our mouths wide and enlarge our desires that we may be filled. Thus do we seek the Lord as our God? We must thirst for Him, "O God, Thou art my God; early will I seek Thee: my soul thirsteth for Thee, my flesh longeth for Thee in a dry and thirsty land, where no water is; To see Thy power and Thy glory, so as I have seen Thee in the sanctuary. Because Thy loving kindness is better than life, my lips shall praise Thee" (Psalm 63:1-3). We must count all things but loss for the excellency of the knowledge of Jesus Christ, that we may be found in Him (Philippians 3:8-9), or we shall not seek Him in a right manner. As the gift of the Holy Spirit virtually contains all spiritual blessings, we must value and desire this above all temporal good things. The invitation is made, "Ho, every one that thirsteth, come ye to the waters, and he that hath no money; come ye, buy and eat; yea, come, buy wine and milk without money and without price" (Isaiah 55:1). The promise is clear, "Blessed are they which do hunger and thirst after righteousness: for they shall be filled" (Matthew 5:6). Without this value for and desire after spiritual blessings, we shall never seek first the Kingdom of God.

3. These desires after promised blessings must be made known to God in fervent prayer.

This seems to be especially intended when it says, "For this I will be enquired of..." We read of seeking God and enquiring early after Him (Psalm 78:34). When God says to us, "Seek ye My face;" our hearts should answer, "Thy face Lord will I seek" (Psalm 27:8). When God, in these promises, declares that He is ready to communicate the best of His blessings to His people, we then must put them at the center of our desires and plead with Him for them. The command is, "Seek ye the Lord while He may be found, call ye upon Him while He is near" (Isaiah 55:6).

God is pleased to manifest Himself to us in His Word and by His providence as the God who hears prayer and does great things for His people in answer to their prayers. Accordingly, our Lord says to us, "Ask, and it shall be given you; seek, and ye shall find; knock, and it shall be opened unto you" (Luke 11:9). We must then, by prayer, make our requests known unto God in the name of Jesus Christ and thus enquire of the Lord concerning the fulfillment of His promises. These promises are not given to supersede but to encourage our prayers. In verses thirty-six and thirty-seven of the context we are told, "I the Lord have spoken it, and I will do it. I will yet for this be enquired of by the house of Israel, to do it for them."

Prayer is one of the means of grace which God will have His people use continually in their closets, in their families, and in the places of their public worship, that He may bless them as their covenant God with all spiritual blessings. In our attendance on this great duty we must prove ourselves the true seed of Jacob who wrestled with the Angel of the Covenant, the Son of God, in humble importunity, refusing to let Him go until He had blessed him (Genesis 32:24-30). Then we shall find that good word fulfilled to us, "I said not unto the seed of Jacob, Seek ye me in vain" (Isaiah 45:19).

4. Enquiring of the Lord may intend that we consult the Word of God as to the way and manner of our seeking the Lord.

The Scriptures are called the Oracles of God (Romans 3:2). They are of infallible truth and given for our instruction in righteousness that we may be furnished unto all good works (2 Timothy 3:17). Therefore, we must consult these living Oracles if we would enquire of God in a right manner concerning the bestowment of promised blessings. We must search the Scriptures that we may know these promises and how we may obtain a title to them. This is needful so that we may seek the Lord so as to find Him and to find life in the light of His countenance. "And this is the confidence that we have in Him, that, if we ask anything according to His will, He heareth us" (1 John 5:14). The will of God revealed in His Word must be our rule and directory while we thus enquire of the Lord. Are we by this method seeking temporal good things? We must observe God's Word as to the manner of attending this duty and not seek them absolutely as the best things but only so far as may be for the glory of God and consistent with our eternal welfare. Are we by this method seeking spiritual good things? Today, as we seek spiritual benefits, we must seek these things with our whole hearts as matters of absolute necessity in order to glorify God in this life and prepare us to enjoy Him in heaven. The Biblical instruction is "Seek ye first the kingdom of God, and His righteousness; and all these things shall be added unto you" (Matthew 6:33). Here our all lies at stake, and we must accordingly seek the more earnestly. While the many and mighty of this world enquire, "Who will show us good?" our great petition must be, "Lord, lift Thou up the light of Thy countenance upon us" (Psalm 4:7). Now we must lie down at the foot of sovereign grace and say with the deepest humility, "Lord, I cannot bear a denial," for we ought not to be willing to perish in the place of torments where the damned curse God and die forever. Nor shall we ever be thus miserable if we seek the grace of God in Christ and the gift of the Holy Ghost in the first and the chief place, with longing desires that cannot be satisfied without them.

5. It intends that we wait upon God in the use of those means which He has appointed for our obtaining the spiritual blessings contained in the promises.

To seek this or other good without looking up to God for it is profane. For men to sit still and say, "Lord Help!" without using the means God has ordained is presumptuous and is a means of tempting the Lord. Therefore, while we pray to God to heal our spiritual maladies and to fill us with His grace, we must also be found in the diligent use of all other means. We must attend to reading and take heed how we hear the Word of God. We must meditate on Divine things, considering their reality, importance, and excellency, that we may be quickened to the more earnest pursuit of them. In a word, we must wait upon God in all ways of duty, that we may receive His Spirit and so His blessing. We must strive to enter in at the strait gate and then to walk in that narrow way which leads to everlasting life.

B. How and After What Manner Should We Attend This Duty?

1. In the exercise of faith in God and our Lord Jesus Christ.

"But without faith it is impossible to please Him: for he that cometh to God must believe that He is, and that He is the rewarder of them that diligently seek Him" (Hebrews 11:6). We must, by faith which is the evidence of things not seen, behold that God who is invisible and realize His divine perfections as manifested in His Word: His knowledge, wisdom, power, goodness, mercy, truth, and holiness. Then we must remember that there is one Mediator between God and men, the man Christ Jesus, through whom we have access unto the Father. Accordingly, we must believe in God and believe also in Jesus Christ, that through Him our faith and hope may be in God. Out of Christ, God is a consuming fire to the apostate children of fallen Adam; in Him, God is the Father of mercies and blesses His people with all spiritual blessings. We must, therefore, look to Jesus as the propitiation for our sins and our Advocate with the Father in our approaches to God. Our dependence must be on the merits and mediation of Jesus Christ when we ask God for the blessings promised in His Word. We must make mention of His worthy name before the Lord and rely upon it as the only name in which we can prevail. "And whatsoever ye shall ask in My name, that will I do, that the Father may be glorified in the Son. If ye shall ask anything in My name, I will do it" (John 14:13,14). All the promises of God in Him are yea, and in Him Amen (2 Corinthians 1:20). They are all confirmed as true and certain, and we must place our trust and confidence in Him accordingly. As our Lord Jesus was obedient unto death that He might purchase all saving blessings for His people, so He ever lives in heaven to make intercession and offer the prayers of the saints with much incense (Revelation 8:3,4). And the prayers of His people, being thus recommended, receive an answer of peace.

2. We must attend the duty with an abasing sense of our sins.
In this respect we should imitate the Father of the Faithful in his pleading for Sodom, "And Abraham answered and said, Behold now, I have taken upon me to speak unto the Lord, which am but dust and ashes" (Genesis 18:27). He acknowledged before the Most High God that he was formed out of the dust and deserved to be consumed in the fire of God's wrath for his own iniquities. Thus must we lie down in the dust before the Lord when we come to ask the best of blessings and confess with Jacob that we are not worthy of the least of all God's mercies. We must abhor the self-conceit of the proud Pharisee, who had the vain confidence to plead his religious performances as if he had made God a debtor to him by them, and join rather with the abased Publican saying, "Lord, be merciful to me a sinner," for every one that exalteth himself shall be abased and he that humbleth himself shall be exalted (Luke 18:10-14). God resists the proud but gives grace to the humble (James 4:6; 1 Peter 5:5). We must then humble ourselves before God under a deep sense of our spiritual poverty and be willing to receive these blessings as the gifts of free grace, if we are to receive them at all from that God who has mercy on whom He will have mercy. In this sense, we may expect that Word shall be fulfilled, "He hath filled the hungry with good things; and the rich he hath sent empty away" (Luke 1:53).

Then there must be in us a penitent confession of sin whereby we have forfeited our lives and all our enjoyments into God's hand. Now we must say with Daniel, when he set his face to seek the Lord by prayer, "We have sinned, and committed iniquity, and have done wickedly, and have rebelled, even by departing from Thy precepts, and from Thy judgments... O Lord, righteousness belongeth unto Thee, but unto us confusion of faces, as at this day" (Daniel 9:5,7). We must mourn with that godly sorrow which works repentance because of our transgressions whereby we have grieved the good Spirit of God and provoked Him to depart from us. We must, with our prayers, offer to God this day the sacrifice of a broken spirit, for a broken and contrite heart, God will not despise (Psalm 51:17). Then shall we be prepared to receive the strong consolations contained in the promise, "Blessed are they that mourn: for they shall be comforted" (Matthew 5:4). In this manner did God's ancient people seek the Lord. The prophecy may look forward even to Gospel times. "In those days, and in that time, saith the Lord, the Children of Israel shall come, they and the Children of Judah together, going and weeping: they shall go, and seek the Lord their God. They shall ask the way to Zion with their faces thitherward, saying, 'Come and let us join ourselves to the Lord in a perpetual covenant that shall not be forgotten'" (Jeremiah 50:4,5).

3. We must attend this duty with holy importunity and persevering diligence.

We must heartily and earnestly engage in this duty, sensible of the great excellency and importance of spiritual blessings, for "The effectual fervent prayer of a righteous man availeth much" (James 5:16). Thus Elias, a man subject to like passions as we are, prayed earnestly, and God answered him both by withholding and giving rain (James 5:17,18). May we seek the Lord with like fervency "till He come and rain righteousness upon [us]" (Hosea 10:12). Our Saviour spoke a parable to this end, that men ought always to pray and not to faint (Luke 18:1). We have a most encouraging example to this purpose in the woman of Canaan. She cried to our Saviour with regard to her daughter who was vexed with a devil, "Have mercy on me, O Lord!" Our Lord appeared to be deaf to her cries. He answered not a word. Then His disciples besought Him to send her away, and our Lord said, "I am not sent but unto the lost sheep of the house of Israel." Notwithstanding this, she came and worshipped Him saying, "Lord, help me." Our Lord seemed then not only to give her another repulse but to deny her request with disdain: "It is not meet to take the children's bread, and cast it to dogs." Carnal reason would have concluded that this poor woman had enough now to have overwhelmed her with despair of ever finding relief, but behold, her persevering importunity rises and grows stronger under these pressures, and she makes a plea of this answer in which our Lord seemed to reproach her as a dog, "Truth, Lord: yet the dogs eat of the crumbs which fall from their masters' table." And then our Saviour's answer is most gracious and full of tender mercy, "O woman, great is thy faith: be it unto thee even as thou wilt." And her daughter was made whole even from that hour. And now, wherever the Gospel is preached, the humble and yet brave and bold importunity of this women is told for a memorial of her and for our encouragement in prayer (Matthew 15:22-28). Let us, as true Israelites, go and do likewise, and we shall have power with God and prevail. Let us pray always with all prayer and supplication in the Spirit, watching thereunto with all perseverance (Ephesians 6:18).

4. We must attend this duty with thankful acknowledgement of blessings received.

When God is pleased to draw nigh to us in a way of grace and favor and to give spiritual blessings with a liberal hand, we must bless His glorious name which is exalted above all blessing and praise, "I will sing unto the Lord, because He hath dealt bountifully with me" (Psalm 13:6). In a special manner we should praise the Lord for that unspeakable gift of His only begotten Son and for the great and comprehensive gift of the Holy Ghost by whom application is made of the redemption purchased by Jesus Christ. We should bless God for the wonderful effusions of His Spirit in the first years of Christian history whereby miraculous gifts, needful for the first propagation of the Gospel, and abundant grace were communicated. We ought also to praise the Lord that He has not left us without a witness of His divine power and grace in the wonderful operations of His Spirit in our times. We are bound by duty and gratitude to obey that word, "Be careful for nothing; but in everything by prayer and supplication with thanksgiving let your requests be made known unto God" (Philippines 4:6). While God's people enquire of Him concerning the bestowment of promised blessings, they must not forget to give thanks. Let the redeemed of the Lord then devoutly say, "Blessed be the God and Father of our Lord Jesus Christ, who hath blessed us with all spiritual blessings in heavenly places in Christ" (Ephesians 1:3).

C. What Are Our Obligations Thus to Enquire of the Lord?

1. In this way God's people must glorify Him as the Author of all spiritual blessings.

God appears in His glory when He gives spiritual blessings to His people. In the works of His Spirit on the hearts of men His glorious power, wisdom, goodness, truth, holiness, grace, and mercy are displayed. We must pray then that God will, in this way, show us His glory and proclaim His name before us. Thus must we give Him glory as the Father of lights from whom comes down every good gift and every perfect gift and adore Him as the God of salvation. When we thus enquire of the Lord we acknowledge that whosoever are the instruments, the excellency of the power whereby sinners are converted must be of God. Thus we give glory to the God and Father of our Lord Jesus as to the Father of mercies; to the Son of God as exalted to be a prince and a Saviour and as having received gifts for men; to the Holy Spirit as the Sanctifier and Comforter of His people.

2. We must attend this duty in obedience to the will of God declared in His Word.

Our Lord says to His people, "I will for this be enquired of by the House of Israel." God commands His people to pray always, with all prayer. In His word He declares that we must wait on Him in the ways of His appointment that we may receive spiritual blessings in abundance: "Ho, every one that thirsteth, come ye to the waters, and he that hath no money; come ye, buy, and eat; yea, come, buy wine and milk without money and without price. Wherefore do ye spend money for that which is not bread? and your labor for that which satisfieth not? Hearken diligently unto me, and eat ye that which is good, and let your soul delight itself in fatness. Incline your ear, and come unto me: hear, and your soul shall live; and I will make an everlasting covenant with you, even the sure mercies of David" (Isaiah 55:1-3). And the commandment is given with a gracious promise annexed to it, "Ask, and it shall be given you; seek, and ye shall find; knock, and it shall be opened unto you" (Matthew 7:7).

3. It is our duty in this way to declare our high esteem for the blessings contained in the promises and to express our longing desires after them.

We must thus acknowledge that the promises are exceeding great and precious and we must reach after the accomplishment of them. "Wisdom is the principal thing; therefore get wisdom: and with all thy getting get understanding" (Proverbs 4:7).

4. We stand in absolute need of these blessings that we may glorify God upon earth and prepare to enjoy Him forever in heaven.

This is the chief end of man, the great errand upon which God has sent us into the world. Unless we mind this one thing needful we live in vain and shall die without wisdom; yea, we must perish in hell forever.

Alas! We have all fallen short of the glory of God as children of apostate Adam. Unless it pleases God, by His Holy Spirit, to fit us to show forth His praise, we shall become vessels of wrath fitted to destruction. Unless the means of grace are accomplished with the divine Spirit and blessing, they will be the savour of death unto death. In that case we shall be like the ground which beareth thorns and briers and so is nigh to cursing, whose end is to be burned. But if we receive this blessing from God, we shall bear that fruit whereby our heavenly Father is glorified.

Thus shall we enjoy the blessings of the kingdom of grace in this world, righteousness and peace and joy in the Holy Ghost, and thus shall we be prepared for the kingdom of glory.

Let us now apply these things to the work and duties of this day.

IMPROVEMENT ONE. We are assembled to ask God for the plentiful effusion of His Spirit upon His people and more particularly, for the flock who usually worship God in this place. We are gathered to bless His name for spiritual blessings already received in the remarkable revival of His work among us and in many other towns. We are also met together to entreat the Lord that He will preserve us and His people from everything that has a tendency to quench His Spirit and obstruct the progress and success of His good work and that it may go on and prosper until the whole land shall be filled with the blessed fruits of the Spirit. This is an important errand indeed! O that there was a Spirit in us to cry mightily to God for this great blessing while we humble ourselves before the Lord for our past unfruitfulness and all those sins whereby we have grieved the Spirit of God! We have formerly once and again observed such days of prayer to seek the Lord for spiritual blessings, the comprehensive sum of which is the gift of the Holy Ghost. And may we not hope that God is now giving a gracious answer to those supplications which have been in this way offered to Him in years past? And ought not this to encourage us now to pray the more earnestly? Yes, most certainly! We wait for Thy salvation, O Lord, who hast reserved gifts for men, even for the rebellious, and are pleased to say unto us, "If ye then, being evil, know how to give good gifts unto your children: how much more shall your heavenly Father give the Holy Spirit to them that ask Him?" (Matthew 7:11).

Let us then, with a high esteem of these spiritual blessings, lift up our hearts with our hands to God this day that He will bless us indeed, bless us with the more abundant effusions of His Spirit. Let us ask Him to convince us more and more of sin so that sinners, pricked to the heart, may say, "What shall we do?" Let us beseech Him to convert us that we may be truly born from above and so enter into the kingdom of God. Let us entreat Him to carry on His work in His children that we may grow in grace and in the knowledge of our Lord Jesus Christ. Let us expect Him to comfort the mourners in Zion that they may rejoice together in the salvation of God. Let us then all unite in our diligent and prudent endeavors to promote this work, each one keeping within his own line.

Let the ministers of our Lord Jesus Christ give themselves continually to prayer and to the ministry of the Word that by you God may delight to give His people the fullness of the blessing of the Gospel which is the ministration of the Spirit (2 Corinthians 3:8). Let us, in the way of duty, wait upon God that we may be strengthened with all might by the Spirit. For who is sufficient for these things? Brethren, pray for us, that the Word of the Lord may have free course and be glorified. Let us seek the promised presence of our ascended Saviour and, in the way of study and painful labor, depend on Him for all that ability and skill we need to make us wise to win souls and lead them unto Christ. Let us unite our endeavors in this great and difficult work, as fellow-helpers to the truth, that we may promote each other's usefulness in the right improvement of those gifts which our glorious Head has in various kinds and degrees communicated to us for the edification of His Body, the Church. And let the success which God has of late given to the ministry of the Word, above what we have known in times past, animate us to labor more abundantly. Blessed are they that sow beside all waters, when the Spirit is poured from on high. Certainly, it will be an abundant recompense for all our pains if God's people may be our crown and joy in the day of the Lord. I mention these things in humility, as one sensible of my own defects in the work of the ministry.

IMPROVEMENT TWO. Let our churches hear what the Spirit says to them in His Word and by His works of grace. Walk together in the faith and order of the Gospel. Obey that word of our lord, "Remember therefore from whence thou art fallen, and repent, and do the first works" (Revelation 2:5). Oh, that our religious assemblies might be as fruitful fields which the Lord has blessed, in which the good seed of the Word plentifully sown shall take root, spring up, and bear fruit an hundred fold! The Lord multiply the seed sown and increase the fruits of your righteousness.

IMPROVEMENT THREE. Let our honored rulers be entreated to give a helping hand to this work by your example and influence and by your authority. God has put honor upon you; do you then honor Him by leading in the great and necessary work of a general reformation? Be not a terror to good works but to the evil. In vain shall we boast of the Christian name if the great things of the moral law are counted as a strange thing among us. Let judgment run down as waters and righteousness as a mighty stream.

IMPROVEMENT FOUR. Let heads of families be exhorted to encourage the work of God by their prayers, example, and authority in their houses. Surely you know that the God who sets the lonely in families and builds the house, has committed this important trust to you with a solemn charge to bring up your children and all under your care, in the nurture and admonition of the Lord. You must therefore take up Joshua's resolution, "As for me and my house, we will serve the Lord" (Joshua 24:15). When God promises to pour out the Spirit of grace and supplication upon the house of David and inhabitants of Jerusalem, it is said that they should look to Him whom they had pierced and mourn; yea, that the land should mourn, every family apart (Zechariah 12:10-14). And then follows the most gracious promise of God's opening a fountain in the house of David and to the inhabitants of Jerusalem to wash away their sins (chapter 13).

Let heads of families, then, call upon the name of the Lord in their houses, that He may pour out His Spirit on them and so bless them in Christ Jesus, in whom all the families of the earth are blessed. Imitate King David, who after he had worshipped God with his people, returned to bless his household (2 Samuel 6:20). Let our family prayer in the morning be set before God as incense and the offering up of our hands as the evening sacrifice, lest that dreadful curse fall upon us and our houses, "Pour out Thy fury upon the heathen that know Thee not, and upon the families that call not on Thy name" (Jeremiah 10:25). Let us all walk before God in our houses with a perfect heart and in a perfect way, saying with the Psalmist, "Oh, when wilt Thou come unto me?" Then call upon all under your roofs to seek and serve the Lord. Travail in birth again with your children until they are born of the Spirit and so have Christ formed in them. Use your best endeavors that your servants may become the children of God and heirs according to the promise, by faith in Jesus Christ. Let your children and servants have leave to attend the means of grace as there may be opportunity and the business of your families will allow it. In a special manner remember the Sabbath day and keep it holy in all your dwellings, for the Lord has blessed this day and hallowed it to be a day of communicating spiritual blessings to His people.

Oh, wait upon God with your houses on the Lord's day, and labor for the meat which endures to everlasting life! On other days abide with God in a diligent attendance upon your particular calling. Do your own business, and let there be no just occasion for that complaint, "We hear that there are some which walk among you disorderly, working not at all, but are busy bodies" (2 Thessalonians 3:11). The great evil of neglecting our own affairs and meddling with those things which do not belong to us is both the parent and nurse of many shameful vices that have a tendency to dishonor God and grieve His Holy Spirit.

IMPROVEMENT FIVE. Let our children and young people go to God for the great blessings promised in the Gospel. Thirst after these living waters and plead that promise with God, "I will pour water upon him that is thirsty, and floods upon the dry ground: I will pour My Spirit upon thy seed, and My blessing upon thine offspring" (Isaiah 44:3). Hear the wisdom of God speaking to you, "I love them that love Me; and those that seek Me early shall find me" (Proverbs 8:17). Hear the Son of God, the essential and eternal wisdom, "Seek ye first the kingdom of God, and His righteousness; and all these things shall be added unto you" (Matthew 6:33). To awaken you, consider how many of your age and time will rise up in judgment and condemn you if you go on walking in the ways of your heart and in the sight of your eyes in this remarkable day of grace. Consider how dreadful it will be for you to be left behind to perish in your sins when others are taken. Look diligently lest any of you should fail of the grace of God, lest there be a profane person, as Esau, who for one morsel of meat sold his birthright, and afterwards, when he would have inherited the blessing, was rejected (Hebrews 12:15-17). But I hope better things of many of you, our dear children. May you imitate Jacob in his holy importunity and bear away the blessing.

IMPROVEMENT SIX. Are there any grown old in years and yet standing as barren trees in God's vineyard? Have you stood more than ten times three years under the means of grace and yet remain dead in trespasses and sins? Hear the word and tremble, "The ax is laid unto the root of the trees: therefore every tree that bringeth not forth good fruit is hewn down, and cast into the fire" (Matthew 3:10). Admire the patience of God and despise not the riches of His goodness and long-suffering, knowing that the goodness of God leads you to repentance (Romans 2:4). Oh, take heed lest after your hardness and impenitent heart you treasure up wrath against the day of wrath! (Romans 2:5). Oh, be sensible of the deep corruption of your hearts which have resisted all the means God has for so long used with you and cry to God for the inward and effectual call of His Spirit that you may be born again, even when you are old, and that in you Christ may show forth all long-suffering for a pattern to them which shall hereafter believe on Him to life everlasting. Oh, remember it will be a most dreadful thing to go down to hell after a long and clear day of Gospel grace. To such is reserved the blackness of darkness forever. Do not then grieve and vex the Holy Spirit any longer but attend to what He says in His Word, "To-day if ye will hear his voice, harden not your hearts" (Hebrews 3:15).

IMPROVEMENT SEVEN. Let such as are under the convictions of the Spirit seek a saving conversion unto God. Oh, beware of quenching the Spirit! Now strive to enter in at the strait gate and press into the kingdom of God. Are you made sensible of the plague of your own hearts? Pray to God to heal your souls. Plead that promise, "I will take away the stony heart out of your flesh" (Ezekiel 36:26). And while you continue in the diligent use of the means of grace, beware of depending on religious duties and outward reformations. Go weary and heavy laden to Christ that in Him you may find rest. The Lord draw you to Him; the Lord make you willing in the day of His power!

Or have any of you obtained joy in believing? Adore that God who has mercy on whom He will have mercy and say, "Not unto us O Lord, not unto us, but to Thy name give glory." Rejoice with holy fear and great humility.

Here give me leave to say that if any of you have been pressed down under uncommon degrees of terror and then been raised with proportional joys, look to it that the foundation of your joy be laid in a graciously broken heart and in a sincere closing with Jesus Christ upon Gospel terms and then that it be followed with a close humble walk with God and with fruits meet for repentance.

As for the outcries, tremblings, and faintings which have been experienced in some places, I apprehend the cause must be judged by the effect. We may not limit the Holy One. The jailor came trembling and fell down before Paul and Silas. Those who heard Peter's sermon were pricked in their heart and said to Peter and to the rest of the Apostles, "Men and Brethren, what shall we do?" (Acts 2:37). A wounded spirit who can bear? If such persons, therefore, have an holy awe of God, a deep humiliation under the sense of sin, an earnest concern about deliverance from it, here is the finger of God. And if it shall please God to impress such a sense of sin and of His wrath on men that they are forced to cry out under it, they are to be pitied and proper means used for their relief and not to be censured as mad and outrageous. But then, if any will indulge themselves in these outcries, especially in time of public worship when there is no real necessity for it and they might restrain themselves, I think they are disorderly and do that which has a tendency to disturb the quiet attentive hearing of God's Word. Nor may we make a judgment of a work whether genuine or not merely by such extraordinary commotions. For there have been tremblings which have not proceeded from the Spirit of truth and holiness.

Let us not then presume to confine the free Spirit of God but regard the substance of the work itself. I do not doubt but what many in our congregation have been deeply wounded for sin without these outcries and that these convictions have in considerable numbers issued in a saving conversion to God. Nor can I suppose that it is the duty of ministers to try to excite these screamings but rather to set the terrors of the law and the gracious invitations of the Gospel before men in the most powerful manner they are able and then to leave it to the only wise God to take His own way in the matter. He can, if He pleases, order these things to the awakening of others. This, we are informed, has been the case in some other places. Those that have not felt this degree of terror ought not to judge those that have. Those that have been thus wrought upon should refrain from judging those that have not. Let both prove their own Christian experience and examine by the Word of God whether the fruits of the Spirit are found in them: fruits such as repentance towards God, faith in our Lord Jesus Christ, love to God and our neighbors, meekness, humility, and the like. If, upon an impartial examination, you find these things in you then you have reason for rejoicing in yourselves and not in another.

Let not any of you who has been made sensible of your perishing condition and then enabled to submit to Christ as your only Saviour, deny the work of grace God has wrought in you because you have not felt such a degree of terror and then of rapturous joys as others may have experienced. Rather be encouraged to wait upon God in the way of duty for the assurance and joy of faith. Let not your eye be evil, because God is good. May not God do what He wills with His own? Do not then behave as the elder son in the parable, who was angry because of the joy expressed in his father's house when his prodigal brother returned a true penitent. There is joy in heaven over the sinner that repents, and there must also be a just occasion for joy upon earth when the dead are made alive and the lost are found.

As to those extraordinary appearances in trances and the things uttered by persons that have fallen under them, no stress may be laid on these things in determining the present or future state of men. Secret things belong to God. His Word is given us for our rule. To the law and to the testimony let us be true.

IMPROVEMENT EIGHT. Let not new converts imagine that they are called and qualified to be teachers of God's Word. Are all prophets? Are all teachers? (1 Corinthians 12:29). No, certainly not! Our ascended Saviour has appointed the Gospel ministry and given to His church pastors and teachers. No man may take this office upon himself. Men must be called to it according to the order appointed in God's Word. Let your zeal then be expressed according to knowledge and sound judgment. It is granted that you may, out of the abundance of your hearts, utter the praises of the great God your Saviour and with humility declare what He has done for your souls in proper time and place. You may edify one another by Christian conference and the like. But there is a great difference between this and setting yourself up as a teacher. I am persuaded that the natural tendency of this, however God may overrule it, is to introduce disorder and to bring the Gospel ministry into contempt. Such men act as if there need be no study, gifts, and learning to qualify them for this difficult and important office. The Apostle's rule is that the office of an elder must not be given to a novice, lest being lifted up with pride, he fall into the condemnation of the devil (1 Timothy 3:6).

IMPROVEMENT NINE. Let even the more private meetings of Christians be encouraged and well regulated. Exercise yourselves in such duties as are proper for you and let good hours be observed, that family religion and closet piety may have their due proportion of time. Solomon observed that to everything there is a season and that God made everything beautiful in its time (Ecclesiastes 3:1-11). Accordingly, that duty is likely to be performed in the best manner which is done seasonably. There is a time for public worship, a time for family and closet devotion, a time for our needful rest in the night, that being refreshed with sleep we may be prepared for the business of the day when man goes forth to his labor. If, for want of due regard to these seasons, our families should suffer in their spiritual or temporal interests, the God of order will be displeased with us. I am not now speaking of extraordinary cases (even the Apostle Paul continued his speech until midnight in order to depart on the morrow) but of the ordinary practice of Christians in their more private meetings. In a word, "Let all things be done decently and in order" (1 Corinthians 14:40).

Avoid all rash judging and censuring of one another as hypocrites and unconverted. Our Lord has said, "Judge not, that ye be not judged" (Matthew 7:1). Indeed, the tree is to be known by its fruits. We ought to exercise such a judgment of discretion and charity towards our neighbor as to watch over him and keep ourselves pure. To pronounce as hypocrites or Pharisees those persons who profess godliness and who live without heresy, moral scandal, or open inconsistency with their profession is a bold invasion of God's prerogative, who alone searches the heart. It is He who warns us, "Judge nothing before the time" (1 Corinthians 4:5). For any one to utter such censures is a great injury and breach of Christian charity. This sin is aggravated when such censures are passed on men of public character, particularly on ministers of the Gospel, for hereby not only is their personal character wounded but also their public usefulness may be obstructed. Let us then avoid this evil. "But why dost thou judge thy brother? or why dost thou set at nought thy brother? For we shall all stand before the judgment seat of Christ" (Romans 14:10). This is not the way to reclaim men but rather the way to exasperate them and stir up that contention which leads to confusion and every evil work.

In a word, let us be zealous for God and good works, and at the same time beware of the dangerous extreme of enthusiasm.

Thus I have taken liberty to touch upon several things which I apprehend are worthy of our serious consideration under the present circumstances if we would avoid giving the great adversary advantage to blemish God's work and if we would stop the mouths of gainsayers. May we resist the devil, not being ignorant of his devices! May we, at this critical juncture, walk circumspectly, not as fools but as wise! In my judgment, the prudent regulation of our religious commotions is of great moment and necessity. Even while we are unworthy instruments in His hand we must defend and preserve the work of God from all evil. This is what I have sincerely designed and endeavoured to do in the present discourse. I have not desired to bring reproach on any persons whatsoever or to discourage any good work. Let no man pervert what has been said or use it to prejudice himself or others against the wonderful work of grace which I truly believe God has accomplished in this town as well as in other places.

It must not be considered a strange thing if frail men are chargeable with imprudence and irregularities. But as for God, His work is perfect. Let us then hear our Lord and Judge, "Woe unto the world because of offenses" (Matthew 18:7). and beware lest we be offended in Christ. Let not God's people be alienated from each other because of some difference in judgment. Be valiant for the truth. At the same time, follow the things which make for peace and things wherewith one may edify another. Let these words sink deep into your hearts: "Let no corrupt communication proceed out of your mouth, but that which is good in the use of edifying, that it may minister grace unto the hearers. And grieve not the Holy Spirit of God, whereby ye are sealed unto the day of redemption. Let all bitterness, and wrath, and anger, and clamour, and evil speaking, be put away from you, with all malice: and be ye kind one to another, tenderhearted, forgiving one another, even as God for Christ's sake hath forgiven you" (Ephesians 4:29-32).

Let us all unite in seeking the advancement of Christ's kingdom among us. Let us pray that ministers and people may have all needed wisdom and grace to know and attend this duty in this day of visitation. Let us pray as the Psalmist: "Let Thy work appear unto Thy servants, and Thy glory unto their children. And let the beauty of the Lord our God be upon us: and establish Thou the work of our hands upon us; yea, the work of our hands establish Thou it" (Psalm 90:16,17). May we be more and more enriched with the showers of blessing from the third heaven! May these holy waters increase and spread far and wide like the waters in Elijah's vision. May they be for the quickening, cleansing, and healing of sinners and for the refreshing of God's children, causing them to abound in the fruits of righteousness! Thus we shall be prepared for the best prosperity. Thus shall we obtain fruits more precious than those which are put forth by virtue of the light and rain of heaven. God, even our God, will bless us, and we shall obtain salvation from the light of His countenance. "Neither will I hide my face any more from them: for I have poured out My Spirit upon the house of Israel, saith the Lord God" (Ezekiel 39:29).

CHAPTER THIRTEEN

The Sad Tendency
of Divisions
and Contentions in Churches
to Bring on Their Ruin
and Desolation

By
Solomon Williams

Solomon Williams, 1700-1776

Solomon Williams, son of William Williams of Hatfield, was born June 4, 1700. His grandfather was the venerable Solomon Stoddard of Northampton, Massachusetts and Jonathan Edwards, a cousin. Like so many of the New-England clergy of his day, Solomon studied at Harvard, graduating at nineteen. In 1722 he was ordained Pastor of the Congregational Church in Lebanon, Connecticut, where he served for fifty-four years.

Williams married Mary Porter of Hadley at about the time he went to Lebanon. They had ten children, two of whom attained some measure of eminence: William was a member of the Continental Congress and one of the signers of the Declaration of Independence; Elphalet, pastored at East Hartford, Connecticut. From 1749 to 1769 Williams was a Fellow of Yale College. In 1773 they honored him with a Doctor of Divinity degree.

Although basically a man of peace, Solomon Williams engaged in two major controversies during his lifetime. The first was with Andrew Croswell on the nature of justifying faith; the second pertained to terms of qualification for lawful communion in the Christian sacraments in which he supported his deceased grandfather's views in opposition to Jonathan Edwards.

According to a grandson, Timothy Stone of Cornwall, Connecticut, "Dr. Williams exemplified his remarkable prudence, not less than his truly Christian zeal, in connection with the great revival of religion which spread so extensively in New England about 1740. He was a decided friend to Mr. Whitefield, and repeatedly, and at different periods, welcomed him to his pulpit; but he was not at all insensible to his tendency to extravagance, especially in the early part of his career, nor was he slow to exert his influence in checking it. The consequence was that while, in some of the adjacent towns and societies many became extremely wild and fanatical, his own people manifested little disposition to depart from Christian order and propriety. "A scene occurred at a private religious meeting at Lebanon during the revival which showed the estimation in which Dr. Williams was held by the fanatics of the day. A boy and a girl, of about ten or twelve years of age, were in different rooms of the house, and each sunk down instantaneously, the same time, into a swoon, and continued apparently insensible for many hours. They emerged simultaneously from their trance; and, when they came to give an account of their experience, they declared they had been to Heaven, where they saw the Lamb's Book of Life. In it were the names of several of their acquaintances, and some of them in large letters; but the name of Solomon Williams was in such small letters to be scarcely discernable and was crowded down to the very bottom of the page." Despite such crude attempts to discredit him, Dr. Williams persisted in identifying and supporting what was right in the movement and in opposing anything that tended to destroy the true work of God.

As a preacher, Williams was described as "grave, solemn, and impressive, but not a Boanerges in voice and manner, like Bellamy, Pomeroy, and Wheelock." His qualifications as a scholar were such that President Clap of Yale College sought to induce him to accept an appointment as Professor of Theology, but the members of the Lebanon Church were very unwilling to have their pastor even consider the appointment. Although described as "exceedingly dignified in all his deportment, never saying or doing anything that involved the least departure from clerical propriety," Williams was obviously a man of considerable personal flexibility, breadth and depth. His final days were marked by great physical suffering with an intense spiritual tranquility. His last words were, "I shall soon be there; and a full blaze of glory will open upon my soul, and swallow it up in God and Christ. At present, we can't have any conception. I hope the time will come, but I must wait." His died on February 29, 1776.

First published as *The Sad Tendency of Divisions and Contentions in Churches To Bring on their Ruin and Desolation As it was Showed in a Sermon Delivered at the West-Farms, Norwich, on a Day of Fasting, February 28, 1750.* Newport: Printed by James Franklin, 1751.

The Sad Tendency
of Divisions
and Contentions in Churches
to Bring on Their Ruin
and Desolation

**"Every kingdom divided against itself
is brought to desolation; and every city or house
divided against itself shall not stand."
Matthew 12:25.**

The occasion of these words is intimated in the first part of the verse from which our text is taken. They are Christ's reply to a blasphemous and scandalous insinuation the Pharisees made against Him. In the twenty-second verse of this chapter we have an account of Christ's casting out a devil from a person who was made blind and dumb by him. The healing of the man was of such a nature that the whole multitude was amazed and glorified God crying, "Is not this the Son of David?" By these words they indicated their belief that only the Messiah could work such miracles. The issue was as plain as the sun. The Pharisees could not deny it, for the miracle was an extraordinary thing and had to be of supernatural origin. There was no way they could avoid the conclusion that Jesus was "the Son of David" except by suggesting that the supernatural power was not of God. Thus they declared that Christ cast out devils by Beelzebub. In this declaration they intimated that there was a compact between Jesus and the Devil and therefore the Devil was not actually cast out but voluntarily retired. This was the last refuge of an obstinate infidelity that was resolved to stand against the clearest conviction. Christ's reply to this base imputation is copious and cogent in order that "every mouth may be stopped with sense and reason, before it be stopped with fire and brimstone."[1]

---

[1]Matthew Henry.

Christ's first argument is contained in the words of my text. In these words our Lord shows that it would be both very strange and highly improbable that Satan could be cast out by such a compact because then his kingdom would be divided against itself. This is a thing, considering his subtlety, that cannot be imagined. Therefore Christ lays down a known rule, which is universally approved by the reason and conscience of all sorts of men, that in all societies a common ruin is the consequence of a mutual quarrel. Every kingdom divided against itself is brought to desolation and so is every society and family. This, the great Roman Orator and Philosopher, observed was an obvious thing and resulted necessarily from the nature of the situation. What house is so stable, what city so firm, which by hatred and dissension may not be utterly overthrown? Divisions commonly end in desolations. If we clash, we break. If we divide one from another, we easily become prey to the common enemy. If we bite and devour one another, we may expect to be consumed one of another (Galatians 5:15). Churches and nations have known this by sad experience.

DOCTRINE. Divisions and contentions in churches as well as other societies of men tend to, and if continued in, bring on their ruin and desolation.

I shall not at present purposely consider how they tend to the ruin of other societies for I design especially to consider how they tend to the ruin and desolation of churches.

Churches are societies of men combined together by religious and ecclesiastical polity. They partake of the common nature of kingdoms, cities and other societies of men. Therefore, the proposition which Christ lays down here, which is a universally known rule, holds with respect to churches as well as to all other societies.

I shall propose several considerations to show and illustrate the truth of this doctrine and shall then make applications of the same.

I. CONSIDERATIONS THAT SHOW AND ILLUSTRATE THE TRUTH OF THIS ASSERTION.

1. Divisions and contentions tend to increase the alienation of particular members from one another.

Churches and church members are joined together according to Apostolic rule: "Now I beseech you, brethren, by the name of our Lord Jesus Christ, that ye all speak the same thing, and that there be no divisions among you; but that ye be perfectly joined together in the same mind and in the same judgment" (1 Corinthians 1:10). When this rule is followed there can be no divisions among believers.

All divisions and contentions must take their rise from differences of sentiments and alienation of affection of one person from another. The continuance of these tend to alienate the persons more and more for they tend to beget and increase hard thoughts and unkind suspicions of one another's actions and principles. When church members are divided they are apt to grow strange to one another, to converse cautiously or shrilly, if at all, and to be afraid to trust one another. In consequence, they are ready to entertain jealousies of one another, supposing that this and that man has some design against them and is aiming to undermine and counteract them. In divisions and contentions the different parties have different designs in view. From these differences naturally arise jealousies of each other and suspicions that their neighbors and brethren who differ from them design to overthrow their purposes and defeat their intentions. Even these jealousies which arise in their minds do of themselves increase the alienation of their affections and set them at still a farther distance from one another. Thus they tend to break off all communication or to render what little they have an angry or a sly, cautious, and designing thing which at length issues in open and declared enmity. Amos wisely asked, "Can two walk together, except they be agreed?" (Amos 3:3).

2. Divisions and contentions tend to result in many sins and sinful carriages of brethren and members toward one another.

As divisions create and increase jealousies and suspicions of one another, these tend to break out into sinful actions. In wrongly interpreting one another's views and designs, they foster the imputation of some crime upon their brethren of which they are not guilty, they aggravate their infirmities and account and treat them as gross and wilful sins. They dispose their minds to put the worst construction upon those actions which seem to be bad and to put bad ones upon those actions which are really virtuous and religious. In short, the tendency of divisions is to stir up anger, wrath, clamor, and evil-speaking.

When the children of Israel heard that their brethren had built an altar on the other side of the Jordan, they quickly concluded that they were running away from the Lord and thereupon readily consented to go to war against them (Joshua 22:12). When Ziba fawned upon David and flattered him, the King let into his own heart evil thoughts about Mephibosheth. David presently gave credit to Ziba's lie and unjustly and without a hearing gave away Mephibosheth's land to that liar (2 Samuel 16:3,4).

Hence such cautions and warnings are given to God's people as,

"Thou shalt not avenge, nor bear any grudge against the children of thy
people, but thou shalt love thy neighbor as thyself" (Leviticus 19:18).
"Hatred stirreth up strifes: but love covereth all sins" (Proverbs 10:12).
"He that hideth hatred with lying lips, and he that uttereth a slander, is
a fool" (verse 18).

**3. In allowing such divisions and contentions to exist, brethren tend
to deprive themselves and one another of the means of their spiritual
edification.**

The next and immediate work of contention is to break off and put to
an end that Christian and brotherly conversation which Christians ought
to maintain in order to instruct, comfort, and edify one another. Contentions break off most, if not all, this sort of spiritually beneficial conversation. If a division is allowed to continue, it will normally turn into a
heated dispute and debate, one side charging crimes, the other side
justifying and defending themselves. The sole outcome of such dissension
may be expected to be increased wrangling and greater division to the
extent that all means of mutual edification is at an end. There then
commonly follows this such alienation of affection and hard thoughts of
one another that they cannot hold communion together any longer. One
thinks the other too bad and too little a Christian to have communion
with him. The other supposes that his principles and practices are so right
that he cannot join with his opponent in anything. Soon they have nothing
but hard thoughts about one another.

It is tragic to observe that contentions often bring on such an
alienation of affection that one will not promote the common edification
of the entire Body lest in doing so his particular enemy benefits. Such an
antagonist may even refuse to fulfill his own responsibilities in the church
in order to guarantee that those he disagrees with will not prosper. Or he
may refuse to do his part, perhaps chiefly because it involves something
an opponent proposed or chose. He concludes it can't be right because
that man or that party which proposed it must needs be wrong. Having
determined before that they are bad men with bad designs, he is well
satisfied that what they are proposing cannot be good.

By such practices cantankerous persons are in danger of dropping the
institutions of Christ and the ordinary means He has appointed for their
edification and salvation. Thus they tend to break the bands of church
societies and crumble them to pieces in full opposition to the direction of
the Apostle: "Let nothing be done through strife or vainglory; but in
lowliness of mind let each esteem other better than themselves. Look not
every man on his own things, but every man also on the things of others"

(Philippines 2:3,4). Acting contrary to Paul's direction and example proposed for our imitation, "Give none offence, neither to the Jews, nor to the Gentiles, nor to the church of God: Even as I please all men in all things, not seeking mine own profit, but the profit of many, that they may be saved" (1 Corinthians 10:32,33). these creators of strife would rather have their own way than to see any entire congregation blessed of God.

4. Divisions and contentions tend to root out true religion and substitute the principles of party quarrels in the place of it.
The advancement of true religion is the great end of the coalition and combination of churches. The bonds which are to hold them together are the terms of the Covenant of Grace. "For the kingdom of God is not meat and drink; but righteousness, and peace, and joy in the Holy Ghost. For he that in these things serveth Christ is acceptable to God, and approved of men. Let us therefore follow after the things which make for peace, and things wherewith one may edify another" (Romans 14:17-19).

When divisions and contentions affect churches and they break into parties, it is common for them to set up the particular party opinions they embrace as the great fundamentals of all religion. In consequence, the main stress of their religion may lie in some peculiar opinions which they hold about slight matters of church discipline, terms of church communion or the peculiar explanation of some non-essential doctrine of religion. By this method, human words and opinions have been made the stamp and standard of numerous religious bodies. The Christian church has often seen sad evidence of the havoc these things have made of religion. While the several parties have sainted and canonized those that came to their standard and have fallen in with their peculiar sentiments and explications, they have at the same time renounced, unsainted, and cursed all that do not agree with them in their peculiar tenants of religion.

Men's disputes and debates turn upon the principles of their party, and they are apt to lay the main stress upon them. By this means the great and essential things of religion are in a manner forgotten or neglected. Truth, faith, real holiness, fervent love to God and man, sincere, universal righteousness, and charity are apt to all be comprehended and thought to be included in some party notions and explications. By this means, true religion, not by slow degrees, dwindles away into form and a furious party zeal. By this same means, the carnal world is either confirmed in its conviction that there is nothing in religion but the passions and worldly interests of men or that it lies in such things as are at best but mere appendages and circumstances of it. Such we see was the tendency of the contentions of the Church of Corinth which occasioned that fervent expostulation of the Apostle Paul: "For it hath been declared unto me of you, my brethren, by them which are of the house of Chloe, that there are contentions among you. Now this I say, that every one of you saith, I am of Paul; and I of Apollos; and I of Cephas; and I of Christ. Is Christ divided? was Paul crucified for you? or were ye baptized into the name of Paul?" (1 Corinthians 1:11-13). And that additional rebuke from the same Apostle: "Ye are yet carnal: for whereas there is among you envying, and strife, and divisions, are ye not carnal, and walk as men? For while one saith, I am of Paul; and another, I am of Apollos; are ye not carnal?" (1 Corinthians 3:3,4).

5. Divisions and contentions tend to quench the Spirit of God and provoke Him to withdraw from them.

The gracious presence of God and the agency of His Holy Spirit is the life of all religion in the church in general and in every individual church in particular. If He is withdrawn the church, may keep up a form of religion, but they will have nothing of the power and life of it. Divisions and contentions are sad means to quench the motions of the Holy Spirit in men's hearts and to drive Him away. The Spirit of God, that blessed Dove, is a Spirit of Peace. He does not dwell and converse with such souls that are much exercised in passion, pride, contention, and strife. These are not His fruits but are infinitely abhorrent to Him. They tend to stifle and bear down the good motions and impressions He makes on the heart and to provoke Him to withdraw.

In Scripture we find reckoned among the works of the flesh, "hatred, variance, emulations, wrath, strife, seditions, heresies, envyings... and such like," and among the fruits of the Spirit, "love, joy, peace, longsuffering, gentleness, goodness, faith, meekness, temperance" (Galatians 5:17-23). We are warned: "If ye have bitter envying and strife in your hearts, glory not, and lie not against the truth. This wisdom descendeth not from above, but is earthly, sensual, devilish. For where envying and strife is, there is confusion and every evil work. But the wisdom that is from above is first pure, then peaceable, gentle, and easy to be entreated, full of mercy and good fruits, without partiality, and without hypocrisy. And the fruit of righteousness is sown in peace of them that make peace" (James 3:14-18). If the Spirit of God is withdrawn from the churches they will not be held together as spiritual fellowships for very long for "the unity of the Spirit is the bond of peace" (Ephesians 4:3). They will soon become carnal societies, having little of God within them, and whether they hold together or break into pieces will hardly matter for that which governs them is not the will of God but what they apprehend to be their carnal interests and worldly designs. Their very ruin and desolation consists in the fact that they serve their passions, prejudices, and party designs rather than the purpose for which God called the church into being.

6. Divisions and contentions tend to make churches contemptible to others and a prey to both Satan and designing men.

To be "terrible as an army with banners" is one part of that fair and beautiful character by which the church is described (Song of Solomon 6:4). When churches are heartily united on the true principles of their union, they give such testimony against sin, such testimony of the holiness of God, of the efficacy of the blood of Christ, and of the virtue of the sanctifying Spirit that they are a terror to evil men and transgressors. Their constancy, courage, and firmness in the cause of God and of the glorious truths of the Gospel of Christ strikes an awe upon the spirits of carnal and wicked men and makes them tremble at the excellency and power of religion so that they actually dread the consequences of unbelief and impiety. But when churches are crumbled, broken, and divided into factions and parties, they become contemptible to men of the world. At such times the carnal-minded look upon professed Christians as merely different parties of hypocrites who are proud, conceited, and designing men. They treat them with scorn. They despise their church discipline and the testimony they pretend to give for religion. They treat it all as a tool to serve the passions and promote the party designs of scheming men. Thus divided, Christians become a reproach to their neighbors and a scandal to religion.

Moreover, they are greatly exposed to the temptations of Satan who watches for advantages. By means of their pride and passion, he is able to betray them into sin. As the result of their love for chief seats, he is able to set them up in the very place of Christ and to substitute their own honor instead of His. He is able to lead them into many mistakes about their duty and the great doctrines and interests of religion. When their eyes are already much darkened by prejudice, self-interest, and self-will, Satan easily gets advantage of their weak side, where there is little guard. He quickly blinds their minds and leads them to mistake self-will and self-interest for pure zeal and the love of God. He can convince them that their own fancies and imaginations and religious motions are the teaching and instructions of the Holy Spirit.

The contentions of the Church of Corinth seem to be the special ground of that great caution and jealousy the Apostle expresses toward them: "For I am jealous over you with godly jealousy: for I have espoused you to one husband, that I may present you as a chaste virgin to Christ. But I fear, lest by any means, as the serpent beguiled Eve through his subtilty, so your minds should be corrupted from the simplicity that is in Christ" (2 Corinthians 11:3,4).

Such divisions also expose individual members to be prey to men of design who have some party interests to serve. By this handle they easily take hold of their passions and make use of the interests of others to draw them into their own designs. Under a notion of religion and zeal for Christ, they may engage them inadvertently to be tools to serve their own designs and the interests of their party. Hence we have many cautions and warnings in the Word of God against such divisions, including Paul's concerned word to the Romans: "Now I beseech you, brethren, mark them which cause divisions and offenses contrary to the doctrine which ye have learned; and avoid them. For they that are such serve not our Lord Jesus Christ, but their own belly; and by good words and fair speeches deceive the hearts of the simple" (Romans 16:17,18).

The Second chapter of Galatians, along with several other Scripture passages, might be mentioned to show that divisions and contentions tend to the ruin and desolation of churches as well as other societies, but these, I hope, are enough to give you some sensible conviction of the truth and the weight of Christ's words, "Every kingdom divided against itself is brought to desolation; and every city or house divided against itself shall not stand."

II. THE APPLICATION OF THIS VERY SIGNIFICANT DOCTRINE TO THE SITUATION AS IT NOW EXISTS AMONG US.

USE ONE. All Christians and churches should dread divisions and contentions among themselves. Since strife and party spirit have such a strong tendency to bring ruin and desolation, we all ought to have a great dread of them. We should particularly watch against the beginnings of such divisions for when once they are started it is not easy to foresee their end. This statement is agreeable with the instruction the Holy Spirit has already given, "The beginning of strife is as when one letteth out water: therefore leave off contention, before it be meddled with" (Proverbs 17:14). One hot word, one peevish reflection, one angry demand, one spiteful contradiction, brings on another, and that a third, and so it continues until it moves like the water that has burst forth from a dam. When a flood starts it is often because of a small leak in the structure, but the rush of the water widens the breach until it bears down all before it as a mighty rushing wall of water. Just so we should dread the first spark of the fire of angry words because we know the terrible damage caused by the raging inferno. Therefore, learn to leave off strife and contention not only when you see the worst of it but when you see the first of it. In addition to what I have just said, let me offer two motives.

1. Divisions and contentions in churches are a great reproach and dishonor to Jesus Christ.

Sometimes men are apt to make light of religious contentions and even boast of them as the natural and necessary result of true religion. They misuse Scripture and act as if Christ had foretold such divisions by declaring: "Think not that I am come to send peace on earth: I came not to send peace, but a sword. For I am come to set a man at variance against his father, and the daughter against her mother, and the daughter in law against her mother in law. And a man's foes shall be they of his own household" (Matthew 10:34-36). But surely we are not to understand that Christ came to make quarrels in His own church or to set His own disciples at variance with one another. We know that He did not come to give temporal or carnal peace and worldly prosperity as many in His day seemed to think He did. His errand was not to give His disciples temporal power, ease, and wealth in this world. No! He came to give peace with God, peace in our consciences, peace with our brethren. Thus He says, "In the world ye shall have tribulation" (John 16:33).

If all the world would heartily receive Christ and His doctrine, there would be universal peace. But while there are so many that reject Him who are the children of this world and of the seed of the serpent, the children of God must expect to feel their enmity. The quarrels and contentions that exist among men are not the fruit of the Gospel but the result of the lusts of those who do not cordially receive it. The most violent and implacable feuds the world has ever seen have been those which have arisen concerning religion. The Gospel proves the occasion of divisions, but it is not because there is any tendency in the religion of Jesus Christ to make men unpeaceable, but rather because men's own lusts oppose the peaceable, pure, and holy doctrines which He teaches them.

All those who are part of the Christian church profess to be disciples of Christ, who is the Prince and Author of Peace. They are solemnly bound by Covenant to obey His will and to be governed by His laws. But their dissensions and quarrels provide sad evidence that they are not what they should be. Such persons are either hypocrites or not as much under the power of Christ's laws and possessed with the true principles of His holy religion as they ought to be. Tragically, professed Christians who war with one another scandalize the name of Christ by making it appear that

He is the passion of their contentions. They bring reproach upon His holy religion by acting as if devotees of it might live in such wrath, variance, emulations, and strife as He declares are not the works of the Spirit but of the flesh (Galatians 5:20). They act as if, when He bids Christians to "earnestly contend for the faith which was once delivered unto the saints" (Jude 3), He gave them license to quarrel with the brethren. They do not appear to hesitate to call them hard names and to injure and hurt them by force or craft because they do not see as they do or because they think differently from them in those things wherein they are persuaded the essence of religion does not lie. But in truth, Christians are only to contend for the faith by sound doctrine, strong arguments, holy lives, pious examples, firm patience, and deep humility in bearing all the evils they meet from an evil world in the way of their steadfast and persevering obedience to the Gospel of Jesus Christ.

2. Divisions and contentions in churches do much harm to others as well as to our own souls.

The divisions and contentions of the visible body of Christ are, as has been said, a great hindrance to its own mutual edification. They are also a sad stumbling block to weak Christians and expose them to many temptations and means of their uncharitable, uncomfortable, and unholy walking.

They may also prove an occasion of ruin to some poor souls, perhaps even to many who are hardened by them in their unbelief and atheism. It is a very common thing to hear the reproach of infidels against religion on account of the unpeaceable behavior of professing Christians. We frequently hear them say that there are such differences among professed Christians in their doctrines and schemes of religion that there can be no certainty about them; that there are such fierce debates, such heats, animosities, and envious and selfish controversies contrary to the doctrines of peace and love, patience and forbearance, which they all pretend to acknowledge, that the evidence is overwhelming that none but the weak and simple believe them. They therefore conclude that all of Christianity is a fraud. When carnal men see the visible body of Christ bringing forth the same fruits as the carnal world produces, fruits that spring from bitter, persecuting, censorious, impatient, revengeful spirits, when they see such like works of the flesh as variance, emulations, wrath, strife, seditions, heresies, they not unwisely believe there is no more religion in one than in the other. Thus many sink into atheism and are confirmed in their rejection and neglect of Christ and His divine doctrine as the result of the divisions and contentions they see among those who profess otherwise.

Churches and individual Christians must avoid all contentions if they truly love and promote the honor of their divine Master. They must dread whatsoever tends to bring reproach upon and scandalize His sacred and precious name. He has bid them be one and even prayed that they might be one as He and His Father are one (John 17:6-26).

If those who have been long engaged in contentions and divisions think it is too late for them to be warned of the danger and excited to dread the beginnings of them, let them at least realize that it is not too late to dread the mischiefs of them and to seek total deliverance from this grievous iniquity.

USE TWO. Christians and churches should be greatly concerned to heal divisions among themselves. No matter how far any churches have gone in divisions, it is to be hoped that it is not too late to entreat you to put an end to them and to use all available means of healing. It is certainly not too late to put the question to you which Abner put to Joab, "Shall the sword devour for ever? knowest thou not that it will be bitterness in the latter end?" (2 Samuel 2:26). If divisions have gone far, it is surely time to see if there is not some "balm in Gilead," if there is not some "physician there" (Jeremiah 8:22).

Hoping that such churches and persons are heartily concerned to have the hurt of the daughter of God's people healed, let me propose to your consideration some means of healing.

1. See that a hearty desire for God's glory and the advancement of the interests of Christ's kingdom rule your hearts.

If, my brethren, you are all actuated and governed by a supreme love for God and Jesus Christ and a sincere desire for His glory; if the advancement of the great, essential interests of religion governs your hearts (and I am persuaded there is no man of you who either does not pretend it does or at least owns it ought to be so) divisions and contentions will then cease. There is nothing in the world that will so calm your passions, sweeten your tempers, and bring all your self-will, worldly interests, and prejudices to the feet of Christ and make you willing to forego them all for that one great and common interest, the edification and salvation of the body, than a true love to God and concern for His kingdom.

A desire for God's glory and the advancement of His kingdom will make you willing to sacrifice every private and party interest to the honor of God and the common good. If the great, necessary, all-concerning things of religion may be preserved and the common good promoted, you will not think it of any great consequence whether it happens in a way exactly and in all circumstances agreeable to your mind or not. God's glory and the common salvation will appear to you to be things infinitely greater than your own will, desire, particular opinions, or peculiar special interests. This will most effectually teach you not to separate any interest, design, or desire of yours from God's interest and Christ's kingdom but to swallow up all in that. This will serve abundantly to convince you that religion disdains the narrow limits of a party, for it is only by true faith and sincere love that men may be brought to union with Christ. If others are made sincerely holy and obedient and you yourselves enabled to abound in Christian virtues, it will be worth more than all the interests of this world, for they are as nothing in comparison with this. All other concerns run into this great one like the rivers run into the sea. Christ shows us we should be ready to part with our lives for His sake and to lay them down for the brethren (1 John 3:16). Thus, for the true Christian, all other interests are transferred to this great and overwhelming concern.

2. See that there be a hearty union in all the things that are necessary to salvation.

All true Christians are agreed in all the things that are necessary to salvation. "There is one body, and one Spirit, even as ye are called in one hope of your calling; one Lord, one faith, one baptism, one God and Father of all, who is above all, and through all, and in you all" (Ephesians 4:4-6). The things which belong to the foundation of the faith are carefully enumerated for us: "repentance from dead works, and of faith toward God, of the doctrine of baptisms, and of laying on of hands, and of resurrection of the dead, and of eternal judgment" (Hebrews 6:1,2).

Christians must beware to make nothing fundamental which Christ has not made so, and in all that he has made foundational, there must be an absolute union and agreement. As already noted, "I beseech you, brethren, by the name of our Lord Jesus Christ, that ye all speak the same thing, and that there be no divisions among you; but that ye be perfectly joined together in the same mind and in the same judgment" (1 Corinthians 1:10). "Now the God of patience and consolation grant you to be likeminded one toward another according to Christ Jesus: That ye may with one mind and one mouth glorify God, even the Father of our Lord Jesus Christ" (Romans 15:5,6). "If there be therefore any consolation in Christ, if any comfort of love, if any fellowship of the Spirit, if any bowels and mercies, fulfil ye my joy, that ye be likeminded, having the same love, being of one accord, of one mind. Let nothing be done through strife or vainglory; but in lowliness of mind let each esteem other better than themselves. Look not every man on his own things, but every man also on the things of others" (Philippians 2:1-4). The great essentials of Christianity are easily stated: that there is but one God, the glorious Jehovah, Father, Son and Holy Ghost; one Saviour, the Lord Jesus Christ; one Sanctifier and Comforter, the Holy Spirit of God; all men must be justified by the righteousness of Jesus Christ and the only means and procuring cause of our righteousness before God must be apprehended by faith; repentance from dead works is required since holy obedience to the whole revealed will of God is a necessary part of this faith; likewise the observance of all God's positive institutions and the sincere exercise of universal righteousness, love, and charity are the genuine and necessary fruits of true faith and actings of holiness. These, at least, are the fundamental truths upon which all must be united and joined together in the same mind and judgment.

3. There must be a forebearing of one another in all those things that are not essential to salvation.

As Christians must all be of one mind in all those things absolutely necessary to salvation, in other matters there is little room to expect they can or should be of the same identical mind. Christians have never all thought alike in any age of Christianity, and it is not likely that it will ever happen in this world. It is almost as common for Christians to differ in their thoughts about one thing and another as it is for them to be distinguished from one another in their looks. If you are resolved to maintain dissention and contention because there are many things wherein you have different apprehensions from others, you may certainly wisely despair of any union taking place. If Christians are resolved to contend over matters of church discipline or the interpretation of every text of Scripture, they may as well give up all thoughts of peace and union and settle down to tearing the seamless coat of Christ into infinite pieces.

It is likely that the Christian church will never be at peace in this world unless it comes about by a kind and charitable forbearance of one another in all those things which are not essential to salvation. This is the only way of being of one mind in these things. It is probable that, among other reasons, God has left these matters liable to disputes and debates for the very purpose of exciting us to the exercise of humility, forbearance, and charity as well as the practice of diligence as ministers of peace, each to the other. "Let us therefore, as many as be perfect, be thus minded: and if in anything ye be otherwise minded, God shall reveal even this unto you. Nevertheless, whereto we have already attained, let us walk by the same rule, let us mind the same things" (Philippians 3:15,16).

4. A patient bearing and ready forgiving of one another for all manner of personal injuries and all supposed unchristian wrongs, so far as the law of Christ allows it.

Scriptures teach that "in the multitude of words there wanteth not sin" (Proverbs 10:19). It is highly unlikely that in the long contentions in which some of you have been engaged you have not wronged your brother with hard speeches and injurious actions. If none of you have, by an unchristian temper in the management of your controversies, dishonored Christ and His religion, you are doubtless a very singular people for there is to be found much of these things within every party. There is a biblical rule in these matters affecting what is personal. It is not becoming to a Christian to have any personal quarrel with any man in the world. Personal injuries are to be born patiently while the believer searches for evidence of the hand of God therein, just as David did when Shimei cursed him (2 Samuel 16:10). We are clearly taught this rule by the Apostle, "Charity beareth all things" (1 Corinthians 13:7). We are further taught to "put on therefore, as the elect of God, holy and beloved, bowels of mercies, kindness, humbleness of mind, meekness, longsuffering; Forebearing one another, and forgiving one another, if any man have a quarrel against any: even as Christ forgave you, so also do ye. And above all these things put on charity, which is the bond of perfectness. And let the peace of God rule in your hearts" (Colossians 3:12-15). Christ did not allow His disciples to bear any grudges or to avenge themselves at all for any injury whatsoever. Whenever injuries are personal, He requires His disciples to forgive absolutely, whether asked or unasked, saying plainly, "For if ye forgive men their trespasses, your heavenly Father will also forgive you: But if ye forgive not men their trespasses, neither will your Father forgive your trespasses" (Matthew 6:14-15).

If you apprehend that the laws and rules of Christ are broken, you must see to it that you do not aggravate matters or treat the fault with any greater severity than is necessary, and then purely to vindicate the honor of Christ and His religion. Your own wills or interests must have nothing whatever to do with your handling of these matters, but you must be motivated purely by the will and glory of Christ. "Brethren, if a man be overtaken in a fault, ye which are spiritual, restore such an one in the spirit of meekness: considering thyself, lest thou also be tempted. Bear one another's burdens, and so fulfil the law of Christ" (Galatians 6:1,2). "I therefore, the prisoner of the Lord, beseech you that ye walk worthy of the vocation wherewith ye are called, With all lowliness and meekness, with longsuffering, forbearing one another in love; Endeavoring to keep the unity of the Spirit in the bond of peace" (Ephesians 4:1-3). "Let all bitterness, and wrath, and anger, and clamor, and evil speaking, be put away from you, with all malice: And be kind one to another, tenderhearted, forgiving one another, even as God for Christ's sake hath forgiven you" (Ephesians 4:31,32).

5. Fervently love and pray for one another and for the special presence of God among you.

You must be, above all other things, concerned that you may have the special presence of God among you by His divine Spirit. If He is with you, His presence will make your way easy and will lighten your path. The gracious presence of God will revive God's work in your own souls as well as in your churches. The manifestations of His presence will make it easy to forgive and you will find that you can and will "confess your faults one to another, and pray one for another, that ye may be healed" (James 5:16).

"If any man see his brother sin a sin which is not unto death, he shall ask, and he shall give him life for them that sin not unto death" (1 John 5:16). If God gives you a hearty love for one another, your party interests and self-serving will wonderfully subside and die away. While you are heartily praying God to forgive your brethren and neighbors, you will not be unwilling or unable to forgive them yourselves. You cannot sincerely say the Lord's Prayer with an unforgiving spirit, for there you entreat, "forgive us our debts, as we forgive our debtors." If God pours upon you a spirit of hearty and fervent prayer for His presence and His Spirit among you, if there were such a spirit of prayer in the churches of this land, it would be a happy omen of the revival of true religion, of the powerful influence of truth, of righteousness and of an abundance of peace which God, of His infinite mercy, grants for Christ Jesus' sake.

CHAPTER FOURTEEN

An Evil
and Adulterous
Generation

By
Andrew Eliot

Andrew Eliot, 1719-1778

Andrew Eliot was born in Boston on December 25, 1719. His father, also Andrew, was a Boston merchant. His grandfather, Andrew Elliott, had come from Somersetshire in England and settled at Beverly, Massachusetts, about 1683. Little is known of his early life. He graduated from Harvard College in 1737, and having felt a call to the ministry of the Gospel, studied theology in preparation for ordination. He began preaching in New North Church, Boston, in August, 1741 as a colleague of John Webb but was not ordained there until April of 1742. He continued in that relationship until the death of Webb in 1750. From then until his own death he carried the sole responsibility for the church.

It may startle some to know that Doctor of Divinity degrees were purchased then, even as today. John Barrett, a close friend of Pastor Webb's and a Deacon at New North Church, purchased the degree for his pastor from the University of Edinburgh in 1767.

Eliot became a member of the Corporation of Harvard College in 1765, and on two subsequent occasions the College sought his services as President. In each instance he declined on the basis of unwillingness to break the tie with his congregation.

One of his sons paid tribute to his father in saying, "The Doctor's memory has been held in great veneration. An upright, honest man he was. The esteem of the wise and good he certainly had. In principle, he was what has been styled a moderate Calvinist. The doctrines laid down in the Assembly's Shorter Catechism he held in high estimation. These he inculcated zealously upon the youth of his congregation, and upon his children, as long as he lived.

"In the pulpit he was a favorite. His discourses were plain and practical, seldom on controversial points. They were delivered without action, but with a pathos and solemnity that commanded attention. He always used notes. His tone of voice was bold and positive, as though he would not be contradicted; nor indeed did he bear contradiction tamely out of the pulpit. Over an highly irascible temper he had acquired a remarkable command. When he felt his passions rising, he would retire by himself till he had controlled them. His influence over his parishioners was great; so that, although there were a number very inimical to him, yet he never was openly opposed to them. They, out of derision, used to style him Pope. Others there were, who disapproved of his prudence in party matters, especially in politics. On no account would he introduce them into the pulpit. One of the maxims which he urged upon those of his sons who went into the clerical profession, was—'When your parishioners are divided in sentiment, enjoy your own opinion, and act according to your best judgment; but join neither as a partizan.' This circumspection acquired for him the name of Andrew Sly."

During the Great Awakening, this circumspection was especially evident as Eliot would neither join forces with Whitefield and the revival nor strongly oppose, albeit the evidence seems clearly to indicate that he regarded the evangelist as a border-line enthusiast. But despite his failure to support the Great Awakening, it is clear that Eliot was an earnest believer who enjoyed a long and blessed life of Christian usefulness. Peter Thatcher said at Eliot's funeral, "In his discourses upon his death bed he always expressed an unshaken faith in those glorious doctrines of the grace of God which he had preached unto others and his firm yet humble confidence in the merits of the Redeemer: resigned to the will of God, nay, eager after His presence and enjoyment of His glory, he would frequently breathe out the pious ejaculation, 'Come Lord Jesus, come quickly—why are Thy chariot wheels so long in coming?' and, with a solemn message to his beloved people on his lips, he expired" on September 13, 1778.

First published as *An Evil and Adulterous Generation: A Sermon Preached on the Public Fast, April 19, 1753 by Andrew Eliot, M.A. Pastor of a Church in Boston.* Boston: Printed by S. Kneeland for J. Winter, 1753.

An Evil and
Adulterous Generation

"An evil and adulterous generation..."
Matthew 12:39.

"An evil and adulterous generation" is the description of the character which our Lord frequently gave to the Jews in His day. It is said of them collectively as a people. Because their sins were general, public and national guilt was contracted by them.

They were not only an "evil generation" but an "adulterous generation." This may be taken in a twofold sense and was doubtless true in both cases. It might intend that they were degenerated from their excellent ancestors. They were not "the children of Abraham," an honorable title in which they gloried. Although they had descended from him according to the flesh, yet in a moral and spiritual sense they were a base and spurious race. Or else it may intimate that by their sins they had become guilty of what is frequently spoken of in Scripture as "spiritual adultery." God had distinguished them from all other nations: "You only have I known of all the families of the earth" (Amos 3:2). He had taken them into a Covenant with Himself. He is even pleased to express it as "married unto you" (Jeremiah 3:14). This singular goodness of God to them laid them under the strongest obligations to holiness and obedience. But their conduct was in no measure up to what it ought to have been. They were guilty of great impiety and wickedness. The most shocking crimes were committed among them with impunity. The heads of the people, their rulers and teachers, taught them to err. They taught them both by their examples and by their precepts. There were many direct breaches of the Law of God which they, by their corrupt glosses and perverse interpretations, made the people to believe were no evil at all.

It is true that all this time they kept up a mighty show of religion. They made a great bustle about those parts of duty which would cost them but little pain and self-denial. They would not omit the smallest religious rites, but they neglected shamefully the substantial duties of morality. This is the testimony which our Saviour bears against them: "Ye pay tithe of mint and anise and cummin, and have omitted the weightier matters of the law, judgment, mercy, and faith" (Matthew 23:23). They were guilty of extortion and most cruel injustice. They "devoure widows' houses" but at the same time "make long prayers (Matthew 23:14) and pretended to a great deal of goodness. Under the show of extraordinary sanctity they perpetrated the worst of crimes. This was especially the character of the Scribes and Pharisees, against whom our Lord pronounced many woes for their hypocrisy and immorality. It is evident, however, that they had taught the people to believe and practice as they did, otherwise they would not have been able to maintain such an exalted character for piety and goodness, notwithstanding all their crimes. They had brought the Jews to believe that duties of the Second Table of the Law were of little or no importance as long as they adhered strictly to those of the First Table. If they believed this way it is most probable that their practice was agreeable to their beliefs. Therefore, our Lord says to a number of the Jews who boasted that they were Abraham's seed, "Ye are of your father the devil, and the lusts of your father ye will do" (John 8:33,44).

If we examine the account given by their own historian we shall be disposed to think that our Lord was not severe in this charge against them and that He had not exaggerated at all the corruption which prevailed among the Jews. The description of the character of the impious and wicked of that age which Josephus gives is so bad that one is ready to wonder that such miscreants were even suffered to live and that God did not immediately, by some final judgment, extirpate them from the face of the earth. "It was," says Josephus, "a time fruitful of all sorts of wickedness among the Jews; so that no evil whatever was left unpracticed. It is impossible for man to contrive any new wickedness, which was not then committed. All were corrupt in their private and public character... They strove to exceed each other in impiety toward God and injustice toward their neighbors. The great men oppressed the people, and the people strove to ruin them. The former were ambitious of dominion and power, the latter had an insatiable thirst of violence and plunder."[1] It appears from hence, as one well observes, that the corruption of this people was general.[2]

The same historian says in another place, "I cannot speak it without regret, yet I must declare, it is my opinion, that if the Romans had

---

[1]The Works of Flavius Josephus.
[2]Lardner, Nathaniel - The Credibility of the Gospel History. Vol. 1.

delayed to come against these wretches, the City, [viz. Jerusalem] would have been swallowed up by an earthquake, or overwhelmed by a deluge, or else been consumed by fire from heaven, as Sodom was: for it bore a generation of men more wicked than those which had suffered such calamities."[3] And having mentioned some of the crimes which were committed in the City while besieged by Titus and the misery to which the inhabitants were reduced, he sums it all up by saying, "To reckon up all their iniquities is impossible: but in short, never did any City suffer so great calamities; nor was there ever from the beginning of the world, a time more fruitful of wickedness than that was."[4] This is the account which is given by one who was himself a Jew and zealous for the honor of his nation, and the facts which he has recorded abundantly prove them to be that wicked and abandoned people he has represented them as.

Indeed, we need no more than the history of the New Testament to convince us that the Jews were at that time sunk to the lowest degree of degeneracy and wickedness. How base, how barbarous was their treatment of our blessed Lord, a man who spent His life in acts of kindness and in the most sincere and disinterested endeavors to serve both their souls and bodies. He appeared with all the marks of a divine Messenger and gave incontestible evidence that He was a Prophet and more than a Prophet. He claimed the exalted character of the Son of God, but in their ingratitude and wickedness, they did not even recognize Him. Think of the obduracy of heart it disclosed in the Jews when they abused and persecuted this great and good Man, this heavenly Messenger, this divine Person! To reject Him, one would think, had been bad enough, but to ill-treat Him only because His Kingdom was spiritual and He did not answer their ambitious expectations from the Messiah and to thirst after His blood and in the most cruel manner to shed it was an act so full of impiety and wickedness as not to admit a parallel.

This murder of Christ was a national act. It was accomplished by the rulers, the teachers, and the body of the Jewish nation who were convened at Jerusalem to celebrate the Passover. It was the people that appeared before Pilate and with such vehemence urged the crucifixion of Christ. It was the nation of the Jews that preferred Barabbas to Him and that uttered that horrid imprecation, "His blood be on us, and on our children" (Matthew 27:25), that compelled the timorous Governor to an act of injustice and cruelty contrary to the light of his own mind, as he

---

[3]Josephus.
[4]Ibid.

once and again declared to them.

When I say this was a national act I do not mean that every individual Jew was active in the death of Christ or consenting to it. Some, we know, were of another mind including the immediate followers of our Lord, Joseph of Arimathea, Nicodemus, and doubtless many others who believed on Him. But the generality of the people, even if they were not active in this horrid crime, consented to it. By their presence and connivance they showed their approbation of what was done. And after the death and resurrection of our Lord, they still resisted the Light which shone around them. The evidence of the Truth of Christianity was stronger and clearer after the death of Christ than it was before. The resurrection of Christ, the effusion of the Holy Spirit, and the gift of tongues and miraculous powers with which the Apostles and others were endowed were all additional proofs that Jesus was no imposter but the promised Messiah. Accordingly, some who had withstood Christ Himself and would not receive Him as the Messiah were convinced under the ministry of the Apostles. But the nation of the Jews, that is the body of the people, persisted in their infidelity. Instead of yielding to the full evidence they now had, they went on to maltreat and to destroy the preachers and professors of the Gospel until they had filled up the measure of their iniquity (1 Thessalonians 2:16), provoked God to unchurch them and to give up their temple and city to such amazing destruction that those who can read the account of it without astonishment and horror must be devoid of all humanity. This being the case, our Lord had much reason to speak of this generation as "evil and adulterous" and to threaten to bring upon them, as He does in another place, "all the righteous blood shed upon the earth" (Matthew 23:35) since in them the wickedness and barbarity of all the persecutors that had ever been in the world seemed to be collected.

I have now considered the words as they relate to the nation of the Jews. The plain meaning of them is that they were a very wicked people, that they were degenerated from their holy ancestors and did not walk answerable to the privileges and advantages with which they had been favored. I shall now take the liberty to apply them to ourselves and to the people of this land.

The character given to the Jews in my text is not peculiar to them. There have been others to whom it has belonged. There have been Christian Churches who have left their first love, sunk into lukewarmness and indifference and proceeded from one impiety to another until God has removed their candlestick out of its place. Such just displays of divine vengeance have doubtless been designed not only to punish the guilty but also for the admonition of others that they might hear and fear and not do so wickedly. It will be happy for this people if God's righteous severity towards others may lead us to repent of our fornications and our departures from that God whose we are and whom we ought to serve.

The character which our Lord gives of the Jewish nation does, I fear, in some degrees belong to us. Even if we are not so bad as they were, and I hope in God we are not, yet may it not with truth be said of us that we are on many accounts "an evil and adulterous generation?"

It is disagreeable but necessary talk to mention the sins we have committed, the aggravations with which they have been attended, and the guilt we have contracted thereby. It is a theme no one would choose to speak on. Nothing could influence me to do so if I did not think it absolutely my duty, especially on such an occasion as this when we are met together to confess our sins and to humble our souls before God on account of them. It is necessary that our wounds should be laid open and searched in order for them to be healed.

Like the Jews, we descend from pious ancestors. The first settlers of New-England were men of exalted goodness. They were not without their faults but they excelled in virtue. What ardent zeal, what disinterested affection to God and His cause possessed their souls when they left a good and pleasant land where some of them had large possessions and sought, in this new world, a covert from the storm of persecution which was raised against them. They were content to dwell in a desert if they might there enjoy that liberty of conscience which was unreasonably denied them in their native country. Nor was their religion confined to those things in which they saw fit to dissent from their brethren. It had influence on their whole conversation. Vice was hardly named, unless to condemn it. A man might live seven years among them and not hear a profane oath or see a man drunk in the street; such was the honorable testimony which was once given of this land.

But "How is the gold become dim! How is the most fine gold changed!" (Lamentations 4:1). Oh, New-England how thou art fallen! We are not the genuine offspring of the first settlers of this land. We are a spurious race, risen up instead of them but very unlike them. We are guilty of great apostasy. We have broken the Covenant which, as we are a professing people, exists between God and ourselves. The glorious God has favored us with peculiar light and advantages. No people under heaven have had greater blessings, but we have not made answerable improvements. He has taken us into a near relation to Himself but we have been unfaithful to Him. He has tried us with mercies. Perhaps there have never been more signal appearances of heaven for the deliverance

and salvation of any people than there have been for this people, but
without right response. He has tried us with judgments. We have been
brought very low. But the methods He has taken with us have by no
means had a suitable effect. His mercies have not melted us; His
judgments have not reclaimed us. We continue as corrupt as ever. There
is to be found among us:

    1. Impiety Toward God.
    2. Sins of Neglect of Jesus Christ and His Salvation.
    3. Contempt Poured on the Holy Spirit.
    4. Vice and Immorality of Almost Every Kind.

What I have further to say upon the subject of our degeneracy will
naturally fall under one or another of these heads.

I. I BEGIN WITH IMPIETY TOWARD GOD.

It must be acknowledged that we still have the appearance of
religion. God, we hope in mercy, still continues our candlestick, our
church state and spiritual privileges, and we make pretenses of regard to
Him. We keep days of fasting and prayer in one season of the year and
of thanksgiving in another, just as our Fathers did. But do we not have a
great deal of reason to think that these solemnities are gradually sinking
into formality and hypocrisy? If we were in any measure sincere, would
there not be a reformation of the evils which prevail in the midst of us?

1. Abuse of the Sabbath.

There is some external regard to the public institutions of religion
among us. It is still a custom with many of our people to come up to the
house of God on His holy day. A goodly appearance is made in our
places of worship when "the tribes come up, the tribes of the Lord, to give
thanks unto the name of the Lord, and to inquire in His temple." These
things are doubtless pleasing to God, but still, is there not an observable
degeneracy with respect to the Sabbath? There are large numbers that
wholly absent themselves from public worship and whose seats are so
often empty when they might conveniently fill them. The slightest
indisposition detains them from the house of God which would not begin
to keep them from paying a visit to the house of a friend. It is a practice
with some, if the disorder is such as makes confinement necessary only
one day of the week, to wait for the Sabbath as the only leisure day they
can find. They think it too much to give to God one day in seven although
He kindly allows them six days for their own employments. Many contract
a habit of loitering at home one part of the day and think they have done
God great service if they afford their presence in the house of God on
another part.

If we look around our religious assemblies we will observe much irreverence and indecency. Some allow themselves to sleep, others spend the time whispering and laughing. Many, by the roving of their eyes, reveal the inattention of their hearts. They are glad when the exercises are over in order that they may have time to mis-spend in idle discourse. It is to be feared that many are able to give a better description of their neighbor's dress than of the sermon they have heard. Would it be this way if we had a serious sense of the presence of God in the assembly? Or if we had a due solicitude for the welfare of our souls? Or if we remembered that we must give an account of every Sabbath and every sermon?

I acknowledge that I have a high opinion of the Sabbath and of its importance. I look upon the religious observance of it as necessary to the very being of religion. The Sabbath is far from being a burden and an unnecessary imposition on mankind. It should be regarded as one of God's greatest possible kindnesses in calling us off from the world, which is so apt to engage our whole soul, and in obliging us to spend one day in seven in meditation and holy exercises which tend to fit us for that eternal state to which we are hastening. Were it not for the public exercises of that day we should soon lose the very appearance of religion. The growing contempt of the Sabbath is with me, therefore, a conclusive argument for our apostasy and an awful symptom that is very likely to grow worse.

2. Another token of our degeneracy is the neglect of family religion.
There are, it is to be feared, heads of families who are never known to pray in their families at all and others who seldom attend to this important duty. The natural accompaniment of this is a neglect of family instruction and family government. Those who do not make it a matter of conscience to pray with their children and servants are not likely to take much pains to teach them the principles of religion or to restrain them from the many vices to which they are prone. We may well expect that children brought up in such families will be careless and indifferent about religion, if they are not altogether dissolute and profane.

3. But if family religion is omitted, is not secret prayer much more neglected?
The reputation of men is not so much affected by the neglect of secret prayer as it is by the neglect of family religion. Therefore, those who have no other purpose in their family devotions than a conformity to a custom or the preserving of their reputations are not likely to be very careful about secret prayer. It is evident that men around us are beginning to lose their sense of dependence on God for both spiritual and

temporal blessings. Only a few employ their thoughts about spiritual blessings, while the general feeling is that temporal blessings come promiscuously upon all, without the direction of any superintending Being. Most men, therefore, seldom or never retire to spread their requests before God. Ignorant and helpless as they are, they do not implore His grace to strengthen and guide them. They enter upon business and engage in vast undertakings and scarce ever ask counsel of God or seek His direction and blessing. Through the distinguishing goodness of Him that made them, they are capable of religion and of making their acknowledgements to Him, yet they rise up and lie down; they eat, drink and transact all the affairs of life, in this respect just like the beasts, with no more thought of God than if there were no such Being.

4. The Sin of Profanity.

Instead of frequently retiring to converse with God in prayer and to seek His favor or by holy meditation to possess their souls with a suitable awe and veneration of Him, too many cast off fear, set their mouths against heaven and take the sacred name of God in vain. It is surprising to observe the degree of profanity to which some have arrived and with what ease and impudence they can toss about the most shocking oaths. Even our children in the streets are adept in this sin. They can swear and curse without remorse and seem to vie with each other in this aggravated crime. Yet profaneness is so ridiculous a vice that no one has ever pretended to vindicate it. There is nothing in our constitution to move us to it. The only temptation I can even think of is that men or children, and in this they are all children, may show their vain companions how bold in wickedness they dare to be, having shaken off those restraints which others are under and perhaps they themselves were under once. If this is the chief cause of profaneness, as I sincerely believe it is, the prevalence of this sin certainly sets a people in a very disadvantageous light, for it is surely a sin which has its foundation in hardness of heart and in the searing of the conscience. The evils I have been mentioning are those which are immediately committed against God and come under the head of impiety.

II. SINS OF NEGLECT OF JESUS CHRIST AND HIS SALVATION.

Many have begun to think our glorious Saviour might have spared Himself the pains of crucifixion and that all He has done for the salvation of fallen man is unnecessary. If they do not declare this in so many words, yet they say that which amounts to as much. Natural religion is placed above the religion of Christ even though we are obviously obliged to Christianity for a great deal we now put under the head of natural religion. The peculiar doctrines of the Gospel are derided, the atonement of Christ in denied, faith in the Mediator and in a future state are looked upon as of no importance and morality is spoken of as being all that is necessary in order to our acceptance with God.

You know, my brethren, that I have always described morality as being of the greatest possible importance, but as highly as I esteem it, I think we set it too high when we speak of it as all that is necessary. I acknowledge that "faith, if it hath not works, is dead, being alone" (James 2:17), but so are works without faith, for they will be a mere lifeless carcass. The great truths revealed in the Gospel, which are the very substance of the Christian faith, are at the foundation of right practice. Without them men may do some things well, but I am persuaded there is not likely to be a sincere, universal conformity to the will of God where doctrine is disregarded. I can go so far as to say that if we may judge by the behavior of men, those who place all religion in morality often show their want of better principles to mend their own lives and make themselves good moralists. The truth is, faith in God, in Christ, and in a future state is necessary to produce that holiness and goodness which we all allow is necessary to happiness. This holiness is the proper, genuine effect of a belief of those truths which the Gospel reveals. Where they make a suitable impression on our minds they will have this effect. To separate these things which have such a close connection with each other is to do the greatest injury to the cause of virtue. If the principles of natural religion prevail, instead of an increase of morality, I expect morality will be banished from among us.

There are others who, although they do not avow such tenets and do have an orthodox creed, yet greatly affront and dishonor our Lord Jesus Christ. They slight His invitations, reject His offers, and break His laws. Alas! How few have cordially submitted to this glorious Saviour! They prefer their enjoyments of time and sense to those infinitely more valuable blessings He is able to bestow. They suffer their hearts to be wholly taken up with the cares and pleasures of life and act as if they had nothing to fear or hope for from Him, although such great promises are made to those who submit to Him and such amazing threatenings are denounced against those who reject and disobey Him.

There are great numbers who have never publicly professed themselves the Disciples of Christ. The table of the Lord is contemned, and but few come to seal their commitments to be the Lord's there. Attendance on the Christian eucharist is beginning to be thought of as a needless thing, although our Saviour has expressly enjoined that we should do this in remembrance of Him. If we continue in the direction we have been going for some time now, our churches are likely to come to nothing, for there will be none to administer the Lord's Supper to. I know it will not universally come to this, as Christ will have a Church in the world and some true disciples to show until He comes, but this may be the case with us here. Christ may unchurch us as He did the seven once flourishing churches of Asia, as well as many others. The present state of things among us, in this respect, certainly argues a great declension. Things did not used to be this way in New-England.

III. CONTEMPT POURED ON THE HOLY SPIRIT.

If, to the things already mentioned, we add the contempt poured on the Holy Spirit, our degeneracy will be still more evident. There is no truth in the whole Bible written in fairer characters than the necessity of the Spirit's influence to fit us for the service of God here and a state of happiness with Him hereafter. Just a little acquaintance with ourselves would bring us to see our own weakness and need of the assistance of this divine Agent. But this glorious Person is grieved and offended in many, many ways. The powers of man are exalted above measure. The necessity of divine influence is denied. The operations of the Spirit in the minds of men are despised and His motions resisted. His convictions, which ought to be carefully cherished, are stifled and suppressed. Even true Christians are not sensible enough of their dependence on the Spirit of God for supplies of grace and strength. They do not consider, as they ought, that they are temples of the Holy Ghost and often, by unsuitable conduct and demeanor, grieve and offend Him. Our degeneracy is in a great measure owing to this disrespect with which the divine Spirit is treated. What makes it even more melancholy is that if we are ever to be recovered out of our declining state it must be by the powerful agency of the very Holy Spirit we are offending. Who can, with reason, expect so great a favor from Him while we, in the grossest manner, displease and affront Him?

IV. VICE AND IMMORALITY OF ALMOST EVERY KIND.

Our guilt is increased by the immoralities which abound in our land. Crimes which were not mentioned among our Fathers are now so common that they are scarcely observed, or if observed they are not discountenanced as they ought to be. Let me list a few in particular.

1. Intemperance is a sin for which the land mourns.

Once our young people were forming religious societies to promote one another's spiritual welfare. These societies were as nurseries for our churches. But they are now greatly diminished, there not being more than two or three in a town like this. But how many societies are there of a different kind—societies for gambling, excessive drinking and the like? I do not say it is unlawful for young persons to meet together to unbend their minds and amuse themselves and one another, providing that under such pretenses they do not go beyond the bounds of reason and religion. But if only they were to sometimes meet to pray to God and to converse on the great things of religion and another world, they would find it time spent to a very good purpose. To speak as kindly as possible about a vile matter, to keep late hours at a tavern can hardly be described as respectable. If it is heads of families who are doing this, such a practice sets a bad example before those who are under their care. It leads to a neglect of family worship and often introduces many other disorders. While they are out drinking, their places must be empty at the religious exercises of the family where they dwell. Many spend money in strong drink that ought to be expended in the support of themselves and their families. The number of private tipplers who hereby quench the Spirit of God, ruin their constitutions, and reduce themselves to penury and want is very great. Their children and servants are brought up in idleness and intemperance and commence to be servants of the devil almost before they come upon the stage of life. Oh, the amazing account such parents, such masters and mistresses, must give before the judgment seat of God! I add mistresses, for although they seem to be but little in the way of temptation, yet even the female sex is awfully infected with this vice. The evidence is clear that large numbers of women are drinking to excess. It is surprising what prodigious sums are expended for spirituous liquors in this one poor Province—if facts are not greatly exaggerated by those who are most likely to know, more than a million of our old currency in a year. Surely much of this might be spared. I am convinced that unless there is a reformation in this particular, strong drink will soon be the ruin of this people. Even if the moderate use of spirituous liquors is lawful, the immoderate use of them is still sinful.

2. Uncleanness is another sin which prevails among us.

There are some who dare to vindicate this vice although it is obviously subversive of society as well as contrary to the plain laws of God. Books which tend to fill the mind with impure ideas and to feed an unlawful flame are frequently and with pleasure read. The conversation of too many, especially young persons, abounds, if not with downright lasciviousness, yet with hints and innuendos which approach very near it and equally reveal the impurity of their hearts. Actual acts of unchastity are increasingly being brought to light! A lasting blot is left upon those who are guilty, their parents and friends are grieved, and all who have a concern for virtue and religion mourn. While we have reason to fear that many deeds of darkness are kept secret from men, we can be sure they cannot be hidden from that God to whom the darkness and the light are the same. Indeed, so vile are these days that some have grown impudent in their vice, they seek no place to hide but declare their sin as Sodom. There are those in this Christian land, if common rumors are to be believed, who openly live in uncleanness and yet are not spurned out of society. If they are not ashamed of such horrid practices I know of no reason why we should be ashamed to bear testimony against them. These things prove that we approach very near to the character of an adulterous generation in a literal as well as in a figurative sense.

3. Oppression and injustice are sins which bring great guilt upon this land.

Men do not consider what is right and fit before God and man but they study how they may take advantage of the necessities of others and how, through the ignorance of their neighbors, they may cheat them. The laborer is defrauded of his hire or paid such a paltry sum for his work that he is rendered unable to procure the necessities of life. The complaints which are being made of this evil are not without foundation. The cry of oppression has gone up to heaven. I will be badly mistaken if the way of dealing we are getting into is not such as tends to destroy the small remains of equity which are among us.

4. Dishonesty is a prevailing sin.

I might mention the disposition there is in many to make promises when they have no rational prospect of being able to fulfil them. Lying or speaking falsely to put off a creditor or to make a bargain is so common a thing that men seem to expect it. It has become necessary, if a man wishes to be safe in business dealings, to treat all as if they were known to be unjust. One must guard against being deceived even when he has dealings with those who appear to be the best type. Surely you are all aware of the tremendous difficulty this creates in our transactions with one another. How evil must a people be among whom there are so few in whom we may safely trust?

5. Pride is another sin of the times.

It appears in our dress, in our furniture, and in all our behavior. Superiors treat those who are below them with haughtiness and contempt. Inferiors affect to make as good an appearance as do those whom

Providence has placed above them.

6. Shall I speak of luxury or that propensity there is in us to gratify our sensual appetites?

Poor as we are, we live high and fare sumptuously every day. This destroys our health, consumes our substance, enfeebles our minds, feeds our lusts, and stupefies our consciences. While we feed and pamper our bodies, we starve our souls. We all agree that frugality is necessary to retrieve us from the difficulties in which we are involved, but no one is willing to begin and to set the example. While recommending it to their neighbor, nearly all seem unwilling to do it themselves.

7. Slander and calumny are prevailing evils.

We are not tender toward our neighbor's reputation as we ought to be. Instead of being faithful monitors to them, when they have done amiss, we publish their failings and propagate every idle story or evil surmise against them. Detraction is so common a sin that those who are guilty of it are hardly aware they do anything amiss and yet there is scarcely anything more injurious to individuals, more harmful to society, or more contrary to that love and charity which the Gospel so strongly recommends.

8. I cannot omit the increasing rudeness and ungovernable dispositions of children and young people.

Many of them are irreverent to superiors and disobedient to those who are placed over them. They possess tempers and behavior which are big with mischief to the community and tend toward subversion of all order, decency, and virtue.

Thus I have mentioned some of those sins which prevail among us. I am not sensible that I have at all exaggerated matters. I am sure I have said nothing which I do not myself believe to be true and which I do not think it my duty to say. I have used plainness because I meant to be understood.

After all, I am not charging the body of this people with the crimes I have mentioned. It is to be hoped that the greatest part of us are not guilty of the more gross acts of immorality and that we have yet among us a goodly number who have escaped the pollutions that are in the world through lust and who adhere to the cause of God and virtue in these degenerate days. "But this," as one observes, "does not wholly excuse us; for we are all faulty in this, that these kinds of vices are too much connived at; at least they are not sufficiently branded and put out of countenance. They pass under easy, not to say, creditable names. And so little a sense have we of them, that a man may keep his reputation among us, though he be very vicious. This very thing, without our personal guilt, makes the sin a national sin." This is especially true of those who by their office or station are called to stand against wickedness but do not bear suitable testimony against the evils which prevail.

I am far from comparing the rulers and teachers of this people with those who sustained these characters among the Jews. Blessed be God, we have magistrates who discountenance vice and with some laudable zeal endeavor to suppress it. We have ministers who preach the pure doctrines and precepts of the Gospel. But might not both do much more than they do? And does not the backwardness of the one in showing to this people their transgression and sin and the remissness of the other in punishing the workers of iniquity tend to increase the public guilt?

Upon the whole, it must be owned that if we are not already, we are in danger of becoming very soon, an evil and adulterous generation. Vice and wickedness make swift and rapid progress and threaten to bear down all virtue and goodness.

Would the time allow, I would now go on to say that the character given in the text is a very dishonorable one. Such sinful conduct as I have described is on many accounts unreasonable. It is to act contrary to all the rules of reason and religion. It includes great ingratitude to God who has distinguished this people by His favors, both spiritual and temporal.

Such a carriage is also very dangerous. It brought awful destruction to the Jews, and God will visit destruction upon us for these things unless we repent. Who of us could bear adultery in the wife of his bosom? And will God bear with our spiritual whoredoms? He may bear long because He is longsuffering and abundant in goodness, but He will at length arise and punish our disobedience and ingratitude. This has been His usual method of dealing, and it is agreeable to the notions which reason and revelation teach us to form of Him. It is most certain that just as God has set the boundaries of the seas, so has He set the bounds of wickedness for every nation, beyond which they shall not pass. When their iniquities are full He will not fail to repay vengeance into their bosom. The Canaanites, the Jews, and many other nations I might name have been sad instances of this kind of proceeding. When a nation is come to that fatal period, none knows it but God. Whether or not we are already near it we cannot tell, but it is something we ought infinitely to fear. It is altogether too evident that things are in a bad posture among us and that our sins have grown to such a height that it is a miracle of divine patience and longsuffering that we are not already consumed.

Let us then humble our souls before God for the degeneracy of this people and for all our approaches to the temper and carriage of the Jews spoken of in my text. This is what our rulers, according to custom, invite us to this day. This is the end for which we sanctify a fast and call a solemn assembly. We are not here merely to put on a show of humiliation, although it is right that we should bow down our heads as a bulrush. It is the heart which God looks at. Hypocrisy at such seasons as this tends greatly to offend Him, for it is to deny His omniscience and to treat Him as if He were altogether such an one as we ourselves are.

We have awful reason to fear that God has been provoked by our former want of sincerity at Solemn Assemblies. Let us this day call our sins to remembrance and the sins of this people. Let us think of the guilt we have contracted. Let us labor to affect our souls with a sense of it, to get into a penitent frame, and to form new and strong resolutions against sin of every kind. It is only by repentance that we can avert the judgments which are brooding over us. If there is true repentance there will be reformation of the evils of which we repent. This is what we must be brought to, or iniquity will be our ruin. God is slow to anger, but He will not always bear it in longsuffering.

The way to bring about a general reformation is for each of us to mend ourselves. Every one of us has helped to make this a guilty people; let us do at least as much to make us a penitent and reformed people. Let us make it our earnest request to God that He will bestow on us the grace necessary to enable us to walk before Him in all holy conversation and godliness. Let us be ever watchful against those sins which do most easily beset us. Perhaps we have been kept back from scandalous crimes, but have we not, many of us, our secret sins? If these are indulged they are likely to end in something worse. We all need to adopt the prayer of the Psalmist, "Cleanse Thou me from secret faults. Keep back Thy servant also from presumptuous sins; let them not have dominion over me" (Psalm 19:12,13).

Having first looked to ourselves, let us do what we can in our respective places to reclaim others. Let us counsel and warn them as opportunity presents. If we can do nothing else, we can bear testimony against their vices. We may, as prudence will admit, show our abhorrence of their crimes and endeavor to shame them into amendment. It will be a glorious reward of our endeavors if we can save a soul from death (James 5:20). It will yield us unspeakable comfort if we are instrumental in delivering our people from ruin.

In particular, let heads of families endeavor to amend what is amiss at home by admonition, advice, prayer, restraint, and above all, by a good example. If ever there is a general reformation, I am persuaded it will begin here. If men are brought to take care of their own homes, things will soon be in a better posture. As the prevailing dissoluteness and immorality is, in great measure, owing to the neglect of family worship, instruction, and government, while these are neglected I cannot hope for better times. There may be some refractory children and servants who will not be restrained, but much good might be done by a suitable care in this particular. He who has attended his duty with respect to those under his charge, although his endeavors fail of success, may, amidst the uneasy reflections this must necessarily occasion, have the satisfactory thought that he has delivered his own soul. But the parent or master who neglects to pray with, to restrain, to counsel and warn his children and servants is, in a great measure, chargeable with the crimes they commit and must expect to answer to God another day.

Let us all pray for the effusion of the Holy Spirit on this ungrateful and sinful people. Without His influence no means we can use will be likely to have any durable effect. His almighty energy can awaken us out of our security, return us from our wanderings, and make us holy. Yes, if He pleases, a nation shall be born at once, a whole people shall immediately be converted to Him, and from the lowest state of degeneracy shall be made a peculiar people zealous of good works. Such a miracle of grace can happen, but it may not be what we should expect at this time. The conversion of all at once is not God's common method of dispensing grace. He usually proceeds in a more gradual way which may not be any less effectual. By the influence of His Spirit accompanying His Word and the dispensation of His Providence, He may restrain bold transgressors and prevent the heaven-defying acts of wickedness they would otherwise commit. Or He can so reform and change them that they fear, obey and serve Him. If provoked by the crimes of any, He suffers them after their hardness and impenitent heart to treasure up unto themselves wrath against the day of wrath (Romans 2:5). Or He can cause their crimes to appear so detestable in the eyes of others as to prevent the influence of their bad example. He can inspire the virtuous and good with courage and fortitude. He can cause them to appear on the Lord's side against the workers of iniquity and by daily additions to their numbers make them superior to those who are enlisted under the devil's banner. By these and a multitude of other ways God is able to stop the progress of impiety and wickedness and to reclaim a degenerate people. And thus, when He sees fit, His grace triumphs over all opposition. This is an event so desirable that I think the friends of Zion ought to unite their requests with the greatest ardency that it may be accomplished.

If we are once, by the influence of the Spirit of grace, brought to a sincere and thorough repentance, God, even our own God, will delight to dwell among us and to bless us, and things will go well with us. If "the Spirit be poured upon us from on high, and the wilderness be a fruitful field, and the fruitful field be counted for a forest. Then judgment shall dwell in the wilderness, and righteousness remain in the fruitful field. And the work of righteousness shall be peace; and the effect of righteousness quietness and assurance for ever" (Isaiah 32:15-17).

CHAPTER FIFTEEN

A
Sermon On
Fasting and Prayer

By
Gilbert Tennent

Gilbert Tennent, 1703-1764

Gilbert Tennent was born in County Armagh, Ireland, February 5, 1703. He immigrated to the United States at fourteen. About this same time he experienced a profound conversion but, because of a deep sense of his own unworthiness, determined to avoid the ministry, actually studying medicine for a year. Around 1725 he received assurance of salvation and felt distinctly called to the ministry. Like his younger brothers, William Jr., John, and Charles, most of Gilbert's education was received at his father's famous Log College, where he also assisted in the training of younger men. He apparently spent at least a portion of one year at Yale College which conferred an M.A. on him in 1725. He began his preaching ministry at Newcastle, Delaware, but left this church so suddenly that he was censored for it. He was ordained by the Philadelphia Presbytery in 1726 and was appointed to start a new church at New Brunswick, New Jersey. Despite the impressiveness of his preaching, the first eighteen months of his ministry were largely without lasting fruits. A severe illness gave him opportunity for careful contemplation, heart-searching, humiliation, and the seeking of an anointing of power. As a result, his preaching took on a new dimension of spiritual consequence, and the Holy Spirit began to use him mightily. During this period, Tennent became friends with, and was greatly influenced by, the godly Dutch pastor Theodorus Jacobus Frelinghuysen. Revival broke out under his ministry in New Brunswick and at other places where he itinerated.

George Whitefield first visited the Tennents in 1739. A strong bond developed between him and Gilbert, who accompanied him on some of his evangelistic missions. During his 1740 visit, Whitefield persuaded Tennent to go on a preaching tour of New England. His three months stay in Boston, in the dead of winter, had tremendous effect. Thomas Prince described Tennent's preaching there as "both terrible and searching. It was for matter justly terrible, as he according to the inspired oracles, exhibited the dreadful holiness, justice, law-threatenings, truth, power, and majesty of God, and His anger with rebellious, impenitent and Christless sinners; the awful danger they were in every moment of being struck down to hell, and damned forever, with the amazing miseries of the place of torment. By his arousing and spiritual preaching, deep and pungent convictions were wrought in the minds of many hundreds of persons in that town; and the same effect was produced in several scores, in the neighboring congregations. And now was such a time as we never knew. The Rev. Mr. [William] Cooper was wont to say that more came to him in one week in deep concern, than in the whole twenty-four years of his preceding ministry. I can say also the same as to the numbers who repaired to me." At least twenty other Massachusetts and Connecticut towns were visited on this tour.

In 1743 Tennent moved to Philadelphia to minister to the new Second Presbyterian congregation formed largely out of Whitefield converts and sympathizers. Here he remained until his death on July 23, 1764. During the years of his Philadelphia pastorate, Gilbert itinerated but little and tended to be less abrasive and much more cooperative with fellow Christians. By 1749 he was laboring to restore unity in the denomination which had badly splintered during his earlier ministry.

Among the most telling critiques of Tennent is that by E. H. Gilbert in his History of the Presbyterian Church: *"With a nature incapable of fear, a burning zeal in defence of what he deemed the truth, a commanding person with powerful delivery, he was destined to exercise, wherever he went, a deep and extensive influence. Yet his charity was sometimes overborne by his zeal."*

First published as *A Sermon Preach'd at Philadelphia, January 7, 1747-8; Being the Day appointed by The Honourable The President and Council, To be observed throughout this Province As a Day of Fasting and Prayer with some Enlargement.* By Gilbert Tennent, A.M. Philadelphia: Printed by W. Bradford, at the sign of the Bible in Second-Street, 1748.

Fasting and Prayer

"And Jehoshaphat feared, and set himself
to seek the Lord, and proclaimed a fast
throughout all Judah. And Judah gathered
themselves together, to ask help of the Lord."
Second Chronicles 20:3,4

When pious King Jehoshaphat heard of the design of the Ammonites and Moabites to invade his kingdom by a formidable armed force, he was affected by the tidings! He feared the outcome! Considering the sins that he and his people were guilty of, he knew they deserved a desolating stroke. He therefore feared it would be inflicted. However, he was determined to use means to obtain deliverance. His just and rational fear stirred him to this.

This was also the case with righteous Noah who "being moved with fear, prepared an ark to the saving of his house, by which he condemned the world" (Hebrews 11:7), that is, the wicked world about him who were stupid and negligent; that neither feared the threatened inundation nor used proper means to prevent their ruin by it.

But what were the means that Jehoshaphat used in his extremity? We are told that he set himself to seek the Lord and proclaimed a fast throughout all Judah. No doubt he prepared his army for defence and set them in array, but knowing that this would be unsuccessful without direction and assistance from heaven, he applied to God by fasting and prayer. This he did with sincerity, earnestness, and resolution. Without these qualities in our supplications, our fasting and prayer at this time are not likely to prevail and to succeed.

This pious prince not only petitioned heaven itself for forgiveness, assistance, and deliverance, but in order to obtain the general concurrence of the nation in this critical and dangerous matter, he proclaimed a fast throughout all Judah. He appointed a day of humiliation and prayer that they might all join together in confessing their sins and asking help of the Lord. Fasting from bodily refreshments upon such extraordinary occasions is a token of self-judging for the sins we have committed. We hereby own ourselves unworthy of the bread we eat and we acknowledge that God might justly withhold it from us. Fasting is also a token of self-denial for the future. Fasting for sin implies a resolution to fast from it, even though it has been a sweet morsel to us in the past.

Magistrates should call their people to the duty of fasting and prayer upon such occasions in order that it may be a national or public act and so that we may obtain national or public mercies.

Jehoshaphat appointed a day of fasting, and the people of Judah, as was their duty, readily assembled in the House of God to ask help of the Lord and to seek His face. Without His protection, the help of man is in vain. Without His help, the best concerted measures for security and defence are in vain. It is the Lord who is the supreme director of all events. He gives to our means whatever success and efficacy He pleases. This great Governor of the whole system of nature and of all the occurrences of time, enjoins His people to call upon Him in the day of adversity. It is in this way that He graciously promises to deliver them.

From the words of our text, considered in their connection with the preceding and following verses, we may observe this proposition: A religious fast, suitably observed, is a means appointed by God for the removal of present calamities and the prevention of them in the future.

In discoursing upon this I shall,

I. Speak of the kinds, causes, nature, ingredients, time, and mode of fasting.

II. Prove the truth of the proposition.

III. Offer improvements.

I. THE KINDS, CAUSES, NATURE, INGREDIENT, TIME, AND MODE OF FASTING.

Fasting is fourfold: natural, civil, medicinal, and religious.

Natural fasting is an abstinence from food, either through want of it or through want of an appetite for it.

Civil fasting is an abstinence from food enjoined by the civil authorities to answer some political purpose. Thus Saul enjoined the people of Israel to fast for a time, lest they should be hindered from pursuing after the Philistines (First Samuel 14).

Medicinal fasting is that abstinence which is required of the sick by physicians to promote the recovery of their health.

Religious fasting is that abstinence from food which is accompanied with religious duties and directed to a religious end. The word fast is rendered in the margin "a day of restraint" signifying that in the time of the fast we should abstain from our ordinary labors, supports, and refreshments such as meat and drink, so that we may better attend upon the service of God. In the fast proclaimed by the King and Nobles of

Ninevah, they were not to taste anything nor even to drink water (Jonah 3:7). This complete form of fasting should doubtless be observed by us as far as it may be consistent with the safety of our constitution and the promotion of the religious worship we are engaged in.

Religious fasting may be said to be two-fold: either public or private.

A public fast is a fast when a considerable number join together in it—a congregation, a province, a city, or an entire nation may be involved. When the cause is public, no doubt the fast should be public also.

A private fast is a fast of particular persons by themselves or by families.

I may again observe that religious fasting is either stated or occasional.

A stated fast is a fast when a particular day or days are set aside for this purpose each year. The fasts of the fourth, fifth, seventh, and tenth months observed by the Jewish Church were of this kind.

An occasional fast is a fast that is kept upon particular emergency occasions, such were those that were kept by King Jehoshaphat, Nehemiah and Queen Esther.

The special causes of occasional fasts include:

1. Extraordinary sins of churches, nations or provinces. All these give cause for public fasts. Thus in the time of Nehemiah and Ezra there were public fasts because of the mixed marriages of the people of Israel with the pagan nations. By a parity of reason we may therefore conclude that most private offenses require private fasts.

2. Another cause of fasting is some judgment of God or distressing calamity inflicted upon a church, nation, or people, or threatened to be inflicted. Thus when a famine, resulting from a plague of locusts and a draught, was upon the land of Israel, they were enjoined by the Prophet Joel to sanctify a fast (Joel 1:14), that is, to keep a day of fasting in a religious manner, with pious dispositions and designs. In our text and context we are informed that when Jehoshaphat understood that the children of Ammon and Moab were coming up against Judah with a numerous army he proclaimed a fast.

3. Fasting may also be employed to obtain success in any notable enterprise or victory over any violent temptation. When Queen Esther was to go into the King's presence to intercede for her nation, she appointed a fast (Esther 4:16). What Christ says respecting demonic possession, "this kind goeth not out but by prayer and fasting" (Matthew 17:21), may be with equal reason applied to other temptations of the enemy.

Fasting, in its general nature, may be described as a branch or influence of religious worship prescribed by God for His own glory and His people's benefit.

As it respects the body, fasting includes abstinence from food and drink as far as it may be consistent with health. The very light of nature teaches this.

Fasting likewise includes an abstinence from all bodily recreations. Hence the Almighty complained of the people of Israel that in the day of their fast they found pleasure (Isaiah 58:3,13). This passage makes it clear that abstinence from pleasure on fast days was essential to a right spirit of fasting and to acceptance of the fast by God.

In addition, a fast includes abstaining from such ornamental dress as is allowable at other times. "In that day," saith the prophet, "did the Lord God of Hosts call to weeping and to mourning, and to baldness, and to girding with sackcloth" (Isaiah 22:12). When Israel heard the awful news of God's refusing to go before them, they expressed their sorrows by laying aside their ornaments (Exodus 33:6). The King of Ninevah was directed to this very thing by the light of nature, for on the day of fasting he laid aside his robe (Jonah 3:6). It is true that we are not under the rigors of the legal dispensation and so are not obliged to these expressions of sorrows which were then practiced, such as rending of the garment, clothing ourselves with sackcloth, covering ourselves with ashes, plucking off the hair, and disfiguring the face. Our Lord observes that the Pharisees disfigured their faces that they might appear to men to fast. He instructs His disciples, however, to avoid all ostentation in their fasting and therefore to wash their faces and anoint their heads (Matthew 6:16,17). This was clearly different from both the conduct of the Pharisees and the practice in the Old Testament fasts. Daniel said, "I ate no pleasant bread, neither did I anoint myself at all" (Daniel 10:3). Although we are freed from the Jewish rigors, nature itself teaches that the dress should be suited to the occasion. A pagan said of purple and scarlet, "non estconveniens luctibus ille color," (such a color is not suited to grief).

Again I observe that fasting, as it respects the body, includes such humble postures as are suited to the solemn service of the day. Although this is not specified by particular precepts, it may be determined by the light of nature and the customs of the places where we live. Fasting is to be conducted in such manner as may best suit the right performance of the duties of that solemnity and are least likely to occasion offence.

Fasting undoubtedly includes our abstaining from worldly labors. Without this abstention we cannot perform the duties required to achieve the purpose of the fast. Hence, under the Old Testament economy, persons were put to death who labored on their fast-days.

As fasting respects the soul, it includes the following duties: humiliation for sin, prayer, and renewing of our Covenant with God.

We should humble ourselves for our sins against God. For want of this humility, the Almighty complained against the fasting of the Jews asking, "Is it such a fast that I have chosen? A day for a man to afflict his soul? Is it to bow down his head as a bulrush, and to spread sackcloth and ashes under him? [outward signs of humiliation without a humble frame of heart] Wilt thou call this a fast, an acceptable day to the Lord?" (Isaiah 58:5). That humiliation for sin which is true and real will express itself in confession of sin, sorrow for it, indignation against it, and fear of the judgments of God, rather than in mere external show.

The humbled soul will confess his sins with childlike simplicity along with all their aggravations. This is indeed the proper work of a day of fasting which may be called a day for atonement. Thus Nehemiah (Nehemiah 1:5-11; 9:5-38), Ezra (Ezra 9:5-15), and Daniel (Daniel 9:5-38) confessed their sins particularly and the sins of the nation, in the day of fasting.

The humbled soul will likewise sorrow for his sins. Thus a day of fasting is called a day to afflict the soul. Daniel assures us that in the private fast which he kept, he mourned three full weeks (Daniel 10:2). Oh, Brethren! Our sorrow should be deep and affectionate upon this occasion! And truly wanting this, a fast without the beauty of mourning, is likely to fail in its purpose.

Is not the humbled person ashamed of sin because of its unreasonableness and ingratitude? Ezra speaks to God on a day of fasting in the following language, "O my God, I am ashamed and blush to lift up my face to Thee my God. Our iniquities have increased over our heads, and our trespass is grown up unto the heavens" (Ezra 9:6).

True humiliation disposes us to an indignation against sin, an indignation against ourselves for sinning, and a godly fear of the richly deserved divine judgment our sins have provoked. This was doubtless signified by the rending of their garments in the Jewish fasts. We are told in our text that Jehoshaphat feared and set himself to seek the Lord and proclaimed a fast throughout all Judah.

Agreeable to this famous precedent was the sentiment, disposition, and practice of the man after God's own heart which he represents in the following language, "My flesh trembleth for fear of Thee, yea, I am afraid of thy judgments" (Psalm 119:120). This fear incited the pious prince to use all proper means for defence against his enemies. This fear incited him not only to pray to his God for deliverance, with humble vehemence, but likewise to bless Him with affectionate gratitude that He had taught his hands to war and his fingers to fight and that He girded himself with strength to battle so that a bow of steel was broken by his arms (2

Samuel 22:35). In a similar vein, Solomon observes that a wise man fears
(Proverbs 14:16). He elsewhere notes, "Happy is the man that feareth
alway: he that hardeneth his heart shall fall into mischief" (Proverbs
28:14).

Is not this fear of God and His judgments, my Brethren, represented
in the sacred Scriptures as the summary, the compendium, the source of
all true piety? Hence this honorable and comprehensive description was
given of Job, that "he was a perfect and upright man, that he feared God
and eschewed [not only moral but penal] evil" (Job 1:1). Where neither
reason nor Scripture restrains the sense of a word to one point, we should
not. Job had a reverential fear of God's majesty and a cautious fear of
His judgments. His fear inclined him, in the course of his daily conduct,
to endeavor to avoid sin, the object of divine indignation, and to endeavor
to escape the penal issues of it in this world and the next. These are
indeed proper objects of our dread and fear.[1]

Another duty included in fasting, as it respects the soul, is prayer.
Fasting and prayer are frequently joined in Scripture. Prayer contains not
only petition for the mercies we need but praises for mercies received.
Our petitions should be both believing and vehement and, therefore, we
are bid on a day of fasting to cry unto the Lord (Joel 1:14). Elsewhere we
are told that the fervent prayer of the righteous man availeth much
(James 5:16). The poor widow prevailed by her importunity (Luke 18:1-8).
Jacob had power over the angel and prevailed, for he wept and made
supplication unto him (Genesis 32:24-29).

Our praises for mercies received should also be affectionate. The due
consideration of mercies vouchsafed tends to heighten our views of sin
and aggravate our sorrows for it. Hence the goodness of God is said to
lead to repentance (Romans 2:4). Thanksgiving for mercies past is a most
effectual way of asking new and needed benefits. Therefore we find that
in the time of Nehemiah the Levites began the solemn fast with praises
and a thankful enumeration of God's mercies toward them (Nehemiah
9:4ff).

Also proper to a day of fasting is the renewing of our covenant with
God. Nehemiah and the princes and nobles of Israel did this. They
entered into a new engagement to walk in the law of the Lord and signed
the Covenant with their hands (Nehemiah 9:38).

While the gospel does not oblige us, by any instance that I know of, to

---

[1]The lengthy digression concerning the current state of affairs which appeared at this point
in the text of the original edition now appears in the appendix to this sermon.

the outward formality of signing and sealing a written Covenant, yet surely the substance intended is binding from the reason and the nature of things. Duty to God and our own safety oblige us to renew our engagements to serve God. It is therefore the proper work of a day of fasting to renew our purposes and promises of forsaking sin in general and more especially those evils by which we have most grieved the Spirit of God and endangered our own safety. We should likewise resolve to renew our performance of the duties we have neglected.

Again, it is proper in a day of fasting to give alms. The Lord Himself informs us, by the Prophet Isaiah, that the fast He had chosen was to loose the bands of wickedness, to undo the heavy burdens, to let the oppressed go free, to deal bread to the hungry, to bring the poor that are cast out into our houses, and to cover the naked (Isaiah 58:6-7). If we do not show mercy to men, we need not expect mercy from God.

I may add that to the right performance of all the aforesaid duties, it is needful in a day of fasting to hear the Word of God. Jonah's preaching was the cause of Ninevah's repentance and humiliation (Jonah 3:4ff). In the fast that Nehemiah observed, they read in the Book of the Law one fourth part of the day (Nehemiah 8:1-13). The Word of God is necessary to direct and assist us in the duties of a day of fasting. It at one and the same time excites both our sorrows and our hopes, by opening before us the infinite evil of sin and the exceeding riches of God's grace and mercy.

As to the time of public fasting, it is to be determined by the magistrates or by such who preside over particular churches. That which is the cause of the fast will determine to a significant degree the appropriate time of the fast. In general, the duty of fasting is enjoined by divine authority and the season of observing a fast is pointed to by divine Providence. Hence, it does not depend merely upon the pleasure of man, otherwise it would be no better than will worship.

As to the mode or manner of fasting, I observe that we should beware of terminating our worship in the fast, which strictly considered, is only a mean designed to prepare us for divine worship. It is sinful and dangerous to rest on externals of religion.

We should beware of fasting for ostentation sake with the Pharisees (Matthew 6:16-18) or with a malicious design like Jezebel's who covered her covetous, cruel intention against Naboth with the guise of a fast. She fasted for strife and debate and smote with the fist of wickedness (First Kings 21:1-16).

On the contrary, our aim should be honest and sincere. It should be to glorify God and to obtain strength to forsake our iniquities. A secret allowance of sin made the Jews' fasting of no avail. If we regard iniquity in our heart, the Lord will not hear our prayer (Psalm 66:18). As our aim should be honest, so should our manner of performing our duty be earnest. We should, with Ephraim, bemoan ourselves and be in bitterness (Jeremiah 31:18).

Moreover all our performances ought to be attended with faith in Christ and hope in the mercy of God through Him, without which they cannot be accepted. Thus in the fast of Ezra, when the son of Jehiel confessed that they had trespassed against God by taking strange wives, he said, "Yet now there is hope in Israel concerning this thing" (Ezra 10:2). But I proceed to the next general head proposed.

II. PROOF THAT FASTING IS A MEAN APPOINTED BY GOD FOR THE REMOVAL OF PRESENT JUDGMENTS AND THE PREVENTING OF SUCH JUDGMENTS IN THE FUTURE.

To this end observe that the light of nature itself dictated the necessity of fasting to divers of the pagans who practiced it when in great calamities. The King and nobles and people of Ninevah are witnesses of this. When destruction was pronounced against them, they betook themselves to fasting, to prevent the execution of it (Jonah 3:5-10). Tertulian likewise informs us that "the Pagans had sometimes their religious fasts."

That fasting is a duty of divine institution, both the Old and New Testaments instruct us. The Almighty enjoined the people of Israel by the Prophet Joel, when they were under a very distressing and general calamity by locusts and caterpillars and in great danger of an invasion by foreign enemies (the Assyrians and Babylonians), to sanctify a fast, to call a Solemn Assembly, and to gather the elders and all the inhabitants of the land into the house of the Lord their God and cry unto Him. Public intimation was to be given of the time. Persons of every age and order were required to convene on that occasion. Seeing all had contributed to the common guilt, it was reasonable that all should join in expressions of sorrow for it and in earnest supplications to God for deliverance from its penal consequences.

The aforesaid duty is enjoined in the following affecting strains of language, "Sanctify ye a fast, call a Solemn Assembly, gather the elders and all the inhabitants of the land into the house of the Lord your God, and cry unto the Lord" (Joel 1:14). "Blow ye the trumpet in Zion, and sound an alarm in My holy mountain: let all the inhabitants of the land tremble..." (2:1). "Turn ye even to Me with all your heart, and with fasting, and with weeping, and with mourning: And rend your heart and not your garments, and turn unto the Lord your God: for He is gracious and merciful, slow to anger, and of great kindness..." (2:12,13). "Sanctify a fast, call a Solemn Assembly: gather the people, sanctify the congregation, assemble the elders, gather the children, and those that suck the breast: let the bridegroom go forth of his chamber, and the bride out of her closet. Let the priests, the ministers of the Lord, weep between the porch and the altar, and let them say, Spare Thy people, O Lord, and give not Thine heritage to reproach, that the heathen should rule over them: wherefore should they say among the people, Where is their God? Then will the Lord be jealous for His land, and pity His people" 2:15-18). It seems probable, from the Scripture now mentioned, that the infants were kept from the breast in a day of humiliation in order that by their cries the hearts of their parents might be moved to repent of sin, the source of their every woe, and that God might have compassion as He did on the infants of Ninevah. Newly married people were likewise to attend, laying aside their mirth and ornaments.

In the prophecy of Isaiah, the nature of that religious fast which God chooses is represented, and surely the fast of the seventh month, observed by the Jewish church, was expressly of divine appointment.

In the New Testament our Lord Jesus Christ enjoins His people to fast in these words, "The days will come when the Bridegroom shall be taken from them, and then shall they fast" (Matthew 9:15). In another place the blessed Redeemer prescribes the manner of fasting saying, "But thou, when thou fastest, anoint thine head and wash thy face, that thou appear not unto men to fast, but unto thy Father which is in secret..." (Matthew 6:17,18).

To talk of fasting without abstaining from food, as far as our constitutions will admit, or at least from pleasant food along with Daniel, is ridiculous, a mere farce and a mockery.

By abstaining from food for a time the soul is better fitted for extraordinary operations. The Apostle Paul kept his body in subjection, least having preached to others, he himself should be a cast away (First Corinthians 9:27).

And indeed, by abstinence from bodily comforts, we judge ourselves unworthy of them and express a decent sympathy with Zion in her sorrows and the laboring state.

That fasting is an appointed means to remove judgments and prevent them is evident from the Scriptures before mentioned and from the words of our text as well as from the account we have in the sacred volume of the fasts observed by Nehemiah, Esther, and Ezra.

But if it be objected that the Papists fast and therefore we should not, I answer: "This objection is hardly worth considering." The Papists believe there is a God. Must we therefore turn atheists that we may be unlike them at this point? The Papists eat. Must we therefore starve ourselves to death? Is this good reasoning? Indeed the Papists do sometimes make a pretence of fasting, but it may be truly said that many of their fasts are mock-fasts, feasts instead of fasts. It must also be confessed that many Protestants sadly neglect this duty of fasting to their great prejudice in religion. All those who would have their corruptions mortified must take pains and use proper means for that end. Fasting is among the most useful means for it has a noble tendency to keep the body in subjection to the mind. But this duty is so contrary to people's keen appetites that they can scarcely be brought to believe in it, and it is still more difficult for them to practice it. Those who do deny themselves and practice fasting as they ought find manifold advantages.

III. I PROCEED TO THE IMPROVEMENT OF THIS SUBJECT.

Here I must highly commend the conduct of the Honorable, the President and the Council in issuing a proclamation for a general fast at this particular time. In this they follow the noble example of pious King Jehoshaphat (mentioned in our text) in a case which perhaps in its main features is familiar and parallel.

I think, dear Brethren, all the causes of fasting before mentioned, concur to invite us to observe it with due solemnity.

USE ONE. Are not the sins of our nation very great? Are not some of them extraordinary? Has not great contempt been cast upon the person and miracles of Christ by some among us? Do not many grow weary of the Gospel and embrace paganism in the place of it? As we are well informed, almost every kind of impiety and profaneness is flagrant in Britain and Ireland, but do not many of the same gross and crying sins abound in this Province? Sins such as lying, swearing, whoredoms, drunkenness, fraud, and Sabbath breaking are all around us.

Are not some professed Christians guilty of pride, censoriousness, worldliness, and backsliding? Have not many forgotten their first love and fallen from their first works? Is it not true that for many the things that remain are ready to die in them?

Does not unfruitfulness under the Word of God and the rod of God generally prevail? Is it not tragic that when God's hand is lifted up against us we do not even see it? When God threatens by His Word, many do not hear and regard. When divers judgments are abroad, only a few seem to learn righteousness. Although, as the proclamation justly observes, the inhabitants of this city and province have been sorely visited with mortal sickness in the summer past, we remain generally unhumbled and unreformed. How many funerals have we had among us? How fast did they sometimes crowd upon each other in an awful and solemn succession? And yet how little effect had this alarming Providence (to all appearances at least) upon the majority? I could not help but think, during the time of these many deaths, that it was more terrible to behold the stupidity of the living than the multitude of the dying. Alas, we come unrefined out of the furnace. Now if we continue to walk contrary to God, has He not declared in His Word that He will walk contrary to us and will punish us seven times for our iniquities? (Leviticus 26:16-29).

Does not the righteous Jehovah threaten to remove the gospel from that nation or people that do not bring forth the fruits thereof? (Matthew 21:43). Has not the Jewish Church been unchurched and their nation dispersed into many distant countries? Have they not been almost destroyed for their unfruitfulness and other impieties, so that there is but a small number of them preserved as a standing and terrible monument of God's righteousness and vengeance? Where are now the once famous Churches of Asia to whom the Epistles in the Revelation were written? What about the ancient Churches in Egypt, Greece, Palestine, and many other places, which the time would fail to enumerate? Where are they today? And even since the great reformation from papal darkness and tyranny, I speak but with sighs and tears, how few are the remains of the once famous Protestant Churches of France and Bohemia which, if I may utter such a thing, were brought to ruin in some measure through the bad conduct of the governing powers of our nation. Oh, how lamentable it is! Has not unfruitfulness, my dear Brethren, brought to pass all the above mentioned desolations? Are not these things for our warning? Ought not our hearts to tremble when we think of them, especially seeing that we do not know how soon their dismal case may be our own. If we think we do not deserve such a stroke, it is but a sad symptom of our ignorance of the general state of our country and nation!

Was it not sin, my Brethren, that brought to confusion and ruin the Caldean, Persian, Grecian, and Roman Monarchies as is beautifully represented in that excellent and seasonable performance entitled, "Britain's Remembrancer?" This is a composition well worthy of your serious perusal. Have not kingdoms and states had their periods of revolution and come to tragic ends? Has not the same thing happened to particular families? And is there not reason to fear that our society is drawing near to some awful crisis? We have been several times lately upon the brink of destruction and yet a gracious God has interposed and unbarred His arm, as in the days of old, and sent undeserved and almost unexpected salvations to us, blessed by His name. Let heaven and earth, let men and angels, conspire in celebrating His praise.

But if we continue to abuse those memorable mercies, His patience will doubtless come to an end. When God is determined to punish a people, He will not be entreated to suspend the falling blow, even though a Moses, a Job, or a Daniel intercede for it. No, when the measure of our iniquities is full, the time of divine forbearance shall expire (First Thessalonians 2:16). Then will the righteous God cut down the fruitless trees that cumbered the ground with the awful axe of His justice (Luke 13:7). Then shall He lay judgment to the line, and righteousness to the plummet, and sweep away the refuge of lies, and the waters shall overflow the hiding-place. Then "your Covenant with death shall be disannulled, and your agreement with Hell shall not stand: when the overflowing scourge shall pass through, then ye shall be trodden down by it" (Isaiah 28:18).

The author to the Hebrews observed that the ground, though often watered, that beareth thorns and briars is nigh unto cursing, whose end is to be burned (Hebrews 6:8). Oh, what cause there is for lamentation over our sins this very day. Surely, Brethren, our whole head is sick, our whole heart faint (Isaiah 1:5). Persons of all orders among us have reason to take up a lamentation and say, "We have sinned, and what shall we do unto Thee, O Thou preserver of men? We have sinned against heaven and in Thy sight, and are no more worthy to be called Thy children."

USE TWO. Are not some awful spiritual judgments already inflicted? Have not some fallen into grievous errors in principle? Have not some already lost their religious impressions and turned with the dog to the vomit and with the sow to the wallowing in the mire? (Second Peter 2:22). Is not the Word preached in general like a miscarrying womb and dry breasts, at least comparatively, and especially in respect to the conversion of sinners?

In regard to temporal distresses, as the proclamation justly observes, do not the calamities of a bloody war in which our nation will engage, seem every year more nearly to approach us? Is not the expectation of the security of our Provinces more and more laid aside. We promised ourselves great matters from the expedition, but alas, we are unhappily disappointed in our own expectations. We have travailed and brought forth nothing but wind. But our disappointments and expense, my Brethren, are the not worst attendants of our melancholy case. No! What unhappy influence our desertion of that enterprise may have upon the Mohawks and other Indian friends, through the instigation of the French, God only knows, and time itself must declare. But this we do know, that if they turn from us, the case of the inhabitants in the less populated areas in particular must be very lamentable.

The late swift and terrible success of the French Army in Flanders, in taking all the frontier towns of Holland, in worsting the Confederate Army, in taking very lately, after a formidable siege, the very Key of that Republic, Bergen-op-Zoom, I say all these things loudly call for our saddest sorrows. The increase of the powers of France is one of the most awful events than can happen in regard of our nation, for it threatens one day or other the utter ruin of our liberties, civil and religious. Except Almighty power interposes and infinite mercy prevents, this will surely happen. Should the French now make a total conquest of Holland, which there is some reason to fear they may, it is not likely that our religious liberty, especially, would long continue after the ruin of our allies. They are so closely united to us by situation, religion, and interest that, considering the divided state of our nation and the dreadful increase of the naval power of France by that acquisition, our situation would be dangerous in the extreme.

And have we not heard, my Brethren, of the designs of our enemies, the French and Spanish Papists, to visit us in this place in the spring of the year ensuing with a considerable naval armament? But alas, how unprepared we are to give them a proper reception. As of yet we have no fort and no great guns to defend us. If our enemies come before we can provide these things, our case will be lamentable indeed. In the meantime, it is a mercy, a comfort in adversity, that divers of the worthy inhabitants of this city are apprehensive of their danger and spirited to do all they can in their present difficult situation for defence against the enemy. May Jehovah bless them! That leads me to mention,

USE THREE. That we are engaged in an important, necessary and noble undertaking. I speak now of the Association of our Defence. Should we not pray to God this day, with all our hearts, that He will be pleased in His great mercy to crown this endeavor with success? Oh, that He would incline the hearts of more and more to join in it and remove all the hindrances that do or may obstruct it.

In a word, my dear Brethren, seeing there is such abundant cause for it, let us keep the fast as it has been represented. Oh, let us be sincere and serious in the performance of the duties of this day. If we regard either the authority of God or our own interests, to say nothing of the interest and safety of others, who knows but what that gracious God who heard Esther and Jehoshaphat and delivered them out of their distresses, may also hear and help us.

And sirs, let us follow our fasting, not with strife and debate as did the wicked Jews whose fast was rejected, but with a holy and humble practice, without which all our external service will be rejected and our souls ruined.

Oh, dear Brethren, let us acknowledge and confess our manifold sins and wickedness with their awful aggravations, as well as the sins of our land and nation.

Let us bewail them with a hearty contrition, "O that our heads were as waters, and our eyes as a fountain of tears" (Jeremiah 9:1) upon this occasion. Surely there is great need that every assembly in this land be a Bochim, a place of weeping and lamentation.

Let us acknowledge that we deserve the just vengeance of God. We deserve to be made desolate as a stroke, to be utterly and forever deprived of all those mercies and privileges which we have so ungratefully and basely abused. Indeed, we deserve to be cast into a place of everlasting pain and misery.

In the meantime, let us with humble, believing, and united ardor, abhor the deserved vengeance of a righteous God and implore His removal of present judgments and His gracious prevention of future miseries.

Let us cry to Jehovah that for Christ's sake He will be pleased to instruct our minds, renew our hearts, reform our lives, and vouchsafe the same blessings upon our nation in general. Likewise let us plead that our good God will preserve our gracious King, the Royal Family, and the Nation. Let us pray that He will be pleased to guide those that manage the helm of the state in this arduous, difficult, and gloomy time. Let us ask Him to take this Province of Pennsylvania under the wing of His special care and protection and bless the laudable measures that are now issuing for that end. Let us beseech Him that the present war may be brought to an honorable and speedy end and that peace will be in all our borders. Oh, that God, even our God, would bless us with all needful good, that He would be pleased to place a wall of fire round about us and His glory in the midst of us.

In the mean time, let me humbly accost the Gentlemen of this Association. Dear Sirs! You must not only pray, repent, and reform, but if necessity requires, fight bravely in defence of your country. As Joab counseled the men of Israel when they drew near to the battle with the Syrians, so I counsel you, "Be of good courage, and let us play the man, for our people and for the cities of our God" (Second Samuel 10:12).

Seeing, dear Brethren, that you are generously preparing for the defence of yourselves, your kindred, and your country, and forasmuch as you do not know what may be the outcome of this undertaking, either to yourselves or others, but you do know that the success of the whole depends upon the divine concurrence, I think you should all, to a man, be aware of the Psalmist's sentiments and with one lip speak his language in the following devout and pious strains, "...In the name of our God we will set up our banners. We will, when necessity requires it for our defence, wage war against the enemies of our King and country, our religion and liberties, in the name of the God of Hosts; and in this we will celebrate our victories, if it pleases the Sovereign Lord of the universe to smile on our attempts in arms. We will eye His honor as our highest end, follow His Word as the rule of our conduct, and depend upon His power and Providence for courage, protection, strength, and success. And to Him we will ascribe the glory of them."

In this way of dependence upon God, in the use of proper means, I may address you, Gentlemen, in the encouraging language of Moses, the meek man of God, when he spoke to pious Joshua, the gallant general of the Jewish Army, and to all Israel a little while before his death and not long before they encountered the enemies of their nation in battle, "Be strong and of a good courage, fear not, nor be afraid of them, for the Lord thy God, He it is that doth go with thee, He will not fail thee, nor forsake thee" (Deuteronomy 31:6). Amen, Amen.

Appendix

We may observe, in passing, that it is not very consistent for those who either really or professedly fear God, to represent their own and their neighbors dangers in a diminutive light and, consequently, not only neglect to prepare themselves for defence but obstruct others who are doing so. I am told that some persons of different denominations in this Province of Pennsylvania are either indifferent about or averse to defensive measures. Might I, in all humility, beg leave to address such persons in the language of Moses to the children of Gad and Reuben, "Shall your brethren go to war, and ye sit here? Wherefore discourage ye the heart of the children of Israel?" (Numbers 32:6). Shall your brethren be at the expense of purchasing military furniture for the defence of themselves and for you? Shall they be at the pains to prepare themselves by military exercises for action in case of extreme necessity even though some of them are not as well able to spare either the money or the time as some of their neighbors? Will you sit still, indulging in shameful ease and negligence, in a time of eminent public danger both by sea and land in a cause so common? A cause so important! In a case so critical! A case so perilous! Is it easy, my Brethren, to reconcile such indolent conduct to that regard you should bear to your country and to your own safety? Is it friendly and neighborly, Sirs, to neglect assisting our brethren in a season of public peril? Or can it be thought kind and generous (however good the intentions may be) to discourage the endeavors of those gallant souls?

There are brave patriots who are nobly composing, through many difficulties, rational, scriptural, and necessary measures for the protection of their country from impending ruin and desolation. I think, Brethren, that the council of Gamaliel to the Jewish Sanhedrin is worthy of your serious notice: "And now I say unto you, 'Refrain from these men, and let them alone: for if this council or this work be of men, it will come to naught: but if it be of God, ye cannot overthrow it: lest haply ye be found even to fight against God" (Acts 5:38-39). If you can't, through scruples of conscience, assist your brethren, you should seek more light and knowledge in this matter. Impartially examine and consider what is offered to you for that end, without the bias of prejudice. You should at least forbear hindering the promotion of a public good in which your own safety and interest are involved as well as that of others. If you object, saying there is no great danger and therefore no need of such warlike preparations as are now being made in this Province, I answer by denying both the premise and the consequence drawn from it.

That we are in a state of great danger at present, plain truth clearly and solidly proves. But suppose we are actually in no great danger. Notwithstanding this, it is our duty as reasonable creatures who hold things in perspective, to prepare for defence before the enemy comes, seeing it is at least possible that he may come. If we wait until he does come, it will be too late. The fatal consequences of our enemies finding us unprepared for defence, I need not mention. Everybody of common understanding may easily imagine this! If the enemy does not come, our preparations will do us no harm; but if he does come, then our preparations will probably, through the blessing of the Lord of Hosts, do us much good. Indeed the great benefit that will in all likelihood issue from our preparation is that the fame of it may well deter the enemy from coming.

We have an instructive and illustrious example of this in the case of Nehemiah who was building the wall of Jerusalem for the defence of the Jewish church and nation. The cruel conspiracy of the opponents of that work against the managers and builders of it was baffled by brave Nehemiah's prudent precaution and preparations for defence: "It came to pass that when Sanballat heard that we builded the wall, he was wroth and took indignation, and mocked the Jews. And he spake before his brethren and the army of Samaria, and said, 'What do these feeble Jews? Will they fortify themselves? Will they sacrifice? Will they make an end in a day? Will they revive the stones out of the heaps of the rubbish which are burned?' Now Tobiah the Ammonite was by him, and he said, 'Even that which they build, if a fox go up, he shall even break down their stone wall'" (Nehemiah 4:1-3). What anger and proud disdain was there. The opponents were not only vexed at the attempt of the Jews, but treated them and it with the greatest contempt and scorn. They looked upon the workmen as ridiculous and the work as weak and improbable and made a jest of both. But pious Nehemiah answered their scoffs with prayers to his God and went on with his work. "Hear, O our God for we are despised" (verse 4). And when he heard of the conspiracy of Sanballat, Tobiah, the Arabians, the Ammonites, and the Ashdodites to come and fight against Jerusalem and to hinder the building of the wall, observe the good measures Nehemiah took in this extremity: "We made our prayer unto our God and set a watch against them day and night" (verse 9). And when he had intelligence that the enemy designed to do them injury by surprise, he set the people after their families, with their swords, their spears, and their bows. He looked up to heaven and round about him. He set guards in proper places and animated the soldiers to bravery in battle by rational and noble incentives. "And I looked, and rose up, and said unto the nobles, and to the rulers, and to the rest of the people, 'Be not ye afraid of them; remember the Lord, which is great and terrible, and fight for your brethren, your sons, and your daughters, your wives, and your houses" (verses 13,14). And what was the fruit of this proceeding? The disappointment of the enemy. When they understood that their plot was discovered and that the Jews were upon their guard in a proper posture of defence, they concluded that it was to no purpose to attack them, and therefore they laid aside their design. They rationally judged, as Nehemiah expressed it, that God had brought their council to naught (verse 15).

Although Nehemiah had received intelligence that the enemy had laid aside their design for a time, he did not think it prudent or proper to drop his watch or lay down his arms. No! By no means! So while one half of his servants wrought in the work, the other half held both spears, shields, bows, and habergeons. "They which builded on the wall, and they that bare burdens, with those that laded, every one with his hands wrought in the work, and with the other hand held a weapon. For the builders, every one had his sword girded by his side, and so builded. And he that sounded the trumpet," said Nehemiah, "was by me. And I said unto the nobles and to the rulers, and to the rest of the people, 'The work is great and large, and we are separated upon the wall, one far from another. In what place therefore ye hear the sound of the trumpet, report ye thither unto us: our God shall fight for us" (Nehemiah 4:16-20).

From the above example, every impartial eye can behold the sweetest harmony and connection between spiritual and outward means, between prayer, watching, a dependence upon God, and the use of martial weapons. Therefore it is unjust and vain to object that those who use the sword do not depend on God.

I think that those who cannot with freedom actually assist the truly generous and noble design of the late Association, should at least be passive, should at least be content to suffer others to protect them and theirs, at the expense of their time, their money, their labor, and perhaps their blood and their lives.

Nor should any object against joining in the Association when they have but little to lose. Should they not value their honor and their liberty at a higher rate? And this, I may add, that the less goods any have to lose, the more generous and noble is their serving, though to the hazard of their own lives, the public interests, and safety of their country.

If any imagine that their faith and piety are sufficient to protect them from a temporal enemy without the use of temporal means, let them try, if they please, by their virtue and influence (separate from temporal or secular means) to build houses, furnish their tables, and keep their money and goods from thieves. Seeing the impossibility of this may possibly convince them of their unhappy mistake. But whither am I led? If I have in any measure digressed from the order of my discourse or been too prolific on this head, you will, I hope, excuse it, my Brethren.

APPENDICES

Appendix A
Salem, Massachusetts
The Covenant of 1636[1]

There was a Church Covenant agreed upon and consented to by the Church of Salem at their first beginning in the year, 1629, on August sixth. This following Covenant was propounded by the Pastor and agreed upon and consented to by the Brethren of the Church in the year 1636.

"Gather My saints together unto Me;
those that have made a covenant with Me by sacrifice."
Psalm 50:5

We whose names are here underwritten, members of the present Church of Christ in Salem, having found by sad experience how dangerous it is to sit loose from the Covenant we made with our God and how apt we are to wander into bypaths, even to the losing of our first aims in entering into church fellowship, do therefore solemnly in the presence of the eternal God, both for our own comforts and those who shall or may be joined unto us, renew that Church Covenant which we find this Church bound unto at their first beginning, viz. That we covenant with the Lord and with one another and do bind ourselves in the presence of God to walk together in all His ways, according as He is pleased to reveal Himself unto us in His blessed Word of Truth, and do explicitly, in the name and fear of God, profess and protest to walk as follows, through the power and grace of our Lord Jesus Christ:

We avouch the Lord to be our God and ourselves to be His people, in the truth and simplicity of our spirits.

We give ourselves to the Lord Jesus Christ and the Word of His grace, for the teaching, ruling, and sanctifying of us in matters of worship and conversation, resolving to cleave to Him alone for life and glory and to oppose all contrary ways, cannons, and constitutions of men in His worship.

We promise to walk with our Brethren and Sisters with all watchfulness and tenderness, avoiding jealousies and suspicions, backbitings,

---

[1]First published as *"A Copy of The Church-Covenants Which Have Been Used in the Church of Salem Both Formerly, and in Their Late Renewing of Their Covenant on the Day of the Public Fast, April 15, 1680. As a Direction pointing to that Covenant of God's Grace in Christ made with His Church and People in the Holy Scriptures."* Boston: Printed at the desire and or the use of many in Salem, for themselves and their Children. By J. F., 1680.

censurings, provokings, secret risings of spirit against them, but in all offenses to follow the rule of the Lord Jesus and to bear and forbear, give and forgive as He has taught us.

In public or private we will willingly do nothing to the offence of the Church but will be willing to take advice for ourselves and ours, as occasion shall be presented.

We will not be forward in the congregation either to show our own gifts and parts in speaking and scrupling or there discover the weaknesses and failings of our Brethren, but will attend an orderly call thereunto, knowing how much the Lord may be dishonored and His Gospel and the profession of it slighted, by our distemper and weaknesses in public.

We bind ourselves to study the advancement of the Gospel in all truth and peace, both in regard to those that are within or without, in no way slighting our sister Churches, but using their counsel as need shall be, not laying a stumbling block before any, no not the Indians, whose good we desire to promote, and so to converse as we may avoid the very appearance of evil.

We do hereby promise to carry ourselves in all lawful obedience to those that are over us in Church or Commonwealth, knowing how well-pleasing it will be to the Lord that they should have encouragement in their places by not grieving their spirits through our irregularities.

We resolve to approve ourselves to the Lord in our particular callings, shunning idleness as the bane of any state, nor will we deal hardly or oppressively with any wherein we are the Lord's stewards.

We also promise to the best of our ability to teach our children and servants the knowledge of God and His will, that they may serve Him also, and all this not by any strength of our own, but by the Lord Christ, whose blood we desire may sprinkle this our Covenant made in His Name.

NOTE: This aforementioned Covenant was often read and renewed by the Church at the end of days of humiliation, especially in the year 1660, on the sixth of the first month.

The Covenant of 1680

The following Covenant was, in several Church meetings in the beginning of this year 1680, considered, agreed upon and consented to by the generality of the Church, to be used as a direction for the renewing of our Church Covenant, as being more accommodated to the present times and state of things among us.

Accordingly, it was made use of in that way at the conclusion of the public fast, April 5, 1680, viz.

We, who through the mercy of God, are Members of this Church of Salem, being now assembled in the presence of God and in the name of our Lord Jesus Christ, after humble confession of our manifold breaches of Covenant with the Lord our God and earnest supplications for His pardoning mercy through the blood of Christ and deep acknowledgement of our own unworthiness to be owned as the Lord's Covenant People, also acknowledging our inability to keep Covenant with God or to perform any spiritual duty unless the Lord enable us thereunto by the grace of His Spirit, and yet being awfully sensible that in these times, by the loud voice of His judgments both felt and feared, the Lord is calling us all to repentance and reformation, we do therefore in humble confidence of His gracious assistance, through Christ, renew our Covenant with God and one with another in the manner following.

1. We do give up ourselves to that God whose name is Jehovah, Father, Son and Spirit, as the only true and living God, and unto our Lord Jesus Christ, as our only Redeemer and Saviour, as the only Prophet, Priest, and King over our souls and only Mediator of the Covenant of Grace, engaging our hearts unto this God in Christ, by the help of His Spirit of Grace, to cleave unto Him as our God and chief good, and unto Jesus Christ as our Mediator by faith, in a way of Gospel obedience, as becometh His Covenant People for ever.

2. We do also give up our offspring unto God in Jesus Christ, avouching the Lord to be our God and the God of our children, and ourselves with our children to be His people, humbly adoring the grace of God in Christ Jesus, that we and our children may be looked upon as the Lord's.

3. We do also give up ourselves one to another in the Lord according to the will of God, to walk together as a Church of Christ in all the ways of His worship and service, according to the rules of the Word of God, promising in brotherly love faithfully to watch over one another's souls, and to submit ourselves to the discipline and government of Christ

and His Church and duly to attend the seals and censures and whatever ordinances Christ hath commanded to be observed by His people according to the order of the Gospel, so far as the Lord hath, or shall reveal unto us.

And whereas the Elders and Messengers of these Churches who have met together in the late Synod to enquire into the reasons of the Lord's controversy with His people have taken notice of many provoking evils as the procuring causes of the judgments of God upon New-England, so far as we or any of us have been guilty of those evils or any of them, according to any light held forth by them from Scripture, we desire from our hearts to bewail it before the Lord and humbly entreat for pardoning mercy for the sake of the blood of the everlasting Covenant. And as an expedient unto Reformation of those evils or whatever else have provoked the eyes of God's glory among us, we do promise and engage ourselves in the presence of God:

1. That we will, by the help of Christ, endeavour every one to reform his own heart and life, by seeking to mortify all our sins and to walk more closely with God than ever we have done, and to uphold the power of godliness, and that we will continue to worship God, in public, private and secret and this, as God shall help us, without formality and hypocrisies, and more fully and faithfully than heretofore, to discharge all Covenant duties one towards another in a way of Church communion.

2. We promise by the help of Christ to reform our families and to walk before God in our houses with a perfect heart and that we will uphold the worship of God therein continually, as He in His Word requires both in respects to prayer and reading of the Scriptures, and that we will do what lies in us to bring up our children for God and therefore will, so far as there shall be need of it, catechize them and exhort and charge them to fear and serve the Lord, and endeavour to set an holy example before them, and be much in prayer for their conversion and salvation.

3. We do further engage, the Lord helping us, to endeavour to keep ourselves pure from the sins of the times and with what lies in us to help forward the Reformation of the same in the places where we live, denying all ungodliness and worldly lusts, living soberly, righteously and godly in this present world, making conscience to walk so as to give no offence nor to give occasion to others to sin or to speak evil of our holy profession.

Finally, giving glory to the Lord our God, that He is the faithful God, keeping Covenant and mercy with His people forever, but confessing that we are a weak and sinful people and subject in many ways to break our Covenant with Him, therefore, that we may observe and keep these and all other Covenant duties required of us in the Word of God, we desire to deny ourselves and to depend wholly upon the grace of God in Christ Jesus for the constant presence and assistance of His Holy Spirit to enable us thereunto. Wherein we shall fail, we shall humbly wait upon His grace in Christ for pardon, for acceptance and for healing for His name's sake. Amen.

Appendix B
Malden, Massachusetts
The Covenant of 1737[2]

We, the members of the Church of Christ in Malden that are in full communion, do humbly acknowledge ourselves in many ways guilty of breaking Covenant with God and with one another and that we have not walked favorably to our profession and engagements, for which we desire to take shame to ourselves and repent in dust and ashes and earnestly seek Him for His pardoning mercy in the blood of Christ and also for the gracious assistance of His Holy Spirit to enable us to reform for the future. And as a means to engage and quicken us to the great and necessary work of repentance and reformation, and to strengthen one another's hands therein, we have agreed according to the many examples we find in the Word of God, to renew our Covenant with God and one another and have chosen this Solemn Day to do it in. Therefore, setting ourselves in the awful presence of the Holy Lord the all-seeing and heart-searching God:

We desire, all of us assembled here today, to take forever the Father, the Son and the Holy Spirit for our God and portion, and professing a serious belief of the Sacred Scriptures to be the Word of God, do rejoice by His grace to take them for the rule of our lives, to guide and govern both our faith and practice, renouncing all that we know to be contrary to His revealed will. Particularly, we do solemnly covenant with our God, through Christ's strengthening us, that we will worship the Lord our God and Him only will we serve; that we will observe and keep pure and entire all such religious worship and ordinances as God has appointed in His Word; that we will make a holy and reverend use of God's name, titles, attributes, Word and works; that we will remember the Sabbath to keep it holy, not thinking our own thoughts nor speaking our own words nor finding our own pleasures on the Lord's day; that we will endeavor faithfully to perform the duties of our several relations; that we will endeavor to love our neighbors as ourselves; that we will be tender of His life, chastity, interests, reputation; that we will endeavor to keep our hearts with all diligence and be very prayerful that we enter not

---

[2]First published as : *"Church Covenant Made On A Day of Public Fasting and Prayer, December 21, 1727, occasioned by a terrible earthquake on Lord's-day-night October 29th, 1727."* Boston, 1727.

into temptation; that we will watch over one another, and be watched over by one another, with a spirit of meekness, love and tenderness and walk together as members of the same body in the holy and diligent observance of and humble submission to the ordinances and discipline He has appointed in His Church.

And forasmuch as a thorough reformation can hardly be hoped for without yet a more express and particular engagement against sundry known evils, and especially against the sins of the times, therefore we do further promise with God's help,

I. That we will seriously endeavor to humble ourselves for and to recover ourselves from our spiritual decay and backsliding, our formality in duties, hypocrisy, sloth, deadness, security, sensuality, worldly-mindedness, and that we will labor to be more real and sincere in all that we profess and practice.

II. That we will be more careful to bring up our children and families in the nurture and admonition of the Lord, instructing and catechizing them, requiring an account of what they learn in public and how they profit, reminding them of their Covenant interest and engagement thereby to be the Lord's and also that we will be more careful to govern them and to see that they do at least outwardly walk in the ways of God and not in the loose and vain ways of the world.

III. Forasmuch as God resists the proud but gives grace to the humble, and we see that pride, particularly in apparel, is become such an epidemical sin at this day and one of those evils for which the land mourns, we engage ourselves, through the help of Christ, to do our utmost endeavor to suppress it both in ourselves and families and to that end we will put ourselves and those under us, into a modest and sober habit and garb, suitable to our rank and condition and to the Lord's present humbling dispensations.

IV. Because a spirit of divisions and contentions has to a criminal degree prevailed in one place and another in the land and in times past in this place, we desire to be humbled before God and to be more watchful for the future that we may live in peace and so have the God of love and peace to dwell with us.

V. Whereas also intemperance, uncleanness and such like heinous and horrible sins have grown too common even in New-England, which has been a land of uprightness, we desire to mourn for these abominations, to endeavor to keep ourselves from these defilements and we will do what in us lies to prevent them in others, at least to bear a due testimony against them.

VI. Seeing fraud, injustice and deceit are evils for which God threatens the land with desolating judgments, we desire to lay to heart these sins and to be careful not to be found chargeable with the guilt of them.

VII. Tale-bearing, backbiting, slandering and taking up reproaches against the innocent being also among the provoking sins of the times and having been found among us, we desire to be humbled for what is past, so far as any of us have been guilty, earnestly begging forgiveness both of God and men and do promise for the future, through the help of Christ, with all care to avoid and watch against such unchristian practices.

"The Lord said unto me, I have heard the voice of the words of this people, which they have spoken unto thee: they have well said all that they have spoken. O that there were such an heart in them, that they would fear Me, and keep all My commandments always, that it might be well with them, and with their children for ever! (Deuteronomy 5:18,19).

NOTE WELL: The preceding articles were chiefly extracted from an instrument composed by the famous and venerable Mr. Wigglesworth and solemnly consented to by the Church in Malden on a public day of humiliation, April 15, 1680 in conformity to many examples in the Word of God and to the advice of the Synod of 1679.

Appendix C
A Call to Solemn Assembly
Massachusetts Bay Colony,
at a Council Held at Boston,
March 10, 1668[3]

The Governour and Magistrates being assembled in Council and in some measure sensible of the many tokens of the Lord's displeasure against us, the cutting short the fruits of the earth for sundry years past and otherwise bringing us low more than formerly, together with the many provoking evils that do abound among us to the great dishonor of God and our profession of His holy name, and that notwithstanding all means used for to reclaim the same, which being in conjunction with sundry other things that are among us, threatening yet more and more displeasure against us if the compassions of our tenderhearted and longsuffering God do not timely prevent: Do therefore commend to all the Inhabitants of this Colony the Twenty fifth day of this instant to be kept a Public Day of Humiliation and spent in Fasting and Prayer to the Lord for pardon of whatever have been or are provoking to His holy eyes, and that He will be pleased to give unto us, from the greatest to the least, truly to repent of all our sins, and to reform the same; and that those uncomfortable Breaches made in several Societies may be again repaired, and we may obtain His favorable Presence with us this following year, and His blessing upon our present seed-time; that so it may appear that the Lord's anger is turned away from us, and that He is yet in our Zion, ruling in the midst of us, uniting the hearts of His poor people to do all His pleasure, and nothing else. Also the present low Estate of the Churches of Christ in Europe, and especially in our own dear Native Country, is to be humbly presented before the Lord.

By the Council,

Edward Rawson, Secretary

---

[3]First printed as a broadside, Boston, 1668.

Appendix D
A Call to Solomn Assembly Massachusetts Bay Colony, at a General Court Held at Boston, March 16, 1680[4]

The Solemn consideration of those awful threatenings that are in the face of divine Providence, both toward the world in general, in respect of that fearful Sight and Sign from Heaven, which hath of late been taken notice of, and towards ourselves more particularly, for that the Lord hath this last year manifested His holy displeasure against us, having by an unusual Flood, by the Blast, and by worms, which His very own hand (who is able by the most contemptible of His creatures to stain our glory) hath sent among us, diminished the fruits of the earth. Having also delivered some of our New-England vessels with those in them, into the hands of such as are enemies to the Christian Name, and more lately frowned upon us by shipwrecks, and considerable losses at Sea; and visited some among us by sudden and unexpected deaths. Being also sensible, that there are in other respects, dark clouds impeding over us. And that the present state of the Protestant interest abroad, and more especially in the Land of our Fathers Sepulchers, doth call for earnest prayer before that God unto whom salvation belongs. The consideration of all these things calling aloud upon us for more than ordinary seeking of the Face of God in Jesus Christ:

This Court doth therefore appoint the 21st day of April next to be observed as a Day of Fasting and Prayer, hereby prohibiting all servile labor upon that day, and exhorting all the Ministers, Churches and People throughout this Colony, religiously to observe the same; and to entreat that the favor of God through Jesus Christ may be towards His people in other parts of the world. And that if it may stand with His good pleasure, we may be hid in the day of the Lord's anger, our public Peace, Health, Liberties still continued. That seed time and harvest may not fail. And that a good success may be to the endeavors of this Court, and particularly for our worthy Agents in their negotiation. And to pray unto Him, that He would order a perfect Lot for us, with respect unto these that are in the approaching Election, to be chosen as Rulers over this His People.

By the Court

---

[4]First published as a broadside, Cambridge: Printed by Samuel Green, 1680.

Appendix E
A Call to Solemn Assembly
Massachusetts Bay Colony
at a Council held at Boston,
March 8, 1680[5]

The Governour and Council, upon mature Consideration of the many loud Calls of Providence, and being also conscious that it is a great duty incumbent on them at all times (but more especially when there are so many solemn inducements) to stir up the People of God to humble themselves before Him, and seek His special favor: And now in particular, that a Spirit of Grace may be poured out upon this people, to convince them of, and humble them for all their sinful prevarications; and in special, those sins so publically borne witness against by the late Synod, and a spirit of Reformation to turn from their evil ways, and make their peace with God, that so these things aggravate not or guilt, nor hasten the wrath of God upon us: That having made our peace with God, He may graciously smile upon, & Crown this Year with His blessing, succeeding the labors of His poor People, and making His paths to drop fatness; favorably preventing those awful frowns, in Blastings, Mildews and Insects, which have consumed a great part of or Labors and abated the quantity and goodness of our principal Grain for many years past, & most of all the last Summer. That the Lord would preside, and so dispose the Lot in the following Election of Magistrates, and give out large portions of His Spirit to His Servants who may then be chosen, such as may witness His gracious presence to be yet with us: That God will graciously indulge and prove us by continuing and upholding our precious and desirable liberties civil and sacred; and utterly disappoint and bring to nought all the malicious devices of any who hate us, that seek and would gladly see the subversion of those things wherein our greatest felicity doth consist. That Heaven's Blessing and Protection may be plentifully afforded to our Sovereign Lord the King, defending His Majesties Person and Kingdoms from all mischievous designs & endeavors of Papists, or any other wickedly bent and engaged: That God would signally appear to uphold and maintain the Protestant interest in the world, and all true Professors of His Name and Glory, in despite of all the Plots and Polices

---

[5]First published as a broadside, Boston, 1680.

wherein the Anti-Christian Party, in combination with Hell are united in deep engagements for their ruin;

Do therefore appoint and Order, that the fifteenth day of April next, be set apart for a Day of Humiliation and Prayer, to be kept throughout this Jurisdiction of the Massachusetts, hereby inhibiting all servile labor on that day; and do commend it to all the Churches and people of the said Jurisdiction to be accordingly observed.

Edward Rawson, Secretary